INFORMATION TECTONICS

INFORMATION TECTONICS

Space, Place and Technology in an Electronic Age

Edited by

Mark I. Wilson
and
Kenneth E. Corey

Michigan State University

JOHN WILEY & SONS, LTD

Chichester • New York • Weinheim • Brisbane • Singapore • Toronto

Copyright © 2000 by John Wiley & Sons Ltd, Baffins Lane, Chichester, West Sussex
PO19 1UD, England

National 01243 779777. International (+44) 1243 779777

e-mail (for orders and customer service enquiries): cs-books@wiley.co.uk

Visit our Home Page on http://www.wiley.co.uk or http://www.wiley.com

OTHER WILEY EDITORIAL OFFICES

John Wiley & Sons, Inc., 605 Third Avenue, New York, NY 10158-0012, USA

WILEY-VCH Verlag GmbH, Pappelallee 3, D-69469 Weinheim, Germany

Jacaranda Wiley Ltd, 33 Park Road, Milton, Queensland 4064, Australia

John Wiley & Sons (Asia) Pte Ltd, 2 Clementi Loop #02-01, Jin Xing Distripark, Singapore 129809

John Wiley & Sons (Canada) Ltd, 22 Worcester Road, Rexdale, Ontario M9W 1L1, Canada

LIBRARY OF CONGRESS CATALOGING-IN-PUBLICATION DATA

Information tectonics : space, place, and technology in an electronic age / edited by Mark
I. Wilson and Kenneth E. Corey.
      p. cm.
    Includes bibliographical references and index.
    ISBN 0-471-98427-2 (cased)   ISBN 0-471-98428-0 (paper)
    1. Information technology. I. Wilson, Mark I. II. Corey, Kenneth E.
  T58.5. I5622 2000
  303.48'33—dc21
                                                                              00–027331

BRITISH LIBRARY CATALOGUING IN PUBLICATION DATA

A catalogue record for this book is available from the British Library

ISBN 0-471-98427-2 (hardback)
ISBN 0-471-98428-0 (paperback)

Typeset in 9/12pt Caslon 224 from author's disks by Mayhew Typesetting, Rhayader, Powys
Printed and bound in Great Britain by Biddles Ltd, Guildford and King's Lynn
This book is printed on acid-free paper responsibly manufactured from sustainable forestry,
in which at least two trees are planted for each one used for paper production.

Contents

Preface   xi

Chapter 1   Space, Place and Technology in an Electronic Age   1
              Mark I. Wilson and Kenneth E. Corey

              Introduction   1
              Emergence of Electronic Space   2
              The Roots of Electronic Space   2
              Geographies of Electronic Space   3
              Overview of the Book   5

I CONCEPTUALIZING ELECTRONIC SPACE   7

Chapter 2   The End of Geography or the Explosion of Place?
              Conceptualizing Space, Place and Information Technology   9
              Stephen Graham

              Cyberspace   9
                  Effect of Spatial Metaphors   10
                  Use of Spatial Metaphors   10
                  Aims of This Chapter   11
              Substitution and Transcendence – Technological
                  Determinism, Generalized Interactivity and the End of
                  Geography   11
                  Towards Areal Uniformity, Urban Dissolution, and
                      Generalized Interactivity   12
                  'Mirror Worlds', the Transmission of Place, and World
                      Transcendence   14
              Co-Evolution – the Parallel Social Production of
                  Geographical Space and Electronic Space   16
                  Articulations Between Place-based and Tele-mediated
                      Relationships   16
                  Telecommunications and the City   17
                      The Co-evolution of Old and New Technologies   18
                      The Interaction of Material Places and Electronic Spaces   19
                  Telecommunications, 'Spatial Fixes', and the Production
                      of Space   20
                      The New Telecommunications Networks   20
                      Social and Spatial Power   21
                      The Exercise of Power   22
              Recombination – Actor Network Theory and Relational
                  Time-Spaces   23
                  The Diversity of Cyberspace   24
                  The Role of Telecommunications Systems   24
                  The Human Element   25
              Conclusions – Space, Place and Technologies as Relational
                  Assemblies   26
                  The City   27
                  Global Networks   27

Chapter 3   Telecom Tectonics and the Meaning of Electronic Space   29
              Mark I. Wilson and Colin A. Arrowsmith

              Introduction   29
              Electronic Space Vehicles   30

Telecom Tectonics   32
  Mapping Electronic Space   33
Implications of Telecom Tectonics   38
  Equity   38
  Production   39
Conclusions   40
Acknowledgements   40

Chapter 4   Human Rights and Welfare in the Electronic State   41
               Stanley D. Brunn

Introduction   41
Some Working Definitions   42
Geography, Rights, and Technology   44
  Human Rights and the Spatial Dimension   44
  Legal Standards and Definition of Community   45
  The Erosion of Boundaries   46
States' Rights and International Rights   48
  Human Rights and Welfare in Electronic Democracies   50
  Legal, Ethical, and Moral Issues   52
Human Rights in an Electronic World   55
Mapping Electronically Connected and Unconnected
  Worlds   57
  Maps of Information and Communication   57
  Social Justice and Welfare Issues   58
Discussion   62

II GLOBAL ELECTRONIC COMMERCE   65

Chapter 5   Telecommunications and Governance in Multinational
               Enterprises   67
               Edward M. Roche and Michael J. Blaine

Introduction   67
Pre-Nineteenth Century – Industrial Structure Formation   69
1860–1960 – Search for Hierarchical Governance   70
1960–1970 – Centralized Data Processing and the Rise of
  Autonomy in Foreign Subsidiaries   72
1970–1985 – The Search for Integration   73
1985–1993 – Re-engineering and Transition of Structures   78
1993 – Strategic Control and the Limits of Hierarchy   81
Prospects for the Future   83
Conclusion   86

Chapter 6   Telecommunications and 24-Hour Trading in the
               International Securities Industry   89
               John V. Langdale

Introduction   89
Internationalization of the Securities Industry   90
Telecommunications and the Internationalization of the
  Securities Industry   91
  Telecommunications and the Centralization and
    Decentralization in the International Banking and
    Finance Industry   93
24-Hour Trading   94
  Options for Achieving 24-Hour Trading   95
    Linking Locations – 'Following the Sun'   95
    Linking Firms   95
    Linking Exchanges   96
  Extending Operating Hours of Securities Exchanges –
    Electronic Trading Systems   97
Conclusions   98

Chapter 7   Japanese Information Services in the Late Twentieth
                 Century   101
                 Barney Warf

                 Information Services and the Global Economy in the Late
                     Twentieth Century   102
                 Japanese Versus United States Telecommunications – A
                     Study in Contrasts   103
                 The Deregulation of Japanese Telecommunications   104
                 New Information Services in the Japanese Economy   107
                     Computer Networks   107
                     Software   108
                     Cable Television, Multimedia, and Videoconferencing   109
                     Cellular Telephones   110
                 The Tokyo Telecommunications Infrastructure   111
                 Conclusion   112

III   URBAN, REGIONAL AND NATIONAL DEVELOPMENT   115

Chapter 8   Cyberstructure and Social Forces – The Japanese
                 Experience   117
                 Tessa Morris-Suzuki and Peter J. Rimmer

                 Introduction   117
                 Early 1980s Vision   117
                 Mid-1990s Reality   122
                 Problems Predicting Social Uses of New Technology   127
                     Internet Japan .jp   127
                     Computer Games and Personal Computer Networks   129
                     Corporate Response and Political Implications   131
                     Cultural and Cost Barriers   132
                 Conclusions   134

Chapter 9   Electronic Space – Creating Cyber Communities in
                 Southeast Asia   135
                 Kenneth E. Corey

                 Introduction   135
                 Part One – Creating Cyber Communities   136
                     Malaysia   136
                         Kuala Lumpur and the City Center Project   137
                         The Intelligent Cities   137
                         Technology Park Malaysia   138
                         Kuala Lumpur International Airport   139
                         Multimedia Super Corridor   139
                         Multimedia Flagship Applications   140
                         Multimedia Development Corporation   141
                         Johor State   142
                     Connecting the Corridor   143
                     Learning from Malaysia's IT and Development Projects   143
                     Singapore   145
                         Internal Spatial Organization and IT Infrastructure 145
                         Technology Corridors   146
                             Southwestern Technology Corridor   146
                             Northeastern Technology Corridor   147
                             Housing and Recreation   147
                             Regional Center Anchors   147
                             Cable Television   148
                         Learning from the Singapore Intelligent City   148
                             The New National Computer Board   149
                             Singapore ONE – One Network for Everyone   150
                             Singapore Inc.   152

Part Two – Controlling the Internet in Southeast Asia   153
   Singapore   153
   Malaysia   157
   Hong Kong, China, and Vietnam   159
   Globalization of Internet Regulation   160
Conclusion   161

Chapter 10   Neighbours – Australian and Indonesian
Telecommunications Connections   165
Peter J. Rimmer

Introduction   165
The Asia–Pacific Region   166
   International Telecommunications   166
Sector Restructuring   169
   First Round Reforms   170
   Second Round Reforms   171
      Privatization in Indonesia   173
      Pro-competition and Deregulation in Australia   174
Performance   176
   Networks and Services   176
      Personal Mobile Telephone Services in Australia and
      Indonesia   177
   Price   182
   International Competitiveness   183
   Industry Development   184
      Private Participation in Indonesia – The KSO
      Contracts   185
Futures   189
   Australia's Communications Futures Project   191
Conclusions   194
Epilogue   195
   Australian Privatization   195
   Indonesia in Crisis   197
Acknowledgements   198

Chapter 11   The Economic Development of Peripheral Rural Areas in
the Information Age   199
Ranald Richardson and Andrew Gillespie

Introduction   199
Incorporating Rural Areas into the Information Society   201
   An 'Endogenous' Model   201
   An Alternative to the Endogenous Model   203
Overcoming Constraints on Enterprises Through ICTs?   204
   Using the Internet   205
Electronic Homeworking and Rural Areas   206
   The Freelance Teleworker   207
   Employed Teleworkers   208
Community Based Telecenters and Telecottages   209
   The 'Telecottage'   209
   The Limited Impact of Telecottages   210
Back Offices and Call Centers   212
   Secretarial Services   213
   Call Centers   213
Conclusions   215

Chapter 12   Telematics, Geography, and Economic Development – Can
Local Initiatives Provide a Strategic Response?   219
David Gibbs, Keith Tanner and Steve Walker

Introduction   219
Overview of European Policies for the Information Society   221
Overview of Technology and Market Trends   223

Developing Local Telematics Initiatives – a Case Study of
   Northwest England 225
   Manchester Case Study 226
   Burnley Case Study 229
   Lancashire College Consortium Case Study 230
Discussion 232
Conclusions 234

References and Bibliography 237

List of Contributors 261

Index 263

PREFACE

The relationship between information technology, space, and place offers social scientists a new application of theory, and challenges us to understand the spatial impact of the new information technologies. The title of this book, *Information Tectonics*, was chosen to reflect the scale of technological change in the information age. The reference to plate tectonics is intentional, capturing the potential immensity of the social and spatial changes resulting from the choices we make about information technology. The term is also associated with building or construction, suggesting the making of something new or different.

Cyberspace offers an appealing research agenda because it requires us to reconsider theory developed in different contexts in the past, and to undertake analysis of a new and rapidly changing phenomenon. For geographers, the very intangibility of cyberspace content offers a new challenge, and contrasts the physical and spatial context upon which the infrastructure is built and continues to grow. In our research over many years, we have come to recognize both the power of the new information technologies, and the need for improved understanding of the social context in which information technology is developed and applied. To formalize our research, we initiated E•Space: The Electronic Space Project in 1995. The broad goal of E•Space is to explore the spatial context of information technology, with emphasis on policy, economy, and society.

As much research has shown, the connectivity afforded by information technology does not erase the need for face to face interaction. One of the core functions of E•Space is the building of an international network of scholars, researchers, and policy makers. In its first year, the Project held a conference at Michigan State University, which emphasized the need for continued attention and interaction around the topic of the social and spatial context for information technology. The success of the first conference led to further conferences in Hakone, Japan (1996), Singapore and Kuala Lumpur (1997), Sophia Antipolis, France (1998) and Cape Town (1999). Each location highlighted the need for awareness of local economic, social, and political norms and institutions in order to understand IT issues.

The idea for this book, and the chapters it contains, are all products of the five E•Space meetings held to date. The chapters reflect the scholarship of researchers from around the world, drawing on different disciplines and interests as they explore the geography of information technology. The network of scholars associated with E•Space now exceeds 150, with those interested in IT issues welcome to join our network. For more information on E•Space, please visit our web site at www.electronicspace.org.

Information Tectonics is possible because of the support of many individuals and organizations. The work of E•Space has been primarily supported by the College of Social Science at Michigan State University, with additional funding from the Global and Area Thematic Initiative of MSUs Center for Advanced Study of International Development. We are pleased to acknowledge the considerable contribution of Louise Portsmouth (Assistant Editor, Wiley) and Robert Hambrook (Senior Production Editor, Wiley) who ably turned our bits into atoms. Finally, we thank the E•Space network of scholars, who have provided an insightful and collegial forum for the exploration of electronic space.

Mark I. Wilson
Kenneth E. Corey
East Lansing, March 2000

CHAPTER 1

SPACE, PLACE AND TECHNOLOGY IN AN ELECTRONIC AGE

Mark I. Wilson and Kenneth E. Corey

INTRODUCTION

What hath God wrought?
First message sent by telegraph May 28, 1844.

Information has always been important, determining economic, diplomatic, and military success and failure. The information age we currently inhabit refers to the preeminence of information as the defining component in many of the economic, social, and political actions that shape our lives. The shift from the physicality of agriculture and manufacturing to the intangibility of information carries with it significant changes in the occupations and industries of most economies and societies. At the same time, technology and organizations shape the world to suit the needs of the controlling forces and markets. The shift from agriculture to manufacturing as the primary employer brought with it urbanization and dramatic changes to the spatial, economic, and social organization of populations across the world. What then can be predicted from an equally dramatic change in production orientation from manufacturing to information and services?

The move from farm to factory, and from tangible to intangible production, characterizes the changing condition of many economies during the past four decades. The ability of land and place to define our identity is also changing with the replacement of the physical by the electronic. The landmarks of places, and the importance of proximity, remain important factors in our daily lives, but what can we expect from the erosion of physical space by electronic space? When Samuel Morse sent the first telegraph message from Washington to Baltimore it was indeed a prescient statement about the electronic future to follow.

Electronic space is defined by the information technologies that shape inter- action and production. These technologies are represented by computers, telecom- munications networks, electronic media, and the Internet. On the surface, there is an immediate disjunction between the intangibility of electronic interaction and the tangibility of physical space. Does the spatial dimension have significance in an electronic world? We believe that space remains important despite the pro- clamation of the death of distance. In fact, the declining friction of distance may diminish the cost of interaction, but it also elevates the significance of the many places that are now accessible. The importance of electronic space, the melding of the physical and electronic worlds, is demonstrated by the chapters in this book, which illustrate the many ways that geography contributes to an understanding of an electronic phenomenon.

EMERGENCE OF ELECTRONIC SPACE

The geographic dimensions of information technologies emerge from the intersection of three distinct but increasingly inter-related phenomena: computers, telecommunications, and the information economy. Computers provide the power to generate, manipulate, manage, and index information. Telecommunications allows the movement of voice and data across space, while the information economy is cause and effect of the development and evolution of both computers and telecommunications. The preeminence of information as the core product of advanced economies was forecast by Toffler (1970) and Bell (1973), and a cause of concern to Gershuny (1978), and rightly considered to carry a significance and impact to rival the Industrial Revolution. The change in the way production is organized carries with it major social, economic, and political change – all with geographic dimensions – that are restructuring the global economy at the end of the twentieth century.

Combining computers and telecommunications revolutionizes the way people interact, by offering the potential of low cost telephony and data exchange. The death of distance, proclaimed by *The Economist* in 1995 and later elaborated by Cairncross (1997), captures the sense that distance no longer matters. The conquering of distance in electronic terms brought for many the dream of low cost and efficient access to people and information worldwide. The death of distance, however, is too simplistic a claim because it misses so many of the nuances of the structure and character of electronic interaction. Distance may not matter for those in affluent countries, or working in information industries, or for those with business or personal reasons to contact others. Those for whom distance may not matter are a small proportion of the world's population. For many of the world's inhabitants, distance remains a source of social and economic friction.

Often associated with the concept of the death of distance is the mistaken assumption that it also refers to the declining importance of place. Low cost electronic interaction has certainly made it easier for residents of different places to interact, but at the same time it has also brought different places into a common realm where differences matter. Harvey (1989, p. 124) notes 'The problem of space is not eliminated but intensified by the crumbling of spatial barriers'. Rather than be seen as a force diminishing distance, low cost electronic interaction underscores the powerful value of connecting places. The reason so much effort and investment has been directed at developing electronic infrastructure is because of the value gained from interacting with different places. There are many reasons for wanting to access different places, such as their markets, the information produced or exchanged there, sale of information as an input to production, or to connect people who have family ties across space.

THE ROOTS OF ELECTRONIC SPACE

In the 1950s, geographer Jean Gottmann conducted comprehensive regional analyses throughout the Northeastern seaboard of the United States. His regional analysis research extended from Virginia northwards to southern New England, and encompassed the metropolitan hubs of Washington, D.C., Baltimore, New York and Boston. Gottman (1961) labeled this new region of coalescing urban and urbanizing places and transportation networks 'Megalopolis'.

Importantly, Professor Gottmann brought to our attention the emergence of new information-driven forces, that later were to have a profound impact on the ways that we perceive space and location in the information and knowledge age of today. Located in the offices of Megalopolitan corporations and government agencies, Professor Gottmann observed workers who were engaged primarily in the processing of information and in decision making based on that information. He noted that there was a qualitative difference between workers engaged in the handling of tangible goods and services, i.e. secondary and tertiary economic activities, and those workers who were engaged principally in the processing of intangibles, i.e. information-based economic activities. He called these latter functions 'quaternary economic activities'. He noted that these activities were being done by white-collar workers. These information-based workers functioned in an era that had not yet been impacted by the nearly ubiquitous influence of desktop information and communication technologies that process so much of a modern economy's information today.

This early geographic research and conceptualization of Jean Gottmann have served to enable us to designate him the 'father of information-age geography' (Corey, 1995). Since Gottmann's pioneering Megalopolis work, information and communication technologies, in fact, have transformed our perceptions of location and space. This book brings together recent research findings and thinking that seeks to advance our collective wisdom. With this selection of work, we seek to develop geographies of electronic space that extend and explicate the understanding and significance of electronic space as we daily attempt to harness and steer these new forces and potentials for the advancement of society.

GEOGRAPHIES OF ELECTRONIC SPACE

The geographic analysis of cyberspace has a short but significant history in its contribution to our understanding of electronic space. A number of volumes have been responsible for initiating or charting our exploration of electronic space. Noteworthy contributions include Hepworth's (1990) *Geography of the Information Economy*, Brunn and Leinbach's (1991) *Collapsing Space and Time*, Kellerman's (1993) *Telecommunications and Geography*, Batty's (1993) *Geography of Cyberspace*, Bakis, Abler, and Roche (1994) on global corporate networks, and Castells' trilogy (1996, 1997, 1998) on the information age. The urban dimension has received attention from Rheingold's (1993) *Virtual Communities*, to Graham and Marvin's (1996) *Telecommunications and the City*, Castells' (1989) *Informational City*, and Mitchell's (1996) *City of Bits*.

The change from the physical to the electronic also carries with it a challenge to explain and illustrate this new phenomenon. The language and techniques used to explain the physical world are hard pressed to provide an immediate conceptualization of the electronic world. How do you show the information economy or the Internet in meaningful ways? As with past innovations, the use of metaphors is an important element in our presentation of new ideas. Among many ways of representing cyberspace, for example Dodge (1999) on the visual forms of cyberspace, while the concept of telecom tectonics termed by Wilson (1995) attempts to capture the electronic equivalent of physical movement. Just as continents drift imperceptibly in physical space, the diminution of distance also means that the relationship between places is also changing, albeit very quickly. In ten years, Australia moved 6c.m. closer to Asia in physical space, but over the same time, its electronic realm more than halved the distance in telecommunications cost terms.

Analysis of cyberspace, however, tends to remain aspatial, ignoring the valuable contribution of geography to understanding this phenomenon. The application of geographic concepts and methods can illustrate and clarify the character and impact of cyberspace. Geographers, urban and regional planners, and regional scientists are well positioned to contribute to our collective understanding of the spatial aspects of cyberspace. By drawing on theories from the past and by inventing new conceptualizations, spatial organization research path-breaking can begin, the results of which can be a fuller explication of knowledge of the principal dimensions of cyberspace and communication technologies-influenced activities.

Geography offers many insights into spatial form and function. There are the geographies of the physical infrastructure that allow electronic interaction, of the flows of information and finance that rely upon electronic infrastructure, and of the economic activities that depend and derive from information technologies. From another perspective, geography offers the perspective of hierarchy. From micro-scale to global-scale, the hierarchy includes: intelligent corridors; cyber communities; cyber conurbations; intelligent megalopolitan development; national-scale information infrastructures; regional-scale information infrastructures; and the global-scale intelligent 'ecumenopolis' (Doxiadis and Papaioannou, 1974). As access to, and use of, cyberspace becomes increasingly important for work as well as leisure, what patterns of hubs and hub hierarchies emerge among these electronic geographies? The networks connecting these hubs are conduits of information flows that also represent different levels and hierarchies.

The geographic aspects of cyberspace include spatial variations and disparities. Comparisons, in this context, might be made between boundaries identifying 'have' from 'have not' areas in virtual space and in real space. One might see this as a geography of inequity, and at various scales ranging from such patterns inside cities at neighborhood scales to large regional variations across the globe producing 'information colonies'. Such disparities exist, and they need measurement, mapping, spatial analysis and interpretation for full understanding.

Geography also is concerned with demarcation of places and interaction. What is the role of boundaries and borders in cyberspace? Some perceive cyberspace as without boundaries, yet jurisdictional borders do, in fact, play a role in political space, and therefore in real space. For example, the current debate in the United States about taxing the sale of goods bought over the Internet has raised these issues to high-profile discussions among inter-governmental officials and business leaders. The spatial organization of regulation, taxation, and enforcement of law in cyberspace demands the perspective and attention of researchers and academics training in spatially oriented disciplines.

Each of these spatial organizational examples lend themselves to the geometric approach of seeking pattern among electronic activities as they are analysed to conform to points, areas, lines, flows, shapes, distance, direction, and so on. These variations over space – as well as over time – represent one of the fundamental conceptual building blocks to systematically identify the spatial organization of cyberspace. As part of this challenge, this volume explores how the application of geographic concepts and methods can advance the state of knowledge of cyberspace and electronic space.

OVERVIEW OF THE BOOK

This volume reflects the studies by scholars from around the world who have an interest in the social, economic, and political dimensions of information technologies. In addition to an interest in IT, the chapters are united in their focus on the geographic scale of electronic space, and on how spatial factors exert influence over the development and impact of information technologies. The book is divided into three parts. Part I addresses the conceptualization of electronic space, while Part II explores the geographic dimensions of electronic commerce, and Part III considers the connections between information technology and urban and regional development.

The first part of the book attempts to apply geographic concepts and analysis to the new 'space' of the electronic age. Stephen Graham, in Chapter 2, explores the challenges established by the development of tele-mediated cyberspaces, and the new ways we think about time, space, and cities. Graham constructs a framework to consider the possible interactions between urban places, the familiar urban world – and cyberspaces – the parallel electronic world of electronic spaces. In the following chapter, Mark Wilson and Colin Arrowsmith apply a traditional form of data presentation, the map and cartogram, to capturing the spatial character of electronic space. This chapter uses the term 'telecom tectonics' to illustrate how declining and low telecommunications costs are remaking the cost space connecting countries and continents. Chapter 4, by Stanley Brunn, considers human rights and welfare in electronic space. Brunn notes that even in a 'borderless world', people still reside in state spaces that have meaning in their daily lives. States and boundaries, real or imagined, still matter as do questions about the access and availability of new technologies, equity, protection, and human rights and welfare.

Electronic commerce is one of the leading applications of information technologies, and the market and profit potential of this form of economic interaction receives a great deal of attention and popular media analysis. In Part II we present three cases illustrating the globalization of commercial activities that are products of the information age and technology. Starting with the transnational corporation in Chapter 5, Edward Roche and Michael Blaine investigate forces shaping both the integration and disintegration of the global corporation. Roche and Blaine, in particular, are interested in the extent to which IT leads to a 'networked' corporation of linked entities, and the degree to which this process can continue before the costs of managing such entities outweigh their benefits. The following chapter, by John Langdale, analyses how advances in telecommunications fuel the development of 24-hour trading in a global securities market. Of note is his investigation of the role of regulation across countries, and the competitive and cooperative strategies used by firms and exchanges that shape the globalization of securities trading. Barney Warf analyses Japan's information services sector in Chapter seven, examining how information technology challenges the traditional model of industrial development.

The urban and regional dimensions of information technology are explored in five chapters of Part III. The first three chapters consider the role and impact of IT in Asia. In Chapter 8, Tessa Morris-Suzuki and Peter J. Rimmer examine the promise of information technology as envisioned by the Japanese Government in the 1980s, and the reality of Japan's 1990s information society. Kenneth E. Corey, in Chapter 9, analyses the processes of creating and controlling cyber communities, emphasizing the national and urban policies used in Singapore and Malaysia. The contrasting and related development of IT and telecommunications in Australia and Indonesia is presented by Peter Rimmer in Chapter 10, with emphasis on the role of services trade between both countries. The two following chapters present the European experience, with Ranald Richardson and Andrew Gillespie addressing the development potential for IT in rural areas, using the case study of peripheral regions in the United Kingdom. IT and local economic development is also addressed by David Gibbs and Keith Tanner in their chapter on European telematics policies for encouraging information based development.

Information Tectonics offers a range of views of information technology, from different disciplines, perspectives, countries and geographic scales. The goal of each chapter, alone and collectively, is to further our understanding of the force and impact of information technology.

PART I

CONCEPTUALIZING
ELECTRONIC SPACE

CHAPTER 2

THE END OF GEOGRAPHY OR THE EXPLOSION OF PLACE? CONCEPTUALIZING SPACE, PLACE AND INFORMATION TECHNOLOGY*

Stephen Graham

CYBERSPACE

It is now widely argued that the 'convergence' of computers with digital telecom-munications and media technologies is creating 'cyberspace', a multi-media skein of digital networks which is infusing rapidly into social, cultural and economic life. Cyberspace is variously defined as a 'consensual hallucination, a graphic represen-tation of data abstracted from the banks of every computer in the human system' (Gibson, 1984); a 'parallel universe' (Benedict, 1991); or a 'new kind of space, invisible to our direct senses, a space which might become more important than physical space itself [and which is] layered on top of, within and between the fabric of traditional geographical space' (Batty, 1993: 615–6).

The recent growth of discourses on 'cyberspace' and new communications technologies, even the very word 'cyberspace' itself, have been dominated by spatial and territorial metaphors. 'Cyberspace', suggests Steven Pile (1994: 1817), 'is a plurality of clashing, resonating and shocking metaphors'. The expanding lexicon of the Internet – the most well-known vehicle of cyberspace – is not only replete with, but actually *constituted by*, the use of metaphors. Debates about the Internet use spatial metaphors to help visualize what are, effectively, no more than abstract flows of electronic signals, coded as information, representation, and transaction. Thus, an Internet point-of-presence becomes a web *site*. The ultimate convergent, broadband descendant of the Internet is labelled the information super*highway*. The satellite node becomes a tele*port*. The Bulletin Board system becomes virtual *community* or electronic *neighbourhood*. Web sites run by municipalities become virtual *cities*. The whole wave-front of technological innovation becomes a Wild-West like electronic *frontier* awaiting colonization. And those exploring this frontier become Web *surfers*, virtual *travellers*, or, to Bill Mitchell (1995: 7), electronic

* This chapter was originally published in the journal *Progress in Human Geography*, 33(2), 165–18: (1998) and is reproduced here by kind permission of Arnold Publishers, memver of the Hodder Headline Group.

flâneurs who 'hang out on the network'. Microsoft seductively invite '*Where* do you want to go today?' And so the list goes on and on.

EFFECT OF SPATIAL METAPHORS

Such spatial metaphors help make tangible the enormously complex and arcane technological systems which underpin the Internet, and other networks, and the growing range of transactions, social and cultural interactions, and exchanges of labor power, services, money, and finance, that flow over them. Whilst many allege networks like the Internet to 'negate geometry', be 'anti-spatial', or be 'incorporeal' (Mitchell, 1995: 8–10), the cumulative effect of spatial metaphors means that they become visualizable and imageably reconstructed as giant, apparently territorial systems. These can, by implication, somehow be imagined similarly to the material and social spaces and places of daily life. In fact, such spatial metaphors are commonly related, usually through simple binary oppositions, to the 'real', material spaces and places within which daily life is confined, lived and constructed.

Some argue that the strategy of developing spatial metaphors is 'perhaps the only conceptual tool we have for understanding the development of a new technology' (Sawhney, 1996: 293). Metaphor-making 'points to the process of learning and discovery – to those analogical leaps from the familiar to the unfamiliar which rally the imagination and emotion as well as the intellect' (Buttimer, 1982: 90, quoted in Kirsch, 1995: 543). As with the glamorous, futuristic technological visions within which they are so often wrapped, these technological metaphors 'always reflect the experience of the moment as well as memories of the past. They are imaginative constructs that have more to say about the times in which they were made than about the real future' (Corn, 1986: 219).

USE OF SPATIAL METAPHORS

But the metaphors that become associated with technology are, like those representations surrounding the material production of space and territory (Lefebvre, 1984), active, ideological constructs. Concepts like the 'information society' and the 'information superhighway' have important roles in shaping the ways in which technologies are socially constructed, the uses to which they are put, and the effects and power relations surrounding their development. Metaphors also encapsulate concepts of how technologies do or should relate to society and social change, as the use of 'shock' and 'wave' metaphors in the writings of Alvin Toffler show (see Toffler, 1970; 1980). They even represent the very nature of society itself, as the spread of 'information society' and 'information age' labels testify. Here, technologies are seen to embody metaphorically the very essence of current cultural, societal or economic change. This brings with it, of course, the attendant dangers of relying on simple technological determinism in thinking about how new technologies are related to social, and spatial, change. As Nigel Thrift (1996a: 1471) suggests, 'in this form of [technological] determinism, the new technological order provides the narrative mill. The new machines become both the model for society and its most conspicuous sign'.

Too often, then, this pervasive reliance on spatial and technological metaphors actually serves to obfuscate the complex relations between new communications and information technologies actually and space, place and society. In some simple, binary allegations that new technologies help us to access a new 'electronic space' or 'place', which somehow parallels the lived material spaces of human territoriality, little thought is actually put to thinking conceptually about how new information technologies actually relate to the spaces and places bound up with human territorial life. Without a thorough and critical consideration of space and place, and how new information technologies relate to, and are embedded in it, reflections on cyberspace, and the economic, social, and cultural effects of growing telemediation, seem likely to be reductionist, deterministic and oversimplistic.

AIMS OF THIS CHAPTER

In this chapter I aim to explore some of the emerging conceptual treatments of the relationships between information technology systems and space and place. Building on my recent work on the relationships between telecommunications and contemporary cities (Graham and Marvin, 1996), and on conceptualizing telecommunications-based urban change (Graham, 1996, 1997), I identify three broad, dominating perspectives and explore them in turn. First, there is the perspective of *substitution* and *transcendence* – the idea that human territoriality, and the space and place-based dynamics of human life, can somehow be replaced using new technologies. Second, there is the *co-evolution* perspective which argues that both the electronic 'spaces' and territorial spaces are necessarily produced *together*, as part of the on-going restructuring of the capitalist political-economic system. Finally, there is the *recombination* perspective, which draws on recent work in Actor-Network Theory. Here, the argument is that a fully *relational* view of the links between technology, time, space, and social life is necessary. Such a perspective reveals how new technologies become enrolled into the complex, contingent and subtle blendings of human actors and technical artefacts, to form actor-networks (which are socio-technical 'hybrids'). Through these, social and spatial life become subtly and continuously recombined in complex combinations of new sets of specs and times, which are always contingent and impossible to generalize.

SUBSTITUTION AND TRANSCENDENCE – TECHNOLOGICAL DETERMINISM, GENERALIZED INTERACTIVITY AND THE END OF GEOGRAPHY

Both the dominant popular and academic debates about space, place, and information technologies adopt the central metaphor of 'impact'. In this 'mainstream' of social research on technology (Mansell, 1994), and in the bulk of popular and media debates about the Internet and 'information superhighway', new telecommunications technologies are assumed to directly cause social and spatial change, in some simple, linear, and deterministic way. Such technological determinism accords with the dominant cultural assumptions of the West, where the pervasive experience of 'technology is one of apparent inevitability' (Hill, 1988: 23). Here, technology is cast as an essential and independent agent of change that is separated from the social world and 'impacts' it, through some predictable, universal, revolutionary wave of change. Thus, that central icon of cyberspace rhetoric, *Wired* magazine, proclaimed in their 1996 (pp. 43–44) *Manifesto for the Digital Society*, that:

> the Digital Revolution that is sweeping across society is actually a communications revolution which is transforming society. When used by people who understand it, digital technology allows information to be transmitted and transmuted in fundamentally limitless ways. This ability is the basis of economic success around the world. But it offers more than that. It offers the priceless intangibles of friendship, community and understanding. It offers a new democracy dominated neither by vested interests of political parties nor the mob's baying howl. It can narrow the gap that separates capital from labor; it can deepen the bonds between people and planet.

In terms of the 'spatial impacts' of current advances in communications technologies, two broad and related discourses have emerged from the loosely-linked group of technological forecasters, cyberspace commentators, and critics, who found their commentaries on simple technological determinism (that is, extrapolating the 'logic' of the spatial impacts of telecommunications from the intrinsic qualities of the technologies themselves). First, there are widespread predictions that concentrated urban areas will lose their spatial 'glue' in some wholesale shift towards reliance on broadband, multimedia communications grids. Advanced capitalist societies are thus liberated from spatial and temporal constraints and are seen to decentralize toward spatial and areal uniformity. Second, there are debates about the development of essentially immersive virtual environments, which, effectively, allow the immersive qualities of geographical place to be transmitted remotely.

TOWARDS AREAL UNIFORMITY, URBAN DISSOLUTION, AND GENERALIZED INTERACTIVITY

The geographical effects on space and place of the supposedly wholesale 'technological revolution', based on new information and communications technologies, become fairly easy to establish if one follows an essentialist, cause-and-effect, and deterministic logic through. As technologies of media, computing and telecommunications converge and integrate; as equipment and transmission costs plummet to become virtually distance-independent; and as broadband integrated networks start to mediate all forms of entertainment, social interaction, cultural experience, economic transaction and the labor process, distance effectively *dies* as a constraint on social, economic and cultural life (*The Economist*, 1995). Human life becomes 'liberated' from the constraints of space and frictional effects of distance.

Anything becomes possible anywhere and at any time (see Graham and Marvin, 1996). All information becomes accessible everywhere and anywhere. The 'logic' of telecommunications and electronic mediation is, therefore, interpreted as inevitably supporting geographical dispersal from large metropolitan regions, or even the effective dissolution of the city itself. As Andy Gillespie argues, 'in all utopian visions, the decentralizing impacts of communications technology are regarded as unproblematic and self evident' (Gillespie, 1992).

Most common here is the assumption that networks of large metropolitan cities will gradually emerge to be some technological anachronism, as propinquity, concentration, place-based relations, and transportation flows are gradually substituted by some universalized, interactive, broadband communications medium (the ultimate 'Information Superhighway'). To Baldwin and colleagues (1996), for example, this all-mediating network, this technological holy grail of fully converged telephony, TV, and data, embellished with virtual shopping and interactive video communications, is already in sight, with the trials of so-called Full Service Networks (FSNs) in cities like Orlando, Florida. 'We now have', they write

> a vision of an ideal broadband communication system that would integrate voice, video and data with storage of huge libraries of material available on demand, with the option of interaction as appropriate. The telephone, cable, broadcast, and computer industries, relatively independent in the past, are converging to create these integrated broadband systems. (Baldwin *et al.*, 1996: 1)

Linked to Virtual Reality technologies, such networks, it is argued, will provide, on-line and instantaneously, all of the richness and subtlety of the immersive communications once available only through place-based interactions in urban areas. 'In urban terms', writes Pawley (1995), 'once time has become instantaneous, space becomes unnecessary. In a "spaceless city", the whole population might require no more than the 30 atom diameter light beam of an optical computer system'.

Such arguments, in fact, have a long lineage. Assumptions that advances in telecommunication will 'dissolve' the city have a history as long as electronic communication itself. Caroline Marvin (1988), in her book *When Old Technologies Were New*, recounts the many assumptions, in the late nineteenth century, that the seemingly fantastical technologies of the telegraph, wireless and telephone would annihilate space constraints through minimizing time constraints. Social, cultural, and geographical differences were to be obliterated in the world-wide shift to ubiquitous telecommunication. According to Edward Bellamy, writing in 1897, 'wherever the electric connection is carried . . . it is possible in slippers and dressing gown for the dweller to take his choice of the public entertainment given that day in every city of the earth' (Bellamy, 1897: 347–8).

Three quarters of a century later, Marshall McLuhan argued that the emergence of his 'global village' meant that the city 'as a form of major dimensions must inevitably dissolve like a fading shot in a movie' (McLuhan, 1964: 366; quoted in Gold, 1990: 23). In 1968, Melvin Webber, in his assertion that society had reached the 'post city age', predicted that:

for the first time in history, it might be possible to locate on a mountain top and to maintain intimate, real-time and realistic contact with business and other societies. All persons tapped into the global communications network would have ties approximating those used in a given metropolitan region (Webber, 1968).

Extending this logic, the Futurists, Naisbitt and Aburdene, see 'a new electronic heartland of linked small towns and cities as laying the groundwork for the decline of cities', and believe that 'in many ways, if cities did not exist, it now would not be necessary to invent them . . . truly global cities will not be the largest, they will be the smartest' (Naisbitt and Aburdene, 1991: 329). Anthony Pascal extends this argument, saying that:

> the era of the computer and the communication satellite is inhospitable to the high density city. What once had to happen in the city can now take place anywhere. With the passage of time [will come] spatial regularity; the urban system converges on, even if never quite attains, complete areal uniformity. The newly emerging technologies will soon begin to provide excellent substitutes for face-to-face contact, the chief remaining *raison d'être* of the traditional city (Pascal, 1987: 602).

Such technologically determinist predictions also resonate surprisingly strongly with some of the more critical recent perspectives of the relationships between space, place and technological change. Paul Virilio (1993), a French urban theorist and critic, predicts that an emerging culture of 'generalized interactivity' is emerging, based on pervasive, ubiquitous, and multipurpose telematics grids, through which 'everything arrives so quickly that departure becomes unnecessary' (Virilio, 1993: 8). Such a transition, suggests Virilio, will amount to nothing less than a 'crisis in the notion of physical dimension' (Virilio, 1993: 9) of space, place, the region and the city. 'The archaic "tyranny of distances" between people who have been geographically scattered', writes Virilio, increasingly gives way to the 'tyranny of real time . . . . The city of the past slowly becomes a paradoxical agglomeration in which relations of immediate proximity give way to interrelationships over distance' (Virilio, 1993; 10). Physical movement through transportation also evaporates in this schema, leaving a growing inertia, a sedentary and secluded dystopian urban landscape where 'the shift is ultimately felt in the body of every city dweller, as a *terminal citizen* who will soon be equipped with interactive prostheses whose pathological model is the "motorized handicapped", equipped so that he or she can control the domestic environment without undergoing any physical displacement' (Virilio, 1993: 11).

'MIRROR WORLDS', THE TRANSMISSION OF PLACE, AND WORLD TRANSCENDENCE

Virilio's predictions of the evaporation of the material, physical dynamics of space and place find support in the more optimistic perspectives of 'cyber-gurus' like Nicholas Negroponte (1995) and Bill Gates (1995). Again, the substitution ethos dominates here, with the assumption that sophisticated Virtual Reality (VR) technologies, switched over broadband global grids, will allow immersive, 3D environments to become so life-like that real places will easily become substitutable. David Gelerntner (1991) imagined that such technological trends will lead to the construction of 'Mirror Worlds', allowing us to 'look into a computer screen and see reality. Some part of your world – the town you live in, the company you work for, your school system, the city hospital – will hang there in a sharp colour image' (Gelerntner, 1991: 1). Nicholas Negroponte asserts that 'digital living will include less and less dependence upon being in a specific place at a specific time, and the transmission of place itself will start to become possible. If I could really look out the electronic window of my living room in Boston and see the Alps, hear the cowbells, and smell the (digital) manure in summer, in a way I am very much in Switzerland' (Negroponte, 1995: 165). Following such logic, Peter Cochrane, an analyst for BT, believes that soon:

> you will buy one terminal that will integrate all of those capabilities (of the phone, the TV, the cam corder and the computer) together. Then we will be able to enter the real world from a distance – to go to the Olympic Games, Wembley Stadium or Wimbledon or whatever from our living room or office. We will be able to have new experiences and go to places we've never been before. I would guess that we will see 40 years' experience crammed into just a five-year period (quoted in Harrison, 1995: 7).

Such technologically evangelistic debates about 'Digital Living' therefore suggest that we are on the verge of accessing a technological infrastructure which will do little less than provide some single, immersive, system to mediate all aspects of human life. The implication is that the very concepts of material space, place and time, and the body, will be rendered problematic, even obsolete. We will shed, as Benedict put it, the 'ballast of our materiality', escaping the physical, corporeal domains of the body, the earth, and space and time in the process (Slouka, 1995: 25). Human societies, cultures, and economies are seen to simply *migrate* into the electronic ether, where identities will be flexibly constructed, any services might be accessed, and any task performed, from any location and at any time, by human agents acting *inside* the limitless domains of constructed electronic environments.

Presumably, as human life becomes more and more dominated by what Thu Nguyen and Alexander (1996: 117) call 'participation in the illusion of an eternal and immaterial electronic world', the material world of space and place would become gradually eviscerated. Pascal's shift towards 'complete areal uniformity', of homes and buildings providing equally-spaced entry points into the pure and liberating cyberspace realm, would be underway. Many cyberspace enthusiasts do, indeed, proclaim the need for what Schroeder (1994) has termed 'world rejection'. Here cyberspace is seen to offer an *alternative* territoriality, an infinitely replenishable and extendible realm of spatial opportunity that counters the finitudes and problems of the increasingly crowded material spaces on Earth. Don Mapes, for example, urges us 'to do away with our territoriality'. To him, 'the good news is: cyberspace is big. It's basically infinite. Earth is limited, it's finite. In cyberspace, if you don't like it, you can move onto the next frontier. There's always another continent in cyberspace' (Mapes on Channel 4, 1994). Hayles sounds even more eager to reject terrestrial space and place. 'In a world despoiled by overdevelopment,

overpopulation, and time-release environmental poisons', she believes, 'it is com-
forting to think that physical forms can recover their pristine purity by being
reconstituted as informational patterns in a multidimensional computer space. A
cyberspace body, like a cyberspace landscape, is immune to blight and corruption'
(Hayles, 1993: 81; cited in Robins, 1995: 138).

CO-EVOLUTION – THE PARALLEL SOCIAL PRODUCTION OF GEOGRAPHICAL SPACE AND ELECTRONIC SPACE

Such extreme cyber-evangelism, of course, perpetuates little but dangerous myth
and fallacy. In proffering new technologies as some complete and simple *substitute*
for the material body, the social world, and for space and place, its proponents do
little to advance understanding of the complex *co-evolutionary* processes linking
new information technologies and space, place, and human territoriality. In allo-
cating to technologies almost magical transformative powers, and in radically over-
estimating the degree to which they can substitute for place-based, face-to-face
interaction, they say more about their own (usually masculine) 'omnipotence
fantasies' (Robins, 1995: 139), than about how complex combinations of place-
based and tele-mediated interactions co-evolve. As Kevin Robins suggests, such
perspectives rest on a:

> common vision of a future that will be different from the present, of a space or a
> reality that is more desirable than the mundane one that presently surrounds and
> contains us . . . All this is driven by a feverish belief in transcendence; a faith that,
> this time around, a new technology will finally and truly deliver us from the
> limitations and frustrations of this imperfect world (Robins, 1995: 135).

A much more sophisticated understanding has been developed recently through
our second broad perspective which explores how the social production of electronic networks and 'spaces' *co-evolves* with the production of material specs and
places, within the same broad societal trends and social processes (see Mosco,
1996: 173–211). Three strands of work have emerged here: analysing the articulation between place-based and tele-mediated relationships; addressing the
linkages between telecommunications and the city; and theoretically analysing
the broader roles that new telecommunications and information technologies play
in supporting the production of new types of spatial arrangements.

ARTICULATIONS BETWEEN PLACE-BASED AND TELE-MEDIATED RELATIONSHIPS

Rather than assuming some simple substitutional relationship, our second perspective suggests that complex *articulations* are emerging between interactions in
geographical space and place, and the electronic realms accessible through new
technologies. The argument here is that, because cyber-evangelists are naïvely

obsessed with the abstract *transmissional* capabilities of information technologies, technologically determinist debates usually neglect the richness and embeddedness of human life within space and place. Sawhney criticizes the 'very transmission-oriented view of human communication [in cyberspace debates]. The purpose of human communication is reduced to transfer of information and the coordination of human activity. The ritual or the communal aspect of human communication is almost totally neglected' (Sawhney, 1996: 309).

Technologically determinist commentators are accused of failing to appreciate the social, cultural and economic dynamics of place and space that cannot be simply tele-mediated through broadband, 3D, or immersive substitutes. Quite the reverse, in fact, because the human construction of space and place is seen to actually ground and contextualize applications and use of new technologies. 'The urban world networked by [Bill] Gates' technologies "strung out on the wire"', writes Denis Cosgrove, 'is not disconnected, abstract, inhuman; it is bound in the places and times of actual lives, into human existences that are as connected, sensuous and personal as they ever have been' (Cosgrove, 1996: 1495). Kevin Robins argues that 'through the development of new technologies, we are, indeed, more and more open to experiences of de-realization and de-localization. But we continue to have physical and localized existences. We must consider our state of suspension between these two conditions' (Robins, 1995: 153).

TELECOMMUNICATIONS AND THE CITY

This 'state of suspension' or articulation between place-based and electronically-mediated realms is especially evident in the large metropolis, which, despite some trends towards the decentralization of routine service functions (OTA, 1995), shows no sign of simple, wholesale evisceration. Globally, urbanization trends are unmatched in history in their intensity; the global urban system continues to dominate the planet economically, politically, socially, and culturally; transportation flows and demands are spiralling at every scale; and even the large industrial cities in the United Kingdom and the United States, that recently were shedding population, are showing some signs of an economic and cultural renaissance, and demographic turn round. In short, new communications technologies are not simply substituting for the experience of, or reliance on, metropolitan places. Rather, a complex co-evolution, articulation, and synergy between place-based and tele-mediated exchange seems to be emerging. Ron Abler rebels 'instinctively . . . against the notion that a digitally-created version of real place constitutes an acceptable substitute for the real thing' (Abler, 1995: 3). Equally possible, he feels, is the emergence of *place virtuality* where urban residents are able to 'tap into the digitally-available resources of the world to enrich reality in real places. By its very nature, virtual reality implies the possibility if not the probability of real virtuality' (Abler, 1995: 3).

As I show in a recent book (Graham and Marvin, 1996), cyberspace is, in fact, a predominantly metropolitan phenomenon that is developing *out* of the old cities. In terms of hard infrastructural investment, demand for services, and rate of innovation, the largest, globally-oriented metropolitan areas are clearly dominant. Thus, whilst New York has around 7% of the US population, 35% of all outgoing US international calls start there. Whilst London has 17% of the UK population, 30% of all UK mobile calls are made there. And whilst Paris has 16% of the French population, it commands 80% of all investment in telecommunications infrastructure in France (Graham and Marvin, 1996: 133).

The Co-evolution of Old and New Technologies

The work of Jean Gottmann (1982) has clearly demonstrated that the incorporation of computer networks into the economic, administrative, and socio-cultural dynamics of the city merely intensifies and adds further capability to the older functions of the post, the telegraph and telephone. The maintenance of control over ever-more complex urban and regional systems, straddling ever-larger distances, and spread over larger and larger metropolitan corridors and regions, becomes possible. Rather than simply substituting or revolutionizing the city, and flows of people and material goods, the evidence suggests that new technologies actually diffuse into the older urban fabric, offering potential for doing old things in new ways. Urban transportation and infrastructure systems can be managed and controlled more precisely, improving capacity. Telecommunications co-evolves with transportation and physical flows, sometimes replacing (telebanking for branch networks, e-mail for post), sometimes generating (travel TV programmes), and sometimes enhancing transport capability (automatic route guidance) (see Graham and Marvin, 1996). The extending and intensifying grids of travel, trade, and tourism actually rely on the enhanced control and coordination capacities of IT at every stage and scale. For example, fifty thousand electronic exchanges of all sorts are estimated to lead up to one flight of one Boeing 747. And within cities, new technologies allow the time and space limits surrounding consumption, work, entertainment, and travel to be managed more flexibly. Thus, the spaces of the city may be constructed within a broader, and more complex, urban field networked together by more sophisticated, integrative technological networks (Boyer, 1996).

New information technologies, in short, actually resonate with, and are bound up in, the active construction of space and place, rather than making it somehow redundant. William Mitchell's notion of 'recombinant architecture' is especially relevant here, because it demonstrates how constructed and produced material spaces are now being infused with cyberspace entry points of all kinds (Mitchell, 1995). Material space and electronic space are increasingly being produced together. The power to function economically and link socially increasingly relies upon constructed, place-based, and material spaces intimately woven into complex telematics infrastructures linking them to other places and spaces. 'Today's institutions' argues Mitchell (1995: 126) 'are supported not only by buildings but by telecommunications and computer software'. Thus, the articulation between widely-stretched telematics systems, and produced material spaces and places, becomes the norm and is a defining feature of contemporary urbanism. 'Constructed spaces', suggests Mitchell (1994), 'will increasingly be seen as electronically-serviced sites where bits meet the body – where digital information is translated into visual, auditory, tactile or otherwise sensorily perceptible form, and vice versa. Displays and sensors for presenting and capturing information will be as essential as doors'. Bookstores, libraries, universities, schools, banks, theatres, museums and galleries, hospitals, manufacturing firms, trading floors, and service providers increasingly become embodied through their presence in both material spaces and electronic spaces. Whilst some substitution is evident – for example with the closure of banking branches paralleling the growth of tele-banking – much of the traditional face-to-face activity within constructed spaces, and the transportation that supports it, seems extremely resilient to simple substitution. In other words, the contemporary city, while housing vast arrays of telematic 'entry points' into the burgeoning worlds of electronic spaces, is still a *meaningful* place economically, socially and culturally (Wilson, 1995).

The Interaction of Material Places and Electronic Spaces

The usefulness of the co-evolution perspective is that it underlines the fact that materially constructed urban places and telecommunications networks stand in a state of *recursive interaction*, shaping *each other* in complex ways that have a history running back to the days of the origin of the telegraph and telephone (and as the continued urban dominance of telecommunications investment and use makes clear; see Thrift, 1996a). Major urban places support dense webs of 'co-presence' that cannot – and will not – be simply mediated by telecommunications (Boden and Molotch, 1994). This is because they are vital supports to high-level business activities in a risky and volatile global economy (Storper and Scott, 1995); because the new urban culture relies on them; and because face-to-face social life derives from them.

The complex articulations between the local and global dynamics of both material places and electronic spaces have recently been explored by Staple (1993). He believes that the Internet and other communications technologies, far from simply collapsing spatial barriers, actually have a dialectic effect, helping to compress time and space barriers whilst, concurrently, supporting a localizing, fragmenting logic of 'tribalization'. Far from unifying all within a single cyberspace, the Internet, he argues, may actually enhance the commitment of different social and cultural interest groups to particular material places and electronic spaces, thus constituting a 'geographical explosion of place' (Staple, 1993: 52). This 'new tribalism', exemplified by the use of the Internet to support complex diasporas across the globe, and to draw together multiple, fragmentary special interest groups on a planetary basis, 'folds' localities, cities and regions into 'the new electronic terrain' (Staple, 1993: 52).

But it is important to stress that the ways in which places become enmeshed into globally-stretched networks like the Internet will be a diverse, contingent process. It is important to stress the diversity of relations that seem likely to exist between the urban structures and systems, and indeed particular cultures, of different nations, and the growth of telemediated interaction. Bolter speculates on the diversity of such relations:

Perhaps the Japanese will construct cyberspace as an extension of their dense urban corridors. On the other hand, people can live in the suburbs and participate in cyberspace from their homes, as many Americans do now. Or, as Americans do, they can commute between one cyberspace location in the workplace (a corporate communications system) and another in their homes (American Online). Thus cyberspace can be a reflection of the American suburbs and exurbs, the Japanese megacities, or the European combination of large and medium-sized cities. Cyberspace need not be the uniform entity suggested by the current metaphor popular in the United States, the 'information superhighway' (Bolter, 1995: 2).

TELECOMMUNICATIONS, 'SPATIAL FIXES', AND THE PRODUCTION OF SPACE

Theoretical perspectives drawing on critical political economy serve to further exemplify the ways in which new telecommunications systems are materially bound up with the production of complex new social and economic geographies. Reacting against the all-encompassing and over-generalized concepts of the 'global village' and 'time-space compression', Scott Kirsch argues that:

> by resorting to the rather cartoonish shrinking world metaphor, we lose sight of the complex relations . . . between capital, *technology*, and space, through which space is not 'shrinking' but rather must be perpetually recast (Kirsch, 1995: 544).

Whilst new information and telecommunications technologies support more flexibility in the way production interests, services and media firms, tourists, and investors treat space, they do not herald some simple shift to a world of pure, absolute mobility. Rather, time and space barriers become reconstituted and reformed within global geometries of flow, incorporation and exclusion. 'The mobility of commerce, organizations, information and people does not make time and space irrelevant, rather, it highlights the extent to which these areas of experience have become more, not less, multi layered, interrelated, and complex' (Ferguson 1992: 79). Places become increasingly shaped and constructed through their incorporation into powerful, corporate networks of flows and exchange. Far from leading to some areal homogeneity, as in some deterministic visions, such a logic accords asymmetric power to global Transnational Corporations (TNCs) to scrutinize and exploit the exact locational attributes of places, as they strive to piece together seamlessly-integrated, and ever-more fine-grained international divisions of labor (Castells, 1989).

The New Telecommunications Networks

Perhaps the clearest exploration of how telecommunications become woven into the creation of new geographical landscapes of production, consumption, and distribution at all spatial scales comes from Eric Swyngedouw (1993: 305). Building on the work of Harvey (1985), he argues that every social and economic activity is necessarily geographical. It is *'inscribed in space and takes place'* (original emphasis). Human societies 'cannot escape place in the structuring of the practices of everyday life' (Swyngedouw, 1993: 305). Within an internationalizing economy, capitalist firms and governments must continually struggle to develop new solutions to the tensions and crisis-tendencies inherent within capitalism, between what David Harvey calls 'fixity' and the need for 'motion', mobility and the global circulation of information, money, capital, services, labor, and commodities (Harvey, 1985). Currently, such tensions and crises arise because increasingly widely-dispersed areas of production, consumption, and exchange, resulting from the internationalizing economy, need to be integrated and coordinated into coherent economic systems. Space thus needs to be 'commanded' and controlled, on an increasingly international scale.

To do this, relatively immobile and embedded fixed transport and telecommunications infrastructures must be produced, linking production sites, distribution facilities, and consumption spaces, that are tied together across space with the transport and communications infrastructure necessary to ensure that a spatial 'fix' exists that will maintain and support profitability. Without the elaboration of ever-more sophisticated and globally-stretched transport and communications infrastructures, Harvey argues that:

> the tension between fixity and mobility erupts into generalized crises, when the landscape shaped in relation to a certain phase of development . . . becomes a barrier to further [capital] accumulation (Harvey, 1993: 7).

Thus, new telecommunications networks 'have to be immobilized in space, in order to facilitate greater movement for the remainder' (Harvey, 1985: 149). Swyngedouw elaborates:

> A communications line . . . liberates actions from place and reduces the friction associated with distance and other space-sensitive barriers. However, such transportation and communications organization can only liberate activities from their embeddedness in space by producing new territorial configurations, by harnessing the social process in a new geography of places and connecting flows. . . . In short, liberation from spatial barriers can only take place through the creation of new communications networks, which in turn, necessitates the construction of new (relatively) fixed and confining structures (Swyngedouw, 1993: 306).

Social and Spatial Power

Crucially, then, the political economic perspective underlines that the development of new telecommunications infrastructures is not some value-neutral, technologically pure process, but an asymmetric social struggle to gain and maintain social power, the power to control space social processes over distance. As any investigation of, say, the growth of global financial centres, or the extending global coverage of corporate telematics networks will soon discover, power over space and power over telecommunications networks go hand in hand. For example, Graham Murdock draws the striking parallel between the 'fortress effect' generated by many postmodern office buildings, and the development of vast, private 'data-spaces' on corporately-controlled networks. He argues that 'here, as in territorial space, continuous battle is being waged between claims for public access and use, and corporate efforts to extend property rights to wider and wider areas of information and symbolization' (Murdock, 1993: 534).

By demystifying, and unpacking, the social and power relations surrounding telecommunications and the production of space, the political economic perspective does much to debunk the myths of technological determinism discussed above. It allows us to reveal the socially-contingent effects of new technologies, the way they are enrolled into complex social and spatial power struggles, and the ways in which some groups, areas, and interests may benefit from the effects of new technologies, whilst others actually lose out. As Swyngedouw suggests, this perspective suggests that 'the increased liberation and freedom from place as a result of new mobility modes for some may lead to the disempowerment and relative exclusion for others' (Swyngedouw, 1993: 322).

The Exercise of Power

Paul Adam (1995) uses the concept of 'personal extensibility' to capture how a person's (tele-mediated and physical) access to distant spaces, services and places may allow them to extend their domination over excluded groups and so support the production of divided spaces and cities. 'One person's (or group's) time-space compression', he writes, 'may depend on another person's (or group's) persistent inability to access distant places'. As Adam states, 'the variation of extensibility according to race, class, age, gender, and other socially-significant categories binds micro-scale biographies to certain macro-level societal processes' (Adam, 1995: 268; see Massey, 1993: 66).

Thus, within cities, forms of 'telematics super-inclusion' (Thrift, 1996b) emerge for élite groups, who help shape cocooned, fortified, urban (often now walled) enclosures, from which their intense access to personal and corporate transport and telematics networks allow them global extensibility. Meanwhile, however, a short distance away, in the interstitial urban zones, there are 'off-line' spaces (Aurigi and Graham, 1997), or 'lag-time places' (Boyer, 1996: 20). In these, often-forgotten places, time and space remain profoundly real, perhaps *increasing*, constraints on social life, because of welfare and labor market restructuring and the withdrawal of banking and public transport services. It is easy, in short, to over-emphasize the mobility of people and things in simple, all-encompassing assumptions about place-transcendence (Thrift, 1996c: 304), which conveniently ignore the splintering and fragmenting reality of urban space.

To Christine Boyer (1996: 20), the highly uneven geography of contemporary cities, and the growing severing of the 'well-designed nodes' of the city from the 'blank, in-between places of nobody's concern', allows fortunate groups to 'deny their complicity' in the production of these new, highly uneven, material urban landscapes. But perhaps the most extreme example of the complex interweaving of new technologies, power relations, and the production of space and place comes with the small, élite group who run the global financial exchanges in World Cities. Here, we find that 'the extensible relations of a tiny minority in New York, London, and Tokyo, serve to control vast domains of the world through international networks of information retrieval and command' (Adam, 1995: 277).

Recombination – Actor Network Theory and Relational Time-Spaces

Our third and final perspective takes such *relational* views of the social construction of technology further. Anchored around the Actor-Network Theories of Michel Callon (1986; 1991) and Bruno Latour (1993), a range of researchers, including those writing of the proliferation of blended human-technological 'cyborgs' (Haraway, 1991), have recently been arguing for a highly contingent, relational perspective of the linkage between technology and social worlds. Actor Network Theory emphasizes how particular social situations and human actors 'enrol' pieces of technology, machines, as well as documents, texts, and money, into 'actor-networks'.

The perspective is fully relational in that it is 'concerned with how all sorts of bits and pieces; bodies, machines, and buildings, as well as texts, are associated together in attempts to build order' (Bingham, 1996: 32). Absolute spaces and times are meaningless here. Agency is a purely relational process. Technologies only have contingent, and diverse, effects through the ways they become linked into specific social contexts by human agency. What Pile and Thrift (1996: 37) call a 'vivid, moving, contingent and open-ended cosmology' emerges. The boundaries between humans and machines become ever-more blurred, permeable, and cyborgian. And 'nothing *means* outside of its relations: it makes no sense to talk of a "machine" in general than it does to talk of a "human" in general' (Bingham, 1996: 17). Nigel Thrift summarizes the approach:

> no technology is ever found working in splendid isolation as though it is the central node in the social universe. It is linked – by the social purposes to which it is put – to humans and other technologies of different kinds. It is linked to a chain of different activities involving other technologies. And it is heavily contextualized. Thus the telephone, say, at someone's place of work had (and has) different meanings from the telephone in, say, their bedroom, and is often used in quite different ways (Thrift, 1996a: 1468).

This linkage of heterogeneous technological elements and actors, strung across distance, is thus seen as a difficult process requiring continuing efforts, to sustain relations which are 'necessarily *both* social and technical' (Akrich 1992: 206). The growing *capabilities* of telecommunications, for supporting action at a distance and remote control, does not therefore negate the need for the human actors which use them to struggle to enrol passive technological agents, into their efforts to attain real remote control. 'Stories of remote control tend to tell of the sheer amount of work that needs to be performed before any sort of ordering through space becomes possible' (Bingham, 1996: 27). Such 'heterogeneous work involving programmers, silicon chips, international transmission protocols, users, telephones, institutions, computer languages, modems, lawyers, fibre-optic cables, and governments to name but a few, has had to be done to create envelopes stable enough to carry [electronic information]' (Bingham, 1996: 31).

THE DIVERSITY OF CYBERSPACE

Thus, there is not one single, unified cyberspace; rather, there are multiple, heterogeneous networks, within which telecommunications and information technologies become closely-linked with human actors, and with other technologies, into systems of socio-technical relations across space. As Nick Bingham (1996: 32) again argues, 'the real illusion is that cyberspace as a singular exists at all', rather than as an enormously varied 'skein of networks' (Latour, 1993: 120) straddling and linking different spaces. Thus, we need to consider the diverse, and interlinked, physical infrastructures of information technologies (cable, Public Switched Telephone Networks, satellite, mobile, Internet, etc.), and how they support the vast panoply of contingent actor-networks. 'Cyberspace' therefore needs to be considered as a fragmented, divided, and contested multiplicity of heterogenous infrastructures and actor-networks.

For example, there are tens of thousands of specialized corporate networks and intranets; the Internet provides the basis for countless Usenet groups, Listservers, corporate advertising sites, specialized Web sites, MUDs, and virtual communities; PSTNs support global systems of automatic teller machine networks, credit cards systems, CCTV, telehealth, teleshopping and telebanking, global logistics, remote monitoring systems, Electronic Data Interchange (EDI) chains, electronic financial transactions, and stock market flows, as well as data and telephony flows; and specialized systems of satellite, broadband, cable and broadcasting networks support burgeoning arrays of television flow. Each application has associated with it a whole multiplicity of human actors and institutions, who must continually struggle to enrol the technologies, along with other technologies, money, and texts, into producing some form of functioning social order. These, and the hundreds of other actor-networks, are always contingent, always constructed, never spatially universal, and always embedded in the micro-social worlds of individuals, groups, and institutions. Such socio-technical networks 'always represent geographies of enablement and constraint' (Law and Bijker, 1992: 301) and always link the local and non-local in intimate relational, and reciprocal, connections.

THE ROLE OF TELECOMMUNICATIONS SYSTEMS

Such a fully relational perspective has important implications for the ways in which we conceptualize space and time. For Actor-Network Theory suggests that, rather than simply being space and time transcending technologies, telecommunications systems actually act as technological networks within which new spaces and times, and new forms of human interaction, control and organization can actually be constructed. As Bruno Latour argues (1987: 228):

> Most of the difficulties we have in understanding science and technology proceed from our belief that space and time exist independently as an unshakable frame of reference *inside which* events and place would occur. This belief makes it impossible to understand how different spaces and different times may be produced *inside the networks* built to mobilize, cumulate and recombine the world.

The continual recombination of the world, within actor-networks and their specific 'different spaces and different times', is possible because the Internet and other information and communications systems are based on 'technological networks', which, despite the rhetoric of universality, are always specific and contingent in linking one place to another. To Latour, such technological networks:

> are composed of particular places, aligned by a series of branchings that cross other places and require other branchings in order to spread. Between the lines of the network there is, strictly speaking, nothing at all: no train, no telephone, no intake pipe, no television sets. Technological networks, as the name suggests, are networks thrown over spaces, and they retain only a few scattered elements of those spaces. They are connected lines, not surfaces. They are by no means comprehensive, global or systematic, even though they embrace surfaces without covering them, and extend a very long way (Latour, 1993: 117–8).

THE HUMAN ELEMENT

The merit of the Actor-Network perspective is its humanism; its emphasis on continuity, humanity, and contingency. In it, humans emerge as more than just subjects whose lives are to be 'impacted', as more than bit-players within macro-level processes of global structural change. It underlines forcefully that 'living, breathing, corporeal human beings arrayed in various creatively improvised networks of relation still exist as something more than machine fodder' (Thrift 1996a: 1466).

Work by Nigel Thrift (1996a, b, c) has used Actor Network Theory to show how cities and spaces like the City of London, far from suffering some simple dissolution, have, over the past century, actually been continually recombined with new technological networks: the telegraph, telephone, and, most recently, telematics trading system. Such new technologies do not produce some 'abstract and inhuman world, strung out on the wire' (Thrift, 1996a: 1480), but are subtly recombined with the spatial and social practices of workers and managers, operating within the complex material and social spaces of the City.

Often, the use of faster and faster telematics systems actually increases the demands for face-to-face contact so that the interpretive loads surrounding information glut can be dealt with competitively. 'The major task in the information spaces of telematic cities like the City of London', writes Thrift (1996a: 1481), 'become interpretation and, moreover, interpretation *in action* under the pressure of real-time events'. Thus, the production of new material spaces, and the social practices that occur in them, is neither some technological cause-and-effect, nor some simple political-economic machination. Rather, it is:

> the hybrid outcome of multiple processes of social configuration processes which are specific to particular differentially extensive actor-networks (made up of people and things holding each other together) and generate their own space and own times, which will sometimes, and sometimes not, be coincident. There is, in other words, no big picture of the modern City to be had but only a set of constantly evolving sketches (Thrift, 1996a: 1485).

Conclusions – Space, Place and Technologies as Relational Assemblies

Two clear conclusions for how we might address the linkages between space, place and information technology emerge from our discussion of the three broad substitution, co-evolution and recombination perspectives.

First, we need to be extremely wary of the dangers of adopting, even implicitly, deterministic technological models and metaphors of technological change. The very notion of a technological 'impact', for example, is problematic. In their extreme form, deterministic approaches deliver little but the 'logic' of apparent technological inevitability, naïve assumptions about simple, cause-and-effect, social and spatial 'impacts', and even messianic and evangelistic predictions of pure, technological salvation.

The co-evolution perspective teaches us that such perspectives fail to capture the ways in which new technologies are inevitably enrolled into complex social power struggles, within which *both* new technological systems and new material geographical landscapes are produced. The recombination perspective, on the other hand, teaches us that such broad-brush transition and 'impact' models ignore the full, contingent, and relational complexity surrounding the social construction of new technologies, in specific places. It argues powerfully that, outside such contingencies, the meaning and effects of new information technologies can never be fully understood. To draw, once more on Nigel Thrift's (1996a: 1474) recent work:

> seen in this light, electronic communications technologies are no longer an economic, social or cultural earthquake, but rather a part of a continuing performative history of 'technological' practices, a complex archive of stances, emotions, tacit and cognitive knowledges, and presentations and re-presentations, which seek out and construct these technologies in certain ways rather than others.

Second, however, we need to be equally wary of the dangers of adopting simplistic concepts of *space* and *place*. Following the arguments of such authors as Giddens (1979), Massey (1993), Harvey (1993), and Graham and Marvin (1996), we need to reject the extremely resilient 'Euclidean' notions, still implicitly underlying many treatments of information technology, that treat spaces and places simply as bounded areas, as definable, Cartesian spatial objects, embedded within some wider, objective framework of time-space. As Doreen Massey (1993: 66) suggests, places need to be defined *in relational terms*, too, as 'articulated moments in networks of social relations and understandings' rather than as 'areas with boundaries around'.

The message, then, is clear. Only by maintaining linked, relational conceptions of *both* new information and communications technology, *and* space and place, will we ever approach a full understanding of the inter-relationships between them. For Latour's 'skein of networks' (1993: 120) involves *relational assemblies* linking technological networks, space and place, and the space and place-based users of such networks. Such linkages are so intimate and recombinatory that defining space and place separately from technological networks soon becomes as impossible as defining technological networks separately from space and place.

THE CITY

The example of the contemporary city illustrates the point. Here, propinquity in material space has no *necessary* correlation with relational meaning, as was always assumed with the concept of distance decay, with positivist urban models like the gravity model, and with many traditional planning treatments of the unitary, integrated city (Webber, 1964). Complex place-based relational meanings – such as access to physical infrastructure, property, labor markets, an 'innovative milieu', social interaction, and the use of cultural facilities – are constantly being recombined with non-local relational connections, accessed via technological networks (telecommunications, long distance transport networks, and, increasingly long distance energy supplies too).

The 'urban' thus can now be seen as a locus for many socio-cultural, economic, and institutional networks, spread out over diffuse and extended regions, and mediated by complex combinations of physical 'co-presence' and technological mediation (see Healey *et al.*, 1995). In some, the interlinkage and superimposition within physical urban space forms meaningful nodes and connections – economic, social, cultural, and physical. In others, the place-based relations are outweighed by the technologically-mediated links to far-off places. Thus, neighbours may, or may not, know each other's names and have meaningful social relations. Adjacent firms may or may not create linkages. Urban public spaces may or may not emerge as common cultural arenas. Complex, subtle, and contingent, combinations of electronic propinquity in the 'non-place urban realm' (Webber, 1964) and place-based relational meanings based on physical propinquity and transport therefore need to be considered in parallel.

Such recombinations of technology and place represent merely the latest processes of urbanism and not some simple post-urban shift (Graham and Marvin, 1996). 'Cities cannot be seen as places which are leaking away into space of floes', writes Thrift (1996b: 6). 'This is to fundamentally misunderstand the ways in which new information technologies have normally acted as a supplement to human communication rather than as a replacement. Innovations like the telephone, the fax, and the computer are used to extend the range of human communication, rather than act as a substitute. It is not either/or but both/and'.

GLOBAL NETWORKS

Complex relational webs emerge here. As the global financial networks linking London, Paris or New York, or the TGV train networks linking Paris and the French provincial capitals demonstrate, the technological networks that support these distant linkages, whilst always local and always embedded in space and place, may actually provide 'tunnel effects' which bring certain spaces and places closer together, whilst pushing physically-adjacent areas further away (Graham and Marvin, 1996). The global divisions of labor and telecommunications networks of Transnational Corporations provide another perfect example. For, as Paul Adam states, 'in this milieu of globalization, the buildings housing the various functions of a transnational corporation, although dispersed around the globe, are intimately connected, yet they may have little or no connection with offices or housing that are directly adjacent' (Adam, 1995: 277).

The relationships between the US, UK, and Japanese urban systems to the global financial capital that happens to be places within their nation are similar. Some of the world's most sophisticated telematics networks now underpin such cities, linking them, 24 hours a day, through trillions of dollars of sub-millisecond global financial transactions, into a global financial marketplace (and, not uncoincidentally, the hubs of the global airline systems). Meanwhile, however, their immediate, provincial 'hinterlands' and domestic urban systems often fail to integrate closely into such global technological networks, despite the fact that they actually pass materially through or by them. Such relational actor-networks strewn across the planet mean, effectively, that 'the centres of two cities are often for practical purposes closer to each other than to their own peripheries' (Mulgan, 1991: 3).

But whilst cities are often spreading out to be vast, multi-centred urban regions linked into global networks, place-based relational webs that rely on adjacency, propinquity and physical flows remain central to the experience of human social, economic, and cultural life. The two rely on each other; they recursively interact. For, as Storper (1995) suggests, shifts toward growing reliance of tele-mediated information, image, electronic transactions, and financial flow, as well as the continuing importance of fashion, art, the media, dance, consumption, leisure, research, play, collective consumption, travel, tourism, education, and governance (Thrift, 1996b), place a premium on reflexivity interpretation and innovation – the key assets of urban areas. As he argues, 'the worlds of action which make up the [reflexive] city economy and society are hybrids, constrained by the machine-like forces of late modern capitalism, but themselves enabled by the ways that system not only permits, but in certain ways, thrives on social reflexivity' (Storper, 1995: 32).

CHAPTER 3

TELECOM TECTONICS AND THE MEANING OF ELECTRONIC SPACE

Mark I. Wilson and Colin A. Arrowsmith

INTRODUCTION

To be digital, Nicholas Negroponte (1995) urges us to consider the difference between atoms and bits. This simple distinction, between the tangible and intangible, between the physical world and the electronic world, is increasingly characterizing many elements of our daily life. The physical world shapes our daily life, work, and interactions, in ways that can be seen. Barriers of mountains and oceans are immediately apparent. But what of the world of bits, of the distinction between physical space and the territory of bits? We know our physical world because we can see it, marvel at satellite images of earth, interpret maps, and explore this space. Electronic space is a far more elusive concept because of its invisibility, or its manifestation as a physical result of electronic media.

In a world increasingly dependent on information generation and flows, the movement of information is determined not by shipping or aviation, but by telecommunications and information technology (Arrowsmith and Wilson, 1997). While shipping, and to a lesser extent, aviation, are tied to specific places by the availability of ports, telecommunications offers far more potential locations for interaction. The economic advantages of global electronic access to reach markets and low cost labor drive the continuous development of telecommunications speed and capacity. As telecommunications costs decline, the global space for telecommunications dependent producers also changes. New opportunities arise for firms to restructure production and its location while lowering operating costs. Information flows and telecommunications access are not unfettered, however, since access to advanced technology depends on willingness to invest and the availability of capital, as well as politically determined rights for telecommunications access.

Passively, telecommunications and information technology can be seen as conduits for information flows, but they are also vehicles for control and access, to reach data bases, clients, and workers distributed across space. These elements are receiving overdue recognition by academics with an interest in the political economy of information, and the impact of technological change on production, spatial patterns, and individuals. Harvey's (1989) concept of time-space compression reflected on centuries of production of physical output, yet the concept is no better illustrated than by the global service economy. Time and space are indeed compressed for manufacturing, and the distinction is even greater for the instantaneous transmission of information products. Hepworth (1990) directs attention to the impact of computer networks and the role of information capital in manufacturing, and the concept of information space. The uneven development stemming from application of information capital is emphasized by Mulgan (1991) in his volume on the ways computer networks transform space. Kellerman (1993) adopts a spatial perspective on how telecommunications affects urban, regional, and international development. The disparity Castells (1996) observes is also a global phenomenon as the information economy incorporates many nations and places.

The character of electronic space is well expressed through the World Wide Web, which allows easy movement through an exhausting range of options, data, and applications of substantial to dubious quality. Seeking and browsing items of interest on the web takes the user from hypertext page to hypertext page. What is less evident is that the browser may also be moving dramatically from place to place at the same time. The source of information may be boldly identified through a place specific home page, but other sources of information may not be easily identified. If not for the occasional two letter identification of a URL as Canada (ca) or Britain (uk) or Singapore (sg) the user may never know the source or circumstances of the information source. Often, the locations are irrelevant, subsumed in the search for information.

This chapter starts with a description of the vehicles that we use to travel through electronic space, the very physical wiring, networks, and facilities that carry bits. Given this electronic infrastructure, the next section asks what our world looks like by distorting the physical to illustrate the spatial relationships of the electronic. Our mental images of the physical world look very different when seen as electronic space, with an unfamiliar global pattern clearly evident. The final section considers the implications of telecom tectonics, of operating in electronic space.

ELECTRONIC SPACE VEHICLES

Electronic space is navigated using a global infrastructure of satellites, cables, and wireless networks that connect billions of telephones and computers. Advanced telecommunications facilities are no longer tied to advanced economies. During the 1980s Ireland completely renovated its telephone system with a digital network. Barbados' digitalized communications system offers direct international dialling for telephone/fax and satellite based high speed data transmission capacity to North America and Europe. Currently, Pakistan is implementing a national fiber optic core telecommunications system to link major centers, while Thailand has awarded contracts for three million additional telephone subscriber lines (Asian Business Review, 1993). In the planning stages is AT&T's project to build a US$2 billion underwater fiber optic network circling Africa, although the coordination required needs agreement by many countries with limited resources (Revzin, 1995).

The ITU (1999a) estimates that the world's almost six billion people share almost 832 million telephone lines, or 14 telephones per 100 inhabitants. This varies considerably across the world, with a dramatic contrast between those countries that are wired and those that are not. For example, the most connected countries include the developed world such as the United States and Canada (64 telephones per 100 inhabitants); Denmark (66 telephones); Germany (57); France (57); United Kingdom (55); Hong Kong (56); Singapore (56); Australia (51). The highest rate is for the financial center of the Channel Islands with 77 telephones per 100 inhabitants.

The wiring of the developed world contrasts dramatically with the state of telephone infrastructure for developing countries. Overall, Africa averages 2.2 telephone lines per 100 inhabitants, and many of those lines are concentrated in South Africa, which accounts for almost one third of all telephone lines in Africa. At the lowest levels are the Democratic Republic of the Congo with 0.04 lines per 100 people; Chad (0.12); Niger (0.18); Rwanda (0.16); Somalia (0.14). A number of Asian countries also have low levels of access to telephones, for example Afghanistan (0.14 lines per 100 people); Bangladesh (0.26); Cambodia (0.23); Laos (0.55); and Myanmar (0.52).

Different patterns emerge when cellular services are included. The ITU (1999b) estimates that the global rate of cellular subscription is 5.38 per 100 inhabitants. Ranging from Africa (0.45 subscribers) to Asia (3.05); the Americas (12.07); and Europe (13.15). While some countries have no cellular service, such as Chad or Niger, others have a significant cellular base. In Rwanda more than half of all telephone services are cellular subscriptions, and in many countries cellular services account for more than a quarter of all telephone subscribers, for example: Côte d'Ivoire (35% cellular); Guinea (37%); South Africa (33%); Paraguay (42%); Venezuela (43%); Cambodia (71%); Hong Kong (46%); Japan (45%); Finland (51%). The United States has a cellular rate of 28.6%; Germany (23%); United Kingdom (32%); and France (25%). Globally, 27.8% of all telephone subscribers are cellular services, which show significant presence in both the most and least developed nations.

The wired and wireless world has also experienced dramatic growth in traffic as access has increased and costs fallen. As an indicator of potential cost saving through technological advance, the Federal Communications Commission (FCC 1999) reports that the first transatlantic cable, TAT-1 in 1956, had an annual investment cost of US$214,000 per circuit equivalent to US$2.44 per minute used. With the introduction of fiber optics and more advanced telephonic systems, the most recent transatlantic cable, AC-1 in 1998, carried an annual investment cost of US$304 per circuit equivalent to US$0.003 per minute.

Technological advances and reduced costs have had a significant impact on revenue and traffic internationally. International traffic data for the United States from the (FCC 1999) show that the average revenue per billed international minute has declined from $3.11 in 1964 to $0.76 per minute in 1997. As prices fell, international calls have increased by an average of 17.7% annually between 1992 and 1997. World traffic in 1997 was 82 trillion minutes, of which the United States accounted for 27.6%. The cost of telecommunications in many countries has declined so much that for businesses and many individuals it is not a significant cost, nor does it exert major influence on operating behavior.

The reduction of real telephone costs has not been equal for all countries, however, with PTTs in many countries slow to pass on the cost savings brought by advances in telecommunications technology. For example, the cost of high speed lease lines using Germany's monopoly telecommunications carrier is five times greater than in the United States and twice the cost in Britain. A London/Frankfurt leased line costing over £40 per month would cost less than £3 as a US equivalent (*Economist*, 1994). The privatization of PTTs in some countries, however, has hastened competition for international calls and brought reduced telephone charges. Recently, the deregulation of Germany's telecommunications sector has brought competition in both domestic and international calls which has led to a rapid increase in telephone use.

Unlike physical space, where distances between two points are not affected by choice of origin and destination, electronic space is very much shaped by differential costs between locations. Differences apply to the direction of interaction, with the cost of a telephone call from Japan to the United States costing more than the reverse call. This means that the United States is farther from Japan than Japan is from the United States. The telecommunications cost surface depends upon the source of the call, with reductions from one country to another not automatically matched for the reverse call. Another difference stems from the timing of telephone calls, with peak hour connections often costing more than off-peak calls. For two countries at the same time, a call in one direction may be at peak rates while the return call would be off-peak.

TELECOM TECTONICS

In geologic terms the world is not changing quickly, and continental drift is apparent in many small and occasionally large changes in the earth's crust. The changes in physical relationships that are occurring tend to be slow, almost imperceptible, while the changes that take place in electronic space are rapid and often dramatic. The deregulation of a country's telecommunications sector can produce almost overnight changes in the structure, efficiency, and cost of electronic interaction. If the defining element of the physical world is distance, then the defining element of electronic space is cost of interaction. At its most simple, the relationship between London and New York can be reduced to a distance of 3,453 miles. In electronic space the relationship can be reduced to a cost per minute. The concept behind electronic space is fundamentally economic, in that decisions are made on cost rather than distance. While traditionally modeled as a linear relationship, cost and distance are often divorced in electronic space. Neighboring Indonesia can cost as much to call from Singapore as calling distant Europe or North America.

Metaphorically, continents and countries are moving closer together in telecommunications cost space, with Britain moving from being over $1 per minute away from the United States to being only 10 cents per minute away. Just as continental drift has brought (and still brings) great physical change, telecom tectonics brings social and economic change. In the same way that the early clippers in the mid nineteenth century brought settlers and prospectors during the Gold Rush days to Australia in record breaking times (Blainey, 1967), so is tele- communications speeding up time-space convergence. Effectively, Australia was brought closer to Europe, driven in part by the desire to reach the Gold Fields as quickly as possible. Again, economic reasons are motivating the forces that bring various countries closer together in telecommunications space.

It is easy to visualize our physical world. We are familiar with maps and descriptions of physical space, and are armed with images of our environment from our experiences, books, film, and television. Each of us has mental images that show the relationships between the physical landmarks used in daily life, and impressions of how the world looks. Our mental maps of the world provide instant, if not always accurate, images of the planet. But if the physical world of atoms is replaced by an electronic world of bits, what images do we carry of this new terrain? How are decisions made about electronic space in contrast to physical space? How can we visualize the ways electronic interaction is altering spatial relationships?

MAPPING ELECTRONIC SPACE

In an attempt to capture the impact of telecom tectonics, the telephone cost space for four countries is presented in this chapter. The aim of these cartograms is to portray how electronic space differs from the familiar physical world we know. Each map shows the relationship between the source and destination countries in terms of the cost of a standard three minute business telephone call. Telecom- munication space is represented by relative movements of countries along predefined directions. Country boundaries move along lines whose bearings have previously been calculated. The distance along this direction is proportional to the communication cost from the source country. The problem with this method is that the topological structure of the newly projected map is not maintained because contiguity is broken. For example, Ireland moves to the east of the United Kingdom when viewed with respect to costs from the United States. In addition, smaller countries can again be obliterated by larger countries with a similar cost distance and bearing. However, the resultant outputs do convey a good represen- tation of electronic space, with differential movements representing the uneven cost structure of electronic space. Arrowsmith and Wilson (1997) present a detailed discussion of the technique used to produce the cartograms.

Four countries are presented as source locations for cartograms of electronic space. Each cartogram shows the original location of each continent, with an overlay showing the location of each continent recalculated in terms of tele- communications cost. The cartograms are presented at the continental level for simplicity, with later examples of greater complexity. Map 1 shows the telecom- munications relationship between France and the world, with Australia moving closer and Africa moving away from France. A similar pattern is evident for Germany in Map 2. The view from Japan (Map 3) is quite different, with North America moving closer, but Asia, Australia, Europe and Africa farther away. For

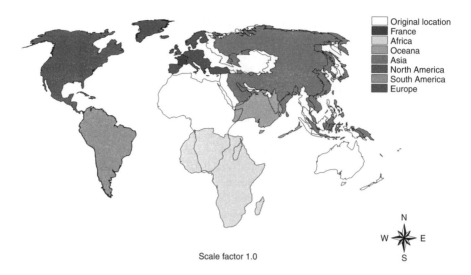

Map 1 *France to the World Continents*

Map 2 *Germany to the World Continents*

the United States, presented in Map 4, Europe and Asia are relatively close, with Latin America further away.

The simplicity of the continental level presentation masks a wide range of differences in telecommunications cost space. For example, at the country level, the relationship between the United States and Asia or Africa (Maps 5 and 6), is far more fragmented, with countries moving closer (Japan, Australia, South Africa) and farther away (Somalia, Mozambique). Telephone costs between Germany and

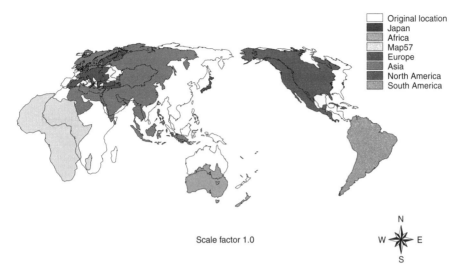

Map 3 *Japan to the World Continents*

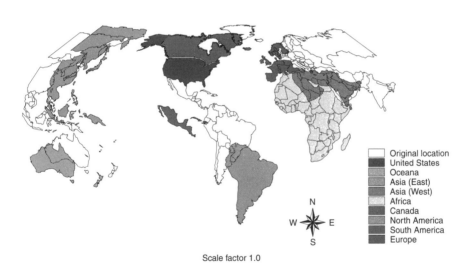

Map 4 *USA to the World Continents*

Asia (Map 7) show cost advantages and a closer location to Australia and Japan, while other countries move further away. From Japan to the Americas in Map 8, the priority and competition of communication to the United States and Canada clearly exceeds other countries. Finally, Map 8 illustrates cost space from Japan to Africa, and also suggests the growing trend to little differentiation in telephone costs based on distance. The distance cost relationship has been eroded greatly in telecommunications cost space, and continues to decline.

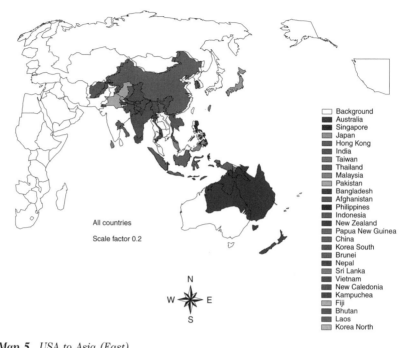

☐	Background
	Australia
	Singapore
	Japan
	Hong Kong
	India
	Taiwan
	Thailand
	Malaysia
	Pakistan
	Bangladesh
	Afghanistan
	Philippines
	Indonesia
	New Zealand
	Papua New Guinea
	China
	Korea South
	Brunei
	Nepal
	Sri Lanka
	Vietnam
	New Caledonia
	Kampuchea
	Fiji
	Bhutan
	Laos
	Korea North

All countries

Scale factor 0.2

Map 5 *USA to Asia (East)*

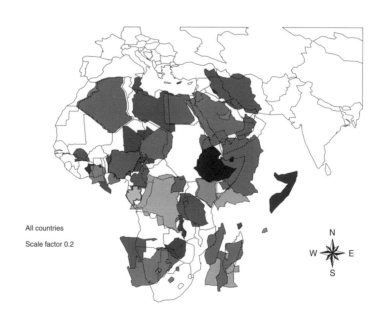

All countries

Scale factor 0.2

Map 6 *USA to Africa and the Middle East*

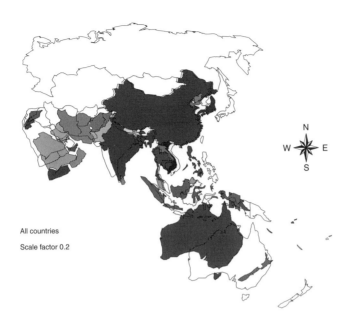

All countries
Scale factor 0.2

Map 7 *Germany to Asia*

All countries
Scale factor 1.0

Map 8 *Japan to North and South America*

IMPLICATIONS OF TELECOM TECTONICS

Mapping electronic space, and the concept of telecom tectonics, are devices to
remind us of the spatial dimensions of the intangible electronic world. The implications of a world based on bits instead of atoms are varied and many. Among
the challenges are human rights, as noted by Brunn in Chapter 4, or the transformation of the firm illustrated by Roche and Blaine (Chapter 5), or the increased
mobility and velocity of international exchange described by Langdale (1991)
in Chapter 6. While there are many significant elements worthy of consideration, in this section we address two elements of telecom tectonics, equity, and
production.

EQUITY

In telecom tectonic terms, not all countries and locations are moving at the same
pace. Many developing countries unable to afford electronic technology remain in
place or lose ground in what Thrift (1995) terms 'electronic ghettos'. It is easy to
be mislead by the maps that show the availability of telecommunications or
Internet access, and conclude that availability means access. Global telephone
systems, such as Iridium, present a world of complete access, yet while availability may approach the universal by place, it does not translate into access
for all.

Many developing countries unable to afford electronic technology remain in
place or lose ground, or have major cities centrally placed in information space
and hinterlands far distant due to outmoded domestic telecommunications systems. For example, using data from ITU (1999a), Africa's 760 million people have
only 17 million telephone lines. If the four most wired countries are excluded
(South Africa, Egypt, Algeria, and Morocco), there remain over 590 million people
in Africa with fewer than 5 million telephone lines, or a rate of 0.8 lines per 100
people. In addition, access is concentrated in urban areas further limiting access to
those distant from cities and towns. The equity issues for developing countries are
immense, but most nations have variations in access to information technology;
parts of Manhattan may well be integral to the information world, while blocks
away such connectivity may be irrelevant or impossible.

Equity considerations are increasingly important as the access, control, and
management of information increasingly become the foundations of economic
growth and development. If information centrality is essential for growth and
development, then the core equity considerations become: Who has access? And is
access possible for those who desire access? While fundamentally an economic
issue of affordability, the ability to access information technologies is also determined by government actions to shape the policies of service providers, or to make
access possible through schools, libraries, and other public facilities. For the
poorest countries, developing access to information technology also begs the question about the most effective way to develop. Are the resources needed to expand
telecommunications better used for other projects?

One way of capturing a dimension of electronic space is through the decisions of firms operating in information and service industries; firms managing and generating information, from research, to currency trading, to call centers. Globalization of services is not a new phenomenon. American, European, and Japanese service firms serve foreign markets from both domestic and international locations. What is growing in scale, however, is the use of offshore locations to produce services used for domestic production, and the real time importation of services, such as toll free reservations or technical support. For example, software can be written by teams in several locations linked electronically; a telephone call to a help desk can be routed to an available agent in one of many locations, or back office tasks can be relocated to the Caribbean or Asia (Wilson, 1997a, 1997b).

One of the most dramatic results of telecom tectonics is the ability to access low wage workers and low cost locations from high wage and high cost countries. The primary motivation for the globalization of information industries is access to low cost labor. Labor costs for information work are not wages alone, but a variety of other factors that influence worker productivity and employer expenses. In addition to wages, labor costs are affected by productivity and worker turnover, worker availability, benefit packages, occupational safety and health considerations, and cultural and social influences. The social and international division of labor offers firms an economic advantage by relocating to gain workforce flexibility and a revised social contract. Information industries seek out low cost and less regulated labor markets. Labor intensive office work in the United States faces wage and cost pressures from declining numbers of young workers and increasing insurance and benefit costs that are not evident in many offshore locations. The resulting high wages and expectations of future wage growth has made low cost labor the central issue for information industry operations.

For some industries, the use of information technologies and telecommunications has expanded the labor market for a firm from local to global areas. The search for engineers, data processing staff, or medical transcriptionists no longer must be restricted to confined geographic areas, but can be extended internationally. From one perspective, the firm is now able to employ workers over a broad geographic and occupational range, and to manage labor costs through use of offshore workers. The reverse view is a concern that lower wages offshore will place downward pressure on wages in developed economies, whose workers may need to compete with well trained staff in lower cost locations.

At a broader level, Internet access can reduce the physical barriers that have prevailed in the past and led to below average growth. Information technologies may be able to remove the barriers that have defined peripheral locations to date. For example, Ireland's peripheral geography has been overcome in many ways through public and private investment in infrastructure, education, and training. Ireland's well developed telecommunications infrastructure provides an electronic way to reduce past disadvantages of location. The shift from peripheral geography to electronic centrality carries great benefits to the people and countries able to engineer a relocation in electronic space. At the same time, electronic space

40
—

challenges those working in high wage locations to increase productivity or face competition from distant locations.

CONCLUSIONS

The concept of telecom tectonics appropriates the imagery of plate tectonics to the invisible realm of electronic space. The use of the metaphor goes beyond the idea of locations changing their relative positions in space. As trade moves from atoms to bits, and electronic interaction offers an alternative to physical interaction, there is significant potential for the realignment of the global economy in electronic space. Plate tectonics involves frequent small, and infrequently massive, adjustments to the physical landscape. The same can be said for the impact of electronic space, which involves daily changes in the scale, form, and location of production and interaction, that over time accumulates to be a major reorganization of the economy.

ACKNOWLEDGEMENTS

The authors thank the assistance of the E*Space Project under the auspices of Michigan State University for providing the initial telecommunication charge data, and for providing a forum to discuss issues relating to the project. The RMIT Faculty of Applied Science provided seed funding for this project, and Michael Black (RMIT Department of Land Information) provided programming assistance.

CHAPTER 4

HUMAN RIGHTS AND WELFARE IN THE ELECTRONIC STATE

Stanley D. Brunn

INTRODUCTION

> Everyone has the right to freedom of opinion and expression; this right includes freedom to hold opinions without interference and to seek, receive, and impart information and ideas through any media and regardless of frontier.

> Article 19 Universal Declaration of Human Rights 1948

The human geographies of postindustrial societies are fraught with fascinating processes and problems, many of which are unprecedented in human history. The human conditions associated with foci on service economies and societies, with a heavy emphasis on the production and consumption of information and communication, raise questions about the nature of personal and interpersonal interaction, the diffusion and exchanges of products and ideas, the impress of technology on a culture, and the roles and responsibilities of governments. At the heart of these issues are concerns about some very basic geographic concepts, concepts that assist us in understanding what is going on where and why. Among the important geographic terms and themes are those defining the meaning of space in multidimensional worlds; place and places within cyberspace, the plastic and elastic nature of distance, the measurement and definitions of communities, human welfare in these electronic states, and the importance of speed or velocity as a new element in fashioning human interaction. It is these juxtapositions of time and space or time and place that are the subject of discussions by academics in various disciplines. These include not only those in communications, journalism and publishing, image processing, and computer based cartography (including GIS, CD-ROM, networked software, and visualization), but those in various forms of electronic commerce, including global finance, long distance learning, telemedicine, human engineering, and electronic or cyberlaw (Gates, 1995).

In assessing the present and future dimensions of electronic space, I address questions about the impresses of ICT (information and communication technologies) on individuals, societies, and governments (Poster, 1990, 1995; Rosenberg, 1994), I am referring to technologies used for word processing, graphics, statistical analyses, education, entertainment, e-mail, and the WWW. Also, I include the use of fax machines, multimedia for instructional purposes, high-density television for teleconferencing and telemedicine, and satellites for sending, receiving, and transferring information. These technologies, by their very nature, have human impacts, *viz.* who uses them and for what? Whom are they designed for? How have they been accepted by various groups? What will be their affects on individuals and groups? What role does the state play in the technology that developed this innovation and production, and also in the sales, regulation, consumer availability and protection?

I would maintain that these are among the most important questions facing societies today, rich and poor, democratic and emerging democratic, as they develop and promote new technologies for the home and workplace as well as for human interaction and leisure pursuits. These are issues facing the producers of these technologies, that is, the economies whose growth and incomes are tied to producing and distributing new products. And they are of concern to those institutions in new societies who wish to see these products introduced, utilized, and perfected. I include those groups and institutions that are responsible for education, safety, health, and caring. Finally, these questions are germane to the state and to interstate relations (Brunn, 1981, 1984; Cohen, 1994; Nye and Owens, 1996). In spite of dramatic changes on the world political map since the end of the Cold War and the introduction of ICTs that have changed the ways people interact, perceive, and behave and that in many cases lead to a 'border-less world', people still reside in state spaces that have meaning in their daily lives. Those may be local spaces, communities, and transborder regions. States and boundaries, real or imagined, still matter as do questions about the access and availability of new technologies, equity, protection, human rights and welfare.

Below, I discuss issues about human rights and welfare at two scales, those affecting existing and expectant electronic democracies, for example, those in Europe and North America and Japan, and the integrated and networked world which is marked by a widespread introduction and diffusion of ICTs. Before examining these scale issues in detail, I want to provide some working definitions of important terms and set a framework where rights and welfare are considered both within state (spaces as 'containers') and interstate (the erasure of borders) contexts. These ideas reflect a current focus of my research, which examines a variety of interfacing issues in political and social geography, information and communications, electronic communities, and human welfare. Many of my ideas stem from research undertaken a couple of decades ago on reorganized political spaces in America, the impacts of time-space convergence on societies, and future cities and settlements. This background has been enhanced by recent information and communications technologies that were unknown even a decade ago and dialogue and discussion with academics from various disciplines and in different countries.

SOME WORKING DEFINITIONS

Three crucial words appear in the title: human rights, welfare, and the electronic state. These are phrases I maintain will be used increasingly in national and international discussions and legislative agendas measuring the impacts of new

ICTs on individuals, groups, and states. *Human rights* refers to those legally defined languages and constitutional statements that stipulate how an individual or group is protected by the sovereign state. Those rights might include an expansion of existing rights to cover new methods of protection from new technologies of surveillance (from telephone, e-mail, camera), defining a new set of protections for those using new technologies in the workplace, definitions of electronic censorship, and the protection of an original map and a piece of traditional music or art. Below, I discuss human rights in a broad context.

Human welfare relates to how groups within a society are protected by the state. I adopt David Smith's human geography query 'Who gets what and where?' as a crucial question to raise and answer (Smith, 1977). In regard to the technologies of information and communication, what group or groups in a state have the information and communication technologies, whether they be computers, telephones, or television, which groups do not, and where are those who have and those who do not have these innovations for employment, education, or entertainment? Here, I am referring both to social classes and regions within a state, such that perhaps those who are wealthy and have middle incomes have the innovations, while those who are poor may not. Or it might be that those living in the capital cities and largest cities are privileged and able to enjoy these technologies and benefits over those long distances away from centers of population or political power. Should a state be concerned about equity and distribution questions; 'why-where' questions become important in the delivery of both goods (computers, telephones, and satellite dishes) and services (fiber optics, hardware upgrades, electricity, data bases, and trained personnel).

The concept *electronic state* refers to those states that are already 'wired' on the Internet or those proposing to implement and diffuse these technologies through a series of information highways. A tightly integrated electronic state would be one in which the above technologies are available. Whether they are provided depends on the political and social goals and priorities of the state. We might envision a 'democratic electronic state' or 'cyberdemocracy' in which the state ensures that peripheral and core areas, rich and poor sections and creative and laggard regions are also connected or networked, so that all benefit from the introduction and diffusion of new goods and services. In a state with less than democratic aspirations, the 'electronic state' may only include those centers of wealth, corporate offices, military, and state power; these could appear both in developed and developing world regions. The linkage pattern would be similar to the primate city networks in which the capital city was often the major and only transportation and information gateway to the outside world. Smaller and less important places on the economic and political map were excluded or perhaps only partially planned for inclusion by those with the power, prestige, and money. The notion of an *electronic world* refers to a global setting that is becoming linked through a host of processes that facilitate cheap and rapid transfer of information and communication. While the concept of a completely wired world may be a long way off, with each new innovation, each extension of the electronic services, and each new link of an information highway, humankind is becoming more electronically connected.

GEOGRAPHY, RIGHTS, AND TECHNOLOGY

In discussions on the realities and consequences of electronic spaces, it is most appropriate to focus on questions about what technological innovations mean to individuals, groups, and the state. Human rights and justice questions are not separated from what decisions are made by the state and corporations, as both make decisions daily that affect the quality of human well being and quality of life as well as individual rights and human welfare, broadly defined. To neglect the study and discussion of such topics in the social and policy sciences and humanities is to separate technology and technological impacts from the places where people work, live, and recreate and the policy decisions of the state. These topics become all the more important when we discuss new technologies that have little precedence in human history or the impact of rapid speed on human lives and livelihood or a state policy whose impacts are changing the very definitions of individual and group rights, and, I would add, the definition and sovereignty of a state.

A useful perspective on questions about rights, justice, and welfare comes from that of the social and political geographer. That is, to look at rights as being defined in terms of people in space. Thus, we can speak of *spatial rights* as those rights or clauses of legal protection that define a person residing in or inhabiting (perhaps only temporarily) specific spaces. Those legal administrative spaces may be counties, cities, or states (Harries and Brunn, 1978). We live in one or more of these territorial or *bounded spaces*, that is, those spaces defined by the national state. Some live most or all their lives in the same spaces, others in transborder spaces that are crossed daily for personal and work reasons. In these situations, the individuals or groups are affected by laws and codes drawn up by those in control of the state and space, be they legislators, courts, quasi-legal groups, or voters.

If we live in one space, we are governed by the rights designated for that space. But many live, circulate, and conduct activities in more than one space, for example, a county, city, and state. And, as noted above, there are *transborder* individuals who reside and work in several different spaces during the course of a month or year. These include states and even regions. The result of this legal complexity may be spaces which define the rights of residents alike or in quite different ways. Maps will display these different 'rights' in different spaces. Those spaces, as we know, are different in the United States from those in Canada and Europe. At another level, the administrative layers of rights may be different at a local level, provincial layers and at the federal or national levels. In an *electronic state*, we are dealing with those places that may be highly connected, less connected, or not even connected by ICTs.

HUMAN RIGHTS AND THE SPATIAL DIMENSION

Those who are concerned about human rights readily acknowledge that rights have a spatial dimension. This observation applies to issues related to women, children, the elderly, disabled populations and subtly or overtly to those of different racial minorities, or have refugee and immigrant status. The rights of a young woman in

Utah are different from California and the elderly receive different state benefits in Florida than in South Dakota or Connecticut. Some states provide a variety of educational programmes for children with special disabilities, others fewer. Health benefits, the legal status of women and immigrants, and protection from environmental risk are additional examples. In an international context, the rights of guestworkers in Italy and Germany are different from Switzerland and Ireland. Each state seeks to protect its own citizens and define the health, education, and welfare benefits of those who are working only temporarily. The same variation applies to those fleeing religious or political persecution.

In this context we are, to use the concept developed by geographer Graham Rowles (1975), all 'prisoners of space'. He applied this concept to his research on the housing of the elderly, as many indeed are prisoners of their own spaces or those spaces created by others. But the concept can be applied to our thinking about human rights in a broad context. In one sense we are all 'victims' or 'prisoners' or residents of bounded spaces; we are under the legal systems and jurisdictions of those who define the rights for people in those spaces.

Some can 'escape' these spaces and live where there are more freedoms; others cannot, so they remain prisoners. Others may choose to live and work where there are improved rights for women, children, the elderly, disabled, and other groups. They have the freedom to move, which may itself be a right for all or specifically designated groups. Thus, the fact that rights are defined spatially and territorially means that issues about human welfare and rights are certain to exhibit a mosaic of geographic variations, within a state or country with a variety of political cultures (for example, within the United States between California, Texas, and Florida) or within a large continent that has experienced various mixes of cultures that have migrated long and short distances over several centuries, for example, in Central or Western Europe. On the world political map there are spaces with varying degrees of *connectedness* to ICTs, some that are densely networked and accessed by all residents, some that are little networked, and still others that have vast portions of area and populations that are not electronically connected. Location is crucial in defining one's human rights in a non-electronic and electronic world.

LEGAL STANDARDS AND DEFINITION OF COMMUNITY

A very interesting issue is being raised with respect to defining rights in electronic spaces. And that is by what *legal standards* will one be judged? Or under what culture is one evaluated? Will the producers of the technology set the standards? These were not difficult questions when one lived in the same place all one's life. That is, one played, grew up, worked, worshipped, recreated, and died often in the same place or perhaps within the same political culture. Today, in a highly mobile world and one in which there is instant contact with spaces once considered a long distance away (in time or space), people move and are regularly being exposed to or confronted with different political cultures or different ways of defining behaviors, societal norms, and acceptable beliefs. One might be living in four or five different political cultures or two or three different countries during a lifetime.

Another question is how one defines one's community? Is that community a bounded place, which is the traditional way we defined community? In this context, it had specific territorial limits. It was a specific jurisdictional, territorial, and legal space. You lived in it, your address was in it, your friends lived in it, and your 'spatial rights' were defined by residents or others for that given territory. Those bounded spaces one could define on a map. We knew 'who we were' by where we were located on a map. But in an electronic world, the spaces become more than systems and networks, not two-dimensional parcels, but three (volumetric) and four (time) dimensions. The appearance of the community may be more akin to a 'web'.

Are we witnessing a *new definition of the community*, in which one's community is defined by a network rather than a place? That is, is one's community not a place or bounded space or territory, but a network in which we are connected by a series of linkages? We can think about those spaces and individuals we interact with during the course of a day, a week, a month, or a year. Do we talk with individuals who are in widely separated locations? In different cities? In different states and countries? We can communicate with them via phone, mail, e-mail, fax, or even using the WWW to access information. A community, in theory and practice, represents a group of individuals who share something in common. Perhaps we share a street or county or city as a place with those near us, but in many cases our community extends beyond it to other places and spaces. Should this be the case, we have much more in common with those who live elsewhere. We share similar views about religion, justice, racial and ethnic minorities (Anderson, 1989), the rights of women, care for the environment, and the role of government in our lives. Those spaces of our community may be 'pockets' of political culture far distant from where we live. The electronic human landscape is constantly changing with new groups that are electronically connected, locally and internationally (Raban, 1988; Rheingold, 1993; Mitchell, 1995).

A new definition of community might include one that is less a territory or specific areal unit and more a network of interests and community of special interests. And in a human rights context, we are interested in the human rights and protection of those rights in those defined and included in our community. Those widely dispersed communities may include children, the elderly, women, refugees, immigrants, farmers, and bankers in other parts of the world than where we live. Special interest groups that are committed to specific social agendas or communities of interest are networks that are not just neatly defined places on social and political maps. Those lobbying or seeking to influence political decisions and government legislation represent networks of individuals and groups often in widely separated spaces, and often in different political cultures and governmental authorities. Borders often mean nothing to those with common (or community) goals. Speed facilitates the communication, networking, and action.

THE EROSION OF BOUNDARIES

We can think of examples of places where electronic and communication networks are replacing those places which had some unique character in the political and legal landscape. Perhaps those places are in widely separated locations. Perhaps the political culture networks among interested groups and institutions represent an additional 'layer' in the legal framework and geography. If that is so, then we need to consider both the traditional and emerging ways in which rights are defined, that is, not only in a place or bounded community, but in a network and interlocking system of varying nodes in the legal hierarchy.

In an international context, we can consider each state on the world political map as a 'container', that is, the state defines the rights and privileges for those within its borders. Those rights may be similar to those in an adjacent state or could be completely different. States with similar histories and cultures may define human rights in a similar manner or differently. In a highly mobile world and one in which there are various media that permit the instant and inexpensive transfer of information across international borders, the states on the world map may lose much of their uniqueness. Boundaries are porous and spaces around borders are permeable, such that people and goods can move across these spaces without restrictions. States may seek to eliminate or reduce differences in order to provide a freer and easier flow of information (electronic and non-electronic) and communications. When this happens, the boundaries that once sharply divided the rights and welfare of residents may become relics in the boundary landscape.

Three examples illustrate the demise of boundaries in the movement of information and the global circulation of people (Deans and Kane, 1992; Dennis, 1993; Gross, 1995). The first is transnational corporations (TNCs) which represent global networks of corporations with branches, affiliates, and offices. Their ease in transferring information, money, and personnel reflects the borderless world in which they operate. While TNCs operate on a global scale and often enter and leave states with relative ease, they are still very cognizant of states as legal spaces on the world economic and political map. That is, even though states may be losing some of their traditional roles and importance on the world scene, and are replaced by loose or tight regional economic and political unions, TNCs still find it necessary to work with governments in selecting places to locate their offices, obtaining attractive financial packages, training labor forces, influencing leaders and legislators, and meeting environmental standards.

A second group that looks at the mosaic of rights and welfare questions includes the many diaspora that constantly are on the move across the planet. These may be individuals who work for IGOs (intergovernmental organizations) such as the UN, UNESCO, FAO, OAU, and NATO or for various NGOs (nongovernmental organizations) including Red Cross and Red Crescent, Doctors Without Borders, Catholic Relief Services, and Amnesty International. This group includes not only bankers, investors, consultants, military personnel, professors, students, missionaries, physicians, but also refugees, construction workers, emergency disaster relief teams, and tourists. Individuals in these groups may be seasonally mobile or their moves may be aperiodic. But they are also cognizant of the laws and regulations of 'foreign spaces' in their travels, specifically how they are protected and provided with services, which may be different from those of the local citizenry.

The third group includes those members of electronic academic communities whose professional identity is linked via messages, data sets, and reports that circulate electronically. These individuals exchange ideas through personal e-mail or contributions on various listservs; they operate, disseminate, and reproduce data sets, and they collaborate on research proposals and projects on local and global topics (Lanegran, 1992; Andersson and Persson, 1993; O'Lear, 1996). Those who are on academic networks learn much about cutting edge topics, either by requesting and sharing information, or simply reading, but not contributing (Brunn, Husso and Pyyhtia, 1999; Brunn, Husso, Pyyhtia and Kokkonen, 1998). In an electronic academic world the on-line requests for data sets and journal contents, as well as electronic publications, are hallmarks of professional networks where state boundaries are meaningless. Speed both in sending and receiving information is a vital ingredient defining the daily worlds of these 'electronic' academics.

STATES' RIGHTS AND INTERNATIONAL RIGHTS

Human rights are important to those living in the state and those outside the state, that is, those governmental and nongovernmental organizations active in broadly defined human welfare issues affecting the international community (Lyons and Mastanduno, 1992). Reports issued by states and by NGOs portray the status of human rights and violations worldwide. That these reports are disseminated via the world media, either as text or as maps, attest to the importance that organizations and states attach to the rights of individuals and citizens, including disenfranchised and discriminated against minorities.

Underlying the world political map are a host of human rights issues, many that relate to the rights of residents within states and others to those who are interested in macroregional or the global human condition (Smith, 1994). No state is immune from issues related to human rights. These issues are raised both by residents with long histories within their boundaries as well as new groups and diasporas, and those in bordering and trading countries.

Human rights issues are especially important today as we are witnessing many new and faster exchanges and movements of people and products across political boundaries as well as new forms of interaction and communication (Figure 1). States do not exist in isolation any more (if they ever did), nor do their residents. The states find that not only are many issues being raised about rights and justice, but also they prompt demands for solutions for violations and problems. Perhaps some states in Africa or Asia once thought that human rights were issues important only in European democracies or in North America or Australia, only to discover that they now have problems raised about new national minorities within their own boundaries, such as slavery, child prostitution, and refugees of wars and famines. And many of these new and emerging minorities and those committed to improving human rights and welfare have networks to groups elsewhere; and many are connected electronically (Brunn, Jones and Purcell, 1994; Sanders, 1995; Brunn and Purcell, 1996).

Three examples illustrate the changing map of human rights. In the United States, a multicultural population for almost two centuries, we now see groups

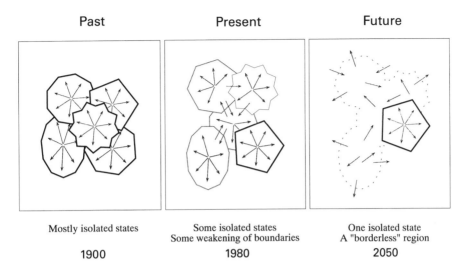

Past	Present	Future
Mostly isolated states	Some isolated states Some weakening of boundaries	One isolated state A "borderless" region
1900	1980	2050

Figure 1 *People and Idea Movements in Europe: Past, Present and Future*

raising questions about the legal status of new immigrants. These are not only new immigrant groups from the Caribbean, Central America, or Pacific Islands, but from South and Southeast Asia. Coupled with the legal status and rights of these groups, as opposed to the traditional Anglo-European immigrant majorities of the last two centuries, we find human rights issues raised by and on behalf of Native Americans, women, the elderly, children, disabled populations, and gays. How are the rights of these new and permanent residents defined? What benefits are they entitled to receive, and their children? Does it make sense to have 50 different state decisions or should there be national policies and programs? Today the discussions about new programs and the sharing of information among state legislatures and legislative commissions demonstrate the ease of long distance communication.

In Western Europe, a continent with multiple states and nationalities, we see issues raised by new groups. Homogeneous states that once had only a small percentage of non-majority members, now find they have guestworkers, new immigrants, and refugees, and are the destinations of new diasporas from other countries outside Europe (Brunn, 1996). Multiculturalism has come to these states and they are faced with questions about absorbing the culture and the settlement of these new peoples in their state-produced educational curricula, how to define citizenship and immigrant status, their rights to own property and vote, their participation in health programs, their coverage in local and national print and visual news, and promoting or inhibiting climates for religious and political tolerance. These newcomers come from eastern Europe, Russia, Central Asia, North Africa, and North America.

In Australia, for long a country with a white majority and European mentality, we find that increased racial and ethnic diversity is changing the face of cities, schools, and the marketplace. Immigrant populations of Japanese, Vietnamese,

Indians, and white South Africans coupled with the rising consciousness of native aborigines are raising a host of legal issues for the country. How these are dealt with will affect the state's education, legal, and political systems.

Issues related to human rights are not restricted only to the individual state, but to regional economic unions and the world community of states. The international dimensions are considered in deliberations about the rights of refugees, the definitions of a refugee, a citizen, a visitor, and a tourist. What are the restrictions a state might enact to keep out an individual or group? Can it be ethnicity, race, medical history, criminal record, political views, work history, family members, or age? How are quotas set? Who sets them and how are they enforced? Who are the gatekeepers that define and enforce human rights? These are no longer questions only for the individual state, but for regions, including the European Union, Pacific Rim, South Asia, and the Gulf States.

One can envisage a host of social justice issues that will call for attention by the international community in the future. These include quarantining individuals with suspected diseases, restricting the travel of those with criminal records (terrorism, drug trafficking, prostitution peddlers, war criminals, and escaped convicts), and suspect political views (however defined). They may also limit the numbers of those seeking work elsewhere or seeking asylum. States and regional organizations may also cooperate to resolve issues, for example, to promote higher standards of living for traditionally defined disenfranchised ethnic minorities as well as new minorities within their borders, to share programmes that promote multicultural education, broadcasting and telecasting, and to co-sponsor legislation to improve the status of women, children, and the elderly (Seager and Olson, 1986).

At issue is whether decisions will be made by individual states, which may result in drastically different laws and protection from neighbors, or whether there will be cooperative efforts at regional or global levels. Efforts to promote and enhance human rights will be among the goals of individual governments, inter-governmental organizations, and NGOs (Brunn and Jones, 1994). These groups will have networks, alliances, affiliations, and chapters around the world, not only within one state. Examples of groups supporting and opposing specific legislation at the state, regional, and global level will be lobbying hard, with money and information (propaganda), to ensure that their views are heard among resident populations, legislators, top level elected officials, and the courts.

HUMAN RIGHTS AND WELFARE IN ELECTRONIC DEMOCRACIES

Next, I want to focus on electronic democracies, and especially on the United States, although many of the specifics apply elsewhere in the developed world, that is, those places that are impacted by advanced ICTs. Also, I believe it is useful to look at the United States as many other countries will experience similar effects and they may look to the United States to observe how the government and groups that influence social legislation respond to technological and social questions (Shelley, Archer, Davidson, and Brunn, 1996). These also include the nature of legislation to finance ICTs in a society and policies that promote social equity and protection.

The United States, as the world's oldest democracy (now entering its fifth century) remains far from perfect, but continuously makes attempts within the democratic process to ensure that social inequities are addressed and corrected through judicial, legislative, and executive processes. And the US Constitution remains a document that is read, studied, and used as a guideline for preparing new constitutions or revising existing constitutions by long-standing democracies. For that reason, much of what is said below about the United States and US society may apply to other emerging *electronic democracies*.

Among the salient issues confronting the contemporary state in the arena of human rights are those related to the impact of the information society and accompanying computer/communication revolutions. The postindustrial society is associated with information industries and economies. We can consider industries and services whose *raison d'être* is producing, collecting, disseminating, manipulating, or mapping information (Garcia, 1997; Wigend, 1997). Some are within the private sector, including finance, real estate, insurance, health, recreation and leisure, marketing, and the print, visual, and sound media. The growth of these economies within the past decade has been phenomenal. In like manner, the state itself has been supporting the growth of these services, whether by favoring deregulation, encouraging megacorporate mergers, or giving financial aid to the growth of information, communication, and computer industries. These economic gains have not occurred in isolation. More often than not, we observe examples where the state is a producer of industries and infrastructures related to the delivery of services and favorable cost environments, whether for selling products or moving products (conversations, goods, digital information, etc.) at bargain rates over long distances (Pickles, 1995). A close examination of the developers of these technologies would reveal close cooperation between the federal state and research grants to state universities and between industrial giants in telecommunications, computer hardware and software, and state universities. Often, research grants support programmes, including graduate students, faculty, and conferences, to promote the goals set by the state.

Many of these state-sponsored information and communication goals are indeed laudable, as they bring worthwhile benefits to many citizens and many locations within a state, thereby promoting human welfare. Examples are satellite information education programmes to those living in isolated areas, an information highway that will permit access to many users for economic and social gains (Maddox, 1994), legislation guaranteeing 'one computer for every five students' and WWW access for those in elementary grades, lower cable television and phone rates, libraries with access to major regional and national data bases and collections, programmes to teach reskillling and retooling to underemployed and unemployed women and men, and high tech medical technology available to physicians and medical specialists anywhere. These are democratic goals that are hard to quibble with, although one might question whether the need and provision of that service is generated by those 'voiceless' individuals and groups at the bottom or those élites at the top who basically are behind the definitions of citizen rights, setting controls on technology, the legislation designed to protect majorities, and the state's acceptable codes (written and unwritten) of conduct.

Legal, Ethical, and Moral Issues

As impressive as the rapid technological and scientific developments in the information, communications, and computer spheres have been in American society during the past two decades, they have not been marked by equal gains in the areas of human rights and welfare. It is almost as if one part of society is being exposed to a blizzard of information and a host of new ways to communicate, calculate, produce, and consume, while another part is struggling to cope with what it means. Entirely new questions relate to issues about the citizen and the state. At issue are a host of legal, ethical, and moral questions about individuals, groups, society at large, regulation, and the role of government. Examples are presented in Table 1.

Many of the legal questions are likely to center on questions of individual rights, liberties, and freedoms, questions that are central to any dialogue in a democracy once new social and technological issues arise. One might even consider cases related to the Bill of Rights, those first ten amendments to the US Constitution that are the hallmark of American democracy. Examples of suggested issues that might be challenged in an emerging electronic democracy are presented in Table 2.

One might even think of a number of very basic questions being raised within states. These might include:

1 How is one's privacy defined when one's entire consumer purchases and one's reading and television preferences are tabulated by marketers interested in regional social behavior and consumer communities?

2 Do I have a right to a computer, modem, cellular phone, videophone, and the WWW, if I want one and am unable to afford it? Are not these basic necessities just as important as a telephone and mailbox? Who pays for it?

3 Will I be protected by the state or a corporation that conducts unauthorized inquiries into my e-mail credit card purchases, checking account, casual and professional phone conversations? 'Knowledge vandals' and computer hackers are hard at work and see golden opportunities ahead for their pursuits.

4 How can we prevent someone from compiling social and behavioral data on a business, county, state or group within a state and selling it to unscrupulous vendors, shady social scientists, or underworld networks? Those data may include detailed company and consumer histories, maps, graphics, photographs, and multiple unauthorized copies. Protection, rights, and free flows of information are at issue.

5 Who 'owns' and has legitimate access to one's e-mail, whether sent from home or office or a third party address? Similar questions arise when making personal and business phone calls from cellular phones or sending faxes from one's private car or a company or state car or international air space.

6 Can a citizen's group file a social discrimination lawsuit because their school was not in the initial plans for the state's information highway network? The consequences are that the children were unable to receive certain educational programmes which assisted those preparing for annual standardized exams. Are we speaking of a form of 'cultural determinism' based on available information and technology?

Table 1 *Legal Issues Facing the Electronic Democracy of Individual States*

1   What is a national? (an Australian, an Irish-American, Vietnamese-Canadian)
2   Will one's genetic code appear on one's national identification card?
3   Does an individual own oneself?
4   What are the rights of temporary asylum seekers? Of refugees? Of undocumented aliens? And extended families?
5   How does one define intellectual property? (What is intellectual and what is property?)
6   How does one prevent counterfeiting and bootlegging materials?
7   Who owns copyrights to new and old patents and information?
8   Who owns translations and which translations are official?
9   What is mail? What is a conversation? What is public and private?
10 What are the rights of the state in transborder data sets? Who owns the data?
11 How enforceable and justifiable are intrastate political borders to spaces supporting individuals and groups with widely different social and political beliefs?
12 Will individual rights be less defensible and supported when issues of the greater public good and welfare are at stake?
13 What are the democratic rights to those limited by the technologies to send and receive information and to form public opinions?
14 Under what conditions are technologies owned by transnational corporations and the information they produce (words, photos, images, symbols) the right of an individual and a state?
15 Will electronic communities, and their national and international subscribers, be accepted as legitimate groups who can vote for political parties within states and international governmental organizations?
16 Will licences for publication, broadcasting, and telecasting be granted to new immigrant minorities, previously 'voiceless' groups, and those with international political agendas?
17 What are the rights of indigenous groups to historic claims: land, water, sacred spaces, and previous injustices?
18 Will minority groups in a state be protected or will states adopt multiple official languages for education and telecommunications?

7   Will an individual be penalized by the state for not installing or turning on the GPS (global positioning system) device in his or her car? If he or she chooses to travel to a location without being monitored by the state surveillance policy, what are his or her rights to protection under the law?
8   As an owner of a company in the information, communications, and computer business that received low interest government loans and benefited from looser government regulations, what information on one's customers must the owner report to proper state authorities? Also, if much of the business is international, what are the legal regulations on reporting transactions from 'offshore information islands'?
9   To what extent are purchases of high tech information, communications, and computer technology and their use against others a violation of law? Here, I am addressing those individuals and groups who obtain ultrasensitive cameras or listening devices to spy on those whose religious beliefs, consumer purchases, lifestyles, and political ideologies may be at odds with the majority population. Related questions about such practices may lead to borderline

54

Table 2 *Questions from the Bill of Rights in the United States Constitution that May Emerge in Electronic Democracies*

Amendment Provisions	Potential Issues
1 No state religion, freedom of speech, freedom of press, freedom of assembly petition to redress grievances	– virtual religion – speech on the Internet – what is speech; censorship – does assembly include electronic communities and communication – official languages – public morality – individual vs. collective rights
2 To keep and bear arms	–
3 Conditions for quartering soldiers	–
4 Rights to search and seizure	– protection of place where information is stored (in machines or international nodes); right to ownership of data (numbers, maps, photos, voices)
5 Private property not taken for public use without compensation; no double jeopardy; no self-incrimination; not deprived of life, liberty, or property without compensation	– what is defined as life? – what are liberties in an electronic state? – what is property (numbers, photos, maps, data, the individual)?
6 Right of the accused to speedy trial; impartial jury of jurors from district where crime committed; rights of accused to know evidence; right to counsel	– trial by jury (electronically) – how jury is selected (random, by computer); witnesses (available electronically); counsel (international witnesses)
7 Right to trial by jury	– how is jury defined? – what is a representative jury?
8 Excessive bail and fines prohibited; no cruel and unusual punishment	– electronically (programmed) determined punishment
9 Rights in Constitution not to be denied	– what are the rights not to be denied?
10 Powers not delegated to US by Constitution are reserved for the states	– what laws (blurring of boundaries); where one lives, works, resides – perhaps multiple locations?

harassment and mischievous acts, including computer hacking and spreading computer viruses.

10 If an individual is found to be in violation of an electronic crime, and is tried by a jury, can he or she request that the prospective jurors be asked about their uses and fears of computers or use of credit card purchases or their familiarity with cellular phones, e-mail, and the WWW? Perhaps the crime was a violation of a copyrighted journal article or blatant plagiarism of a Third World colleague's work or the videoproduction of wedding festivities in a remote culture in the Central Andes.

11 If a pregnant woman is carrying a foetus with a physical or mental defect, is
    there a responsibility to correct it with the latest technology? Who makes that
    decision? The mother? The mother and father? The physician? Or the state?
    Correcting it will probably ensure that the baby is born healthy and will live a
    long life, not correcting it may result in the baby being born with deformities
    and living a short life.

12 Who decides if a child will receive artificial organs and animal transplants?
    Will the mother or both parents decide? The physician? The court? Will the
    decisions on the availability of artificial organs be based on a lottery, the
    income of the parent or parents, ethnic and race mixture, religion, or political
    affiliation? Do CEOs and presidents have a higher priority than those who are
    unemployed laborers, elderly Republicans, new immigrants from Haiti, citizens
    without criminal records, and Buddhists?

HUMAN RIGHTS IN AN ELECTRONIC WORLD

Next, I would like to extend our thinking about the rights of individuals and groups
in an individual state to that of a world where there is more interaction and
connectedness through ICTs. While much of the entire world or maybe cities in it
may be electronically connected, it is important to remember that in a global
context some individuals and groups might not be (Brunn, 1993). A number of
issues that might arise are presented in Table 3.

There are three main points to make in this discussion. The first is what model
or schema will be used to define human rights and welfare in the emerging electronic worlds? One might assume, and I question this assumption, that it will be
the Western model, that is, one based primarily on the way European states or new
Europeanized parts of the world, including the United States, Canada, Australia,
New Zealand, and South Africa, look at the world. The present emphasis on human
rights and welfare, as is reflected in international documents, including the UN
Declaration of Human Rights, is based on how Europeans consider the rights of
individuals versus groups in an open and representative democracy. Those
declarations and rights are more concerned with the rights of individuals rather
than those of groups. The languages of constitutions of these states and revisions
have emphasized the right of the individual to certain freedoms, whether in public
assembly, expression, or worship. In other states, and especially in Africa and
Asia, there are stronger interests in community and collective rights, less on those
of individuals. Among the questions that will emerge in global law and legal
thinking are whether Western thought will continue to dominate the language of
human rights and welfare or whether we are likely to witness some or more
acceptance of non-Western norms (Saunders, 1991; Vasquez et al., 1995). Perhaps
two or three acceptable norms will develop.

The second point is that alternative voices want to be heard within states and in
international arenas. Frederick (1993) defines these as times when there is an
'evolving right to communicate'. That is, the 'rights' of people and the 'right to
communicate'. One can see examples of these issues in calls for self-determination

Table 3 *Legal Issues Affecting an Electronic World*

1 Defining nationality and international citizenship or status.
2 Excluding or censoring, undesirable or unwanted 'foreign' media; symbols, words, television programs, news, advertisements, and entertainment.
3 Rights and regulations of transnational institutions: corporations, religious organizations, banking, and entertainment.
4 Rights and protection of diminishing minorities (religious, language, cultures).
5 The exploitation of traditional weak groups in homes, workplace and schools: women, children, the elderly, disabled, immigrants, religious minorities.
6 Removing barriers to discrimination: racial, gender, age.
7 Territorial demands of stateless groups.
8 Protection of endangered populations, cultures, and historic landscapes.
9 Rights of 'voiceless' groups to information technologies and channels to communicate within national and international arenas.
10 Prohibition of propaganda produced by states and NGOs: propaganda that is racist, sexist, violent, exploitative, abusive, and insensitive.
11 Enforcement of violators of international information laws.
12 Banning of genocide, destructive military weapons, weapons testing, biological weapons, slavery, and sex tourism, media, and trafficking.
13 Right to express political opinion (voting, representation) on national and international issues and to maintain multiple citizenship that permits voting.
14 Right to inform populations of impending disasters: environmental, health, natural.
15 Humanitarian intervention in the event of famine, persecution by the state, epidemics, ecological disasters and threatened biosphere reserves.
16 Rights of individuals versus community in pluralistic states.
17 Establishing quotas for victims of oppression, famine, disasters at regional and international levels.
18 Appropriate legal and court systems for suits against ecommerce and multinational corporations, interstate organizations, and NGOs.
19 Affirmative action efforts to ensure greater representation of Third and Fourth World states in global information and communications decisions.

on the part of indigenous groups within old and new states; peoples are concerned about their own destinies. They are seeking not only to be heard, but also seen and represented. A number of stateless groups and unrecognized nations, whether in Middle America, Southwest Asia, South Asia, or Europe, wish for an end to long periods of domination by the rich, powerful, and traditional groups.

The third point is related to the second, and that is the rights of people to communicate, that is, those long denied a right to communicate. These one might consider 'voiceless' members of a society. They may be individuals or groups, including ethnic, linguistic, and religious minority groups within a majority society, women, lower classes, long-standing indigenous groups, and new immigrants. They are seeking ways to express their views and opinions and they may be distinctly different from those of the majority populations or even of the state itself. Since it is the state that defines access to the media, it is these groups who seek their rights to assemble, broadcast, telecast, publish, travel, and organize. Many of these newly established communities and support systems are seeking allies with other voiceless groups, both within their own state or those in adjacent states or with NGOs around the world. The relative ease in networking with other groups and the low costs of such endeavours, whether by listservs, e-mail, WWW, or fax, have broadened the solidarity of their efforts and also questioned the 'containerized' and traditional bounded-space limits of individual and group rights.

Mapping Electronically Connected and Unconnected Worlds

In looking at collapsing space and time, a key feature of electronic worlds, we need to remember that the world is a varied environment with some places and locations being connected more than others, and also some places that are unconnected. The same holds for people, offices, schools, and governments in cities and rural areas in those spaces. These worlds of humankind can also be depicted on maps. If we think about the contents of many world atlases, they depict, for example, maps of language, culture, settlement, and types of government, as well as world maps depicting variations in incomes, belief systems, natural resources, pollution levels, industrial performance, and population growth. Many of these are familiar choropleth maps of countries or nodes within countries. But there are also the worlds of communication and information which merit inclusion in national and world atlases.

Maps of Information and Communication

There is a crying need to include maps in atlases that depict information and communication themes (for example, see Seager, 1990). Topics might include not only the number and residences of newspaper and television reporters on all continents, the plans for information highways, availability of international news, international trade in Hollywood films and television series, and overseas investments by foreign companies, but also computers and phones per 1,000 population, WWW sites or places (countries and cities with home pages), usage of the Internet, sales of hardware and software, electronic data bases and base services, and electronic commerce, including the daily movement of money (which is information) around the world. Electronic commerce includes not only the transfer of information by e-mail and listservs (Wigend, 1997; Choi, Stahl, and Whinston, 1997; Leinbach and Brunn, unpublished manuscript; Garcia, 1997; Hill, 1997; Auger and Gallaugher, 1997), but also the use of the WWW to promote business and 'sell' a state (Cronin, 1996; Brunn and Cottle, 1997). An atlas showing maps of the quaternary and quinary sectors would also include financial centers, legal offices specializing in citizen, corporate, environmental, and international law, 'Silicon Valleys' around the world, creative regions (see Carmel, 1997) for medicine, military, entertainment, and education, major 'information sheds' of global newspapers and satellite news (Sky Channel and CNN), the 'world' of MTV, information offices of governments and NGOs, and centers of political power (in this case information and communication power).

These maps would be combinations of networks, systems, and hierarchies. Mapping these data for these existing and emerging worlds of ICTs may require some new representations of space and time (Batty and Barr, 1994). Places that are widely separated in absolute space may not be in the same communication and time space. 'Speed' maps and the implications of speed in commerce and communication, for example, global time-space and cost-space convergence maps, could be additional themes to depict. A cyberspace atlas would want to map or graph the meanings and measures of distance (*The Economist*, 1995). Distance is measured by time (minutes and seconds) for those individuals, offices, organizations, and governments that are 'wired' or 'connected' in cyberspace (Brunn, Jones and Purcell, 1994).

SOCIAL JUSTICE AND WELFARE ISSUES

It also bears mention in any cyberspace discussion to note that there are other sets of worlds 'out there' that are not part of the tightly connected and interconnected worlds. These represent those individuals and groups who are without electricity, telephones and televisions; schools, businesses, and government offices without computers, fax machines, e-mail, and WWW access. They are places outside cyberspace and where connections to the electronic world are only dreams and fantasies and where the concept of an electronic state or democracy means little or nothing. These places may be households and rural communities and even large cities (only a very small part of the human population owns computers and has access to the Internet). The patterns may not be displayed in national or world atlases, that is, 'maps of unconnected places', but they exist on all continents (some in greater volume than others), not only in imaginary or virtual space. There have always been such places and there always will be. An example of a contemporary map depicting these variations is Figure 2. One needs to keep these maps in mind when discussing questions about rights and welfare and the electronic state.

The patterns of both sets of maps, that is, of connected and unconnected locations, often depict the same locations, especially in large states where there are vast differences in well being, incomes, and social class. For example, in a large city, there may be offices and households that are connected to the state and world daily via computer, e-mail, and fax machines, while other shops and homes are without electricity as well as regular phone service and mail delivery (Figure 3). Cost and access may be the reasons behind the usage of certain information and communication technologies in some homes and offices, but so may questions of privilege, that is, those with power are provided the services and technologies. Power may be associated with access to electricity, a communications infrastructure, and ability to purchase and obtain instruction in using new technologies. The power of those in the informational city (Castells, 1989) may extend to those with close friendships with favored political officials and parties, those working for international corporations or NGOs, those in favored universities and state laboratories, and those receiving state subsidies because their interests serve the state

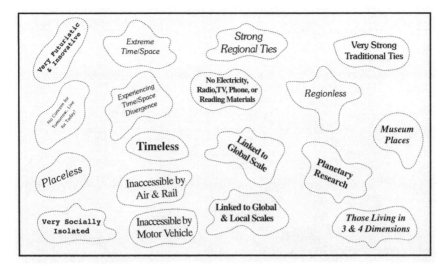

Figure 2a World Time Regions

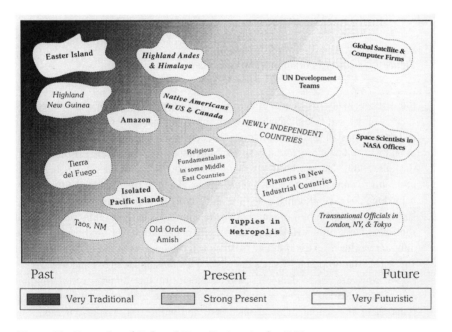

Figure 2b Examples of Cultural Time Regions in the 1990s

directly. Others may be denied such favoritism and electronic access. Thus, they are unconnected or poorly connected, with the direct result being that they are less influential and powerful.

The result of these social differences is that there is certain unevenness in the production, distribution, diffusion, and utilization of new technologies. In essence,

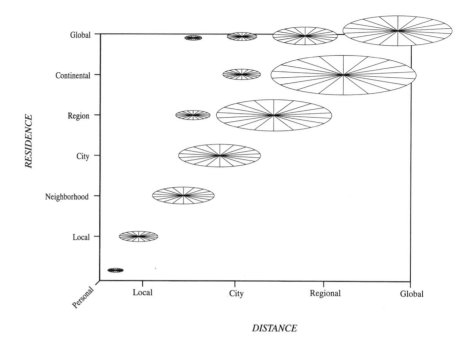

Figure 3 *Scale of Information Transactions*

the patterns exhibit both sets of hierarchies of time and space. Within a large city there will be some individuals without these technologies or gadgets (whether cellular phones, or global minitelevision receivers), some with a few technologies, others with a few more, and a very few individuals with everything (Brunn, 1993; Castells, 1989). The 'worlds of interaction' include those at local scales using word-of-mouth to communicate while others will be global in their extensibility, that is, using long distance phoning, e-mailing, and faxing to literally anyone who is similarly connected (Figure 4). Some worlds are connected early via innovations, some somewhat later, others very late and still others perhaps never. And because these different worlds of space and time exist, so will the impacts of the technologies and any legislation proposed by the state when questions about rights and welfare are raised. Any attempt to democratize technologies or the diffusion of information and communication of new technologies will have to look at social justice questions about the spatial rights of majorities and minorities, gender differences in usage of ICTs, and rural–urban variations, as well as acceptance rates among diverse cultures within the state's jurisdictions.

In our thinking about these welfare issues, we should keep in mind the diverse human geographies that exist on the planet. These issues are among those receiving the attention of geographers and others these days. They are raised in our discussions about acceptable modes and models of economic development, environmental protection and ecojustice, the consequences of diffusing technologies without questions of human impact, the rights of women, children, and

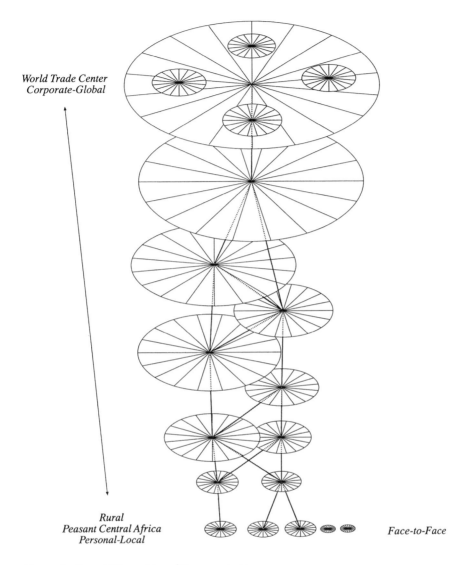

Figure 4 Nested Hierarchies of Communications

minorities, and indigenous cultures, and the responsibilities of multicultural corporations, states, IGOs, and NGOs. In quaternary and quinary economies and societies, the politics of human rights, values, and welfare occupy center stage, and they are global, not only local. The special interest groups and political parties of the agrarian and industrial eras of human history are gradually losing their importance, albeit it sometimes slowly. Gone are the days when farmers, railroads, and mineral companies, and one might even add manufacturing, governed the political agenda. They are being replaced by new lobbies and special interest groups looking at information and communications technologies (band frequencies for radio and television, deregulation of telecommunications industries, intellectual patent protection, the protection of hardware and software markets, and favourable legislation permitting access to global marketing) and the protection of individuals and groups in society. All of a sudden, 'people and the places they live matter', that is, what they believe, choose to have (or not have), and wish to reside and be protected (from polluters, greedy corporations, terrorists, and hegemonic political interests).

The above issues about human rights and welfare not only face the United States and Canada, but also France, Germany, United Kingdom, Switzerland, Japan, Australia, and elsewhere. Groups within states, often at very local scales, and political parties, are raising social and equity questions in many places where these new technologies are being introduced. These include 'watch dog' groups concerned about consumer product safety, the content of programming on television (suitable for children or adults), the introduction of unwelcome and outside (usually means Western or Hollywood) products that are sold or advertised on television or billboards and the Internet, the negative impact (usually means deterioration) of Western commercialism on local values and cultures, and the 'selling out' of the state to foreign investors. At the very heart of many of these concerns are three questions: the pace of change accompanying the introduction and availability of these new technologies (how fast?), the direction of change (where is it headed?), and the consequences of these changes (what do they mean?) (Smith, 1980; Brunn and Leinbach, 1991).

DISCUSSION

Some of the above questions may be hypothetical, but they also may be real. It is certain that there will be an increasing number of such issues in the local and national courts and also in regional and world courts within the next decade and beyond (Murphy, 1994; Boyle, 1996). These issues will emerge as significant among traditional majority groups in a society, but also for the many new and potentially vocal groups. Good examples are those who serve as advocates for the elderly, children, abused and disabled populations, new religious sects, political fringe (left and right) groups, women, gays and lesbians, stateless groups, eco-activists, and countercultural fanatics, many of whom have their own information networks, economies, web sites and delivery systems. Some might call these networked groups 'electronic tribes' as they seem to increase in number and visibility with more channels of communication open than previously. In some ways, the new ICTs, many of which appear impersonal and almost inhuman, are seen as liberating some groups within our society who previously were trapped by a legal system defined by majority élites who sought to establish, regulate, and retain societal norms and their privileged positions of power. That is, technology is a liberator to some, especially within an information/communications context. The cornucopia of new specialized magazines, newsletters, videoclubs, and listservs, WWW home pages, the plethora of new radio frequencies granted to local groups, and the nearly 100 television channels provide ample evidence of the 'narrowcasting' of information packaging within society (Smith, 1990). It might be argued that each of these new avenues of communications represents a new and different voice which believes it has the right to publish, broadcast and telecast, and transmit information to its supporters, even if in a democratic society numbers may be restricted (Agnew and Corbridge, 1995).

Questions about rights will revolve around the meaning, uses, and misuses of a host of information, communication, and computer technologies. Previously, legal questions in these spheres were restricted to the telephone hookups, newspaper and magazine subscriptions, and then cable television subscribers. But the introduction of the computer, and increasingly more powerful and personal computers, ushered in many new problems for those who developed profitable businesses that collected, processed, transported, manipulated, sold, and mapped (even GIS) data. Also included are the credit card purchases of any product or service, the ease of monitoring phone calls, the frequency of unauthorized and unsupervised uses of photocopying, the confidentiality of faxes, cellular and beeper phones and e-mail, the hundreds of corporate and personal home pages added to the WWW daily, and the zooming sales of new and used hardware and software raise questions about regulation, governance, protection of commerce and the rights of producers, consumers, and society at large.

I believe that we are slowly witnessing in contemporary society the questions I raised at the outset: that governments have to confront head-on a series of messy and tangled legal and ethical questions about human rights in the electronic state. Examples in recent years include the rights of librarians to protect those who check out X-rated books and videos, 'citizen police' groups who wish to photograph those entering establishments they consider do not meet community standards, students who access the data bases of schools, corporations and the military, school districts who consider their students to be at an inherent disadvantage because they lack computer instruction, ample hardware, and access to the Internet, professional associations who are reluctant to provide data on their members to potential vendors, and governments and corporations who destroy potentially damaging evidence on groups facing environmental risk. One could also add those international banks who refused to identify their depositors, be they terrorists, tyrants, or with links to global drug trafficking and organized crime.

As I see these dilemmas unfolding, I believe that traditional democracies, such as the United States, are faced with three challenges. First, how can it protect its citizens in the face of threats to rights of privacy and protection, which are constantly being tested by the private sector? Second, will the legal and legislative arms of the electronic democracy be able to take the lead in defining human rights for the new and old majorities or must the state continue to lag behind the technological advances? And, third, will these patterns of 'electronic human rights' be defined unevenly across the country, with the result being another messy patchwork of state and local laws? That is, citizens in some states are better protected and served than others. Or will there be congressional legislation and landmark Supreme Court decisions that will ensure equal protection for citizens, regardless of economic station, social class, ideology or location? To be sure, questions about human disparities on and off the information highway and access to the Internet, the rights of those marketing private information about consumers,

64
—

the regulations of companies in the information/communications infrastructure, and the penalties for electronic pirates, computer hackers, and information spies are only a few of the problems facing social scientists and engineers, policy-makers, jurists, and media/information executives as we embark on the journey 'towards a more perfect "electronic" union'.

PART II

GLOBAL ELECTRONIC
COMMERCE

CHAPTER 5

TELECOMMUNICATIONS AND GOVERNANCE IN MULTINATIONAL ENTERPRISES

Edward Mozely Roche and Michael James Blaine

INTRODUCTION

In multinational enterprises, four major structural innovations have occurred over the past two centuries: the vertical hierarchy, the multi-divisional (M) form, the matrix, and the network. These innovations have been a response to the external environment and technological innovations in telecommunications and information processing capabilities which greatly increased the complexity, scale, and scope of the firm's activities, enabling it to take advantage of opportunities as it adapted to the changing external environment.

Telecommunications and international trade have a relationship that goes back more than a century to the first use of the telegraph, telex, and telephone in conducting international commerce. In the Multinational Enterprise (MNE), headquarters locations have been tied together with overseas subsidiaries in order to coordinate management control over manufacturing, finance, sales, distribution and other functional areas. Data processing and telecommunications infrastructures have enabled companies to build very large vertically-integrated enterprises spanning the globe, often operating in as many as 100 countries on a 24-hour basis.

This chapter examines the evolving relationship between telecommunications and information systems, geographical expansion, and internal governance of the MNE. It argues that these factors can be understood only within a larger context of how economic opportunity drives strategy. Strategy, in turn, drives that organizational form enabled by the structure of an internal bureaucratic information system. Governance in large geographically distributed enterprises is exercised by management efforts expressed and communicated through the organization's information system in a complex cycle of information creation, processing, decision taking, and control. The information infrastructure of the MNE – defined as the set of rules governing the hardware and software infrastructure supporting the creation, processing, storage and distribution of information and data, including voice, video and multimedia signals – suffers from a paradox of complexity, and this is related to the overall distribution of data processing sites, and the type of information architecture in place (see Deans and Karwan, 1994; Palvia *et al.*, 1992).

Although information and telecommunications systems are critical enablers of governance in support of strategy, the underlying organizational logic of MNEs has

Table 1   *Telecommunications and Governance in Multinational Enterprises*

Structural Innovation	Historical Period	Enabling Telecommunications Technologies	Data Processing Architectures
Vertical Hierarchy	Before 1960s back to early international trading companies	After 1860s, telegraph; followed by telex, telephone, and limited radio communications; introduction of telephone into business was controversial	No significant automation. Firms were organized according to a Weberian type hierarchy as railroads and telecommunication allowed them to coordinate over greater distances
Multi-Divisional Form	Early twentieth century to 1970s	Telecommunications operated as 'natural monopolies'; development of modems and point to point leased lines for data communications; Centrex and PBX technology improves	Installation of mainframe technologies with IBM System 360. Centralization of architectures. Inability to communicate significantly over distances, resulting in 'islands' of processing
Matrix	1970s to mid-1980s	Packet switching made computer networking to many points easier; continued sophistication of modem, compression and multiplexing technologies; heavy use of leased lines point-to-point; LANs, WANs, MANs	Powerful mainframes; introduction of departmental minicomputers (mid-sized machines) [e.g. Sys/3x, 43xx]; introduction of client-server model; significant integration problems; Unix time begins in 1970
Network (Virtual)	1990s	Global service alliances serving MNEs; SMDS and other high speed services; Asynchronous Transfer Mode; Frame Relay; Systems Network Architecture	Internet, intranet and World Wide Web breakdown information sharing barriers; rise of eBusiness; desktop teleconferencing and multimedia

Note: As a result of differing competitive factors these general forms were adopted at different points in time in different industries and in different countries, based on competitive factors.

changed through different historical periods. We have chosen historical periodization based on advances in information technology and telecommunications, and secondarily on macroeconomic and global events. For each historical phase of growth of the MNE, we discuss the general economic environment, the enabling communications and information processing technologies available, and the type of governance and related organizational structure possible to support the underlying strategy of the enterprise. (see Table 1).

PRE-NINETEENTH CENTURY – INDUSTRIAL STRUCTURE FORMATION

The early development of multinational enterprises took place to the greatest degree in Europe, particularly with the rise of 'medieval super-companies' (Hunt, 1994) followed by the Amsterdam bourse and the growth of large shipping and investment companies to support formation of capital. As the Dutch Republic rose to prominence in the early seventeenth century, its commercial activities were based on linking together several major areas of commerce. Timber, tar and other raw materials were taken from Russia and Scandinavia and brought to Amsterdam where they were handled by a complex warehousing operation. Wines, oils, and (especially) salt from Spain, Portugal, and France were brought north for further trading. Germany was served through shipping up the Rhine.

With the rise of Protestantism and the desire for independence from the Spanish Crown, the resulting war (The War of the Spanish Succession) cut off access to supplies from Spain and Portugal forcing a search further afield for tradable resources, leading to the Far East and in particular to the Indonesian 'spice islands' (Braudel, 1979; Israel, 1995, 1989). As the East India Company (*Verenigde Oostindische Compagnie*) and the West Indian Company (*Westindische Compagnie*) developed, supplemented as they were by the previous activities of the Hanseatic League, as well as rival trade from the English and Spanish, a sophisticated mechanism of technology and governance came into being centered in the seventeenth century. Carlos (1986) compares the Chartered Trading companies to modern multinational enterprises.

With the exception of short distance carrier pigeons, corporate communications during this period were carried at the pace of the horse or boat. Due to the great distances involved (from Europe to the Far East), the information system was slow and incomplete, making it impossible to evaluate remote events having either a positive or deleterious effect on the invested enterprises, thus raising risks in international commerce. As a result, emergence of the joint stock company, allowing purchase of 1/16th up to 1/32nd shares (there are reports of 1/64th shares) in any overseas venture allowed merchant investors to spread their risks across many different enterprises, thus raising the overall rate of return (see Parry, 1967 for a history of these early ventures). Control was exercised in a completely centralized fashion for the dispatch of trading ships. Without telecommunications, however, difficulty in communications made it obligatory to allow company agents located in remote company ports considerable autonomy in service as governor. The auxiliary roles assumed by overseas agents as political figures (backed by military force) both facilitated the MNE overseas subsidiaries acting autonomously, and set a political tone that would erupt later.

A relationship existed between the velocity of information (speed of ships and horse) and the control of enterprises (centralized in strategy, but local in implementation and autonomy). Even as global trade expanded, and enterprises became more complex, the same technology of communications was dominant throughout the seventeenth century, and onwards, until a series of disruptive developments served to change it. The technologies responsible for introducing change (in communication and control governance patterns) were the railroad and the telegraph. These two forces for change had their greatest impact from the middle of the nineteenth century.

Years later, Chandler, Bruchey and Galambos (1968) would argue that the archetypal structure of the modern industrial corporation was a direct outgrowth of the rapidly changing infrastructure of the late nineteenth century. According to Chandler, the creation of a national system of railroads and canals between 1830-70 was responsible for a revolution in management practices that shifted business activities away from firms run by individual entrepreneurs to corporations run by formal, bureaucratic management. Growth of canals and railroads fostered a number of structural innovations including the functional department, the geographic division, and the holding company. Railroads precipitated separation of long range, strategic activities from day to day operations of the firm, thus establishing management as a separate activity demanding the full attention of skilled personnel. This new structure is called the 'multidivisional' form (M-form).

1860–1960 – Search for Hierarchical Governance

The rise of industrial production and long distance transportation, both powered by steam, heightened the intensity of international competition. As railroads expanded, so too did the telegraph system rapidly grow, providing for the first time in history a velocity of information divorced from the physical limitations of transportation. As a side note, it was during this time that the word 'communications' in its traditional meaning was separated into 'transportation' and 'telecommunication', these two now becoming separate phenomena.

The new telecommunications, quickly enhanced by the telex and telephone, allowed firms to rapidly expand their 'scale and scope' achieving a size never before possible as command and control allowed perfection of a complex management information system (see Figure 1). The 'information cycle' in hierarchical enterprises involved top management forcing strong control down through the hierarchy of trained specialists optimized to carry out business orders. Transactions were processed at the bottom of the hierarchy, thereby creating raw data which was processed at middle levels and passed along for 'final consumption' at the top by decision takers.

At the international level, the relationship between telecommunications and business goes back more than a century to the first use of telegraph, telex, and telephone in conducting international commerce (Roche, 1992). In the MNE headquarters locations have been tied together with overseas subsidiaries in order to coordinate manufacturing, other activities, financial reporting, and management control. Data processing and telecommunications infrastructures which evolved made it possible for companies to build large, extended enterprises, spanning the globe and operating in many countries on a 24-hour basis (Vignault, 1987; Harasim, 1993).

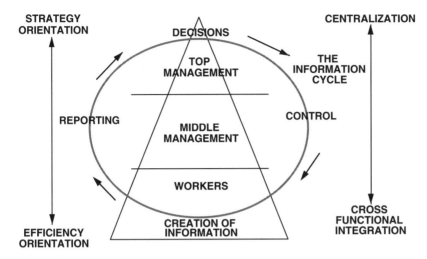

Figure 1 *The Information Cycle in the Classical Weberian Hierarchy*

Egelhoff (1991) has applied this 'information-processing' perspective to the MNE noting that, '. . . the information-processing perspective calls for translating strategic and environmental conditions and organizational design features into their respective information-processing implications' (Egelhoff, 1991: 345). Egelhoff argued that organizational effectiveness is a function of 'fit' between the information-processing *requirements* in the environment and the information-processing *capabilities* in the firm. He identified six basic types of information systems:

1. 'centralized' in which all information processing occurs at headquarters;
2. 'decentralized' where separate data processing centers are in all locations;
3. 'regional' where information-processing capabilities are concentrated in regional centers;
4. 'hierarchical centralization' in which lower order processing takes place locally or regionally and is centralized in specific sites as processing becomes more complex or comprehensive;
5. 'client-server' in which most information-processing occurs locally but within a central context; and
6. the 'network' which has no centers and in which information processing capabilities are evenly distributed to all points in the system.

Although writing years later, Egelhoff's typology closely resembles standard descriptions of the organizational structure of the MNE. After all, the control systems firms build to manage and process the flow of information within the firm or between the firm and its external environments help to define both the firm's structure and its capabilities to adapt to changing external conditions.

Evolution of organizational structure in the MNE has reflected the firm's increasing need to manage and process increasing amounts of complex information. During this period, introduction of telecommunication equipment and computers enabled MNEs to complement organizational structure with an 'information (infra-)structure' to aid coordination and control of the international activities of the firm over great distances. Information 'networks' linking head-quarters with their subsidiaries have been known for quite some time, but these systems have been difficult to study due to their complexity and scale. In the days before computers, methods of coordinating the flow of information within and between firms included the telegraph, the telex, and the telephone. Surprisingly, these 'primitive' technologies were the primary means of coordinating the activities of MNEs until the end of the 1960s.

At the end of this period, MNEs were busy expanding their geographical scope at a very fast rate as Europe and Japan recovered from the devastation of the war. However, the handling of information in a strictly hierarchical manner had to be compromised because of geographical distances. With MNEs, it was impossible to have an internationally centralized headquarters with the complete information reporting envisaged by the traditional model. As a result, overseas subsidiaries continued to adopt the model so familiar from the past, that of semi-autonomous operations. This was not a question of strategic priority, but rather of technical necessity, as international telephony and telex (there were no international computer networks during this period apart from a very few cases) did not have enough capacity to support the same level of information flow as needed by the information cycle within a single company at a headquarters location.

As a result (of this inability to efficiently transfer the required vast amounts of information to headquarters due to technical limitations), MNEs were forced to create semi-autonomous subsidiaries in which all principal functional areas (sales, marketing, finance, human resources, etc.) were replicated at least in each country, if not in each overseas location.

It was at this time that automated data processing, without significant data communications, came into being and changed the nature of headquarters operations. However, the result was different for domestic enterprises in comparison to the MNE. For domestic enterprises, data processing allowed vast increases in information-handling efficiency, particularly for routine transactions such as bank statements and billing, etc.

1960–1970 – CENTRALIZED DATA PROCESSING AND THE RISE OF AUTONOMY IN FOREIGN SUBSIDIARIES

During this period a variety of forms have evolved. In *Markets and Hierarchies*, Williamson (1975) examined three organizational structures: the unitary (U) form, the holding company, and the multidivisional (M) form. In general, U-form organizations are simple, vertical hierarchies in which all decisions and planning are made by a chief executive officer. The holding company is a diversified organization containing a number of relatively autonomous business units loosely controlled by a central management. Finally, the multi-divisional structure is a diversified organization that contains several lines of business coordinated in order to achieve economies of scale and scope. Based on this analysis, Williamson advanced the 'M-form hypothesis', which suggests that the performance of M-form organizations will exceed the performance of either U-form organizations or holding companies. Williamson argued that the division of tasks inherent in the M-form allowed top management to engage in strategic planning and coordination of related activities in a much more efficient manner. Companies that adopted a multidivisional structure should achieve superior performance.

As a result, a new level of complexity was added to the firm's operation, as foreign activities of many companies shifted from exporting to foreign production. The resulting multinational enterprises (MNEs) were viewed as being a response to specific conditions in the international environment which encouraged firms to conduct transactions through internal rather than external markets (Hymer, 1960; Kindleberger, 1968; Buckley and Casson, 1976; Dunning, 1977, 1979, 1980). At the scale needed, these internal transactions could only be carried out by firms making an intensive use of international telecommunications.

As they became internationalized, firms had gone through an initial phase in which their new foreign subsidiaries were linked to the parent through loose financial ties, resembling a holding company (Stopford and Wells, 1972). During the second phase, separate international divisions were created to consolidate foreign activities. This division acted as an autonomous part of the organization and engaged its own strategic planning. In the third phase, foreign and domestic activities became more closely linked and strategic planning was developed world-wide on an integrated basis. Dymsza (1984) traced the spread of the multinational enterprise from the United States, to Western Europe, then Japan, and finally the Third World, noting that foreign corporations often follow the same pattern of multinationalization described by Stopford and Wells.

As MNEs expanded abroad, they undertook major structural rearrangement in an effort to coordinate the firm's international operations to simultaneously achieve global integration while retaining the differentiation needed to be responsive to local economic, socio-cultural and legal characteristics of each host nation. As a result, these organizations were architected according to 'industrial logic' with the information flow converging on rapidly expanding headquarters locations. For the MNE, however, the lack of sufficiently robust data communications (computer to computer connections over international borders) guaranteed the emergence of a different form of enterprise. It was necessary to develop methods of corporate governance which would allow a 'data poor' style of decision taking at corporate headquarters, supplemented by a 'data rich' style in overseas subsidiaries.

1970–1985 – THE SEARCH FOR INTEGRATION

During this period, technical developments in both telecommunications and information technology greatly increased the flexibility of firms in ordering their internal bureaucratic and control structures. Telecommunications not so much fueled geographical expansion of the firm, but helped to connect together the data processing centers that heretofore had stood autonomous throughout the world of the MNE. The amount and sophistication of data transmitted from subsidiaries to headquarters increased dramatically. However, serious problems remained including lack of compatibility between data centers; complexity and difficulty of staffing specialists capable of long-range global systems integration efforts; tremendous problems with basic data definitions; and problems in managing the organizational transformation towards a more centralized model.

It did not take long for the 'centralized' model of data processing to become obsolete as the IS function found it increasingly difficult to develop applications systems within budget and schedule. In addition, the rise of the departmental minicomputer began to erode the power of IS. A third development is that data communications began a rapid development that even today has scarcely subsided.

The role of telecommunications in this period was one of extending the geographical reach of the IS function, but not of the enterprise, which in most cases had already approached its geographical limits. The newly minted information system was linked together on top of an existing 'brick and mortar' structure of the firm. Telecommunications first allowed existing data processing centers to offer geographically dispersed processing. Afterwards, it became possible to link together the CPUs of dispersed data centers. This possibility (of linking together different heterogeneous data centers) was of critical importance since, as pointed out earlier, the technical limitations of long-distance data networking had forced enterprises to build up autonomous (e.g. non-cooperating) data centers (whether or not the subsidiary was organized on an autonomous basis). McFarlan et al. (1983) had called these 'islands of automation'.

In the 1970s, the first remote terminal linkages had been established when Texas Instruments built the world's first private satellite network linking its Texas plants with semiconductor manufacturing operations in the Far East. Later technologies made it possible to use terminals and cluster controllers placed at distant locations, but this approach was relatively expensive since it relied on analog networks supplied through the telephone companies. These early forms, however primitive they appear today, allowed remote locations to share information with headquarters or with regional centers. The velocity of information was accelerated and decision making was improved by the faster transfer of information and feedback cycles. Theoretically, this translated into more accurate decisions (Rapoport, 1985), although it has been difficult to measure and verify these effects (Egelhoff, 1991).

These (and other) problems led firms to experience a 'learning curve' in their efforts to build integrated global systems: acquiring international telecommunications networks to link together geographically dispersed data centers was only a first step. After networks had been put into place, even more severe challenges arose: it was necessary to link together the applications (not only the centers) into meaningful networks of cooperative processing – all with the goal of supporting the overall strategy of the corporation.

This raised many managerial dilemmas for the IS function, particularly as political problems emerged in the wake of the increased need to coordinate systems development and planning at the international level. As these many initiatives were put into place, the IS function in many organizations took on the appearance of an uncoordinated giant, inefficient and unresponsive to the corporation. These 'images' of the IS function persisted throughout the next generation of technology, and in many cases are still with us today.

During this period, there was, however, a complex interplay between environmental factors and the potential improvements in organizational structure being opened up by advances in information technology. Researchers were attempting to determine what drives changes in organization. Joan Woodward was among the first to directly challenge this general organizational approach by showing how firms with similar organizational structures exhibited widely divergent performances. In a pivotal study of British manufacturing firms, Woodward (1958) identified a clear relationship between a firm's performance, its organizational characteristics, and the type of technology it employed. Based on this analysis, she concluded that a firm's system of production was an important determinant of its organizational structure. During the 1960s, a number of researchers examined the impact of various environmental factors on the structure and performance of the firm (Chandler, 1962; Thompson, 1967). In general, these researchers attempted to identify critical characteristics of the environment and match them with appropriate characteristics of the firm.

Based on a study of Scottish firms entering the electronics industry, Burns and Stalker (1961) defined two 'ideal types' of organizations: mechanistic – in which hierarchical control and vertical communication patterns coordinate clearly defined, specialized tasks; and organic – in which collaboration and open communication are used to continually restructure tasks and adapt to novel problems. They show how each form is appropriate for a different environmental context. Mechanistic firms are well suited for stable environments since the hierarchical control of specialized tasks yields various economies, but is only practicable when future contingencies can be accurately predicted. On the other hand, the free flow of information and the lack of specialization in the organic firm enable it to quickly respond to environmental or technological change making it appropriate in highly unstable or uncertain environments.

Contingency theory suggested that an organization's performance is directly related to the 'fit' between its structure and environment. In their book *Organization and Environment*, Lawrence and Lorsch (1967) developed a formal theory regarding the relationship between a firm and its environment. Viewing the organization as a complex system, they argued that as organizations became large, they differentiated into parts that later needed to be integrated.

The task of integrating diverse sub-units is a difficult one and becomes more difficult as sub-units become differentiated. Successful organizations are those that develop an appropriate method of integrating their disparate parts and resolving the conflicts between sub-units. In more stable environments, integration tends to occur at the top of the firm's hierarchy, while in uncertain environments, integration takes place at lower levels. Lawrence and Lorsch proposed a 'contingency theory' of organizations and noted,

The basic assumption underlying such a theory . . . is that organizational variables are in a complex interrelationship with one another and with conditions in the environment. . . . [W]e have found an important relationship among external variables (the certainty and diversity of the environment, and the strategic environmental issue), internal states of differentiation and integration. If an organization's internal states and processes are consistent with external demands . . . it will be effective in dealing with its environment (Lawrence and Lorsch, 1967: 157).

The overwhelming complexity of the environment has made it difficult to identify relevant environmental variables, let alone correlate them with organizational structures. Consequently, contingency theory has been criticized for a number of reasons, including: it is static rather than dynamic; it does not clearly address problems of environmental uncertainty, technology, or size; and it has encouraged an unending search for new 'contingency' variables. Lawrence (1981) addressed many of these criticisms by proposing an 'adaptive' model of organizational structure that draws heavily on the biological concepts of evolution and natural selection, and the 'population ecology' model of Hannan and Freeman (1977, 1988). According to this model, existing organizations represent survivors that have been 'selected for' in the sense that they possess a unique set of resources and organizational capabilities not present in the larger group of organizational casualties.

One way of conceptualizing this process of adaptation is to focus on the flow of information between the firm and the environment. Kilduff (1992) notes,

An organization is a complex adaptive system that interacts with its environment, storing the cumulative results of its interactions in routines. These routines are the result of learning processes . . . and can be modified by feedback from the internal or external environment (Kilduff, 1992: 133).

This view of the firm as a learning, adapting, open system relies on the notion that organizations are constantly receiving and processing information from their environments. The 'routines' an organization develops to gather, process, and store this information are a critical determinant of its 'structure', and more importantly, its capacity to process information. Galbraith (1973) examined various structural features and ranked in increasing order of their information-processing capacity first rules, then programs (routines), hierarchical referrals, goal-setting, vertical information systems, and lateral relations.

The traditional justification for organizing international economic activities within the MNE has been brought into question. Diffusion of technologies and management practices and the growth of international competition have substantially eroded the basis of many firm-specific advantages. At the same time, the declining importance of natural resources in the production process has diminished the need for vertical integration. During the 1980s, changes in the international political economy included the growing similarities between national and product markets, the emergence of large and fluid international capital markets, falling trade barriers, advances in technology, the increased dissemination of information, and the rise of new global competitors. These changes eroded many of the traditional advantages of large, vertically-integrated firms. As social, economic, and political developments have improved the efficiency of international markets and promoted the convergence of technology and consumer tastes, many have argued that the MNE with its characteristic system of international sub-sidiaries had become increasingly obsolete. Robinson (1981) argued the costs of using internal markets to transfer capital, skills, technology, and goods between countries may actually be higher in some cases than costs associated with exchanges in the open marketplace. While one set of factors improves efficiency of external markets, another reduces hierarchical governance benefits.

According to Dunning (1989), vastly different organizational forms and resource endowments may be required to take advantage of the technological advances of the 1980s and 1990s. He noted, 'It is by no means certain that the . . . hierarchical structure of firms evolved through the 1960s and 1970s will be suitable for the remaining years of the twentieth century' (Dunning, 1989: 26). But if the tradi-tional hierarchical control of an international production and distribution system is no longer suitable, what type of organization is appropriate for today's turbulent economic environment?

It has become popular to argue that long term, contractual arrangements between independent firms are the answer. They, presumably, are more flexible than the traditional hierarchical form of governance. Over a decade ago Root (1984) suggested

> . . . firms will move away from 'internalization' and toward 'externalization'. They will more freely transfer non-strategic production processes to firms, say, in the developing countries under arrangements that are based far more on cooperation than on control by the international firm (Root, 1984: 23).

These latter forms of inter-firm cooperation have been called 'new forms of investment' (NFIs). According to Hennart (1989),

> 'New Forms' include arrangements that fall short of majority ownership, such as various forms of contracts (licensing, franchising, management contracts, turnkey and product-in-hand contracts, production sharing-contracts, and international subcontracting) as well as joint ventures (Hennart, 1989: 212).

From an information technology point of view, more intensive coordination with partners located in proximity to overseas subsidiaries places considerably stronger demands on the telecommunications network, since the amount of data flow will be vastly increased.

The growing body of literature on joint ventures, strategic alliances, and other contractual arrangements (Killing, 1983; Mariti and Smiley, 1983; Harrigan, 1985; Anderson and Gatignon, 1986; Morris and Hergert, 1987; Contractor and Lorange, 1988; Kogut, 1988) further suggested opportunities presented in the 'new' inter-national environment did not readily lend themselves to the traditional structures. Has the model of the firm (MNE) based on the internalization of markets, vertical and/or horizontal integration, and the central control of an international system of subsidiaries been replaced by a new paradigm which stresses 'externalization', cooperation with host governments and other firms, and coordination of activities through contractual agreements between independent companies? Drucker (1988) foresaw the development of 'information-based' organizations and argued that through use of computers and telecommunications, organizations could overcome that increased complexity and bounded rationality which limited earlier organizational forms. This, in turn, would lead to smaller, flatter organizations controlled by highly trained specialists rather than middle managers. His vision led to a large, complex 'network' of independent organizations loosely linked through R&D, production, and distribution agreements.

It was the proliferation of leased and dedicated telecommunications lines that allowed companies to build increasingly large and complex information 'networks' needed to support these innovations. These networks were primarily within individual nation states – generally the United States. Although this technology made it possible to link together sites in other countries, national legislation, standards, high costs and many practical matters inhibited the growth of these linkages (Rada and Pipe, 1984; Junne, 1988; Jussawalla, 1987; Ives and Jarvenpaa, 1991).

During the latter half of the 1980s the growth of networks accelerated on an international scale, as user groups such as the International Telecommunications User Group (INTUG) worked to ease nation state imposed restrictions. Although many problems associated with international computer networking have been eased in the most recent round of trade negotiations, national goals, being divergent as they are, virtually guarantee a continuing struggle between the firm and the nation state, making it more expensive and complex to create, enhance, or expand such international networks (see Wallenstein, 1990). It is unreasonable to expect these transborder data flow problems to be completely resolved before the end of the first or second decade of the next century, if ever. This may throttle the international expansion of the virtual corporation in the near-term, as it has generally inhibited progress in the past.

1985–1993 – RE-ENGINEERING AND TRANSITION OF STRUCTURES

As these intra-organizational networks expanded in the 1980s, advanced computer systems made it possible to establish external linkages between companies. For the first time this created a schism in the management of the firm's information infrastructure. Before, there had only been internal networks, now many firms had to manage external networks as well. At the time, few recognized that the development of these external information networks had potential to change the structure of the firm and even entire industries (Piore and Sabel, 1984; McGee, 1991; Konsynski, 1993).

These external information networks – inter-organizational systems (IOSs) – were initially termed 'strategic systems' in the MIS literature (Wiseman, 1988). Strategic information systems were said to provide advantages to the firm since once they were installed it became more difficult and costly for the customer to switch to another vendor (McFarlan, 1984). Others argued that this type of computer linkage resulted in 'information bonding' (Venkatraman and Loh, 1994) which further tied the customer to the firm, creating a 'barrier to entry' to firms attempting to establish competing linkages (with the same customer). Following this logic, the strategic advantage Citibank gained from its invention of the automatic teller machine has often been hailed as one of the most important strategic innovations in information technology (White, 1979; Blackwell, 1983; Mulqueen, 1987).

Efforts to build strategic inter-organizational linkages and the breaking apart of large, industrial structures has only been possible because of rapid advances in computer and telecommunications systems. It is only with the rapid and efficient transfer and manipulation of information between firms and their counterparts – customers, sub-contractors, outsource service providers, etc. – that the virtual company can exist (Gilroy, 1993). Technically, these connections between 'components' of the firm are carried through either private or public telecommunication networks, or through third-party, intermediary networks which are in the business of linking firms together. An example of a third-party network is the clearing system and credit card authorization and billing system shared by banks.

Perhaps the greatest irony of these inter-organizational information systems is that many MNEs are probably moving in the opposite direction.[†] Much of the literature in the 1980s focused on 'globalization' – the process of consolidating available functional areas of the firm in order to obtain economies of scale and scope. Globalization is the antithesis of 'dis-integration' through information and telecommunications technologies.

Some writers claimed that much of the strategic advantage associated with these systems had been an accident (Clemons and Row, 1988) and that firms were building these networks out of 'strategic necessity'. This was a very different argument to the popular notion that the firm's information system was the center of innovation and strategic planning. The latter view of information technology-based competitive advantage was further dampened by a number of studies which suggested that investments in information technology did not increase productivity. According to Roach (1994), by the end of the 1980s, almost one-half of the capital investment in the US economy was going into information technology, but many argued there was little improvement in productivity.

Rapid advances in information technology inevitably led to outsourcing, as the IT functional area was unable to show adequate returns on investment. As the personal computer and workstation had entered the corporation, layers of networks and support structures were of necessity added to the IS function. 'Information centers' and 'help desks' became popular 'buzz words' (commonly discussed issues). Although intended to add flexibility to information processing, these small devices caused a further weakening and ossification of the IS function, making it very difficult to recover. Weakening took place by default as end-users (and their managers) rapidly moved towards the client-server model of distributed computing, fueling a quantum increase in number of end-user devices needing management. It quickly became clear the client server model was extraordinarily expensive, more than four times more per user than any other architecture. The IS function as a whole, particularly in the mid-1980s, was required to spend more to

---

[†] Note: Much more research on this needs to be done.

keep pace with technology, but without substantial productivity gains to show for justification, the result being that IS was turned into an eventual cost cutting target. This led (because it appears less expensive) to a rise in outsourcing of data processing, telecommunications, systems development and applications integration, data entry, fundamental legacy programming (typically COBOL or other legacy mainframe languages), and many other functions typically managed by the IS function. In many cases, companies chose to outsource their entire data telecommunications function, and this trend has grown. None of these internal machinations had any substantive effect on the geographical scope of the MNE.

Other functional areas (besides IT) were also subject to outsourcing. Corporations became more facile at working with external partners. This lead inevitably to the concept of a firm in which outsourcing was the norm, not the exception. Firms started experimenting with novel ways of linking companies together electronically. These experiments ultimately gave rise to the network or virtual firm. Breakthroughs in understanding the social impact of the network form of governance came from academics such as Castels (1989), Scott (1993) and Saxenian (1994) who compared the economic efficiency and competitive power of the network firm to that of the traditional hierarchical company. Saxenian compares the computer and other high technology companies around Route 128 in Boston with those in Silicon Valley. In explaining the demise of Digital Equipment and Wang versus the success of Hewlett Packard, Sun Microsystems and Silicon Graphics, she concluded that these differences could be explained by the way these companies organized their external relationships.

At the heart of this analysis is the idea that the hierarchical, centralized, vertically integrated firm was actually a weak and vulnerable form of organization. With shorter product life cycles, for example, firms were being forced to bring products to market faster, resulting in time-sensitive competition (Stalk and Hout, 1990; Anderson and Tushman, 1991). The Silicon Valley firms were successful because they retained their 'core competencies' (Kesler et al., 1993; Prahalad, 1993; Bakker et al., 1994; Kozin and Young, 1994; Simpson, 1994) and sub-contracted out everything else. In short, they replaced the equity control of their value-adding chains with contractual arrangements linking independent suppliers. Sun Microsystems is an ideal example of a network company where much basic manufacturing is done by others. Adopting this form of organization meant that the smaller virtual firm could often out-manoeuvre its larger rivals. With Compaq versus IBM, Sun versus DEC, and many other cases, this form of company appeared to succeed.

As realization of the network model spread, larger firms began to reexamine their operations. Re-engineering, down-sizing, and outsourcing are each an aspect of the re-examination of the Fordist model – that the most survivable and successful form of industrial organization was the massive, vertically-integrated firm. In their efforts, many firms 'dis-integrated' so that business functions which were not central to the firm's core mission or competencies were either spun off into separate companies or sub-contracted out to others (Morton, 1991).

In passing, it is important to note that this new approach to industrial organization can have severe repercussions for the firm's 'stakeholders', particularly labor. Since much of the virtual firm's production is transferred to suppliers overseas or in low-wage, non-union domestic sites, the widespread adoption of the network model may weaken and impoverish domestic workers. Consequently, industrial re-organization has often had the effect of depressing wages and reducing employment through the elimination of middle managers and production workers. In America, the job security of the 1950s–70s now appears to be an artifact of a bygone age (Newman, 1993; Bridges, 1994; Handy, 1994).

1993 – STRATEGIC CONTROL AND THE LIMITS OF HIERARCHY

By the early part of the 1990s the ravaging waves of re-engineering and out-sourcing were already showing early signs of calming. The casualties had been great, and many IS functions had been devastated beyond recognition. De-skilling of the workforce, slashing of middle management, and not so occasional enrich-ment of top executives continued to erode the strong sinews of the grand MNEs which had been so carefully constructed during the past quarter of a century (and more). In many cases the appearance of what remained was beyond recognition.

Entirely new forms of industrial structure have emerged. Nearly three-quarters of a century after Weber had published his study of bureaucracy (see translation, 1968), based on observations of the Prussian military, an organization which *did* have the efficiency he wrote of, technological and business forces had conspired to break down the 'Weberian hierarchy' as the dominant paradigm of organization. Telecommunications allowed firms to more easily establish inter-organizational 'horizontal' linkages between themselves, and the rise of outsourcing, not only within the IS function but throughout the organization, had led to the creation of a new industrial form – the 'networked' or 'virtual' corporation.

In a 1986 article entitled 'The Hollow Corporation', *Business Week* proclaimed the emergence of a new type of organization – 'the post-industrial' or 'network' corporation. They noted, '. . . these new corporations are "vertically disaggre-gated", relying on other companies for manufacturing and many crucial business functions. They are industrial companies without industrial production' (*Business Week* (1986) 3 March: 64). Among the early adopters of this 'new' form of econ-omic organization were Nike, Esprit, Liz Claiborne, Emerson Radio, TIE, Schwinn, Sun Microsystems, and Lewis Galoob. In 1985, these companies generated revenues ranging between \$50 million and \$1 billion using workforces of less than 3,500 – and in some cases less than 150 – employees. Further, in most cases the proportion of manufacturing employees to total employees was under 20%. A decade later, the 'network' – or 'virtual' corporation as it is also called – had captured the imaginations of managers and academics alike, and was viewed by many as the appropriate response to competitive environments characterized by high levels of uncertainty and rapid rates of technological change.

A 'network' or 'virtual' firm is a company that provides goods and services without directly owning the assets – and in many cases the knowledge – required to produce those goods and services. Instead, the network firm serves as the 'nexus' of a complex set of corporate or contractual relationships with asset owners, and adds value by providing the 'vision' or design for a new product, service or technology and by assembling and managing the relationships required to deliver that vision to customers.

By coordinating the firm's (international) activities through contractual agreements with host governments, other MNEs, and local firms, the firm becomes the nexus for the exchange of capital and information within this larger network of independent organizations (Blaine, 1994). By externalizing the firm's value-adding chain in this way, the firm may be in a better position to respond to rapidly changing threats and opportunities in the international competitive environment. By replacing routines and hierarchical referral with flexible lateral relations between independent entities, the network form greatly increases capacity to process information.

The network model represents a unique form of governance difficult to explain using the traditional theory of the firm (Hakansson and Johanson, 1993). Accepted economic analysis suggests alternative means of organizing economic activities – the market and the firm (Coase, 1937; Richardson, 1972; Williamson, 1975). A sharp contrast is drawn between markets and hierarchical organizational structures but a vast middle-ground of 'intermediate' or 'hybrid' mechanisms with both 'conscious planning' and 'arm's-length exchanges' is often ignored. These 'new forms of investment' are contractually-based and include such arrangements as licensing, management contracts, joint production or R&D, subcontracting, and minority joint ventures. Kester (1992) suggested that various forms of contractual governance span a continuum ranging from explicit contracts enforceable in a court of law to implicit, 'relational' contracts based on trust and informal sanctions. The network firm appears to lie at the latter end of this spectrum. Powell (1990) noted 'In network modes of resource allocation within firms, transactions occur through networks of individuals engaged in reciprocal, preferential, mutually supportive actions' (Powell, 1990: 303).

Network firms are the consequence of two occurrences that have radically altered the relative costs and benefits of hierarchical governance. The first involves the growing complexity and uncertainty associated with many traditional business activities, including shortened product life cycles, increased international competition, converging national and product markets, and rapid advances in technology. As Halal (1994) notes,

> The rise of a complex environment challenges our most basic assumptions about management. Hierarchy is too cumbersome under these conditions, so modern economies require organic systems composed of numerous small, self-guided enterprises that can adapt to their local environment more easily . . . (Halal, 1994: 69).

The theory argues that replacing equity control of the firm's value-adding chain with flexible contractual arrangements between itself and partners allows reduction of high production and overhead costs, increased rates of innovation and product introduction, and adaptation to unstable demand or shifts in technology.

The virtual corporation provides an alternative to the traditional, hierarchical coordination of internal economic transactions. As the exchange of products and information within the network grows, it becomes increasingly difficult to identify boundaries between individual entities. Davidow and Malone (1992) underscore this point in their description of the virtual corporation, noting that:

> To the outside observer, (the virtual corporation) will appear almost edgeless, with permeable and continuously changing interfaces between company, supplier, and customers (Davidow and Malone, 1992: 5).

Consequently, the network or virtual firm violates the most basic assumption of traditional economic theory – that transactions occur between discrete actors.

Although the theoretical rationale for the network is compelling, there are several reasons to question the adequacy of this form of governance. We argue the 'network' is fundamentally a costly and inefficient form of organization for a simple reason: as the number of components – or nodes – in the network increases, the cost of managing the complex contractual relationships which compose the network becomes unbearable regardless of the efficiency of telecommunications. Thus, while firms may be able to reduce administrative and production costs, increase flexibility, and access unique expertise by adopting the network form, at some point the need for additional safeguards to protect the interests of individual entities and the problem of dividing responsibilities and benefits between constituents will outweigh the potential economies gained from this form of organization. As the size and complexity of the network expands, so does the problem of managing the technological infrastructure or 'information architecture' that supports the exchange and processing of information among constituents. Thus, at some point the network form of organization may become too expensive to govern.

PROSPECTS FOR THE FUTURE

The 'network' or 'virtual' corporation has been seen as a structural response to changing conditions in the (international) competitive environment, particularly the growing uncertainty associated with many business activities due to rapid advances in technology, increased global competition, and constantly evolving national and international laws and regulations. By increasing the flexibility and information-processing capacity of the firm, network governance, theoretically, enables the firm to adapt to these highly complex and uncertain external conditions more quickly and at far less cost than large integrated firms. As a result, network firms should exhibit superior performance, and over time challenge the archetypal hierarchical firm for organizational dominance.

There are, however, costs associated with all forms of governance. Although these costs are difficult to measure, transaction cost analysis (Williamson, 1975, 1985) provides a tool for comparing the relative costs and benefits of alternative methods of organizing economic activities. According to Williamson, transaction cost analysis entails, '. . . an examination of the comparative costs of planning, adapting, and monitoring task completion under alternative governance structures' (original emphasis) (Williamson, 1985: 2). Traditionally, only two forms of economic organization were recognized – the market and the firm. Coase (1937) was perhaps the first to recognize that the firm was the product of the costs associated with market-mediated exchange. He cited the cost of discovering relevant prices, the cost of writing and enforcing contracts, and the cost of uncertainty, and noted that in some cases these costs could be high enough to justify the 'suppression of the price mechanism' and the coordination of economic activities through the firm.

Although hierarchical governance (the firm) may generate certain economies – such as economies of scale and scope (Chandler, 1990) and the reduction of contracting and enforcement costs, the firm also incurs unique costs, the most important being the costs of creating and maintaining the administrative apparatus that controls the firm. As the size of the firm increases, so does the cost and complexity of managing its activities. Thus, at some point, the firm may grow so large that it begins to experience 'transactional diseconomies' as Williamson (1975) calls them. These include internal procurement bias, internal expansion bias, programme persistence bias, communication and information distortions, and employment disincentives. Taken together, these 'diseconomies' could raise the cost of hierarchical governance above that of market-mediated exchange so that the firm could no longer provide an efficient alternative to the market.

In the end, it is frustrating to explain why cooperative mechanisms – including the network firm – should have an advantage over either market or hierarchical governance. Williamson (1979, 1985) develops a scheme that explains the advantages of alternative forms of governance based on the nature of the transactions involved. Market exchange, in his view, is appropriate for any transaction that is nonspecific in nature – such as buying and selling basic commodities. As transactions become more idiosyncratic or require more specialized investments, alternative forms of governance are preferred. If transactions are less idiosyncratic and occur frequently, various types of 'relational contracting' – or 'bilateral' governance as Williamson calls it – are favored. These more cooperative arrangements between firms arise because the moderate idiosyncrasy of the transaction gives parties an incentive to continue their relationship, but no incentive to shift the exchange to the market or to 'internalize' it within the firm.

It is not at all clear why the cost of managing a complex set of contractual relations, intermediated at arm's length by the telecommunications network, should be less than the cost of managing a large integrated firm, nor why a network firm should be better able to manage these relationships than a traditional firm. A large firm may be able to forge more advantageous relationships than a network firm due to its ability to engage in more comprehensive search activities and its bargaining power relative to potential partners.

There are, however, four conditions under which network governance may be preferred:

1. when the value of a particular product does not justify the costs of owning the physical assets required to produce it;
2. when large firms experience high 'transactional diseconomies' due to the nature of their activities;

3. when the returns associated with a particular activity are so high that the form of governance becomes irrelevant; and
4. when the cost of negotiating and enforcing contracts are lower for a network than an integrated firm.

The first condition is relevant in 'sunset' industries or in industries which have experienced a radical change in product or process technologies or consumer tastes. Although the value of the firm's product no longer justifies the firm's investment in existing plant and equipment, the firm still possesses valuable knowledge, relationships, and goodwill that may be profitably employed in another way. By replacing the cost of internal production with contractual agreements between more efficient, low-cost suppliers, the firm may be able to substantially reduce its cost of production and continue operating without a large portion of its assets and workforce.

The second condition – when large firms experience high 'transactional dis-economies' – may also produce network firms through the process of 'disintegration'. Large firms may become unable to accurately assess their environment and ignore critical threats to their activities. Performance declines and the firm may eventually have to 'down-size', 'right-size', or 're-engineer' its operations in order to survive.

The third condition – when returns are extremely high – represents a contrary view of network governance. The network firm emerges not because it offers advantages over hierarchical governance, but because the products or knowledge created by the firm generate such high returns that *any* form of governance would suffice. The bulk of network companies are in fields that generate large monopoly profits associated with unique technologies or knowledge such as biotechnology, computers and information technologies, entertainment, even fashion. Could the high returns associated with certain proprietary knowledge – not the advantages of network governance – explain the apparent success of these firms?

The fourth condition is when network firms find a less expensive way to negotiate and enforce contracts and manage relations between partners. Hill (1990) suggested that traditional economic theory has grossly exaggerated the need for extensive safeguards against opportunism, and thus the cost of writing and enforcing contracts. There may be additional economies associated with long-term reciprocal trading which traditional economic analysis does not recognize (Elg and Johansson, 1993; Blaine, 1995). More efficient methods of trading or the administrative apparatus used in coordinating one exchange may lower the cost of a second related exchange. Network firms employ 'trust' or similar informal mechanisms to reduce the cost of 'writing and enforcing contracts under conditions of uncertainty' (Ouchi, 1980; Johanson and Mattson, 1987; Powell, 1990; Grabher, 1993). To the extent that trust between parties is well founded and maintained, the need for costly contracting is clearly abrogated. To the extent that contracts may be informal rather than explicit, the firm's flexibility is enhanced. Thus, by providing an inexpensive alternative to explicit contracting, trust – when it is well founded – may lower the cost of network governance relative to traditional hierarchical governance.

Ghoshal and Nohria (1993) identified three structural mechanisms in the MNE that can be used to integrate the activities of diverse sub-units. They are: centralization, formalization, and normative integration (socialization). Centralization is well known and involves the use of authority to manage the firm's internal relationships. Formalization involves the use of rules and procedures to maintain cohesion and resolve internal disputes. Finally, normative integration uses a strong set of behavioral norms (e.g. corporate culture) to manage internal relationships. These three mechanisms may also be used to manage relationships and resolve disputes between members of a network firm. For example, when the firm at the center of the network has greater bargaining power than its partners, then its decision-making and dispute resolution can be centralized. This situation could arise when the center controls key knowledge or technologies, or is the only partner capable of assembling and coordinating the network's components. Over time, the use of authority may create tension and animosity within the group, increasing the need for formal contractual safeguards, thus raising governance costs. Formalization would require network members to develop a formal set of rules to manage internal relationships, resolve disputes between partners, and divide responsibilities. This would require lengthy negotiations, however, once a set of rules had been agreed upon, managing internal relations would be less problematical. Unfortunately, adoption of rules makes it more difficult for the network to adapt to changing external conditions. They may also make it difficult for the firm to incorporate new members.

In the case of normative integration (socialization), members of the network develop a strong set of norms, myths, or behaviors that give the group a unique identity. If this identity is strong enough, partners will place the interests of the group above their own individual interests, and 'trust' may evolve. This sense of trust among network members may significantly lower the cost of governance and provide the network with a key advantage over traditional hierarchical mechanisms (although trust can also exist in a hierarchy). This approach is more appropriate in cultures that are strongly group-oriented, tightly knit, or employ strong social sanctions – such as reputation effects. But whatever the external conditions, a critical factor in the success of the network form of organization lies in its ability to manage internal relationships and disputes, and coordinate activities among partners in a way that is less costly than either market exchange or hierarchical control.

CONCLUSION

What can we say of the near future? Many of the corporations we study will continue to exist, even beyond our lifetimes, yet for many death will come as surely as a new organizational paradigm establishes loftier benchmarks of efficiency. The end of employment as a certainty for many, the continued pauperization and proletarianization of the masses as well as the strengthening of the virtual form of organization will usher in the new age of the next century. It is not for us to hold advances in telecommunications as the culprit. True, it has enabled these vast changes in the structure and organization of the MNE, but it is the greed in human nature which has so used technology to prevent the spreading of benefits which is at the root of our problem.

The 'network' or 'virtual' firm is the most recent in a series of structural innovations designed to more closely align the capabilities of the firm with the demands of its environment. In general, these innovations have been designed to increase the 'information-processing' capacity of the firm, enabling it to expand operational scale and scope and coordinate increasingly complex activities.

Network governance is enabled by advances in telecommunication and computer communications systems, including the Internet, which have made it possible for firms to orchestrate their activities across electronic inter-organizational linkages. What is new is that for the first time, these linkages provide a useful substitute for the equity and hierarchical control of the MNE.

It is true that vast efficiency improvements in large complex business organizations can be obtained through the intensive use of telecommunications and information technologies, and that these efficiencies are driving some corporations to evolve into smaller 'networked' organizations. However, the calculus of governance suggests that the process of 'dis-integration' can proceed only so far before the additional costs of managing both the complex set of external supplier relationships and the complex information structures which link these parts together begin to outweigh the potential benefits of this new form of organization.

Is the network model a transitional organizational structure appropriate only for the early stages of industry creation? Certainly, network flexibility enables it to adapt to changing technologies, standards, and regulations, and to substantially reduce the costs of accessing the 'complementary assets' needed to commercialize new products or technologies. These advantages far outweigh the costs of managing complex relationships among partners. Since only a few firms survive this early stage of industry competition – generally those whose products or technologies become widely accepted, the costs of network governance are more than offset by the gains of those fortunate few, and are irrelevant to the casualties. Network firms appear to populate the early stages of rapidly evolving, often high technology industries. Can we find that once standards become widely accepted, innovation-based competition shifts to production-based competition, with cost becoming an ever increasing concern? The advantages of hierarchical control might begin to outweigh the advantages of flexibility and innovation. Over time, the successful network firm may revert to a more traditional structure. As the survivors of the early stages of industry competition become apparent, large firms could absorb these network firms into their own organizations, which has the effect of obliterating their network features.

Network firms appear well suited for highly complex, rapidly shifting environmental conditions. Network firms may continue to perform highly complex tasks in small niche markets, while integrated firms continue to perform more clearly defined tasks in large, increasingly global markets. It is not unreasonable to envision a bifurcated organizational environment in which large, integrated (multinational) firms and smaller, flexible network firms coexist more or less peacefully in largely unrelated worlds, performing vastly different activities and functions. The outcome is one of peaceful coexistence. Piore and Sable (1984) suggest these two types of organizations have coexisted and in some cases supported each other for some time, that in many industries traditional 'craft' or 'small batch' production – which is similar in some ways to the production processes used by network firms – has continued to occur alongside mass production typical of large integrated firms. These two ways of organizing production are appropriate for very different activities which do not compete directly with each other, and in some cases may support each other.

It is important to note that the types of organization we have considered here consist of small centers controlling larger peripheral activities through mainly non-equity means. They are *not* large centers holding hands with other large centers through strategic alliances and joint ventures, nor are they large centers controlling 'networks' of small suppliers through equity and non-equity arrangements. This distinction is important because proliferation of global alliances between multinational enterprises has been an important – and perhaps disconcerting – development. What makes network governance unique – and contradicts traditional organizational theories – is that it coordinates complex activities without the use of hierarchical or equity control.

Will MNEs continue to consolidate their operations and power, relying in the globalization process on even more sophisticated telecommunications linkages? Or will they follow the course of the smaller successful Silicon Valley firms and begin to dis-integrate into smaller 'networked' organizations, linked together in an eBusiness industrial network? Certainly, the continued rapid advances in electronic networks would appear to favor further dis-integration. If the 'virtual' firm truly represents a superior form of organization, what forces are stopping the wholesale disintegration of giant firms?

Telecommunications continues to strengthen the internal nervous system of the MNE which has been able to make tremendous strides in spreading its economic power around the world, and has reached the limits of geographical scope while still able to maintain, even strengthen, managerial control. Telecommunications has enabled it to make vast improvements in coordination and efficiency as well as simplification of specialized internal bureaucratic functions. Finally, it has enabled the MNE to begin the difficult process of managing the relationships with smaller units, and the outsourcing and subcontracting of what in the near past were considered to be critical functional areas. Perhaps it is an irony that the very force – telecommunications – which has played such a pivotal role in building up the structures of the present day hierarchical MNE is now a key driver in its transformation.

CHAPTER 6

TELECOMMUNICATIONS AND 24-HOUR TRADING IN THE INTERNATIONAL SECURITIES INDUSTRY

John V. Langdale

INTRODUCTION

The stockmarket crashes of October 19–20, 1987 and October 13, 1989 illustrated the strong global interdependency of international financial markets. The ripple effects of both crashes continued during the week as various participants in the international financial community reacted to developments in their local markets and in other countries (US OTA, 1990: 23–4). Stockbrokers and investors in many countries waited anxiously for trading to commence in New York and in Tokyo. While the crash illustrated the global interdependency of financial markets, it also illustrated that national factors are very important in influencing the local response to global forces. For example, some markets, such as Japan, did not decline as far as others.

The role of telecommunications and computer technology is central to an understanding of the nature of global trading in the securities industry. Firms are able to use telecommunications to buy and sell securities in major exchanges globally. The use of these technologies has both positive and negative impacts: on the positive side, they allow for responses to take place quickly, so that peripheral locations are able to access better quality information. Conversely, the speed of response allows financial crashes to spread very quickly and perhaps overwhelm the ability of regulators to control developments. As one trader pointed out: 'What you have is an electronic information system that lets everybody enjoy the benefits of panic equally' (Sesit, 1987).

It is often argued that the barriers of distance have now been overcome with the internationalization of industry and the introduction of new telecommunications and other information technologies. As a result, it has been argued that distance is no longer a barrier to international transactions. Banking and finance is often used as an example of a highly internationalized industry which has overcome the barriers of distance with 24-hour trading in global financial markets. In particular, some consider that new information and communications technologies have effectively removed spatial and temporal constraints on 24-hour global securities trading (Hepworth, 1991; O'Brien, 1992).

This chapter argues that while the introduction of new telecommunications and information technologies has had an important impact on the global operations of the securities industry, it is simplistic to argue that the barriers to distance have now been overcome and that there is seamless global securities trading. The adoption of technological change must be examined in the context of the competitive and cooperative strategies of major participants as well as the changing nature of regulation in the industry.

This chapter considers the role of telecommunications and other information technologies in the emergence of 24-hour trading in the futures industry. It focuses on futures exchange-based trading rather than other areas of trading, such as stock exchanges and over-the-counter derivatives. This chapter examines the internationalization of the futures industry and the role of telecommunications and other information technologies on the level of centralization and decentralization of futures trading. While telecommunications and other information technologies are important in shaping internationalization of the futures industry, the chapter argues that it is also affected by the:

- nature of competitive and cooperative strategies among and between major firms and futures exchanges; and
- changing nature of regulation in various countries.

The geography of the global futures industry is being shaped by the complex interplay of these forces. Growth of futures trading in major cities needs to be seen partly as a result of local and national factors but also in the context of global developments. At present, local and national factors dominate, but global forces are likely to play an increasing role in the future. However, it is simplistic to argue that national economies will be dominated by global forces; the geography of the futures industry (and other industries) needs to be seen as a result of a balance between forces operating at different geographical scales, ranging from the global to the local. The balance is changing over time, with global forces becoming more important in many industries and in many countries; however, this does not mean that forces operating at a local and national level are no longer important.

INTERNATIONALIZATION OF THE SECURITIES INDUSTRY

Internationalization in the banking and finance industry has been proceeding rapidly since the 1970s. One definition of internationalization is that national markets are becoming integrated into a world market that operates on a twenty-four hour basis. The trend towards internationalization of securities markets is being driven by a combination of factors, such as the:

- deregulation of government controls;
- emergence of huge institutional investment funds needing cross-national diversification;
- internationalization of production (manufacturing and more recently service industries); and

- technological change, particularly in telecommunications and other information technologies (US OTA, 1990: 11).

However, internationalization is also being driven by other factors. Trends towards securitization reflect a move away from bank lending and towards capital market borrowing. Large borrowers are selling securities directly to investors rather than obtaining bank loans. In addition, banks are tending to convert the loans they make into marketable securities (Savage, 1988).

The internationalization of securities markets is used to refer to various types of activities (US OTA, 1990: 29). These include:

- cross-listing of stocks and bonds issued in one country in a second country;
- investors of one country buying and selling foreign stocks in foreign markets, through foreign brokers;
- opening a country's stock markets to foreign brokers and dealers who serve foreigners and nationals;
- ties between exchanges in different countries;
- 24-four hour trading, or shifting the control of trading to colleagues in other countries and time zones;
- multinational offerings of bonds and equities;
- international mutual funds; and
- cross-national stock index derivative instruments.

This chapter focuses on a limited range of these activities: it examines the development of 24-hour trading via after-hours electronic exchanges as well as linkages between futures exchanges in different countries.

In the mid-1980s the United States dominated 95% of world futures trading. However, over time Chicago's dominance has declined, so that for the first nine months of 1994, US futures and options exchanges had a cumulative volume of 498.2 million contracts, whereas the rest of the world had traded 594.8 million contracts over the same period (Morse, 1994). Rapid growth of national futures exchanges has occurred in European countries (e.g. United Kingdom, France, and Germany), as well as in selected Asia–Pacific countries (e.g. Australia, Japan, and Singapore). It is likely that there will be rapid growth of futures trading in other countries as liberalization of financial services continues on a worldwide basis. At present, many countries' governments prohibit or severely restrict the operations of futures trading.

TELECOMMUNICATIONS AND THE INTERNATIONALIZATION OF THE SECURITIES INDUSTRY

New telecommunications and other information technologies are major factors underpinning the internationalization of the banking and finance industry. This is particularly true in the corporate or wholesale area of the industry: this sector of banking and finance serves medium-sized and large businesses including major transnational corporations (TNCs), many of whom are rapidly internationalizing (Langdale, 1985).

The impact of new telecommunications and other information technologies on the securities industry has been very significant (Hepworth, 1990). The impact may be seen in terms of the adoption of information technology by the securities companies themselves. Large securities firms from the United States (e.g. Merrill Lynch, Salomon Brothers, and Goldman Sachs), Japan (e.g. Nomura, Daiwa, Yamaichi) and the United Kingdom (e.g. Barclays de Zoete Wedd and County Natwest) have substantial global operations and invest heavily in telecommunications and information technology. One stockbroker pointed out that:

> securities companies are no longer companies that buy and sell shares and need a bit of information to do it. They are global information companies that happen also to buy and sell a few shares (Anon, 1990).

The securities industry relies heavily on telecommunications and information technologies. Securities markets are driven by information; there are strong incentives to use advances in communications technology, especially those that allow a speedier response (Coates, 1992). However, given that these technologies often threaten the roles and skills of established participants, the internationalization of securities industries is being shaped by the complex interactions between new technological developments and the strategies of major participants (e.g. banks, investment banks and securities firms as well as securities exchanges) as well as by government regulatory developments.

Furthermore, securities exchanges are becoming more heavily computerized and brokers are linked electronically to these exchanges. In addition, business and financial information providers such as Reuters and Telerate are also electronically linked to these exchanges; they rely on obtaining a rapid flow of electronic information from stock and futures exchanges before distributing it worldwide to their clients. Speed of information is vital to their competitive success. For example, Reuters complained for some years that it was disadvantaged in obtaining information from the Tokyo Stock Exchange, because the exchange provided the local Japanese information provider, QUICK, with its information feeds a number of seconds faster than it did to foreign companies such as Reuters.

The use of telecommunications and computers to speed the clearing and settlement processes makes possible global trading of securities. At the same time information technology stimulates international trade in securities, since it improves the information that investors have about foreign markets.

There has been little research examining the degree to which the international securities industry makes use of international telecommunications. Many financial firms use leased circuits for a significant part of their international telecommunications needs (Langdale, 1989). Yet the trading of securities is still overwhelmingly dependent upon the public switched telecommunications network (PSTN). Dealers' final buy and sell decisions from customers (both wholesale and retail) are generally transmitted over the PSTN. Staple and Mullins (1989) examined the linkage between demand for voice traffic on the PSTN and trading volumes on the New York Stock Exchange (NYSE). There was a significant relationship: doubling of inter-exchange activity on the NYSE led to an increase of approximately 4% in the growth rate of telecommunications traffic (Staple and Mullins, 1989).

TELECOMMUNICATIONS AND THE CENTRALIZATION AND DECENTRALIZATION IN THE INTERNATIONAL BANKING AND FINANCE INDUSTRY

Telecommunications technologies have exerted both a centralizing and a decentralizing force in the international banking and finance industry. They centralize the industry in that they give headquarters of large firms or major securities exchanges the capability of extending their influence to distant countries. Reductions in the cost of transferring information and a growing diversity in the means of achieving communication thus assist in the centralization of economic activity. Martin (1994) points out that new technologies allow firms even greater possibilities to develop economies of scale and scope through concentrating activities in a relatively small number of leading financial centers, as well as selling and servicing global products from a few strategic locations. The agglomeration economies generated by the established nexus of institutionalized financial skills, expertise, and supporting specialist cognate services in leading financial centers gives them a strong competitive advantage over national or provincial centers. New electronic trading systems based on computer and telecommunications technologies thus provide the capability of centralizing international securities trading in major exchanges.

However, telecommunications technologies also decentralize economic activity, since they allow peripheral regions and countries access to information formerly held by the center. Thus, the geographical spread of telecommunications and information technologies throughout the world has allowed trading to take place in these countries. There are no major technological barriers to the establishment of nationally-based securities exchanges. Decentralization forces are particularly strong in the international securities industry. Information about firms is primarily nationally based; securities exchanges are in a sense clearing houses for such information.

Furthermore, communications difficulties caused by time-zone differences are a traditional decentralizing force in the growth of cities as financial centers. Time differences have supported the development of various financial centers in different regions, since many financial transactions require interactive communications (Kindleberger, 1974: 10–11). The problem created by long-distance interactive communications by telephone between people in widely different time zones involves a dislocation to the working day for at least one party. It has only been with the advent of new telecommunications technologies (e.g. telex and electronic mail) that communication (although not interactive) is possible between distant parties with minimal disruption.

The importance of time zones in the development of financial centers may be seen in the growth of tax havens and offshore financial centers (Johns, 1983). Johns considered the close relationships between major international financial cities (onshore centers) and their associated offshore centers. Because of the differences in the levels of regulation and taxation, the Eurocurrency market has developed in these offshore centers, which are islands or small countries (e.g. Luxembourg) in similar time zones to the major onshore financial centers (London, New York, and Tokyo). The offshore centers are closely connected via modern telecommunications systems with their respective onshore centers. These close relationships between onshore and offshore financial centers may be seen in a number of regions. The numerous offshore centers in the Caribbean and Central American region (e.g. Panama, Bahamas, Caymans and Bermuda) are in similar time zones to New York and other large US onshore centers (Johns, 1983: 191). Luxembourg performs a similar function for Germany and Belgium, Bahrain for Saudi Arabia and Hong Kong for Japan.

24-HOUR TRADING

The role of 24-hour global trading in various financial markets has grown rapidly. This reflects the growing internationalization of the banking and finance industry and the ease with which international electronic funds transfer can take place. However, not all financial products have moved towards global trading. Global trading is encouraged by products that are homogeneous, familiar and tradable in large quantities, as, for example, trading in foreign exchange and US government bonds. A fully internationalized banking and finance market would operate on a 24-hour basis with information flowing between different countries with minimal institutional and regulatory barriers. Clearly, this situation has not been reached and there are numerous barriers still in existence.

The development of 24-hour trading using telecommunications and information technologies was seen by a number of groups in the industry as a means of defending existing positions or entering the industry. A powerful group is the Chicago futures exchanges, who saw by the mid-1980s that their existing dominance of the industry was likely to decline. Global electronic trading was seen as a means of defending their dominance of the industry. Their vision was a single after-hours trading system anchored and governed in Chicago, uniting a confederation of exchanges on a world-wide basis (Morse, 1994). A second group is the information vendors, such as Reuters, Telerate, and Bloomberg. These firms emerged initially as collectors and sellers of business and financial information; however, they have moved towards establishing electronic securities markets as a natural outgrowth of their business. These firms also saw global trading as a means of dominating the industry. For example, Reuters backed the electronic trading system, GLOBEX, as a means to this end.

The Chicago futures exchanges' vision of a global system has not happened. Instead, numerous competing futures exchanges oriented primarily to national markets have expanded across Europe and Asia. This result occurred partly because the demand for many futures contracts was primarily local not global in character. In addition, local futures exchanges were jealous of protecting their turf.

They saw that a global system would reduce their local autonomy. In addition, there was considerable infighting between the various Chicago exchanges, as well as suspicion between floor traders and brokers and the proponents of electronic trading.

Options for Achieving 24-Hour Trading

Firms and securities exchanges have followed a number of options in moving towards 24-hour trading. These options may be classified as:

- Linking locations: following the sun:
  (i)   linking firms;
  (ii) linking securities exchanges.
- Extending operating hours of securities exchanges:
  (i)   extending hours of floor trading;
  (ii) electronic exchanges.

Linking Locations – 'Following the Sun'

One option that firms and markets have followed is to electronically connect different locations and transfer information as the working day follows the sun on a 24-hour basis. This option has been followed to a limited extent in foreign exchange and securities trading. Foreign exchange trading tends to be most active during the time period when the East Coast of the United States and the Western European trading day overlaps, although trading in the East Asian region has expanded rapidly in recent years, reflecting the growing importance of Japan and other East Asian countries as international financial centers. It is important not to overemphasize the importance of this strategy, since it is practised only in some financial services. However, it has considerable importance for the Asia–Pacific region in terms of the rivalry between financial centers to be the financial center for the Asian time zone.

Linking Firms

TNCs in banking and finance often link locations around the world on an intra-corporate basis. For example, a bank operating in New York City could pass on its foreign exchange position in various currencies to an office in Tokyo, Singapore or Hong Kong to cover the Asian trading day. At the close of trading, this office then passes its position to London for the European trading day and it finally comes back to New York for the cycle to begin again.

A similar system also exists in securities trading. A number of large securities firms trade on their own account or on behalf of clients 24 hours a day. To achieve this they have set up operations in three time zones (East Asia, Europe and America) so one branch is always open. In fact, only a few large firms have introduced this strategy. For example, Merrill Lynch passes its book in US government securities from one center to another, so that each in turn is responsible for trading the company's position. During that period deals originating in other branches are passed to the current book manager for local completion. In the mid-1980s Merrill Lynch's New York office passed its Japanese 'book' of securities trading onto Tokyo. Another stock 'book' was traded via Hong Kong instead of Tokyo; still others shuttle between only two cities. However, most US stocks are traded largely by the Merrill offices in the United States and London because they remain thinly traded in Japan. This type of global trading is telecommunications intensive, since traders in passing the 'book' need to swap information on the latest developments (Anon, 1987).

However, it is unlikely that this type of global securities trading will become the norm. Trading in securities continues to be driven by national forces; the greatest liquidity for most companies' stocks continues to be in their local market. Most information affecting companies is released during the operating hours of the national markets in which they are headquartered. While it is possible to buy Japanese stocks in London and later the same day sell them in New York, the price of Japanese stocks is driven from Tokyo, not London or New York.

There are many other problems inhibiting the rise of global securities trading. Most securities are not as international as US bonds, and most dealers do not have a global coverage of offices. Equities, in particular, are hedged around with a maze of regulatory and settlement problems. Clearing and settlement of each trade presents a major problem and there are foreign exchange risks inherent in any delay. A further difficulty is in deciding where to book a profit (or loss) if stock is bought in one center and sold in another. National revenue authorities find it difficult to accept that a (taxable) profit, apparently made in their jurisdiction, should be attributed to someone in another country (Waters, 1989).

Linking Exchanges

24-hour trading may also be achieved by linking securities exchanges located in different time zones. For example, futures exchanges in different countries have linked contracts in a mutual offset system: thus, a contract bought in the Chicago Mercantile Exchange (CME) may be sold in the Singapore futures exchange (SIMEX) without additional commission fees. The advantage of the system is that it is possible for a contract to be bought or sold over a longer period of time in any day; this reduces uncertainty since many financial markets show major fluctuations on an hourly basis.

While a number of linkages have been developed and some are quite successful, most have never moved past the planning stage. There are a variety of technical and regulatory problems in linking exchanges. Regulatory difficulties are a particular problem in a number of cases. One of the major problems relates to the competition between exchanges; each exchange wants to hold its own business. Exchanges are less enthusiastic about internationalization than their clients. Larger exchanges fear that a link with a smaller exchange will sap liquidity and provide no real benefit for their own market. Smaller exchanges fear that they may be swallowed up by larger exchanges, although they would not be interested in linking up with other small exchanges. In addition, there may be conflicts between large versus small traders and brokers. However, a factor encouraging cooperation between different exchanges is the threat from electronic trading systems.

Major futures exchanges in the Asia–Pacific region (Tokyo, Singapore, Hong Kong, and Sydney) are competing with each other to attract business from North America and Western Europe during the hours that the latter exchanges are closed. Conversely, these Asia–Pacific exchanges are also facing competition from US and European futures exchanges, which are expanding the number of hours they operate each day in order to attract trade from the Asia–Pacific Region and from each other. While the potential business resulting from 24-hour trading has been exaggerated, there is significant competition between exchanges, particularly between Chicago and Tokyo.

Extending Operating Hours of Securities Exchanges – Electronic Trading Systems

Securities exchanges are able to extend their reach into additional time zones by extending their hours of operation. One option is to extend the hours of operation of the floor trading. A number of US exchanges have extended their trading into the evening in order to be able to provide trading opportunities for Asian investors. However, the drawbacks of longer hours are high costs of employing staff outside normal working hours and thin liquidity. One way around these disadvantages is to use electronic trading in hours outside floor trading.

Chicago futures exchanges have been particularly interested in the possibilities of extending opening hours because their relative dominance of the global futures industry has been steadily declining as international futures exchanges in other countries emerge. In addition, futures exchanges in general are facing growing competition from the largely unregulated over-the-counter derivatives markets.

The emergence of electronic securities exchanges is complicated by: issues of competitive rivalry of firms and securities exchanges; rapid technological change; as well as dramatic changes in the nature of the internationalization of the banking and finance industry. Consequently, in order to understand the geography of 24-hour trading, it is necessary to examine these competitive rivalries.

Most futures exchanges around the world have been exploring since the mid-1980s the options of whether to link their floor trading or electronic trading operations on an exchange to exchange basis, or whether to link to GLOBEX, a multi-participant electronic trading system. GLOBEX, jointly developed by Reuters and the Chicago Mercantile Exchange (CME), opened in 1992 after a number of years of development and trials. GLOBEX allows traders and their customers to deal using their screens after trading closes on the CME. GLOBEX automatically matches orders at the best price as they come in. This development avoids the costs of operating a physical exchange 24 hours a day and the regulatory and institutional problems of trading 'following the sun'.

The international linkages between futures exchanges have been quite complex over the past decade. Most exchanges have considered joining GLOBEX at one time, but as of late 1999, the three major participants are the EME, the French Exchange, MATIF and Singapore's SIMEX.

The reasons for exchanges not joining GLOBEX are complex, but are related to the domestic and international competition between exchanges. The Chicago Board of Trade (CBOT) joined GLOBEX for a time, but dropped out of the system in 1994 and has developed its own electronic after-hours trading system, Project A. It has expanded use of the system to an overnight session in March 1995. In addition, CBOT is connecting to Bloomberg, an electronic information provider.

The London-based futures exchange, LIFFE, considered joining GLOBEX, but decided against it when it found out that its ability to offer particular contracts and to establish its own international links would be severely circumscribed by GLOBEX. LIFFE established a mutual offset arrangements with other exchanges which allow contracts to be bought or sold in either exchange; however, each exchange retains local autonomy.

GLOBEX has been less successful than expected. Aside from commercial rivalries with other futures exchanges, there are a number of other problems. One reason for the slower rate of development of electronic trading has been that there have been considerable difficulties in developing technologically sophisticated trading systems. GLOBEX has particularly suffered in this respect because by the time that it was finally launched in 1992, it was no longer technically advanced. In addition, obtaining regulatory approval has taken a lengthy period. More fundamentally, questions have arisen about the extent of demand for 24-hour trading; it appears that demand is much smaller than what was expected in the late-1980s.

Conclusions

New telecommunications and information technologies are having major impacts on the nature of the internationalization of production. At the same time, these technologies are transforming the nature of distance, given that the costs of overcoming distance are lower and there is a greater diversity of telecommunications services available. However, a central argument in this chapter is that it is simplistic to assume that the barriers of distance have been overcome and there is now a fully-developed 24-hour trading network in the securities industry. There certainly have been some developments along these lines and more are likely in the future. Global developments must be seen in the context of the enormous growth of trading that is taking place within cities and countries. Securities trading remains dominated by nationally-based factors.

In general, research on the internationalization of economic activity has often simplified what is a complex pattern of processes working at different geographical scales ranging from the global to the local. Geographers need to unravel the role of these processes in order to understand the changing geography of economic activity.

A further theme in this chapter is that the nature of the adoption of new telecommunications and information technologies raises complex issues. The shift towards global 24-hour trading has been advocated by some participants as a means of defending their current position or as a means of entering the industry. New technologies have the potential to change the balance of power between firms and securities exchanges, with some participants benefiting more than others. Complex patterns of cooperation and rivalry are shaping the geography of the international securities industry. Consideration of the geographical implications of the adoption of new technologies needs to be examined in the context of this institutional perspective.

Government regulations are also a major factor in shaping the emergence of 24-hour trading. Differences in regulations from country to country raise the costs of global trading. While there are moves to harmonize these regulations, it is likely that many will persist. The geography of the industry needs to be examined in the context of national regulators moves, as well as developments to harmonize regulations on a global basis.

CHAPTER 7

JAPANESE INFORMATION SERVICES IN THE LATE TWENTIETH CENTURY

Barney Warf

The late twentieth century was a period of exceptional turmoil in the global economy. Rapid technological change – particularly as a result of the micro-electronics revolution – has been reflected in the growth of information services worldwide. The growth of telecommunications and related information services has been the object of much recent scrutiny (Akwule, 1992; Graham, 1992; Graham and Marvin, 1996). Many observers trace the emergence and dissemination of such functions to the birth of a post-Fordist economic order, marked by a highly complex division of labor, vertical disintegration, deregulation, and flexible production systems.

Japan, a world leader in industries such as electronics and automobiles, has been curiously reticent to adapt to this environment, with a poorly endowed information services infrastructure and relatively inactive in global markets in services, even in Asia (Spinks, 1991). Perhaps for this reason, the literature on information services in Japan has been scanty. Late to deregulate its information services compared to the United States or Britain, Japan has nonetheless witnessed significant changes in its information services over the last decade.

This chapter examines recent technological and regulatory changes in the Japanese information services industries, focusing upon new corporate strategies in the increasingly competitive global environment, particularly joint ventures. These changes have occurred hand-in-hand with a mounting globalization of this sector, including foreign penetration and the formation of transoceanic fiber optic networks. The chapter argues that the origin and impacts of these trends within Japan cannot be divorced analytically from that nation's attempts to remain competitive internationally. Thus, the highly regulated, oligopolistic market structure so common in other Japanese industries, which worked so well in the era of Fordist production, has become progressively unfeasible in the competitive, post-Fordist global market of tradeable services.

The chapter opens with an overview of the role of information services in the global economy, noting the increased mobility afforded to capital by this phenomenon. Next, it contrasts the magnitude and sophistication of the US and Japanese information services infrastructures, noting the high degree of development of the former relative to the latter. Third, it turns to the deregulation of the Japanese information services sector, specifically the break-up of Nippon Telegraph and Telephone (NTT), the rise of new competitors in specialized market niches, and NTT's attempts to rebuff these challenges through a series of foreign ventures.

Fourth, it focuses upon recent technological changes in Japan's information services markets, including increasing corporate and personal access to the Internet, the growth of packaged software, multimedia services, and the introduction of videophone and cellular telephone services. The fifth part examines the Tokyo telecommunications infrastructure, particularly the teleport, which have been central to Japan and Tokyo's international prominence. The conclusion reiterates the fundamental roles played by internationalization, deregulation, and technological change in this sector.

INFORMATION SERVICES AND THE GLOBAL ECONOMY IN THE LATE TWENTIETH CENTURY

The global economy in the late twentieth century became progressively structured around an increasingly dense network of international telecommunications systems (Gillespie and Williams, 1988; Dicken, 1992; Warf, 1995). The breakdown of the Bretton-Woods agreement in 1973 and subsequent shift to floating exchange rates, widespread deregulation, including telecommunications, the recycling of petrodollars, the steady expansion of multinational corporations, and the globalization of banking and securities conspired to make electronic communications vital to international trade and commerce. In part, these changes may be seen as aftershocks of the microelectronics revolution, which initiated widespread changes in production systems around the world. Such networks – including satellite, fiber optic, and leased telephone lines – have become instrumental to the globalization of numerous industries, particularly finance, as they seek to penetrate foreign markets, reduce costs, cope with mounting uncertainty, and respond to growing competitive pressures at home and abroad. In such a context, many corporations, especially in financial and business services, must be able to procure, process, and transmit vast quantities of information instantaneously, with access to suppliers and clients around the world. For financial firms, the digitization of capital permits electronic funds transfer, allowing large sums to be moved across the earth at a moment's notice (Langdale, 1985, 1989).

Many observers have situated the growth of information services within the broader shift from one regime of production, Fordism, to another, post-Fordism, characterized by vertical disintegration, the shedding of layers of management, collaborative joint ventures and strategic alliances, high levels of uncertainty, niche marketing, just-in-time inventory systems, and a whole slough of new technologies that thoroughly reshaped inventory control, communications, and interfirm linkages (Wood, 1991; Amin, 1994).

The geographic consequences of the post-Fordist informational economy, however, are poorly understood. Castells (1989, 1996) argues that information technologies have created a 'space of flows' in which capital enjoys unsurpassed mobility. It is evident that telecommunications systems have allowed some functions, such as unskilled clerical and data entry jobs, to be decentralized to low-wage Third World nations (Warf, 1993). Simultaneously, the global information network has spurred the growth of dense agglomerations of skilled headquarter functions in so-called 'world cities', most notably New York, London, and Tokyo (Moss, 1987; Sassen, 1991). Thus, the conventional topologies of production radically reconfigured in the late twentieth century.

For public policy-makers, these networks present both challenges and opportunities. The decline in technological barriers to capital flows has raised the importance of political ones. National governments, for example, may lose a large measure of control over their money supplies as financial institutions electronically import and export large sums at will. Equally important are the implications for local authorities, which seek to carve a competitive niche in the new political and technological environment. Finally, the rise of an 'informational' mode of production has dramatic consequences for everyday life, language, and the social construction of identity and the self as culture becomes restructured around the hyperactive, disembodied information of electronic landscapes (Virilio, 1995; Morley and Robins, 1995).

JAPANESE VERSUS UNITED STATES TELECOMMUNICATIONS – A STUDY IN CONTRASTS

Although the United States and Japan constitute the world's two largest economies, the differences in their national commitments to telecommunications and information services are startling. By any measure, Japan lags behind the United States in this arena (Table 1). For example, personal computer usage per 100 workers in the United States is more than four times that in Japan, indicating an undercapitalized service sector there. Japanese computers connected to the Internet in 1995 measured a mere 39,000, in comparison to the 1.18 million in the United States. In the retail markets, cellular phone usage per 100 people in the United States is three times greater than in Japan, and the percentage of US households subscribing to cable TV (60%) vastly exceeds the share in Japan (2.7%).

The relatively poorly endowed Japanese telecommunications infrastructure is surprising considering that nation's prominent role in other industries such as electronics, steel, or automobiles. Japanese information services firms have not been considered highly competitive internationally (Culp and McIntyre, 1994). In information services, United States–Japanese trade relations depart radically from the norm of American deficits and huge Japanese surpluses. In 1991, for example, the United States exported $398 million of information technologies to Japan (a tiny fraction of the total market there), but imported only $16 million (Survey of Current Business, 1992). US firms control 55% of the Japanese market in gateway services, (Culp and McIntyre, 1994) and 96% of the packaged software market (Ishizawa, 1994a).

In addition to trade, American firms have done reasonably well in Japan despite persistent government attempts to minimize foreign competition, as well as numerous cultural and linguistic barriers. Many Japanese firms have engaged in joint ventures to enhance their access to new technologies and to reduce the risks of marketing (Lakshmanan and Okumura, 1995). Numerous foreign information services firms have established joint ventures with Japanese firms (Table 2), while

Table 1 *Contrasts between United States and Japanese Information Services*

	US	Japan
% PCs Linked to LANs	52.0	8.6
PC Ownership Rates	15.8	5.7
CD-ROM Titles (thousands)	1,276	216
Cable TV Operators	11,075	149
Cable TV Subscribers (millions)	57.2	1.1

Source: Johnson 1990.

Table 2 *Joint Ventures of Japanese and Foreign Information Services Firms*

Japanese Partner	Foreign Partner	Partner's Nation	Purpose
Fujitsu	AT&T	US	phone service
Teleway Japan	AT&T	US	phone service
NTT	Microsoft	US	multimedia services
NTT	Nextel	US	cellular phones
KDD	Int'l Digital	US	SE Asian cables
AT&T Japan	Motorola	US	wireless WANs
KDD	AT&T	US	transPacific cable
KDD	France Telecom	France	transIndian ocean cable
KDD	Singapore Telecom	Singapore	transIndian ocean cable
Sega	Oracle	US	software development
Mitsubishi	Northern Telecom	Canada	ATM switching
Toshiba	Hagenuk GmbH	Germany	cellular phones
Toyo Digital	Nokia	Finland	cellular phones
Hitachi, Sanyo, Sharp, Sony, Canon	AT&T	US	videophone service

Source: compiled by author.

others, such as IBM and Sprint, have subsidiaries there. IBM Japan has 25,000 employees, not including two subsidiaries, IBM Japan General Business Co. and IBM Japan Service Business Co.

THE DEREGULATION OF JAPANESE TELECOMMUNICATIONS

Recently, Japanese policy-makers have realized the social and economic costs of their inadequate investments and stifling regulation in this sector and have emphasized policies designed to boost their competitiveness. Chief among these was the deregulation of the monopoly long held by Nippon Telegraph and Telephone (NTT) beginning in 1985, one year after the United States broke up the similar position held by AT&T, opening the NTT monopoly up to competition. The process also saw steps by the Ministry of Posts and Telecommunications to build a nationwide fiber optic cable by the year 2010. Indeed, the formation of a national 'infostructure' linking every home, office, and hospital, which is expected to cost roughly 53 trillion yen ($510 billion), is widely viewed in Japanese policy-making circles as instrumental to the nation's future competitiveness internationally.

Deregulation saw the emergence of nine regional telephone firms in Japan (similar to the nine Regional Bell Operating Companies in the United States), and excluded NTT from offering international communication service. Despite deregulation, NTT remains the giant of Japanese telecommunications (Culp and McIntyre, 1994). One of the largest carriers in the world, its revenues in 1994 amounted to more than 5.89 trillion yen ($55 billion). With 1.15 million km of conventional copper cables throughout the nation, it has a formidable infrastructure. The firm is still predominantly government-owned: two-thirds of its stock is owned by the Finance Ministry, its rates are publicly regulated, and major decisions must be cleared with the Telecommunications Ministry.

Domestically, NTT has faced mounting competition to its commanding market share. For example, Tokyo Telecommunications Network (TNN) compete head-on with NTT throughout Japan. However, TNN is so small, with only 10,000 subscribers, that telephone services bring only 3% of its revenues; the balance derives from leased circuits to businesses (Kageki, 1994). While TNN's revenues are less than 1% of NTT's, it too has a colossus in its corner, the Tokyo Electric Power Company, which may enable TNN to utilize the 21,000 km of fiber optic lines that it has laid alongside its power lines. Indeed, electric power utilities are leading shareholders in Japan's nine regional telephone firms and generate profits via leased circuits. Similarly, the railway operator Tokyo Corporation owns 77% of Japan's largest urban cable TV operator, Tokyo Cable Television, which serves 82,000 households in the Tokyo metropolitan region, and Kinki Nippon Railway is the sole owner of Kintetsu Cable Network. Smaller firms, such as Teleway Japan, and cable television operators, such as Yokohama TV, also offer phone services as the lines between these industries have evaporated. While competition of this sort has pushed down rates of domestic calls to the break-even point, margins on international calls are still considerable, albeit declining, leading NTT into the international arena.

Following deregulation, NTT was banned from providing international telecommunications service. This policy opened numerous opportunities for other firms, especially Kokusai Denshin Denwa (KDD), which holds about 70% of Japan's 300 billion yen ($2.86 billion) annual international telephone market (Kageki, 1994a). However, KDD's near-monopoly in this market is challenged by newer firms, such as International Telecom Japan and International Digital Communications, as well as by American firms. For example, USF Pacific (with a mere 1,500 clients) offers the service for 40% lower rates than Japanese carriers, and AT&T's service USADirect shifts the origin of calls from Japan to the United States at substantially lower cost (Kageki, 1994a). AT&T also joined forces with the financially strapped Teleway Japan Corp., the weakest of the domestic long distance carriers. Outbound foreign calls from Japan are destined primarily for the United States, followed by South Korea, China, the Philippines, and other Southeast Asian nations (Table 3). While total international calls increase by 10% annually, calls to China have risen at more than 50% per annum. Domestic and international

Table 3 *Distribution of Outgoing
International Phone Calls from Japan, 1993*

	Percent	Minutes (millions)
United States	24.0%	307.2
South Korea	10.7%	136.9
China	7.5%	96.0
Philippines	7.2%	92.2
Taiwan	6.3%	80.6
Thailand	4.5%	57.6
Brazil	3.9%	49.9
Hong Kong	3.6%	46.1
U.K.	3.4%	43.5
Iran	2.9%	37.1
Malaysia	2.5%	32.0
Singapore	2.4%	30.7
Other	21.1%	270.1
Total	100.0%	1,280.0

Source: Kageki 1994.

carriers have been prohibited from entering each other's markets, but future deregulation is widely expected to break down this barrier. Another sign of the complementarity of deregulation and internationalization is the recent presence of 18 foreign firms among the 254 members of the Communications Industry Association, including two on its board of directors, Northern Telecom Japan and Nippon Motorola.

NTT has not been lethargic in the face of its competition. In 1994, it applied to the Ministry of Posts and Telecommunications for permission to reduce line charges for high-speed digital transmission, which currently serve 3,000 companies and generate annual sales of 80 billion yen ($714 million). NTT and Microsoft formed an alliance to develop multimedia technology to allow Japanese software houses to distribute their products more efficiently by linking NTT's F-Net fax network using Microsoft's AT Work multifunctional telecommunications software; they will also use the same system to bring multimedia games to millions of Japanese households (Ishizawa, 1994a). NTT also launched an ambitious alliance with Nextel Communications, an American telecommunications services firm, to provide advanced digital cellular telephone services in the United States.

NTT moved aggressively into the East Asian telecommunications market. In 1993, it acquired 20% of Thai Telephone and Telecommunications Corporation (Kageki, 1994a); it had long shared the Thai market for switching equipment with the Swedish firm Telefonaktiebolaget LM Ericsson. Thus, although NTT is banned from providing international phone calls, there is no restriction on its participating in domestic business in foreign countries. Not to be outdone, KDD is currently acquiring 150 telephone lines between Hong Kong and Vietnam, and 360 lines between Thailand and Hong Kong. KDD, International Telecom Japan, and International Digital Communications currently have a joint venture to lay a 3,400 km,

560 megabit fiber optic cable linking Thailand, Hong Kong, and Vietnam at an estimated cost of $166 million.

New Information Services in the Japanese Economy

The emergence of a post-Fordist Japanese economy witnessed the birth of new information services and markets, including computer networking, software, cable television, multimedia services and videoconferencing, and cellular telephones. Each is briefly examined in turn.

Computer Networks

Computer markets in Japan remain considerably more complex than in the United States. While the US market gelled in the 1980s around IBM and Macintosh standards, in Japan a half dozen PC makers still compete for roughly equal market shares (O'Toole, 1993b). Problems of compatibility are thus significant obstacles, especially as lower prices have made PCs affordable for the middle class, greatly expanding the PC market. However, IBM's market share has improved with the introduction of DOS/V, a bilingual operating system that enables IBM compatible machines to handle Japanese (O'Toole, 1994a). With DOS/V, Japanese computer giants, including NEC and Fujitsu, began to move away from their proprietary operating systems and to bring them into line with the *de facto* IBM international standard.

Much as personal computers reshaped office work in the 1980s, so too has networking radically transformed the world of computing in the 1990s. In office work, Local Area Networks (LANs) have been joined by Wide Area Networks (WANs), including, more recently, wireless versions, which are increasingly common in the United States but rare in Japan. Motorola and AT&T Global Information Solutions Japan lead the Japanese market in this regard, although the Ministry of Posts and Telecommunications has a large one. American firms have done well in the Japanese LAN equipment market: the market leader is Nihon Cisco Systems, a subsidiary of Cisco Systems of California, and the US firm Wellfleet Communications ranks second.

The most important form of networking – access to the Internet, the largest electronic network on the planet – came astonishingly late to Japan. Only in October, 1993 did the Japanese Government permit full commercial connections to the Internet. Until then, only universities or corporate computers could access the Internet, and then only for non-commercial purposes. Deregulation opened up opportunities for new providers of Internet services. In 1994, the three largest providers in Japan included NEC's PC-Van, with 640,000 members, Nifty-Serve, with 590,000 members, and AsciiNet, with 85,000 members. While PC-Van caters primarily to corporate workers, Nifty-Serve's market consists primarily of individual users. Problems of compatibility between the two systems hindered interaction until 1994. The tiny domestic service provider Internet Initiative Japan is also active in this arena. NEC and Fujitsu each invested 10% of the $288,000 in start-up capital to establish the firm Ultra-High Speed Network and Computer Technology Laboratories (the remaining 70% came from MITI), which is developing technology to transmit 2.4 gigabits of information per second.

Global computer links have encouraged joint ventures between Japanese and foreign firms. For example, AT&T and KDD laid a transPacific submarine fiber optic line between Los Angeles and Tokyo in 1988 (Warf, 1989). Currently, they are planning a similar line between Japan and the United Kingdom. KDD, France Telecom, and Singapore Telecommunications are jointly studying the feasibility of a trans-Indian Ocean fiber optic cable. These lines, are part of AT&T's Fiberoptic Link Around the World (FLAG) network linking 13 nations in Europe, the Mideast and Asia. When completed, the FLAG project will create the world's longest submarine telecommunications network, a system augmented through aggressive pricing and marketing. However, while telecommunications prices around the world are falling, prices of international networking services are high in Japan compared to the United States. For example, the lease of one T1 (1.5 megabit) line from Tokyo to Silicon Valley costs US$88,000 per month, or six times the cost of an equivalent line to Tokyo rented in San José (O'Toole, 1993a). In 1993, AT&T Jens Corp. – a joint venture formed by AT&T and a consortium of Japanese firms – forged the first transPacific link for commercial Internet users. One fledgling American provider of this service in Japan is Performance Systems International, which purchased InterCon International (itself a subsidiary of another American firm), and is extending the availability of commercial Internet connections beyond Tokyo, Nagoya, and Osaka, cities served by InterCon (O'Toole, 1994b).

Networks not only permitted Japanese firms' entrance into global markets, but also facilitated the movement of foreign firms into Japan. France Telecom and Deutsche Bundespost Telekom have sought to ride the global wave of deregulation into the Japanese market. In addition, IBM Japan started connecting Japanese computers to the Internet through various communication services, including Prodigy, which will accelerate sales of IBM personal computers in Japan and allow a variety of services such as mail order shopping, library referencing, and photographic transmission. Nonetheless, compared to the computer-rich environment of the United States, these numbers are minuscule: as O'Toole (1993b) noted, 'The tsunami of open networks is just reaching the Japanese shore'.

SOFTWARE

For years, Japanese software houses prided themselves on writing unique, customized programs for large business users. The shift from mainframe to personal computers, however, encouraged the growth of standardized software packages such as word processing, graphics packages, and operating systems. Accordingly, sales in the Japanese packaged software industry grew by 40% between 1985 and 1993 (Figure 1). However, this market remains one that Japanese firms have yet to discover: overseas vendors hold 96% of Japan's packaged software market

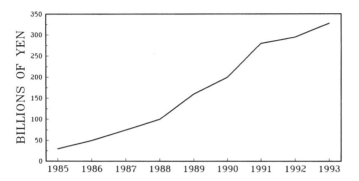

Figure 1 *Shipments of Packaged Software to Japan, 1985–1993*
Source: Ishizawa 1994a

(Ishizawa, 1994a) including the ubiquitous Microsoft. The US software house, Oracle, for example, has established alliances with key Japanese manufacturers such as Sega Enterprises and Pioneer Electronics to develop and market software.

CABLE TELEVISION, MULTIMEDIA, AND VIDEOCONFERENCING

Multimedia services have expanded beyond their beginnings in data transfer to include more sophisticated services such as cable TV. An enormous and well-developed market in the United States, cable television only reaches about 20% of Japanese households. Curiously, while American firms have embraced the market potential of multimedia wholeheartedly, risk-averse Japanese firms have been remarkably reticent. One notable exception, is NTT, which hopes to extend its fiber optic system to every home and office in the nation, and has itself initiated digital cable service. Indeed, NTT has jumped enthusiastically on the multimedia bandwagon, converging its telephone, computer and television functions. It currently spends 280 billion yen ($2.5 billion) annually on research and development of such functions, including 12 laboratories staffed by 8,500 researchers. An NTT subsidiary, Data Communications Systems, formed a joint venture with Softbank and Mediabank to launch an interactive television station, commercializing a video-on-demand service (Kageki, 1994b). NTT's alliance with Microsoft will link the former's infrastructure with the latter's software to sell retail multimedia services (Ishizawa, 1994a).

The blurring boundaries between cable television and telephone operators have encouraged railroads such as Kinki Nippon Railway, which own many cable television firms, to pursue this market as well. Conversely, cable TV firms such as LCV Corp. in Nagano prefecture and Yokohama TV have pioneered the move into realms beyond broadcasting to offer local telephone service. Finally, after years of inaction in this market, Mitsubishi Electric entered the multimedia race by teaming up with the Canadian firm Northern Telecom, a pioneer in the development of asynchronous transfer mode (ATM) switching systems and a keystone of future multimedia networks (Iguchi and Nagura, 1994). Northern Telecom had long sought a presence in the Japanese market, an opportunity afforded by deregulation and the rapid market and technological changes of the 1990s.

Satellite services, which improved markedly in quality worldwide following deregulation, have joined fiber optics in the provision of advanced digital services. In the United States, deregulation of the satellite industry began with the FCC's Open Skies decision in 1972. In contrast, private Japanese satellite services, led by Japan Satellite Broadcasting, began only in 1991. Similarly, Jusco Co. recently started a multimedia satellite network to supersede its existing terrestrial system. The government has also encouraged research in the development of low-orbit satellites to transmit weak mobile phone signals. Teleworking pilot projects such as the Shiki Satellite Office system have encouraged the decentralization of office functions by providing common access to centralized databases and expertise, and have accelerated office development in Kyushu, Chiba prefecture, and suburban Tokyo (Spinks, 1991). Finally, Japan has also been active in the East Asian regional satellite network, ASIASAT.

A related spin-off of multimedia services has been videoconferencing. The Japanese Government has encouraged videoconferencing by fiber and satellite to facilitate telecommuting, a strategy designed to reduce energy consumption and automobile-induced pollution. Following the sale of NTT stock in 1985, the government used part of the proceeds to establish the Japan Key Technology Center, which promotes industry research by investing up to 70% of the start-up capital for small research firms. Nippon Life Insurance has the world's largest private videoconferencing system, which started in 1990 and today connects 1,900 employees in Tokyo and Osaka. The videophone market is likely to increase rapidly in the future: AT&T, which produces the VideoPhone 2500 – a video telephone that can use the infrastructure of the existing telephone system – has signed licensing agreements with Hitachi, Sanyo, Sharp, Sony, and Canon.

CELLULAR TELEPHONES

The market for cellular phones in Japan has long been hamstrung by restrictive regulations. Direct sales of cellular phones were permitted only as of April 1, 1994, when manufacturers were permitted to supply handsets directly to consumers. Even now, the domestic market is uneven. NTT has sought to dominate this market much as it has conventional telephone service through its alliance with the American firm Nextel Communications. NTT does have competition, however. Japan Telecom, a domestic telephone company, jointly set up a firm with Nissan Motor Company to provide cellular telephone service in Kyushu (Kageki, 1994a). The two firms are also entering the lucrative markets in and around Osaka and Nagoya. Nissan also teamed up with another firm, DDI Corporation, Japan Telecom's competitor, to provide the same service in Tokyo.

The cellular phone market has been firmly internationalized throughout its short history. In 1989, the United States and Japan signed a bilateral agreement in which Japan pledged to grant American firms 'comparable market access and non-discrimination' in the allocation of radio frequencies in lucrative metropolitan markets, particularly Tokyo. Of US firms seeking to compete in the Japanese cellular market, Motorola, the largest cellular phone producer in the world, with 3,000 Japanese employees, has been by far the most aggressive, spending the last two decades struggling for access to the Japanese cellular phone market and setting up a system incompatible with that of the reigning giant, NTT. However, IDO Corp., a cellular telephone company, utilizes both the Motorola and NTT systems, although the latter's is far more extensive.

Japanese firms are well poised to sell cellular phones worldwide because they produce 70% of the world's supply of quartz crystal components, oscillators that are indispensable to cellular phone handsets. Firms such as Toyo Communication Equipment, Nihon Dempa Kogyo, and Kinseki are global market leaders. A world-wide shortage of oscillators has resulted from the explosion of cellular phone sales around the world. Japanese firms have reacted to the growth in this market by teaming up with foreign companies. Toshiba, for example, signed an agreement with the German electronics firm Hagenuk GmbH to jointly develop digital cellular phones using the European format GSM, which will be exported to 40 countries, including China and Latin America, but not Japan or North America. Tokyo Digital Phone sells terminals made by Nokia of Finland at half the suggested retail price; Nokia is second only to Motorola in the Japanese cellular market.

THE TOKYO TELECOMMUNICATIONS INFRASTRUCTURE

The three 'global cities' – Tokyo, London, and New York – have come to symbolize the global information economy powerfully, particularly as command and control centers (Sassen, 1991). In 1990, the Tokyo metropolitan region was home to 31.7 million people, one of the largest urban areas in the world. The Tokyo region accounts for 25% of Japan's population, but a disproportionate share of its economic activity, including 60% of the nation's corporate headquarters, 65% of its stock transactions, 89% of its foreign corporations, and 65% of its foreign banks (Cybriwsky, 1991).

Tokyo's growth is clearly tied to its international linkages to the world economy, particularly in finance, a reflection of Japan's growth as a major world economic power (Tokyo Mondai Kenkyukai, 1988; Masai, 1989; Hattori, 1990; Cybriwsky, 1991). In the 1980s, Japan's status in the global financial markets was unparalleled as the world's largest creditor nation (Vogel, 1986; *Far Eastern Economic Review*, 1987). Because such financial transactions require close proximity to one another, these firms formed highly dense concentrations within the financial district. In Tokyo, 80% of firms participating in foreign financial markets are concentrated in the area bounded by a 1 km radius from the center (Otemachi, Marunouchi, Yurakucho, and Yaesu districts), forming a new, internationalized sector of the city that rivals the old, domestically oriented one.

In the 1990s, however, like London and New York, Tokyo's bubble burst, and its financial sector suffered a particularly severe downturn in profitability and employment (*The Economist*, 1993; Leyshon, 1994): since 1989, the Nikkei average of stocks has dropped by 60%, bankruptcy liabilities have skyrocketed, and real estate values have stopped growing. In Tokyo, as throughout the industrialized world, large, multinational firms have steadily trimmed staff to reduce costs. The recent downturn in Japan's economic fortunes has renewed calls to regain the nation's competitive edge, leading to increased public and private investment in information services (echoing the US 'information highway' initiative under the Clinton Administration).

Tokyo's role as a center of information-intensive activities includes a growing telecommunications infrastructure, including the CAPTAIN (Character and Pattern Telephone Access Information Network) fiber optic system (Nakamura and White, 1988). Like France's Minitel system, however, CAPTAIN has been rendered obsolete by rapid technological changes in information services, leading to experimentation with newer generations of systems. In keeping with the Japanese tradition of close cooperation between the public and private sectors, the government has recently initiated a series of high technology 'technopolises' that form part of a long-term 'teletopia' plan to encourage decentralization of firms out of the Tokyo region to other parts of the nation (Lipman *et al.*, 1986; Rimmer, 1991; Graham, 1992).

In 2000 the city is scheduled to complete the Tokyo Teleport on 98 hectares of reclaimed land in Tokyo Harbor (Tokyo Metropolitan Government Planning Department, 1989). The teleport's 'intelligent buildings' (which accommodate fiber optics and advanced computational capacity), particularly its Telecom Center, are designed to accommodate the international Integrated Services Digital Network (ISDN) (Ishizawa, 1987). Wide Area Networks provide local telecommunications services via microwave channels, as do Value Added Networks on fiber optic routes. The site was originally projected to expand to 340 hectares, including office, waterfront, and recreational functions, and employ 100,000 people (Figure 2), but may be scaled back in light of the recent recessionary climate.

CONCLUSION

The post-Fordist revolution has had a dramatic impact on production systems around the world. Rounds of vertical disintegration, an expanding world market, deregulation, and mounting uncertainty have encouraged the growth of information services in most economically advanced nations. However, this sea-change has unfolded in different ways in different places. Compared to its prowess in manufacturing, in which Japan is one of the world's leaders, the nation's information services sector is relatively poorly developed. Both residential and commercial access to services such as cable TV, personal computers, and the Internet lag far behind the United States.

Following the bursting of the 'bubble economy' in the 1990s, three interlinked sets of forces have reshaped the face of the Japanese information services industries, including deregulation, technological change, and internationalization, which have been simultaneously determinant, mutually reinforcing processes. Japan's successes in the era of Fordist production, ironically, hampered its

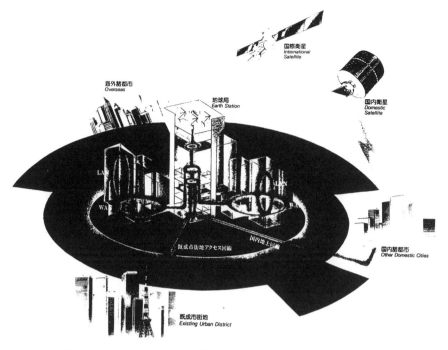

国際衛星
International Satellite

海外諸都市
Overseas

地球局
Earth Station

国内衛星
Domestic Satellite

既成市街地アクセス回線

国内地上回線

国内諸都市
Other Domestic Cities

既成市街地
Existing Urban District

Figure 2 *Representation of the Tokyo Teleport*
Source: Tokyo Metropolitan Government Planning Department 1989.

movements into an information-intensive era. Only the collapse of financial markets in the 1990s provided sufficient incentive to upgrade the nation's information services infrastructure. The nation's policy-makers belatedly realized that the highly regulated policy environment that proved so successful after World War II restricts national competitiveness in the fluid global economy of the late twentieth century. Japan's deregulation of its financial and telecommunications industries was late compared to that in Europe and North America's, and despite the breakup of NTT, is still relatively poorly advanced. Several restrictions remain: for example, the Ministry of Health and Welfare's Medical Act prohibits video medical checkups or teleconferencing of board meetings, while the Education Ministry denies video home schooling. Restrictions also remain on foreign ownership of Japanese common carriers, including up to 20% of NTT and KDD and one-third of other carriers.

Technological changes, particularly the digital revolution, have accelerated competition in new markets, encouraged foreign suppliers, and eradicated many boundaries between industries. Personal computers, fiber optics, new satellite systems, cellular phones, and videophones offer prime examples. Multimedia services have led to a gradual merger of cable television and telephone firms in Japan, as in the United States. There is little reason to doubt that the pace of technological change will not slow down in the future. Indeed, a host of new products lies just beyond the horizon. Paging devices, for example, common for years amongst American doctors and drug dealers, are primarily consumed in Japan by stylish high school girls.

Digitization has opened the world of Japanese information services to international competition to an unparalleled degree, breaking down the mercantilist set of protectionist measures that served it so well during the post-World War II Fordist boom. For many Japanese firms, joint ventures with foreign companies are particularly attractive. Thus, Japan has been forced to open up to the world economy, encouraging competition from foreign suppliers in its domestic market, a process likely to reduce consumer prices. The microelectronics revolution has, unintentionally, served as a digital Commodore Perry, and the mercantilist tariffs and quotas that protected its Fordist regime are being swept away like the Tokugawa shogunate.

PART III

URBAN, REGIONAL AND NATIONAL DEVELOPMENT

CHAPTER 8

CYBERSTRUCTURE AND SOCIAL FORCES – THE JAPANESE EXPERIENCE

Tessa Morris-Suzuki and Peter J. Rimmer

INTRODUCTION

Millennium fever gripped Japan early. Interest in futurology among its people has been intense ever since Herman Kahn spoke in the late 1970s about the twenty-first century being Japan's. The Japanese Government – as the leader-in-waiting – was bequeathed the task of charting the future course of economic, technological, and sociological organization that would supersede the American-led, industrial society of the twentieth century. The work of commissions and research groups appointed by Prime Minister Ôhira was presented in the 1983 publication 'Beyond the Modern Age' (*Kindai o koete*). Subsequently, numerous books and papers have provided a flood of ideas and images about the next stage in universal social evolution (Pyle, 1988). These images of the future were packaged as the 'information society' (*jôhôka shakai*) or 'high level information society' (*kôdo jôhôka shakai*), and were underpinned by the Ministry of Finance's new theory of 'softnomics'.

Japan's information-centered society promised to provide a new urban and regional geography. Simultaneously, this Utopian vision pledged to enhance national competitiveness, foster social integration, and supply low-cost welfare. It is pertinent to examine how far these predictions have been realized. Has Japan enhanced its international position; has social harmony been fostered; and has low-cost welfare been provided? How far has Japan's geography been transformed by the promise to reduce regional disparities?

Attention in considering these issues is focused on the key elements highlighted in mapping-out the contours of the information society during the early 1980s. Then, departures from the original vision by the 1990s are examined in an analysis of the contemporary information environment. Particular attention is paid to changes in the production and consumption of a variety of new media technologies, especially the Internet. Finally, an explanation for these deviations is advanced, highlighting the difficulties of making predictions about the social uses of new technologies.

EARLY 1980s VISION

The National Land Agency's (KK, 1984) vision of Japan's future geography showed urban and regional areas linked by a main trunk optical fiber network (Figure 1). The ideal central city possesses office automation and a local area network. South of

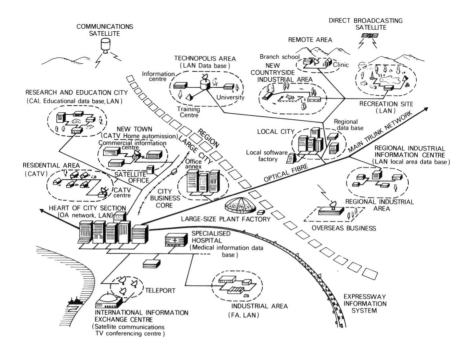

Figure 1 *The 'informatization' city and region of the twenty-first century*

Source: Rimmer, 1988: 228. Acronyms: CATV Community Atenna Television; CAI Cable Instruction; FA Factory Automation; INS Information Network System; LAN Local Area Network; and OA Office Automation.

the city there is a large-size factory, a specialized hospital with its own medical diagnosis center, teleport, international exchange center for satellite communications and television conferencing center, an industrial area with factory automation, and an expressway with an inbuilt information system. North of the city there is a residential area with community antenna television, a freestanding city business core, a new town with a cable television network, and research and education city with cable instruction television, educational data base and local area network. Within the southeast part of the region there is a regional industrial information center with a local area network and data base, and a free-standing overseas business enterprise with its own teleport. In the northwest part of the region there is a local city with a regional data base and local software factory; a technopolis area with a local area network and data base serving a university, training center, and information center, a new countryside industrial area, a designated remote area branch school and clinic, and a recreation site with its own local area network.[1]

Stripping away the surface detail from Japan's idealized city and region of the twenty-first century reveals the underlying communications networks more clearly

---

[1] The technopolis was developed by the Ministry of International Trade and Industry in 26 regional areas as a means for diffusing the most advanced technologies (MRI, 1993).

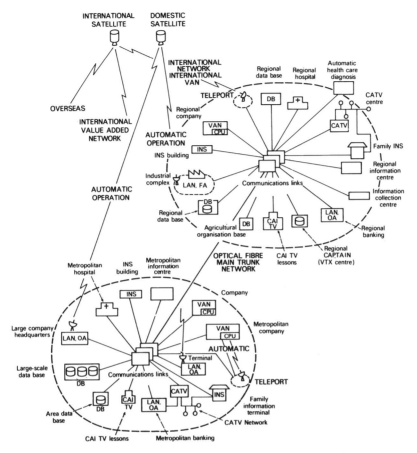

Figure 2 *A schematic diagram showing the key telecommunications features in an idealized city and region*

Source: Rimmer, 1988: 227. Acronyms: CAPTAIN Character and Pattern Telephone Access Information; CATV Community Atenna Television; CAI Cable Instruction; CPU Central Processing Unit; DB Data Base; FA Factory Automation; INS Information Network System; LAN Local Area Network; OA Office Automation; VAN Value Added Network; and VTX Video Text.

(Figure 2). The plan shows the international value added networks and domestic satellites, with the optical fiber main trunk network linking city and regional cores from which minor connections emanate. Although videotext using the character and pattern telephone access information network figures prominently in these underlying communications networks the key elements of the infrastructure for the twenty-first century are the information network system buildings and cable television.

The information network system shown in Figure 3 was pushed by the then state-owned Nippon Telegraph and Telephone (NTT) Corporation in 1982 (TSKJSK, 1982; Kitahara, 1983; Baark, 1985; Murakami, 1985). Although the NTT Corporation was partly privatized and subjected to competition from other carriers in

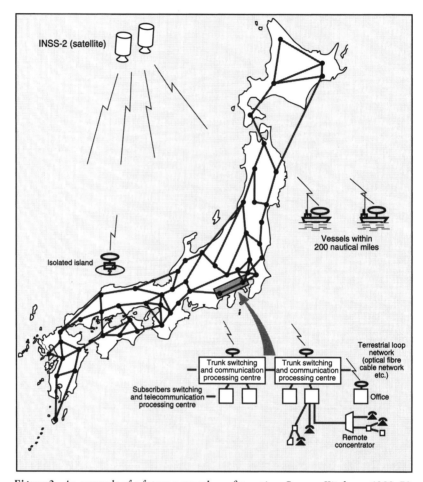

Figure 3 *An example of a future network configuration. Source: Kitahara, 1983: 72.*

1985 the ex-monopolist has remained dominant in the market and pursued the narrowband information network system – more commonly known as an integrated services digital network (Hatta and Takeuchi, 1995; Van der Staal *et al.*, 1995).[2] Between 1984 and 1987 the NTT Corporation conducted its much reported small

---

[2] Since the regulatory reforms in 1985 there has been a rapid growth in new common carriers (NCCs) in the Japanese telecommunications market. The three largest are the long-distance carriers – DDI Corp, Japan Telecom Corp and Teleway Japan Corp (Budde, 1995). Although the NCCs captured more than 50% of telephone traffic between Tokyo and Osaka, the NTT Corporation's overall share still exceeds 75% and its huge excess capacity gives the company a huge cost advantage. Also the NTT Corporation monopolized local calls which accounted for over 70% of Japan's domestic traffic (Hatta and Takeuchi, 1995; Stewart, 1996). In late 1995 the NTT Corporation agreed to open its local telephone network to competitors. This move was designed to stave off the Ministry of Posts and Telegraph's plans for dismembering the NTT Corporation as happened to the American Telephone and Telegraph (AT&T) Corporation in 1984 (*Nikkei Weekly*, October 2, 1995).

INS Network

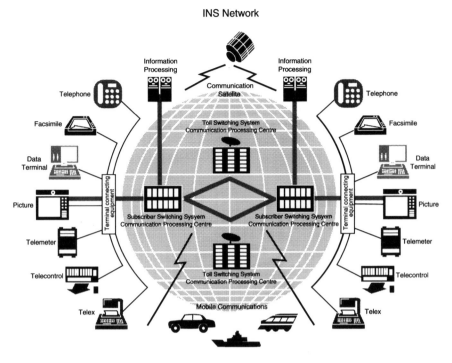

Figure 4 *The NTT Corporation's Information Network System (INS). Source: NTT, n.d.: 3.*

scale trials with the model information network system in the Tokyo suburbs of Mitaka and Musashino (NTT, n.d.).[3] When the NTT Corporation commenced information network system operations in 1988 it was the first practical example of the digitization of data, pictures and sound, and transmission between users by optical fiber, digital switching systems, and satellite communications.

The information network system offered the prospect of every factory, house-hold, and public office being integrated into a single system, by 1995, without the need for prior subscription to individual services (Figure 4). Businesses were promised a complete communications system by the information network system with teleconferencing facilities and the opportunity to develop 'satellite offices' (NTT, n.d.). Householders would be provided by the information network system with home banking, home shopping, and home study. Local government officials would have a local information service, an on-demand service for issuing residence

---

[3] As part of the NTT Corporation's experiment some 2,000 households in Mitaka and Musashino were linked to a digital optical-fiber network and given the opportunity to test advanced information and communications equipment. Local government, social service agencies, and private enterprises were given the opportunity to experiment with software. The facsimile had the greatest appeal and home shopping the least. This result prompted the NTT Corporation to shift its focus from home services to business users (Van der Staal *et al.*, 1995; Morris-Suzuki, 1996).

certificates, and capacity to provide video displays of important events. Advance publicity for the system even offered the prospect of 'remote medicine', using a variety of electronic equipment to link elderly and housebound patients to hospitals, so that they could be examined by a doctor without leaving their own homes. Although information overload and invasion of privacy were foreseen, the net effect for users was expected to be increased creativity, reduced waste and more leisure time. Generally, low priority is given to the negative social consequences of technological development in Japan. The information network system was justified to enable Japan to get ahead in the 'information revolution' – and these plans to 'wire the nation' scared the Americans.[4]

MID-1990S REALITY

Japan's transition from an industrial to an information society was expected to take 20 or 30 years. A stocktake of progress by the mid-1990s suggests all has not gone according to plan in realizing the original urban and regional development goals.[5] The familiar litany of a rapidly ageing population, overconcentration of population in urban areas, environmental problems, the need for structural economic change, and demands for a more comfortable lifestyle and more open society still persist.

Japan's Telecommunications Council (1994) sought to tackle these multifarious problems through its Japanese Information Infrastructure Plan (Latzer, 1995). Specifically, the Council proposed to maintain and reinforce existing urban and regional arrangements while transforming the monocentric configurations of metropolitan areas into polycentric ones (Figure 5). By 2010 homes in the seven metropolitan areas will be linked by an integrated broadband system (i.e. a fiber-to-home system). Peripheral areas will be connected by satellites by 2010; but the infrastructure for the interstitial micropolitan zone is still under discussion (Gershon and Kanayama, 1995).[6] The key feature of all regional development plans is the information park in which universities and other R&D facilities, such as studios, convention and residential facilities, and supporting facilities, have central roles (MRI, 1993).

This revised programme suggests the NTT Corporation's information network system backbone and its integrated services digital network technology have developed steadily in Japan, though below initial expectations.[7] Operation of the

---

[4] As Japan's wired television has not competed with conventional television the acronym for Japan's cable television is CATV (Sugaya, 1995).
[5] There is only a small gap in telephone traffic between leading and lagging prefectures in telephone calls per subscriber but the overall regional disparity has decreased only slightly (Van der Staal, 1994).
[6] Japan's Telecommunications Council proposed most prefectural capitals would be part of the network by 2000 (20% of the population; cities with populations over 50,000 by 2005; 60% of the population; and the whole of Japan by 2010).
[7] The information network system covered 50% of Japan and reached 86% of its population in September 1992 (Van der Staal et al., 1995).

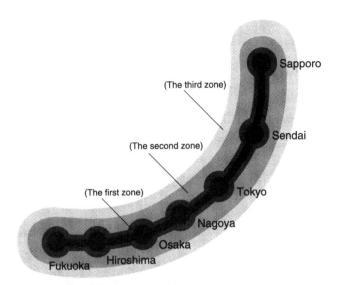

Figure 5 *Proposed regional structure in the 'networked' society. Source: Based on Takahashi, 1995.*

INS network and platforms by the NTT Corporation has proven more expensive than envisaged. Apart from the high price of equipment, the other reasons given for the slow diffusion have been its unattractiveness to subscribers because of lack of interconnectivity and services; and tension between the universal equal access aspirations of the Ministry of Posts and Telecommunications and the NTT Corporation's desire to receive rates that cover costs (Van der Staal *et al.*, 1995). Also, the sluggish demand for an information network system stems from its being too versatile for average Japanese users and having too few unique features.[8] The information network system appeals to the corporate market but video-on-demand and games would be required to capture the mass consumer market.[9]

Upgrading the information network system has been required to make it more flexible, and to keep up with the increasing sophistication of communications content (Figure 6).[10] The original information network system was superseded by the information network system Net 1500 to provide a faster carrying speed from

---

[8] The NTT Corporation's teleconferencing services launched in 1985 flopped in Japan because it undermined corporate hierarchies and etiquette (*Nikkei Weekly*, October 23, 1995).

[9] In October 1995 the NTT Corporation had 1 million integrated services digital network channels used mostly by corporations (*Nikkei Weekly*, December 25, 1995 and January 1, 1996).

[10] A broadband integrated services digital network experiment has also been underway to carry the large amounts of data required for high-definition television. Great resource wastage would be brought about by broadband integrated services digital network's construction unless attention is paid to the investment behavior of the carriers, especially the NTT Corporation (Hatta and Takeuchi, 1995).

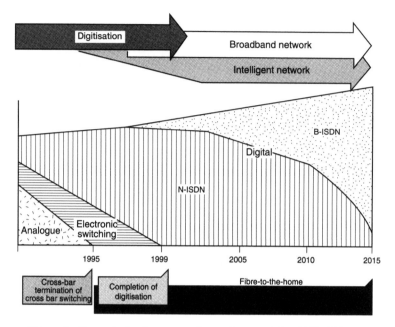

Figure 6 *Network development scheme. Source: Aoki, 1995: 131.*

64kbit to 1.5kbit per second.[11] Also, the NTT Corporation reinvigorated its information network system in 1990 by promising the creation, by 2015, of a broadband integrated services digital network system – incorporating the latest asynchronous transfer mode technology – under the motto 'visual, intelligent, and personal'.[12] The NTT Corporation's revised vision was mistaken by observers in the United States as a definite Japanese strategy, and may have inadvertently prompted President Clinton's own Information Superhighway Plan, also due for completion in 2015 (Latzer, 1995).[13] There will not, however, be a broadband integrated services digital network system in every Japanese home by 2015!

---

[11] The information network system's Net 1500 has proved to be economical because of its data-intensive circuits. This facility is particularly useful for electronic-image processing, plate making systems for the print industry and videoconferencing (Budde, 1995: 118).

[12] Originally, the NTT Corporation planned to launch broadband integrated services digital network for corporate customers in 1993. One-third of the networks were to be converted to broadband integrated services digital network by 2005 and optical fibers would be available to homes in major cities. The target completion date was 2015. In 1992 the fiber-to-home vision was abandoned. Then broadband integrated services digital network was postponed in 1993. Under a revised schedule broadband integrated services digital network would now be offered to corporate customers by 1995. Home use would start in 1998 and it would still be completed in 2015 (Van der Staal *et al.*, 1995).

[13] Even if the NTT Corporation's integrated services digital network meets the government target in connecting Japan's information superhighway it may be still several years before consumers actually experience multimedia. This delay has allowed some firms to develop video CD players as an alternative to the information highway offering video-on-demand, news-on-demand, and on-line shopping.

It is instructive to compare current experiments (using the latest broadband integrated services digital network technology) with the earlier trials of the model information network system conducted in the 1980s. The 'Multimedia Communications Common Use Experiment', launched by the NTT Corporation in September 1994, looks at first very much like a repeat performance of earlier experiments, although with improved hardware. Like the 1980s model system trials, it is a scheme that gives selected users access to the most up-to-date communications services in order to try out potential uses of the information network system. It will also be used to develop and test the asynchronous transfer mode technology necessary for the shift to the broadband integrated services digital network. The publicity surrounding the experiment lists a familiar catalogue of potential social benefits that might flow from these trials: home shopping, instant access to news, remote medicine, and distance education (Ôtsuki, 1995: 55).

But a closer look suggests that some lessons have been learnt from the previous decade's experiments. The earlier emphasis on household use has now been replaced by a recognition that many of the services offered by the information network system will be too expensive for normal family use in the foreseeable future. Also, social as well as technological barriers hamper the development of the more revolutionary social uses once predicted for the system. In the current experiment the users are not individual households but 127 consortia of businesses, universities, and other research groups. 'Remote medicine' now refers not so much to the use of the system to examine individual patients at home, but rather to the electronic exchange of sophisticated medical information (such as three-dimensional scanned images) between one hospital and another. Distance education experiments, too, are tending to focus less on the provision of education to individual households than on the exchange of lecture programs and other teaching material between universities (Ôtsuki, 1995). One of the few household services for which a bright future is predicted is video-on-demand (see, for example, TSKJSK, 1994: 19). This would combine features of cable television with an interactive element, so that users could choose which programs to watch at any given time.

Meanwhile, interest in the broadband integrated services digital network has been distracted by the promise of multimedia embodied in the 'National Information Infrastructure' and 'Global Information Infrastructure' (Van der Staal et al., 1995). The broadband integrated services digital network system is no longer the ultimate goal but merely one link in the multimedia network. Some observers even suggest that it, too, may become obsolete before the network is fully in place. As the rapid and largely unplanned spread of the Internet has overtaken some of its Utopian plans for the communications future, the NTT Corporation itself has responded by pursuing the development of a new, more flexible network for electronic data, the 'Open Computer Network'. This would represent a step away from the conventional communications system, whose architecture is based on the needs of telephone users, and would involve the creation of a 'connectionless system' better adapted to the needs of computer communications (Asakura, 1995: 127).

Cable television's penetration rate of 5% in Japan has also fallen below expectations. Cable represented only 26% of all households with television and the average channel capacity of urban cable television is 26 (Budde, 1995; Sugaya, 1995; Van der Staal *et al.*, 1995).[14] The low penetration rate has been attributed to the good quality of the existing free-to-air system, and the poor programming and relatively high charge for cable television (*Nikkei Weekly*, December 12 1994). Although there are no marked entry barriers to cable television, an advanced system offering 100 channels and a multimedia or interactive video service would compete with the NTT Corporation's own plans for multimedia services.[15] As the average Japanese household already spends US$58 per month on information services the demand for cable television may not seem promising. However, cable television is still growing in Japan and there are large expectations for its future boosted by the Ministry of Posts and Telecommunications, particularly as providers could enter other telecommunications businesses (e.g. telephony).[16] The fact that few households yet have access to cable television also means that there is a large and untapped potential market for video-on-demand, as this begins to become available in the late 1990s.

Technological adjustment to the information network system and the sluggish demand for cable television were not anticipated. Further, the government forecasters of the early 1980s seriously miscalculated some of their predictions for businesses, households, and public bodies. Businesses made good use of the information network system to integrate their logistic chains (e.g. offices-factories-wholesaler-retailer) and develop automatic funds transfer, but satellite offices and homeworking have been slow to develop (MRI, 1993). Household targets have been reduced to cable television, video-on-demand, and electronic newspapers, as home shopping has shown little growth and the opportunities for distance education and home healthcare are, at best, ambiguous. A pilot study of a compact videophone communications system using the integrated services digital network in home health care of the disabled has shown improved communication interdependence, family health, and accessibility to medical consultations (Takano, Nakamura and Akao, 1995). The possibilities of reinvigoration of local communities through new local government communications networks have yet to be proven. These outcomes have prompted the Ministry of International Trade and Industry to be far more cautious than in 1982 when predicting the social uses of new technology in

---

[14] There are 1.5 million cable subscribers in Japan compared with 57.2 million in the USA (Budde, 1995: 127).

[15] The NTT Corporation has established GrR Homenet, a planning company. with Sega Enterprises Ltd, Sony Corp., Yamaha Corp. and Victor Corp. to conduct feasibility studies and investigate the market for one-to-one interactive video games, shopping, electronic mail and news-on-demand. In 1995 alone the NTT Corp. also made eight separate alliances with US multimedia firms (Hayes, 1996).

[16] Yokohama Cable Television has been formed by Nynex, the regional US holding company, and several Japanese firms in a new cable project and in Tokyo's central business district Suginami Cable Television will obtain cable network technology from the US's Telecommunications Inc. (TCI) to serve a subscriber base of 240,000 homes (Budde, 1995; Sugaya, 1995).

its 'High Level Informisation Program' (TSKJSK, 1994).[17] The Ministry's programme for advanced information infrastructure has targeted education (multimedia software bases), research and development (interministerial research
information networks), medical care and welfare (pharmaceutical data bases and
exchange of X-ray photographs), administration (local area network and data
bases), and libraries (electronic library systems) (MITI, 1994).[18]

PROBLEMS PREDICTING SOCIAL USES OF NEW TECHNOLOGY

The apparent failure of bureaucratic visions to enhance domestic competitiveness,
boost social integration, and supply low-cost welfare stems from a lack of appreci-
ation of the complex trade-offs between consumers and producers in the total
'information environment' covering television, radio, telephones, cable television,
computer networks, books, software, post, and face-to-face communication (Van
der Staal, 1994; Gôtô, 1990). Despite relatively high education levels, knowledge is
unequally distributed in Japan, as in other countries, because of inequalities in the
possession of monetary, social, and cultural capital. This reality is obscured in folk
tales about the ordered information superhighway and the alternative anarchistic
vision of cyberspace. More realistically, an awareness of the political economy of
knowledge sees the arena of new information networks as a 'cyberstructure', where
invisible but powerful distortions exist in the distribution of pre-existing knowledge. The approach underlines the fact that individuals meet on structured and
unequal terms (Morris-Suzuki, 1996). A good example is the case of the Internet.

INTERNET JAPAN .jp

The NTT Corporation's information network system experiments had focused on
businesses and households and paid relatively little attention to the academic
sector's information needs. Independent experiments by researchers, however,
led Tokyo University, Keio University, and Tokyo Institute of Technology to
establish the JUNET (Japan University Network). Reflecting its international
orientation, the English language JUNET was linked in 1986 to the US forerunner
of Internet, the ARPAnet (Advanced Research Projects Agency). A Japanese language version was developed largely by a graduate student (Murai, 1995). In 1988,

---

[17] In mapping out this program Ministry of International Trade and Industry planners were
conscious of the US's National Information Infrastructure (NII) plan and Europe's Trans-
European Networks (TEN) plan. They were also aware of the State of California's Smart
Valley project, the State of North Carolina's Information Highway Project and Washington
D.C.'s Netplex.
[18] The Ministry of International Trade and Industry's Programme 21 identifies information
and communications as one of eight promising markets for the twenty-first century (MITI,
1994). Particular attention is paid to video software, electronic museum, tele-education
and mobile communications.

the universities, in collaboration with communications and publishing interests, developed the WIDE (Widely Integrated Distributed Environment) network which was fully compatible with the Internet. Then, in 1993, links were established between the WIDE network and Japan's commercial computer networks. Although vulnerable to blackouts and damaged telephone networks, the e-mail and the Internet proved very effective after the Kobe earthquake of January 17, 1995 (*Nikkei Weekly*, February 20, 1995; April 3, 1995; Noam and Sato, 1995).[19] All of these developments have intensified corporate interest in the Internet. Although the commercial internet service provider market was started by smaller companies it is now targeted by the major Japanese computer corporations, notably Fujitsu, Hitachi, and NEC.

By the mid-1990s Japan had the largest Internet network in Asia. In July 1995, Japan had an estimated 100 internet service providers. Many providers were supplying access over integrated services digital network lines as well as providing analogue access for Internet subscribers. About 75% of the providers are located in Tokyo. Some providers are also developing trans-Pacific backbones to link the United States and their Asian neighbours, Hong Kong and Singapore.[20] Japan had 159,776 Internet hosts – a figure which surpassed South Korea but still lagged behind Australia (Table 1).

In 1995, Japan had four-to-five million Internet subscribers (Mesher, 1996). Less than 16% of Japanese homes, however, have personal computers (Table 2).[21] This low rate of diffusion seems to reflect at least two characteristics of the spread of information technology in Japan. The first is the widespread use of dedicated wordprocessors. In most English-speaking countries, personal computers have come to be very widely used in homes and offices for wordprocessing. Wordprocessing programs for the Japanese language, though, have been relatively expensive and often cumbersome to use. As a result, many Japanese users opted to buy cheap and user-friendly dedicated wordprocessing machines.

It was only in 1994, as the use of e-mail and other computer networks began to take off, that sales of personal computers in Japan outstripped sales of dedicated wordprocessors (Figure 7). Even today, the diffusion of personal computers in public institutions is surprisingly limited when compared with many other industrialized countries. For example, a survey conducted at the end of 1995 by the news magazine *Aera* found that less than 17% of Japanese parliamentarians used personal computers (Hamada, 1995).

---

[19] The Nifty computer network service in Kobe became a major meeting point. Both Nifty and its rival PC-VAN established special earthquake bulletin boards. They enabled 'information volunteers' to operate (Noam and Sato, 1995).

[20] In December 1995 Interconnected Associates of Seattle and Starr Direct in Japan established the Tokyo–Seattle Bridge – a T-3 Trans-Pacific Internet link. The Tokyo–Washington Internet Railroad and a consortium of internet service providers are also providing a T-3 Trans-Pacific link between Japan, Hong Kong and Singapore (Mesher, 1996).

[21] Major banks in Japan are just beginning to invest in personal computers for their marketing employees (*Nikkei Weekly*, December 26, 1994; January 2, 1995).

Table 1 *Internet Host Distribution by Top Level Domain Name in Asia-Pacific Region, July 1995*

Country	Domain	Hosts
Australia	.au	207,426
Japan	*.jp*	*159,776*
Korea	.kr	23,791
New Zealand	.nz	43,863
Taiwan	.tw	16,166
Singapore	.sg	8,208
Thailand	.th	2,481
Malaysia	.my	1,087
China	.cn	1,023
Indonesia	.id	848
India	.in	645
Philippines	.ph	365
Macau	.mo	47
Nepal	.np	19
Guam	.gu	18
Fiji	.fj	9
Pakistan	.pk	6

Source: Mesher (1996: 28).

Table 2 *Households in Japan with Personal Computers, 1987–1995*

Date	Number per thousand households	Rate of growth
1987	12.4	11.7
1988	10.2	9.7
1989	12.2	11.6
1990	11.2	10.6
1991	12.7	11.5
1992	13.2	12.3
1993	13.6	11.9
1994	15.8	13.9
1995	17.8	15.6

Source: Japan Information Network (citing Current Consumption Survey, The Business Statistics Research Division, Research Bureau, Economic Planning Agency).

COMPUTER GAMES AND PERSONAL COMPUTER NETWORKS

The same pattern of specialization appeared in the use of computers for games and entertainment. While many US families used cheap general-purpose personal computers such as the Mac Plus for entertainment, in Japan the market was dominated by Nintendo's single chip game computer 'Family Computer' (Famicon) and its imitators. These, it is true, were used not only by children to play multiple-

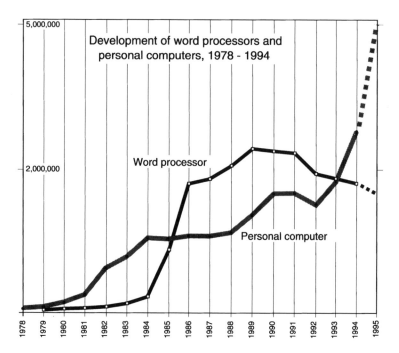

Figure 7 *Development of word processors and personal computers, 1978–1994.*
Source: Ôzaki, 1995: 16

user fantasy games such as 'Mario Brothers', 'Super Mario Brothers', and 'Dragon Quest' but also came to be linked into networks used by adults, mainly to speculate on the share market through 'Famicon Trading' (Morris-Suzuki, 1996).[22] However, the wide diffusion of word processors and game computers undoubtedly slowed the spread of programable personal computers in Japan throughout the 1980s and early 1990s.

The low household computerization rate was paralleled by the low penetration diffusion of cable television. Thus, Japan does not have a grassroots tradition in info-communications or wide experience with computer networks or cable television (Latzer, 1995). The introduction of Microsoft Word's Windows 95 operating system software on November 27, 1995, however, has helped the personal computer to become a standard household appliance.[23] Sales of personal computers

[22] Unlike the information network system experiments Famicon was cheap (US$100), simple to operate and fitted the physical and social infrastructure of Japanese households. Famicon has succoured fantasies rather than promoted community values (Morris-Suzuki, 1996). Game machines in Japan still cost less than US$300 whereas the personal computer costs US$2000.

[23] The introduction of Windows 95 in Japan boosted sales by Apple Computer Inc. (*Nikkei Weekly*, February 5, 1995).

soared to an estimated 5.3 million units in 1995 with 14.3 million units being anticipated in 1999 (*Nikkei Weekly*, 23 October 1995).

By 1995, rapid progress was being made with personal computer networks and the growing popularity of the Internet and compact disc read only (CD-ROM) software. Internet activity on the Web is increasing in Japan. Business and the public sector (central and local governments) are compiling home pages.[24] Major bulletin board services are offering Internet access for their members.[25] Small entrepreneurial ventures have also been developed which allow individuals to link to the Internet if they lack access to terminals at large firms or universities.[26] An estimated 50 Internet cafés have been established – three-quarters of them being in Tokyo. A whole new generation of young hackers and computer enthusiasts is providing an expanding market, not only for personal computers and software, but also for a rapidly expanding range of personal computer and Internet magazines (Greenfeld, 1994: 230–242). New services are being developed for on-line banking and on-line shopping.[27] The latter is being facilitated by the development of a Japanese language 'cybermall'. The Big Four security houses in Japan are using the Internet to provide on-line investor data.[28]

In response to the new threat to their market share, game computer makers have been competing to produce simple, cheap machines with Internet connectivity. Bandai's Pippin communications terminal, for example, offers access to the Internet at a cost of about US$600. Critics, however, question the appeal of these simplified machines, which lack hard drives to download data, and are generally much slower than standard PCs (*Nikkei Weekly*, February 19, 1996). It remains to be seen whether these variants on the 'Internet box' will enable game computer makers to stem the growing market dominance of the PC manufacturers.

CORPORATE RESPONSE AND POLITICAL IMPLICATIONS

Corporate Japan has been slow to adopt e-mail, as it undermines the way senior managers obtain information. More than ten managers, for example, may screen a business proposal. Each adds his chop, signifying agreement. The Internet is also alien to the traditional way of targeting investors through information meetings.

The political implications of the Internet have attracted considerable attention in Japan, as in other countries. The Internet offers a channel for political parties,

---

[24] The Economic Planning Agency, the Ministry of Posts and Telecommunications, the Prime Minister's official residence and the Science and Technology Agency have opened sites on the Internet (*Nikkei Weekly*, May 10, 1995).

[25] The major bulletin boards include Fujitsu Ltd, IBM Japan Ltd, NEC Corp's PC-VAN and Nifty Serve (*Nikkei Weekly*, May 10, 1995). In 1994, there were 2.59 million subscribers to Japan's on-line services (*Nikkei Weekly*, November 7, 1994).

[26] The small ventures firms include Bekkoame Internet and Rimnet (*Nikkei Weekly*, July 31, 1995).

[27] US firms Digital Media Lab, People World and Shopping 2000 have established a joint-venture for on-line shopping (Mesher, 1996).

[28] The Big Four are Daiwa Securities Co., Nomura Research Institute, Nikko Research Center and Yamaichi Research Institute of Securities & Economics.

local government, and citizens' movements to communicate directly with the public, bypassing the intervening power of newspapers and television. The major Japanese political parties all have Internet home pages, as do most Prefectural governments, while services such as the 'NGO Park' provide information on a number of Japan's leading non-governmental organizations (NGOs). During the recent protests against US bases on Okinawa, the Okinawan Prefectural government used the Internet to distribute information about its demands for a scaling down of the American military presence on the island, and in return received hundreds of e-mail messages of support from throughout the world.

There is obvious potential for the emergence of new forms of 'electronic democracy' but these developments will take time to mature. As we have seen, Japanese politicians have been slow to adopt computer technology. This is partly because of a reluctance to abandon traditions of face-to-face political negotiation, and (in some cases) because they fear being overwhelmed by e-mail from voters (Hamada, 1995). Their concerns are understandable. Political parties that establish Internet home pages have discovered that, without new structures to deal with public demands, they are quickly swamped by piles of unanswered messages from frustrated members (*Daily Yomiuri*, January 1, 1996). In short, the use of electronic communications by themselves will not revolutionize political life. For creative change to occur, it will be necessary for technological innovation to be accompanied by changes in the structure and behavior of political institutions themselves.

CULTURAL AND COST BARRIERS

There are important ways in which the Internet diverges from the earlier image of the information revolution despite its use of the technology's interactive communications and educational uses. Widespread Internet traffic in Japan is restricted by the need to possess a personal computer, modem and communications software and the level of skills required to create a home page. Earlier visions of the information network system focused on nationwide communications networks, where the language barrier was not an issue. The Internet, however, is above all an 'international-net', and one dominated by the use of the English language. Many Japanese observers see this as representing an unforeseen reassertion of US cultural supremacy in the last decade of the twentieth century. Nishi Kazuo of the ASCI Company, for example, argues that US promotion of the Internet is part of a conscious attempt to maintain the worldwide dominance both of the English language and of a US dollar based economic system (since many services must be paid for in dollars) (Nishi, 1995: 46). In the long term, language problems may be reduced by the development of translation software, or of various forms of 'Internet pidgin'. For the immediate future, though, effective use of the wide range of available Internet services depends on an ability to communicate easily in English, and this clearly restricts access for many Japanese people, particularly older people and those without tertiary education.

A further barrier to wider Internet use in Japan has been the high cost of telecommunications by international standards. Communications charges have fallen substantially in recent years, but are still around twice the cost of US charges for many comparable domestic services. As a result, while each US phone is used for an average of 53 minutes per day, each Japanese phone is used for just 22 minutes (Honma, 1995: 104). Costs have been kept high in Japan partly by peculiarities in Japan's telecommunications oligopoly. The NTT Corporation uses profits from trunk line intercity telephone services to subsidize unprofitable intra-metropolitan services. It therefore has to keep prices on its long distance services relatively high, and this creates little incentive to the NTT Corporation's competitors to cut their charges for these services. The Japanese government and the NTT Corporation are making serious efforts to reduce and restructure telecommunications costs, but in the meantime they remain an impediment to the spread of Internet services which may involve lengthy long-distance or overseas telecommunications connections.

It is not surprising, then, that use of the Internet, and particularly the more creative uses involving the sending as well as receiving of information, is confined largely to the young and well-educated sections of the population who have access to computer technology through their work or study. A survey by the company Cyberspace Japan found that over half of all users were in their twenties, and that about two-thirds were using computers in colleges or workplaces (Tamura, 1995). This pattern is not, of course, unique to Japan. One international study of World Wide Web users suggests that over 80% are technicians, researchers, university students, managers, or consultants, and that 90% are male (Newfield and Hôjô, 1996: 38).

Early Utopian visions of the 'Information Society' emphasized the role of new communications technology in integrating national society. The Internet, however, is a communications medium which crosses boundaries, but whose use is very unevenly spread within Japanese society itself. This is, of course, partly a reflection of its novelty; as the technology becomes cheaper and more familiar, we can anticipate a wider spread amongst household users. Diffusion, though, is likely to be limited by social factors as well as by problems of cost and of access to the necessary range of skills.

As Julian Stallabrass (1995: 14) has observed, 'the virtual community demands a real one prior to it in order to function successfully'. Internet communities tend to be international communities based on occupation, educational status, and age. They are also, it should be noted, communities sustained and reinforced by face-to-face contact: it is precisely the groups who travel most widely, and interact most frequently with their international counterparts through face-to-face contact, who are the most likely to use the Internet for communications. It remains to be seen whether other groups, such as full-time parents, the unemployed, part-time workers, and farmers can develop the international communities needed to sustain such networks. If not, it seems likely that we may see a divergence between different social uses of the new communications technologies. Some groups make greater use of services like the Internet, while others make greater use of emerging services such as video-on-demand. Although the Internet communities transcend national boundaries new barriers may be created within Japan between the 'information rich' and the 'information poor'.

CONCLUSIONS

Scepticism has been expressed by the authors over the realization of a new urban and regional geography derived from bold Utopian visions of the information society. Not all of the possibilities outlined by the planners have been realized because of the resistance of social systems to technological change. Yet communications networks are spreading rapidly in Japan and their uses may confound our caution, particularly about the spread of cable television.

The preoccupation with integrating many forms of communications networks has to be matched by a concern for the ways in which different groups of people have made use of the services offered (Morris-Suzuki, 1996). The variable uses of the networks by consumers and producers of knowledge have reinforced the existing disparities in its social distribution. Partly, this is the result of the unequal access to material wealth. Even if there is a reduction in the price of technology, the staff of large corporations and élite research institutions are always better placed to take advantage of them. The persistence of this unequal distribution of knowledge not only excludes people from the skills required for knowledge creation, but precludes them from benefiting from technologies originally targeted at them. Disparities between the 'knowledge rich' and the 'knowledge poor' will be a crucial focus of attention as the global information infrastructure network spreads.

These disparities in knowledge will be reflected in a different sort of urban and regional development than envisaged in the early 1980s. A stocktake of the advanced information society in the mid-1990s suggests a three-speed Japan – 'fast' metropolitan areas, 'medium' micropolitan areas, and 'slow' periphery – rather than the original single speed. This division masks Tokyo – the unchallenged center of knowledge – travelling at 'superspeed'. Within Tokyo, a new tri-level class structure is emerging comprising those controlling the production of electronic information, those dependent on telematics in their work place, and those who do not and will not use a personal computer. Generally, the controllers are associated with the central business district and residential districts of the 'high town' (*yamanote*), the workers with the sprawling suburbs, and the newly dispossessed with the 'low town' (*shitamachi*) and unrevitalized industrial suburbs. Will socio-spatial polarization be with us forever?

CHAPTER 9

ELECTRONIC SPACE – CREATING CYBER COMMUNITIES IN SOUTHEAST ASIA

Kenneth E. Corey

INTRODUCTION

A revolution is underway around the world. The revolution is driven by the convergence of electronic and information technologies. This convergence is beginning to transform communities and ultimately societies. These kinds of computer-stimulated transformations long have been forecast, but in recent years there is evidence that revolutionary change, in fact, is gaining momentum. The term, 'information technology' has come to mean the convergence of various information-based, telecommunication, broadcast, and mass media communication technologies. Conventionally, these technologies include and refer to: computers and computerization, telecommunication, multimedia, and data technologies and their interdependencies (Keen, 1991: 98). Throughout the rest of the chapter, IT is used to include these multimedia technologies and their increasing, organizational, and technological convergence.

The goal of this chapter is to examine the processes of creating and controlling cyber communities. In the planning of IT-based development, a wide range of factors must be taken into account. Based on prior empirical research, these include the following:

- vision and leadership;
- modern information infrastructure investment;
- facilitative regulatory environment;
- human resources development and trained personnel;
- early and late experience in IT public policy implementation;
- essential and unique nature of a country's political economy and culture in executing urban and national IT policies;
- organizational/spatial synergies and their catalytic and coalescing dynamics.

These factors have been demonstrated to be critical in the implementation of IT programmes in community, urban and regional development (Corey, 1998).

The notion of 'cyber communities' as used here is simply that commonalities among people and across location and space can be induced and enhanced by widespread use and application of information and telecommunication technologies. Somewhat analogous to transportation systems, IT and their networking systems can serve to connect and bind together people, such that electronic or cyber communities represent an additional social construction and reality that overlays all of the other pre-information age social constructions of 'communities', as based on highways, manufacturing, housing, and so on.

Based on prior comparative IT development and policies research of selected Southeast Asian countries, a number of factors and lessons were derived. Among these were the importance of planning and implementing a facilitative regulatory environment for the IT development. Until recently, the principal focus of such environments revolved around the re-regulation and liberalization of telephone and other telecommunication environments (Stiglitz, 1997: 21–22). The explosion in the use of the Internet, however, has stimulated additional changes among the regulatory policies environments of various countries.

These changes are underway around the globe, from Germany to Hong Kong to the United States. The focus here is on the Southeast Asian region and its several formative national approaches to regulating the Internet. By analysing the processes of some of the world's early innovators in Internet regulation, one may better understand national values, priorities and approaches to development by means of their efforts at harnessing new information technologies.

The chapter consists of two parts. Part one is an examination of the current strategies and tactics employed in Malaysia and Singapore in planning and implementing IT programmes in the development of their community, regional, and national areas. Part two of the chapter includes a comparative analysis of the cyberlaws being used by countries in Southeast Asia. Both the processes of creating and controlling cyber communities contain important lessons for contemporary development and planning.

PART ONE – CREATING CYBER COMMUNITIES

MALAYSIA

Malaysia's IT policies are articulated from the highest level of government. Speaking before the private-sector business leadership of Malaysia in 1991, Prime Minister Datuk Seri Dr. Mahathir Mohamad pointed the country toward the year 2020 with his 'Way Forward' strategy.

> In the information age that we are living in, the Malaysian society must be information rich. It can be no accident that there is no wealthy developed country that is information-poor and no information-rich country that is poor and undeveloped (Mahathir, February 28, 1991: 12).

The strategy, Vision 2020, broadly conceptualized IT by specifying that Malaysia needed to stay abreast of high technology generally, and specifically Malaysia needed to be competitive in those technology industries where the country had comparative advantages. Microelectronics is one of those industries. By these means, and by developing a scientific, innovative, and producer society, Malaysia intends to become a fully developed nation by 2020.

Relying heavily on investment in modern infrastructure and public–private partnerships, the government of Dr. Mahathir has moved boldly and quickly to operationalize the vision of having Malaysia be a developed nation by the year 2020. In the last several years, plans for massive development projects have been unveiled. The Multimedia Super Corridor strategy is the overarching development concept organizing these plans. The development plans rely on science, high technology and IT. They have included:

1. landmark mega-construction initiatives in Kuala Lumpur (KL);
2. the new Kuala Lumpur International Airport (KLIA);
3. the intelligent cities of Putrajaya Bandar Bistari, Malaysia's new administrative capital, which is planned as an intelligent city to spearhead the development of the new Multimedia Super Corridor and Cyberjaya, the living community;
4. Technology Park Malaysia; and
5. the development of the Johor Information Infrastructure in Johor State, immediately across the strait from the 'intelligent island' city-state of Singapore (Mahathir, August 1, 1996).

Kuala Lumpur and the City Center Project

Malaysian strategies are being designed both to relieve the growing congestion of Kuala Lumpur (KL), and to generate new urban development in the city's center. The Kuala Lumpur City Center project is planned as a new downtown complex of 22 office blocks, the centerpiece of which is the 446 meter twin towers. Owned by the national oil company Petronas, these towers are the two tallest buildings in the world. This mega-urban project symbolizes Malaysia's growth and future potential for realizing the 2020 Vision of being a developed country.

KL is being re-developed by means of such projects as a light rail system; the 421 meter Kuala Lumpur Tower; and the country's first 'cyber township', Bandar Sri Pemaisuri in KL; it is to be completed in the year 2002 (*The Straits Times*, May 25, 1996: 21); and the KL Linear City, a 1.9 km long, planned 10-storey development of offices, condominiums, restaurants, shopping malls, parking, and even a canal, all to be built above the Klang River. This extraordinary project, known as 'Giga World', is planned to take 24 years to complete (Pura, July 11, 1996).

The Intelligent Cities

The Multimedia Super Corridor is planned to have two intelligent cities, Putrajaya, the administrative capital, and Cyberjaya, an education, residential, research and development center. The elements of the Multimedia Super Corridor began to be put in place in 1995. The new city, Putrajaya was one of those key elements. Putrajaya is named after Malaysia's first prime minister, Abdul Rahman Putra Al-Haj. Putrajaya is planned to become Malaysia's administrative capital by the year 2000.

With KL becoming more congested yearly, Malaysia's policy of encouraging urbanization outside the city took a major leap in 1995 with the inauguration of the new administrative capital city project, Putrajaya. The new city area of 14,780 hectares is located 25 km (18 miles) south of KL; its construction cost is estimated at more than US$8 billion. By the year 2000, the city's population is planned to be in excess of 75,000. Putrajaya is scheduled to be completed by the year 2008; ultimately, the city will have a population of 250,000; the surrounding area will have a population of 570,000 people. Putrajaya is planned as an electronic government center, and its design will be that of an intelligent garden city. The following federal government entities will move to Putrajaya: prime minister's office and official residence; the finance ministry, the federal courts, and most other federal government agencies (Pura, September 4, 1995: 11). This will involve the movement of an estimated 76,000 government employees. With this administrative and governmental relocation, it will enable KL to assume its role as Malaysia's principal commercial center.

Cyberjaya is a 400 hectare site, and will be the focus of the first 200 companies to be invited into the Multimedia Super Corridor. Cyberjaya is designated to be the major living community in the Corridor. By means of zoning, the surrounding environment of rainforests and plantations are accessible to the city's residents. A range of housing types and styles is to be available. These facilities will be supported by shopping, recreation, hotels, and transportation linkages within the MSC and to Kuala Lumpur. This intelligent city also will be the site for Multimedia University.

Cyberjaya will be built by a joint venture company named Cyberview. The Japanese telecommunications multinational corporation, Nippon Telegraph and Telephone, will be the only foreign stakeholder of Cyberview, with a 15% stake. The other corporate stakeholders are Malaysian. Renong is the largest stakeholder at 55%; the others include: Peremba, Embay, Country Heights, the Selangor State Government, Permodalan Nasional, Golden Hope, and the Multimedia Development Corporation (Kynge and Nakomoto, May 7, 1997).

Technology Park Malaysia

Pre-dating the announcement of the MSC strategy, the Technology Park Malaysia was established in 1988. Among its objectives are to promote research and development, and to commercialize innovation. Technology Park Malaysia takes on significance in the MSC era because it recently has become the venue for several of the key organizations leading Malaysia's IT drive. These include: satellite broadcaster, MEASAT Broadcast; Tenaga Nasional, the national power company; and the Malaysian Institute of Microelectronic Systems (MIMOS). The latter organization was established in 1985 as Malaysia's center for excellence in microelectronics and information technology. MIMOS has evolved from being a unit of the Prime Minister's Department, and became a fully-fledged government department, and a corporate organization in late 1996. MIMOS serves as the secretariat for Malaysia's National Information Technology Council (NITC). The Technology Park Malaysia is surrounded in convenient proximity by a number of Malaysia's top universities and national research institutes.

Kuala Lumpur International Airport

The Kuala Lumpur International Airport (KLIA) will be Asia's largest airport. At the southern end of the corridor is located the KLIA at Sepang, 45 k.m. south of KL. This project also is intended to stimulate significant development throughout its surrounding area. The KLIA occupies about 100 square kilometers. 1998 was the opening year for the airport. The airport was planned to have a cargo capacity of one million metric tonnes, and to include commercial, industrial and residential development (Pura, September 4, 1995: 11). The KLIA will form the core of Malaysia's aerospace industry.

Multimedia Super Corridor

The Multimedia Super Corridor will 'give the world a place where the full potential of the Information Age can be explored without any artificial limits' (Mahathir, Third Quarter 1996: 55). The Malaysian Multimedia Super Corridor (MSC) encompasses a 750 square kilometer area, a 15 km wide by 50 km long corridor which includes the planning and development of the Kuala Lumpur City Center to the north, the KLIA to the south, and in between, the MSC is anchored by Putrajaya, the new administrative capital of Malaysia. Premier Mahathir has stated that 'the new city will be designed as a high-tech, hard-wired information hub with a state-of-the-art telecom infrastructure' (Pura, September 4, 1995: 11). The MSC is to be completed by the year 2020.

The Multimedia Super Corridor strategy has grown in area from its early announcements to the strategy at the present time. During 1996, the MSC was stated to be 15 by 40 km, or an area of 600 square kilometers. It may be noted that Singapore's total national land area is 647.5 square kilometers. In early 1997, the area of the MSC was stated to be 750 square kilometers, because the new linear dimensions were stated to be 15 by 50 km. The web site for MSC's Multimedia Development Corporation states 'the nation has devoted this massive corridor – larger than Singapore – to creating a perfect environment for companies wanting to create, distribute, and employ multimedia products and services' (Multimedia Development Corporation, April 17, 1997).

The MSC concept, based on intelligent infrastructure, is intended to mobilize government and corporate private sector resources so as to capitalize on the evolving critical mass 'to create the foundation for the country's competitive edge in the coming decades'. Technologically, the MSC 'can be fitted with a high-speed single backbone integrated telecommunication network to cater for advanced value-added telecommunications, information services and multimedia services' (Nun, September 4–6, 1995: 5). The IT infrastructure plan is for a fiber optic backbone with 2.5–10 gigabits per second capacity.

The MSC vision puts a priority on the consumer applications of IT with objectives of: universal access to the 'national superhighway' and the 'global network'; intelligent interactive multimedia kiosks; telebooths; community telework centers; and other IT-mediated public services as in education and health care. These objectives are intended to result in a higher quality of life for Putrajaya's citizens. Additional benefits are expected as a result of intelligent infrastructure investments (Nun, September 4–6, 1995: 4–5). Those include: reduction in traffic; reduction in air pollution; and most importantly, the Putrajaya initiative is expected to enhance Malaysia's global competitiveness. The critical technologies of the networked digital economy include 'wide-band internetworking and interactive multimedia applications' (Nun, November 3, 1995: 5).

Prime Minister Mahathir has stated, 'One day Kuala Lumpur, Putrajaya and our new airport will become one mega-city that can be compared to centres like Tokyo–Yokohama' (*The Economist*, September 2, 1995: 39). As these kinds of visions get translated into urban developments and corridors throughout eastern Asia, the seeds of megalopolitan growth are being sown from Japan to Indonesia. In addition to bold vision, the MSC's implementation is stimulated by some of the world's first cyberlaws; including: the Malaysian Multimedia Convergence Act; the Digital Signature Act; the Computer Crime Act; and the Telemedicine Development Act.

The services and amenities that will be developed as a part of the MSC are intended to attract investment from around the world to Malaysia. IT, telecommunications and multimedia corporations with marketing, and research and development needs for locations in Southeast Asia are the principal investment targets. By linking those global corporations with Malaysian corporations, there is the intention to stimulate developmental synergies for the creation of a globally competitive Malaysian information technology economy.

The vision for the Multimedia Super Corridor includes software development firms, regional headquarters for manufacturing operations located in other parts of the region, research and development activities, and personal computer vendors. In short, the MSC encompasses all companies that create, distribute, integrate, or use multimedia products and services. The IT infrastructure for the MSC is critical to the success of this strategy. The fiber optic backbone supports virtual boardrooms, remote CAD/CAM operations, and live multimedia Internet broadcasting.

Multimedia Flagship Applications

The government of Malaysia has identified eight multimedia Flagship Applications to be developed in the MSC by the year 2000:

- electronic government;
- national multipurpose smart card;
- smart schools;
- telemedicine;
- borderless marketing centers;
- world-wide manufacturing webs;
- research and development clusters;
- financial services.

(Multimedia Development Corporation, April 17, 1997; and Johnstone, February 1997: 51).

Plagued by the 1997 currency crisis, Prime Minister Mahathir announced that the Government of Malaysia would proceed with the MSC infrastructure. He indicated that there would be no delay in the project because so much of it is to be built by the private sector (Ho, September 20, 1997). In early 1998, the fragility of Malaysia's IT mega projects, especially their financial stability, was suggested. The principal problem was said to be that the companies charged with building Putrajaya and Cyberjaya are no longer able to raise adequate capital. Most of the financing was expected to be derived from share issues, but the stock prices slide since the middle of 1997 has closed this avenue (McNulty, January 14, 1998).

The Malaysian company Cyberview announced that it would seek to borrow US$380m for infrastructure investment to develop 2,800 hectares into an 'intelligent city'. This plan to take on such additional debt at this stage in the country's financial crisis is said to be indicative of the importance that the government of Malaysia is placing on the continuing plans for implementing the Multimedia Super Corridor (McNulty, January 21, 1998).

Multimedia Development Corporation

The Multimedia Development Corporation (MDC) is the organization that was created to implement the Multimedia Super Corridor strategy. The Corporation has the power needed to insure that the requirements of investors are satisfied. In addition to working with companies in the Corridor to get operations underway, the Corporation is responsible also for attracting investors to the Corridor from around the world. In short, the Multimedia Development Corporation is expected to fine tune arrangements so as to insure operational success for the Corridor and its investors, with concern for laws, technical standards, and the timely execution of the Flagship Applications for the Multimedia Super Corridor.

The mission and key roles of the MDC are:

- super-one-stop-shop for all government contacts to facilitate entry and operations of MSC companies;
- world class marketeer of the MSC to overseas and Malaysian companies; provision of quality client service;
- master strategist to guide MSC development and recommend, together with the National IT Council (NITC), how the MSC can catalyze other required changes across the country;
- financier and concessionaire that manages the request for proposal processes, awards contracts and regulates the provision of world-class infrastructure and services (Nun, August 29, 1996).

The MDC was establishing ten offices around the world to market and attract foreign investors to the Multimedia Super Corridor. The Corporation is a one-stop organization designed to facilitate, coordinate, and cut red tape. Its overseas services are to provide advice to firms for moving into the Corridor. The MDC overseas staff advise on cyberlaws, immigration laws, office space in the MSC, and provide a listing of Malaysian firms interested in joint-venture projects (*The Straits Times* Weekly Edition, March 15, 1997).

MSC status is conferred for companies supportive of the Corridor's intent which is for IT and multimedia firms engaged in such services or such production, and willing to transfer such technology into the Malaysian economy. MSC status corporations also must have at least 15% of their employees as engineers and the other non-manual occupations. With such MSC qualifications, Corridor firms are exempt from corporate tax for ten years (*The Nikkei Weekly*, May 5, 1997).

In its early marketing stages, the MSC has attracted a great deal of interest. More than 900 companies, both foreign and Malaysian, have bid to participate in the development of the MSC program (*The Nikkei Weekly*, May 5, 1997). By April 1997, 29 companies had been given MSC status; 14 of these were foreign, including IT and telecommunications corporations from Japan, such as NEC Corporation, Fujitsu Limited, Mitsubishi Corporation, Sharp Corporation, and Nippon Telegraph and Telehone Corporation (NTT). NTT is 'the most committed foreign participant' in Malaysia's MSC. The Japanese company, which is actively seeking opportunities in South-east Asia, is also expected to join forces with Malaysian companies to set up within the MSC a 'multimedia university' to concentrate on teaching and research in many aspects of information technology (Kynge and Nakamoto, May 7, 1997: 1). Geographically, with the ultimate development of the centrally-located MSC, further development attention can be turned to the northern Pengang-Kulim region and the southern Johor region.

Johor State

Separated by the narrow Johor Strait, there long has been a functional symbiosis between Malaysia's southernmost State of Johor and the Republic of Singapore. As a consequence, Johor State has been a traditional location for investment from Singapore. In 1994, capital investment in Johor totaled S$786 million in 194 projects. Singapore was the largest foreign investor with S$196 million in 104 projects. These investments in manufacturing, especially in the electronics sector, have been judged to be successful by the Johor State Economic Development Corporation. This performance is seen to have 'been the result of the policies and strategies of the government to create a broad-based, efficient and export-oriented manufacturing sector' (*The Straits Times* Weekly Edition, April 15, 1995: 11). Relative to Singapore, Johor Baru has comparative advantages in 'land availability, lower rental, better access to first class recreational facilities, cheaper housing, good infrastructure' (Awang, 1995: 8). The combined population of Singapore and southern Malaysia is likely to approach ten million people, and Johor Baru, with its easily accessible space for further development, is well positioned to take advantage of the future opportunities offered by the synergies of the Singapore–Malaysia–Indonesia growth triangle strategy (Awang, 1995: 8).

Much of Singapore's planned development over the last two decades has sought to incorporate IT into its strategies. With nearby and increasingly interdependent Singapore continuing to grasp the many value-added opportunities of the information age, it is natural for Malaysia's Johor State to consider similar IT development strategies. Now, the time is seen as right for planning even further twinning between Johor and Singapore; this timing is stimulated by a second causeway, the upgrading of the international airport in Senai, a new port for Johor, and increasing tourist and real estate demand. By taking strategic advantage of

Singapore's spillover effects, Johor is seeking to upgrade, internationalize, and grow its local economy. The planned Johor Information Infrastructure will enable the State's IT goals to be pursued.

The Johor Information Infrastructure Study (JII) recommended that the private sector build the JII and state government should be the anchor tenant. This approach was designed to serve the needs of four communities of users: government; providers and producers; users and buyers; and the public and citizens. The goal is to enable Johor State to contribute to Malaysia's national objective of 'building an information rich society, where information reach and range is virtually at its maximum' (IBM World Trade Corporation and Institute Sultan Iskander, March 30, 1996: 151).

In order to be able to have Malaysia's national IT agenda implemented in the regions throughout the country, State IT Councils (SITCs) have been established to enhance nation-wide cooperation. The goals for the National IT Council (NITC) and SITC network are:

- to promote IT development and use throughout the nation;
- to set up an IT policy formulation and implementation mechanism in line with the National IT Agenda (NITA);
- to set up a feedback mechanism to evaluate and review IT policies and implementation strategies at both state and national levels;
- to determine the impact of IT programmes on society and the government, business, and non-profit sectors;
- to establish channels of communication between the NITC and the SITCs;
- to encourage cross communication among SITCs.
  (Source: http://www.jaring.my/nitc/sitc.html)

By early 1998, five of 14 Malaysian states had activated SITC hot links. These permit the monitoring of IT development progress.

CONNECTING THE CORRIDOR

The major MSC elements of KL, Putrajaya and KLIA will be knitted together by the North–South Expressway, the planned Express Rail Link, and a planned dedicated highway. The recently completed national north–south highway serves to link the MSC to the length of the Malaysian peninsula. Putrajaya will have its own light rail system and tram network to facilitate internal connectivity.

LEARNING FROM MALAYSIA'S IT AND DEVELOPMENT PROJECTS

In the end, these technology-based and landmark development projects are intended to build the nation and its communities. Not just any nation or some generic country is at issue here; these public policies are those of the government

Table 1 *World Wide Web Addresses on Creating Cyber Communities in Malaysia
and Singapore*

On community networks:
http://www.sils.umich.edu/community/what.html
http://www.rmsd.com/comnet/wwwvl_commnet.html
http://alberti.mit.edu/arch/4.207/comnetworks.html

On Electronic Space:
http://www.ssc.msu.edu/~Dean/espace.htm

On freenets and community networks worldwide:
http://duke.usask.ca/~scottp/free.html
http://www.nptn.org:80/about.fn/

On preparing inner-city communities for information age:
http://www.urbantech.inter.net/Default.htm

On impact of information technology in planning:
http://www.plannersweb.com/
http://www/bway.net/~urbandev/apaid

On information technology developments in Asia:
http://www.atip.or.jp/

On Malaysia:
http://www.jaring.my

On Multimedia Super Corridor:
http://www.mdc.com.my/msc/
http://www.jaring/msia/md/msc.html

On Singapore:
http://www.ncb.gov.sg/ncb/press/newncb.html
http://www.singapore-inc.com
http://www.sl.gov.sg/general-info.htm
http://www.sl.gov.sg/faq.htm1#11
http://www.sba.gov.sg/newarel.htm#p26

On Smart Valley and Connect 96:
http://www.svi.org
http://www.svi.org/connect96

of Prime Minister Mahathir for Malaysia. While there are some generic characteristics across countries, and their IT policies, it also is the unique societal and
cultural attributes of a country that make for holistic nation building. For example,
Premier Mahathir has stated:

> It is not mere development that Malaysia wants. She aims at an entire value system of
> the highest magnitude that blends into the cultural order that is uniquely Malaysian
> (MIMOS, 1995: 17).

In short, it is the integration and synthesis of the rational and the technological
with the cultural, organizational, societal, economic, and political that produces
'community', and 'nation'. To be able to monitor progress on Malaysia's IT policies,
refer to Table 1 for addresses on the World Wide Web.

SINGAPORE

Because of Singapore's early, innovative use of IT as a centerpiece of its development policies, and because Singapore is a city, the Singapore case at this point in time represents the best case in the world in urban IT policy planning and IT programme implementation. While many countries around the world, particularly in eastern Asia, have begun to focus on IT and telecommunication technologies in their development planning, the results of these plans have not been in place long enough to see the full benefits and costs of such implementation – when compared to the earlier and fuller results from Singapore's sustained IT investments and experiments.

INTERNAL SPATIAL ORGANIZATION AND IT INFRASTRUCTURE

With only 646 square kilometers in national area, Singapore has had to be extremely careful in the ways that its land is used. In 1991, the Urban Development Authority (URA) issued a concept plan that updated the 1971 'ring' concept plan. The broad objective of the current revised concept plan is 'to plan for the physical development of Singapore into a Tropical City of Excellence, an exotic island and an international investment hub' (Urban Redevelopment Authority, 1991: 11). The new concept plan provides the framework for Singapore's future spatial development well into the twenty-first century, i.e. to year x. By that time, the plan assumes that further land reclamation will have increased the city-state's land area to 730 square kilometres; in the year 2030 Singapore population is assumed to be about 3.7 million. The current population is about three million. In order to support Singapore's strategies for internationalization, the 1991 concept plan allocates land use for future 'high-technology and information-based industries'.

The revised concept planning framework has three phases: (i) to year 2000; (ii) to year 2010; and (iii) to year x. The spatial planning framework consists of five regions with commercial centers as foci: central; east; north-east; north; and west. This planned decentralized pattern has been adopted so as to decongest the business and commercial-dominated central area. Commercial functions that do not require central area location will be encouraged to distribute to the four other regions according to a constellation plan that is to be well connected by the Mass Rapid Transit (MRT), light rail, and expressway systems. By locating industrial areas in close proximity to the locationally peripheral housing concentrations, journey to work volumes will be better managed.

Singapore long has been noted for its innovation in the provision of public-constructed housing and the facilitation of high levels of home ownership by means of the personal savings mechanism of the Central Provident Fund. Under the revised concept plan, housing improvements would continue by creating more low- and medium-rise housing options. Additionally, the tropical greening of the central and outlying areas would receive further development. Throughout the plan, the intent is to up-grade and improve on current levels of amenities, such as housing, cultural, and recreational opportunities.

TECHNOLOGY CORRIDORS

As to intelligent infrastructure, the revised concept plan provides for the development of two technology corridors. Business parks are important elements of the planned technology corridors. The plan calls the business parks 'the industrial estates of the future'. The notion underpinning these corridors is to create 'science habitats' comprised of holistic and synergistic high-quality working–living–learning and recreating environments that 'attract and retain top talent'. These environments would be highly integrated by means of the application of the most modern transportation, communications, and information technologies.

> A Business Park is an area specifically set aside for non-pollutive industries and businesses that engage in high-technology, research and development, high value-added and knowledge-intensive activities. . . . the two main features that distinguish business parks from industrial estates are: (a) the range of permitted uses that are generally non-production in nature but are characteristic of high-technology and research-oriented industries; and (b) the emphasis on landscaping, quality building designs and provision of amenity facilities to reflect the importance placed by companies on the image of the Business Park and the welfare of their employees (Urban Redevelopment Authority, March 1993: 2).

The revised concept plan states that the existing Singapore Science Park is suggestive of the business park of the future. '. . . although it does not have that integrated work/home recreation quality' (Urban Redevelopment Authority, 1991: 21).

Southwestern Technology Corridor

The Southwestern Technology Corridor is planned to provide world-class research infrastructure. It is anchored at either end by Singapore's two universities, the National University of Singapore (NUS) at the eastern end, and the Nanyang Technological University (NTU) at the western end. The eastern end also has the Singapore Science Park, which is now in its second phase of development. The Science Park is adjacent to NUS.

TeleTech Park is part of phase two of the Singapore Science Park development. It is part of the Southwestern Technology Corridor and is designed for IT-related research and development firms 'developing new telecommunications products and services' (TeleTech Park, 1996). The world-class designed building incorporates sophisticated infrastructure such as on-site global satellite links, broadband ISDN, and optical fiber links, among other contemporary IT facilities. TeleTech Park is an investment project of the Telecommunication Authority of Singapore, along with joint-venture actors: Singapore Telecommunications Ltd, Singapore Technologies Pte Ltd, and Technology Parks Pte Ltd. Sixty per cent of TeleTech Park is taken by six tenants in mid-1997 (VISTA, 1997: 21).

Over the span of the full three planning phases of the revised concept plan, six business parks are planned along with high-quality housing, a regional center, and high connectivity via information technology, telecommunications, and excellent transportation facilities. The intent is to catalyze synergy and creative interaction among the scientists, the investors, and their living and working environments such that this mix stimulates innovation and entrepreneurship.

Northeastern Technology Corridor

The Northeastern Technology Corridor has Changi International Airport at its eastern end; at the western end of the corridor will be a regional center, concentrations of high-quality housing, industry, and seven business parks. The functional theme of this corridor is focused on aviation and aero-space high-technology industries.

Housing and Recreation

Singapore long has been known for its innovation in housing (Wong and Yeh, 1985). Under the revised concept plan housing innovation will continue. More low-rise and medium-rise housing options will be provided. Household sizes are planned to be decreased from persons per dwelling levels in 1990 of 4.2 to a year x level of 3.1. A goal is to develop, in the residents, the feeling of living in a natural tropical island environment. Many options in recreation, leisure, and culture are planned for integration with inner city living, waterfront housing, and park and garden living. Marinas, boating, beaches from reclaimed land, pedestrian and bicycle paths, greenery, natural environments, and seascapes, are to be combined so as to reinforce the feeling of tropical island living. Complementing these environmental enhancements are a continuation of conservation of historical and architectural resources such as: the shophouses of Chinatown and Little India, the neighborhood of Kampong Glen around the Sultan Mosque, and the old godowns, warehouses, and quays along the Singapore River.

These many physical and spatial designs plan for the knitting together of the island's major regions and various precincts, including ultimately the development and connection of the northeastern and southwestern islands by MRT and light rail transit respectively, by year x. The timing of each of these concept planning elements is dependent on actual demand. A reinforcement of Singapore as a unique 'intelligent' and Asian city is an objective of these technological and physical programmes.

Regional Center Anchors

As Singapore's various development strategies have evolved, regional centers have emerged as anchors to the corridors. Tampines New Town is one of these regional center anchors. Tampines, at the eastern end of the Northeastern Technology Corridor, has become the site for the back-office space 'Finance Park', based on the new town hosting and being a regional computer center. This opportunity came from feedback provided by the Monetary Authority of Singapore (*Tan*, May 24, 1996). As a result of the concerted and opportunistic initiatives of these Singaporean actors, Tampines New Town has become a testbed for IT-community development applications such as Telepark and Tampines Webtown. The Telepark in Tampines 'is a unique facilities management centre exclusively designed to house . . . computer systems and data communications equipment', and it is advertised as

'Asia's first telecommunications park for computer and communications systems' (Singapore Telecom, 1995). The Telepark is 40,000 square meters in size and has been designed for the special needs of IT and telecommunications tenants, including the provision of satellite antennae for the tenants. Telepark is not an isolated IT facility. It is imbedded in Tampines New Town which is part of the Northeastern Technology Corridor; it is on the Mass Rapid Transit system and quite close to the global accessibility provided by Changi International Airport. These are the kinds of locational and spatial synergies that characterize Singapore's IT development; and they, at the same time, are both planned and opportunistic.

Tampines Webtown is a recent Internet project created to link the residents of Tampines New Town. The objectives of Tampines Webtown are two-fold: (i) 'to allow residents to get to know each other, fostering a deeper sense of community', and (ii) '. . . they can get to know their leaders in a more personal way, and help them shape the community into an even better one' (Tampines Webtown, July 11, 1996).

Cable Television

Cable television is another one of the means, among many, that is intended to have a technological and community integrating effect on Singapore. Cable television user surveys and tests have been conducted, and the whole island is planned to be wired soon. The small scale of Singapore and its well connected, modern infrastructure in IT and telecommunications makes it an ideal testbed for piloting national information infrastructure (NII) applications and other experiments such as video on demand, interactive television, and the government control of information and communications flows to Singapore's citizenry (National Computer Board, 1995). The Government of Singapore will continue to be selective in the content of the information coming into the country by means of mass media. It has long-stated goals of promoting Asian values; consequently, controlling electronic satellite communications, and broadcast communications media, including the Internet, is an important means in attempting to safeguard the nation's stated values. Cable television is a technological means, by government, both to enhance the Singaporean's quality of life and to preserve the moral values of the nation.

LEARNING FROM THE SINGAPORE INTELLIGENT CITY

Digital, smart, and intelligent technologies are an important part of Singapore's development. Singapore was one of the earliest countries to adopt explicit public policies and programmes of information technology (IT), and for the computerization of the economy and the city-state's institutions as a pillar of its national and urban community development. Singapore's leaders, as early as 1968, began to state publicly that science and technology-driven development was critical to the city-state's future policies.

Today, Singapore already is in its fourth generation of IT public policies implementation. First, from 1981 to the present, the Computerization of the Civil Service

Scheme has been implemented; it is a means of modernizing and making more productive the public sector. The National Computer Board (NCB) was charged in 1981 with managing and implementing the scheme. Second, from 1986 to 1992, the National IT Plan was pursued. Its various elements served to put in place the foundation and framework for the effective utilization of IT as a productive sector of society as well as of the Singaporean economy. The plan addressed needs in: human resources and trained personnel; telecommunications and IT infrastructure; industry; applications; culture; creativity and entrepreneurship; and inter-organizational coordination and collaboration. Third, IT2000 consisted of goals to: develop a national information infrastructure; create the technology corridors; link communities locally and globally; develop Singapore as a competitive global IT hub; enhance the potential of individuals; transform the economy; and in the process, improve Singaporeans' quality of life. Fourth, in September 1995, the National Computer Board (NCB) began the 'Restructuring for IT2000' phase.

Under the April 1, 1996 'Restructuring for IT2000' initiative, the NCB's new role is to corporatize those NCB functions that lend themselves to participation by the private sector. This shift was possible because of the increasing growth and maturity of Singapore's IT industry. 'Today, after 14 years, a total of 800 application systems valued at [S]$655 million have been put in place under the Civil Service Computerization Programme (CSCP)' (Teo, September 7, 1995: 3).

There no longer is the need to rely principally on NCB expertise to advance Singapore's IT public policies; that expertise now is better distributed throughout the economy and society. More public–private partnerships and strategic alliances will characterize Singapore's IT future. NCB's restructured role also will continue to promote IT for Singapore, but in more focused ways. Business and industry clusters form the reorganization theme for the NCB's new role. In order 'to accelerate the pace of IT2000', a new NCB IT Cluster Development Fund can stimulate 'flagship projects' by eight industry clusters. Four policy 'thrusts' comprise the restructured IT2000 vision: (i) IT for the masses; (ii) IT in government; (iii) IT in support of industry; and (iv) IT as an export industry. Researchers should monitor and measure the results of these policy thrusts so as to provide systematic feedback to improve future IT public policy-making. The above actions and applications of the restructured IT2000 vision are intended to generate these results for Singapore's society: business spin-offs to enhance the competitiveness of the economy, and in the end, these IT policies, as implemented, should enable Singaporeans to recognize the difference in their quality of life.

As part of the on-going process of restructuring IT2000, three refinements have been initiated over the 1996–97 period. The NCB was transferred; an internet-working hub public–private strategy was initiated as Singapore ONE; and Singapore Inc. was begun as a continuous improvement for coordinating and marketing government support for IT-development investment.

The New National Computer Board

As competition in the IT sector in Southeast Asia increases, Singapore continues to re-structure and refine its economic and technological performance. This includes re-organization, such as the 1997 transfer of Singapore's National Computer Board from the Ministry of Finance to the Ministry of Trade and Industry.

The Ministry of Trade and Industry also includes: the Economic Development Board; the National Science and Technology Board; Singapore Productivity and Standards Board; the Trade Development Board; and the Singapore Tourist Promotion Board. With the National Computer Board organizationally functioning among these economic development agencies, it is intended 'that there will be more effective coordination and synergy of economic development and industry promotion efforts at the national level' (*IT Asia*, March 1997). Most of these agencies are integral to the Singapore ONE initiative. 'Together, these agencies will be able to work even more closely to help nurture the local IT industry and develop Singapore into the IT Mega-Hub of the Asia–Pacific' (National Computer Board, February 15, 1997).

The NCB transfer was preceded by earlier changes in 1996 when it 'refocused its efforts to further accelerate the realization of IT2000'; this re-structuring meant that the National Computer Board set out to meet three challenges, to: (i) increase Singapore's competitiveness; (ii) improve the lifestyle of Singaporeans; and (iii) develop a vibrant local IT industry (National Computer Board, April/May 1996: 1–2). The Singapore ONE project has enabled further movement on these new NCB challenges.

Singapore ONE – One Network for Everyone

While Malaysia has been marketing, modifying, and tailoring its MSC concept, Singapore has been updating, fine-tuning, and re-packaging its IT2000 strategy. Singapore ONE was initiated in 1996.

> Singapore ONE is a national, high capacity network platform that will deliver a potentially unlimited range of multimedia services to the workplace, the home and the school. It comprises two distinct but interrelated levels – an infrastructure level of networks and switches, and a level of applications and multimedia services (http://www.sl.gov.sg/general-info.htm).

> The infrastructure level of Singapore ONE will consist of a core broadband network platform connecting several local access networks. The initial thrusts for applications development will be in the areas of government, home, education and business (http://www.sl.gov.sg/faq.htm1#11).

Therefore, the goal of Singapore ONE is to have Singapore be the first country to have a nationwide broadband infrastructure in 1998. By the end of 1998, all 800,000 households will be wired by means of hybrid fiber coaxial network (VISTAS, 1997). Businesses, schools and public kiosks also are part of the network. By April 1997, 17 local companies and multinational corporations had agreed to develop broadband enabling technologies for Singapore ONE. This represented an additional S$115 million in development investment (VISTAS, 1997: 14).

By January 1997, Singapore ONE had grown into a public–private partnership of S$182 million among five government organizations and 14 multimedia multinational corporations. These partners included:

National Computer Board
National Science and Technology Board
Telecommunication Authority of Singapore

Economic Development Board
Singapore Broadcasting Authority

Anderson Consulting
Bloomberg
Electronic Arts
Hewlett Packard
IBM
Microsoft
Motorola Multimedia Group
Music Pen
NEC Singapore
Oracle
Reuters
Sun Microsystems
Yahoo

Deputy Prime Minister Lee Hsien Loong stated that Singapore ONE will give IT corporations persuasive reasons to continue to invest in Singapore. It will offer companies a nationwide test-bed before they expand into the region. A Pioneer Club was targeted as content, service, and technology providers and membership was open to all companies which could commit to launching a commercial service or application by June 30, 1998 (*The Straits Times* Weekly Edition, February 1, 1997: 6).

By means of an internetwork Hub, the goal of 'Singapore ONE, one network for everyone' provides a wide range of multimedia service to each Singaporean home (Lee and Goh, September 7, 1996). These services include: teleshopping; video conferencing; high-speed Internet; access to libraries, and entertainment-on-demand. After trials, these services were expected initially to be available in 1998. Currently, 600 pilot users are able to access higher-speed Internet and 50 or so other multimedia applications (VISTAS, 1997: 35). By the end of 1997, there were 5,000 pilot households and offices, with access to 100 services and applications.

The implementation of Singapore ONE was planned to be executed in two phases: Phase 1 from 1996 to 2001 focused on government, education, home, and business; and Phase 2, starting in 1999, will have more commercial services. The government offered early adopters incentives. One of these, for example, included preferential tariffs for broadband connectivity support under the Innovation Development Scheme (IDS). And there are many other incentives. Earliest members of the Pioneer Club have to pay 'only S$12,800 a month for a basic 155 megabit per second line compared to the market rate of S$22,000 a month' (*The Straits Times* Weekly Edition, February 1, 1997: 6).

In early 1997, the NCB solicited applications for trial participants of individuals to test the high-speed transmissions via (i) a television connected to an Internet device; (ii) home computer linked to a special modem to permit video over standard telephone lines; and (iii) computer linked to the fiber optic cabling being laid throughout the city-state by Singapore Cable Vision. Trial participants received smart cards for use in making purchases and for identification on the network. Initially, the NCB estimated that the Singapore ONE monthly fee would be under S$100 (*The Straits Times* Weekly Edition, February 1, 1997).

Users can access Singapore ONE by two means: (i) asymmetric digital sub-scriber line (ADSL) modem, or (ii) a cable modem, or both. The first makes use of the telephone lines provided by SingTel, the second uses the cable television network provided by Singapore Cable Vision (SCV). Monthly subscription fees from SingTel for the use of the ADSL modem are S$25 plus 5 cents for every minute of network usage; SCV's fee is S$35 plus about S$40 for the 10 BaseT Ethernet card (VISTAS, 1997: 34).

The ADSL telephone exchanges, the cable network, and the service providers are linked by means of a high-speed broadband optical fiber backbone based on Asynchronous Transfer Mode (ATM) technology. An infrastructure consortium, 1-Net Singapore Pte Ltd, is building, owns and operates the core broadband (VISTAS, 1997: 35).

Singapore Inc.

Similar to the ways that the various units of a large corporation function together, the institutions of the city-state strive to work together in harmony to achieve the country's economic and development goals. Each element of Singapore Inc. functions to discharge its own responsibility so that it contributes to Singapore's overall promotion and development.

This technology investment approach, combined with close inter-organizational coordination, long has been a characteristic of Singapore's government-led development processes. In early 1997, Singapore Inc.'s new web site was launched by Dr. Tony Tan, Deputy Prime Minister and Minister for Defense. The web site is <http://www.singapore-inc.com>. It touts the high degrees of functional interdependencies and seamless customer-oriented coordination among seven select Singapore boards and organizations. These include: Economic Development Board; Jurong Town Corporation; National Computer Board; National Science and Technology Board; Singapore Trade Development Board; Singapore Tourist Promotion Board; and Singapore Productivity and Standards Board. The marketing brochure for Singapore Inc stated:

> Through the cooperation and support of all parties – political leaders and government, institutions and academia, chambers of commerce and trade associations, industrialists and labor, foreign investors and local companies, the people, and all who have identified themselves to be the nation's stakeholders – the vision for Singapore will be achieved in harmony with measurable success for each party (http://www.singapore-inc.com).

The web site for Singapore Inc provides the browser with profiles of each agency. Each agency also has its own web site. The Economic Development Board has been promoting investment in Singapore and packaging its coordinative one-stop services since 1961. This extraordinary long-term experience gives Singapore a significant lead and comparative advantage over its emerging competitors in the region. By constant renewal and review of its approaches, the Economic Development Board has been able to maintain its effectiveness in attracting foreign investment to Singapore. In recent years, foreign investment promotion has been complemented by activities intended to help local Singaporean businesses to invest overseas. These Singapore-based firms have invested increasingly in the near-neighbors of Malaysia and Indonesia, as well as in the emerging economies of China, Vietnam, India, and Myanmar (Hamlin, March 29, 1997).

This multi-faceted development approach from Singapore's location serves to benefit both Singapore and its neighbors in the region. The Singapore Economic Development Board refers to this as a 'borderless view beyond Singapore, and into the region' (Economic Development Board, 19 March 1997). Singapore's modern infrastructure, its skilled workforce, and its location among the emerging economies of Asia have combined to confer a strong competitive advantage on the city-state. To be able to monitor progress on Singapore's IT policies, refer to Table 1 for a URL address on the World Wide Web.

PART TWO – CONTROLLING THE INTERNET IN SOUTHEAST ASIA

Malaysian Prime Minister Mahathir, in promoting the country's new Multimedia Super Corridor (MSC), has pledged not to censor the Internet for those enterprises with MSC status. What are the implications for the lack of regulation and for regulation in Southeast Asian IT development? The governments of Southeast Asia are on record publicly as being concerned about cyberspace content in smut, and potential religious and racial incitement. In September 1996, the Association of South East Asian Nations (ASEAN) agreed that their broadcasters should block material from the Internet that undercuts Asian values. The Association made a point of urging the West to understand these concerns in the region. ASEAN members varied on Internet policing approaches. Singapore emphasized stringent Internet monitoring by the city-state's three Internet service providers. Other members of ASEAN encouraged self-regulation (*The Asian Wall Street Journal Weekly*, September 9, 1996: 11).

As other countries around the globe struggle with regulating the Internet, the countries of Southeast Asia have taken their own approaches to controlling cyberspace content. These approaches are guided by the individual national application of their unique blend of Asian values. One can discern these by examining the several cases analysed below. However, according to Mr. Virgilio Labrador of the Asia Broadcast Center,

> . . . the principle that must guide content regulation, . . . must be the United Nations Universal Declaration of Human Rights. In essence, the UN Declaration states that everyone has the right to seek, receive, impart and disseminate information by any form, means or channel regardless of frontiers or borders (Asian Media, Information and Communication Centre, January–February 1997: 20).

SINGAPORE

It is important to understand how Singapore is approaching the regulation of the Internet. This is the case, not only because Singapore is a pioneer in Southeast

Asia in inventing many IT innovations, but also because Malaysia is marketing its new Multimedia Super Corridor by suggesting that its cyberlaws are less restrictive than its competitors, i.e. Singapore. As part of Singapore's early engagement of, and experience with the use of IT in the country's development, cyberlaws were created and instituted. The Computer Misuse Act of 1993 is an example. The purpose of this law was to secure computer material against unauthorized access or modification (Parliament of Singapore, March 18, 1993).

In 1995, public discussion in Singapore began to address the rapid growth of the Internet and legal controls that should be created to enable both the exploitation of IT for Singapore's development and the protection of its values (Datta-Ray, June 24, 1995: 32). By early 1996, public discussion had shifted to calls for Singaporeans to self-police their behavior in cyberspace. The Singapore Broadcasting Authority went on record that it intended to take a pragmatic and evolutionary approach to formulating Singapore's Internet regulatory framework. The outline of this approach to regulate the Internet's use in Singapore would be to encourage responsible use by means of public education, and to regulate by exception rather than to attempt to fully control the Internet's content. Industry self-regulation and community policing were advocated for the future development of the Internet in Singapore. By maintaining regular discussions with selected actors in the industry, the Authority intends to continue to perfect the development of Singapore's regulatory framework (Shuhaimi, March 23, 1996: 23).

In mid-July 1996, the Singapore Broadcasting Authority issued guidelines for the regulation of the Internet in Singapore. The regulations take the form of a licensing scheme, the purpose of which is 'to safeguard public morals, political stability and religious harmony' (Pereira, July 13, 1996: 1). This event was preceded by the formation of the Singapore Broadcasting Authority (SBA). The SBA's function is to encourage the development of a creative and responsible broadcasting industry in Singapore and is expected to insure 'that broadcast material is not against public interest or order, national harmony, good taste or decency' (Pereira, March 6, 1996). The authority of the SBA comes from the SBA Act of 1994; it is a statutory board of the Ministry of Information and the Arts.

The SBA developed a regulatory framework both for the traditional broadcast services, and for the new broadcast medium of the Internet. Under the regulatory framework, SBA issues two types of licenses for broadcasting services: individual and class. Broadcasting services that have a major impact on the general public are individually licensed by SBA. They include the nationwide free-to-air radio and television services. SBA also lays down conditions for programme content and programming mix. SBA introduced a class licence approach for some categories of services including audiotext, videotext, and teletext services, broadcast data services and Internet. This approach, while requiring the industry to comply with SBA's guidelines, is administratively efficient as it does not require these service operators to apply or be issued with individual licenses (Singapore Broadcasting Authority, March 1996: 14–15).

The class license scheme includes two types of Internet providers: Internet service providers, and Internet content providers. The first type sell or provide access to the Internet; the second type provide information content. The service providers have to be registered with SBA; of the content providers, only those must register which provide local political and religious content on the Internet, and on-line newspapers that target Singapore subscribers. Registering entails giving SBA the names of editors and publishers, and information on the organization; such information provision is intended both to promote responsible behavior on the Internet and at the same time to encourage its development in Singapore. Regulation is intended to focus on content provided on the Internet on an organized basis. The Internet service providers also must pay a licensing fee. (Pereira, July 13, 1996: 1).

Singapore's Internet services are provided by three corporations: Cyberway; Pacific Internet; and Singnet. Cyberway, the most recent Internet service provider, is a joint venture of SPH Multimedia and ST Telecommunications. Sembawang Media operates Pacific Internet. Singapore Telecom, the former direct-line telephone monopoly, operates Singnet (Singapore Broadcasting Authority, May 1996: 9).

There is sensitivity over content of some news groups such as religion, sex, violence, and graphic content that is objectionable. The service providers have the SBA guidelines to instruct them on what content to provide and what content to block. When the SBA directs it, these Internet service providers must block objectionable content. This is content 'which tends to bring the government into hatred or contempt, or which excites disaffection against the government' (Kynge, July 12, 1996: 7).

Schools and other places which offer access to children will need tighter control; the SBA said it was working with the Education Ministry and the National Library Board on this. Internet Content Providers (ICP); the term refers to anyone who provides information on the WorldWideWeb, including those who put out their own home pages (Periera, July 15, 1996, e-mail).

One of the additional concerns that has emerged from the issuance of these regulations may be a bit of confusion among Singaporeans over how the new laws apply. For example, the new rules require 'men of standing on formal editorial boards' for all groups which incorporate religion and politics on the Internet. These board members must be of good standing in the community (Lee, T., May 31, 1996: 58). Also, 'the public is unclear as to what constitutes illegal possession of pornography, and what does not' (Ng, October 5, 1996: 23). As the SBA guidelines get implemented over time, clarity can be expected to sharpen with practice.

By the Autumn of 1996, the Singapore approach to regulate the Internet's use, and at the same time to allow the free flow of information on the Internet, was articulated further:

> The approach was to leave private communications alone, while concentrating on the few dozen sites which were of mass appeal and easily accessible, to ensure that the plazas, or open areas in cyberspace, were relatively pristine and wholesome (*Singapore Bulletin*, November 1996: 13).

In the case of political and religious web sites, these had to be registered by the owners of the sites 'to encourage a sense of responsibility' (*Singapore Bulletin*, November 1996: 13). Shortly after the Government of Singapore introduced its initial regulation of the Internet, it also launched a computer system, i.e. a proxy server, to monitor objectionable sites. As of September 15, 1996, Singapore's Internet service

> providers must channel Singapore's more than 120,000 Internet subscribers through the proxy servers, preventing them from seeing about a dozen sites known to contain nudity and sexual topics (Shuhaimi, August 15, 1996: 2).

Additionally, according to SingNet's Richard Villanueva, the proxy servers match the government's banned sites against the sites that are accessed by Singaporean Internet subscribers. This approach supplements the threat of punishment and the government's exhortations against what it sees as misuse of the Internet. 'Corporations which intend to provide Internet solely to their employees for business are excluded' (Goh, September 7, 1996: 2) from the requirement that public subscribers to the Internet have to be channeled through filter systems such as proxy servers. Access to the Internet is unrestricted if it is for internal business purposes.

Additionally, the SBA clarified that it was interested in the broadcast of objectionable material on the Internet and not the private access of such information. It was not an offence for individuals to access pornography on the Internet; 'we do not track, nor do we monitor individuals' access, and neither do the Internet Service Providers' (*Singapore Bulletin*, November 1996: 14). Singapore has formed a National Internet Advisory Committee to assess Internet privacy and promotion of Internet use. The Committee's principal subcommittees and their emphases were on legal, industry and public education functions.

Singapore's approach to Internet regulation was tested in September 1996. A Singaporean man was convicted of possessing obscene films that had been taken from the Internet. This was the first such case in the city-state. The man was fined US$43,310 (S$61,500). He was charged under the Films Act; the Computer Misuse Act had not yet been changed then to accommodate such behavior. As a result of this case, and the questions that it stimulated among Singapore's public, government officials responded in the local newspaper with some of these points.

Singapore Internet users 'were assured . . . that they are not being monitored when they surf in cyberspace'. SBA spokespersons iterated that the Authority does 'not interfere with what individuals access on the Internet in the privacy of their homes . . . we do not track nor do we monitor individuals' access, and neither do the Internet Service Providers'. However, the Authority is interested in the broadcast and distribution of pornographic information in Singapore and the control of pornographic sites with mass impact.

The case cited above was uncovered as a result of an externally-stimulated operation against international child pornography distribution by Interpol, but not from Singapore's monitoring of individuals' usage of the Internet. The SBA's position is that 'the Internet is a growing medium and issues of privacy are important . . . We are prepared to recommend measures such as laws to strengthen privacy on the Internet' (Pereira, September 28, 1996: 2). A resulting *Straits Times* editorial stated that 'Singapore's nearly 150,000 Netizens will be relieved to learn that all those fears provoked by a single Internet prosecution are groundless' (Editor, October 12, 1996: 12). The editorial went on to state that the honor system for Singapore's Internet users is an effective means of enabling the Internet to evolve in Singapore.

In sum, after more than half a year of implementing its evolutionary and experimental approach to regulating the Internet, Singapore's Ambassador to the United States, Chang Heng Chee, described Singapore's approach as enlightened. She depicted her government's policy as that of a gatekeeper acting to insure that Singaporean Internet users use it responsibly. She was quoted as saying that 'the global Internet community cannot be dissected from the people, or have free flow over and above their values' (Koh, February 8, 1997: 4). As a consequence, the government would not permit the technology to dictate the direction of Singapore's society.

In October 1997, the National Internet Advisory Committee (NIAC) gave its first report. The report called for a more 'liberal atmosphere' (Koh, October 11, 1997: 15). The report included several recommendations for the Singapore Broadcasting Authority to consider:

- The SBA should be more specific in its rules.
- The responsibilities of Internet Service Providers (ISPs) and content providers should be spelt out clearly.
- The regulators should clarify what vague terms like banning 'prohibited material' mean.
- The SBA should step up efforts to protect the young.
- An additional layer of 'filter' should be set up at places where school-children are the major users of the Internet, such as schools.
- There should be a 'light-handed approach' to enforcement.

'The Internet is a new medium, we definitely don't want the regulators to come down like a ton of bricks' (Chua, October 4, 1997: 6). Additionally, the SBA Committee said that these were objectionable content areas: pornography; violence; promotion of ethnic and religious intolerance; and promotion of criminal activity. The committee said that the SBA regulation which bans contents which 'bring the Government into hatred or contempt, or excites disaffection against it . . . may curtail free speech, and it is best to take it out'.

The NIAC's report is quite congruent with Singapore's incremental and experimental approach to controlling the new phenomenon of the Internet. And the Committee observed that provisions that already are covered by other laws also should apply to cyberspace. The Committee believed that the above-referenced clarifications would operate to make Singapore an 'influence hub' in the region. The goal is more likely to be realized by having a balance between control and creativity.

MALAYSIA

Malaysia is one of the Southeast Asian countries that prefers self-regulatory approaches by Internet service providers. Malaysia's Deputy Prime Minister Datuk Anwar Ibrahim said: 'Censoring the Internet is not the solution. Simply closing our doors will not only hurt us but push us back in the race for growth and prosperity' (*The Straits Times* Weekly Edition, March 16, 1996: 10). However, the Government of Malaysia is concerned about the Internet being used as a medium of libel and disparaging comments about the country. Rumors, racist comments, and uncensored remarks on Malaysia and its politics on the Internet are of particular concern.

Stimulated largely by Malaysia's need to attract investment to its Multimedia Super Corridor, in 1997, a package of cyberlaws was developed, debated and passed by Parliament. Eighteen people working six months on the Malaysia cyberlaw project was the foundation for this effort. Such regulations are essential to give Malaysia and the Multimedia Super Corridor the required legal and stable environment for the facilitation of such activities as software development and the intellectual property protection to safeguard such creativity and investment (*The Straits Times* Weekly Edition, March 29, 1997: 10).

Malaysia's Minister for Energy, Telecommunications, and Posts, Datuk Leo Moggie, has stated that each country needs to have its own specified cyberlaws to suit local market conditions. Malaysia has '. . . to have our own cyberlaws in order to make sure that what we plan to do in this country can be started'. As to the enforcement of the cyberlaws, Minister Moggie said:

> . . . we are more interested in encouraging and facilitating multimedia companies to grow in the MSC, . . . the objective of the special policies and laws is to be very liberal to allow multimedia companies to be innovative in doing what they need to do within the multimedia environment and the high technology industry (Kang, October 29, 1996).

Malaysia's Multimedia Super Corridor's Bill of Guarantees and cyberlaws were derived in part from a process of detailed interviews with representatives of over 150 multimedia and information technology companies. The Multimedia Development Corporation of the Multimedia Super Corridor intends that these policies, laws, and Bill of Guarantees 'will make Malaysia the regional leader in intellectual property protection and free information' (cited from Multimedia Development Corporation, home page, <http://www.mdc.com.my/faq/qa/index.html>, 26 March 1997). In fact, one of the ten guarantees of the Bill of Guarantees for companies with Multimedia Super Corridor status is to 'become a regional leader in intellectual property protection and cyberlaws' (cited from Multimedia Development Corporation, home page, <http://www.mdc.com.my/incent/bill/index.html>, 25 March 1997).

To attain this regional leadership role in regulating the Internet, Malaysia has developed six policies and cyberlaws:

1 The Multimedia Convergence Act which creates an up-to-date communications framework. It was scheduled for implementation in 1997.
2 The Digital Signature Cyberlaw enables businesses and the community to use electronic signatures instead of their hand-written counterparts in legal and business transactions.

3 The Multimedia Intellectual Property Cyberlaw gives multimedia developers full intellectual property protection through the on-line registration of works, licensing, and royalty collection.

4 The Computer Crime Cyberlaw provides law enforcers with a framework that defines illegal access, interception, and use of computers and information; standards for service providers; and outlines potential penalties for infractions.

5 The Telemedicine Development Cyberlaw empowers medical practitioners to provide medical services from remote locations using electronic medical data and prescription standards, in the knowledge that their treatment will be covered under insurance schemes.

6 The Electronic Government Cyberlaw allows politicians, public servants, and the public to communicate electronically with each other using established and secure formats and standards. (Cited from Multimedia Development Corporation, home page, <http://www.mdc.com.my/infras/cyberlaw/index.html>, 17 April 1997).

Bills 2 through 5 were passed in May 1997 (*The Star*, May 16, 1997). The Digital Signature Act required the formation of a new regulatory body to enforce it. The Act enables the use of electronic signatures in place of handwritten signatures by means of computers. This enabling legislation is intended to facilitate electronic commerce and electronic legal transactions. The new regulatory department, under the Ministry of Energy, Telecommunications, and Posts, would authorize and certify digital signatures. The above other three cyberlaws that were passed already have their respective regulatory bodies; the police enforce the Computer Crime Act; the Domestic Trade and Consumer Affairs Ministry enforces the Copyright (Amendment) Act; and the Telemedicine Act is regulated by the Health Ministry (*New Straits Times*, May 14, 1997).

HONG KONG, CHINA, AND VIETNAM

In Asia, the range of Internet regulation is extreme. Hong Kong's colonial government had a policy of no regulation of the Internet (Arnold, January 27, 1997); the Special Administrative Region government has continued this policy. At the other extreme, China's Internet regulatory policies both tightened and loosened during 1996. Earlier in the year, over 100 WorldWideWeb sites were blocked. The types of blocked sites included: English language news; Chinese language information from Taiwan; Hong Kong-based, China-watching organizations; overseas dissident groups; and some sexually explicit sites. However, the several academic networks in China went unblocked (Chen, September 9, 1996: 10). Later in the year, after checking some of the blocked sites, an official of China's State Council said that some of the Western-media web sites were unblocked. He stated also that officials would continue to monitor, selectively, 'politically suspect or pornographic material' (*Asian Wall Street Journal* Weekly Edition, January 20, 1997: 16). Now that Hong Kong has been returned to China, with time, these divergent Internet practices of Hong Kong and China are likely to be reassessed by the respective regulatory authorities.

At the end of 1997, the People's Republic of China unveiled a battery of new Internet controls that will affect China's users of 250,000 personal computers and 49,000 host computers. These additional regulations specify the following as Internet crimes: defaming government, leaking state secrets, political subversion, computer hacking, spreading pornography and violence. China's government, by these rules, seeks to guard against computer viruses, and computer crimes in general. Punishment for these crimes include fines, both for users and Internet providers. Internet service providers are expected to assist the government's Public Security Agency in enforcing the controls. These regulations apply to businesses, as well as individual Internet users. It is noteworthy that these controls 'are intended to cover information transmitted from Hong Kong, Macao, and Taiwan' (*Far Eastern Economic Review*, January 8, 1998; and Harding, December 31, 1997).

Vietnam has all of the Internet regulation issues ahead of it. 'So far, no one in Vietnam offers direct access to the full Internet' (Chua and Zisiger, September 9, 1996: 1). Issues of Internet security, business rivalry, and Internet responsibility questions seem to be the principal impediments to the development of an Internet policy. In 1996, the regulator, the Department General of Posts and Telecommunications drafted regulations requiring

> Internet providers and users to register with the authorities and report any illegal activities or damaging information they stumble across. Service providers must allow the Ministry of Interior to monitor traffic; users are liable if they send or receive data deemed to harm national security or the social order (Chua and Zisiger, September 9, 1996: 11).

The central government must license Internet service providers. Private companies and a provincial posts and telecom agency have established local networks; limited e-mail services were used by the approximately 2,000 users of NetNam and VARENet. Other e-mail and/or electronic news services were offered via ToolNet, Vietnet, and VINet (Chua and Zisiger, September 9, 1996: 1 and 11).

GLOBALIZATION OF INTERNET REGULATION

In Southeast Asia, issues of Internet security came to the fore when a principal Malaysian Internet service provider, Asia Connect, issued a challenge and a reward for anyone who could break into its Internet security system. Two Malaysians took up the challenge, and intercepted Asia Connect's e-mail in two-minutes' time. In Singapore, two of the city-state's Internet service providers assured its users that they had the 'best security systems available' (Hau, January 20, 1996: 7). Internet security concerns are not limited to Southeast Asia.

Given the high degree of economic and technological interdependencies between the countries of the world, there has been and will continue to be a great deal of international cross learning and Internet regulatory experimentation. This will be the case particularly for Singapore and Malaysia because foreign investment is sought and domestic business entrepreneurs are encouraged to venture outside their home borders. The cases analysed above enable one to discern some of the cultural and ideological differences among the countries. Over time, however, driven by the focus of globalization, one might expect a narrowing in the range of approaches, not only among Southeast Asian countries, but also among many other nations elsewhere.

With recent World Trade Organization initiatives, trade in telecommunications, IT, and related multimedia services around the world will grow and restructure (Williams, March 27, 1997; Andrews, February 16, 1997). Related to regulating the Internet for purposes of development and protecting the national culture, there also are concerns for security and privacy. This is the case particularly as global trade in these multimedia services expands. Consequently, the next phase of Internet regulation attention can be expected to emphasize such issues as security and privacy. The Organization for Economic Cooperation and Development (OECD) has adopted guidelines for securing information and transactions on the Internet (Schenker, March 27, 1997). Today, there are software solutions available to better protect electronic communications (Asia, Inc., March 1997; Arnold, April 29. 1996). And with the development of the first global codes of privacy by the International Labor Office (ILO) and the Global Information Infrastructure Commission (GIIC), there is a globalization of privacy controls underway. These recent privacy codes, recommendations, and encryption issues were reviewed by G. Russell Pipe in *I-Ways* (Pipe, First Quarter 1997).

CONCLUSION

This chapter has focused on the interdependencies of societal, economic, and political forces with information technologies. The linkages between urban and national policy planning and policy implementation have been explicated using case material from Malaysia, Singapore, and the Southeast Asian region. IT development cases have enabled us to compare and contrast the sequencing, timing, and relative effectiveness of IT public policies across time and space.

Prior comparative research has demonstrated the criticality of vision and leadership, modern information infrastructure investment, and human resources development and trained personnel in the planning and implementation of IT and telecommunications policies (Corey, 1996). The present chapter has extended these findings by demonstrating the additional importance of early, pioneering experience in IT public policy implementation; the essential and unique nature of a country's political economy and culture in the execution of urban and national IT policies; and the organizational/spatial synergies and their catalytic and coalescing dynamics. Part two of the chapter explicated the role of the recently emergent facilitative legal and regulatory environment.

Lastly, the case studies of the chapter have demonstrated two converging forces that are representative of the political economies of their respective countries. The mini-dragon cases of Malaysia and Singapore are characteristic of state-led policy and programme planning, while the US cases, for example, are characteristic of market-led initiatives that manifest themselves locally. In future policy improvement terms, each political economy probably has something to learn from the experiences of the other. In turn, third parties also may benefit from observing and studying these two IT and economic forces, especially as their best and most appropriate qualities might be integrated into new, value-added policy and programmatic interventions. This challenge for increasing innovation in electronic community development needs to be taken up by urban and national policy makers and business leaders around the world. By meeting this challenge, urban policy practitioners and academics will be contributing to the creation of new urban development paradigms.

As to the importance of a facilitative regulatory environment, the control of the Internet in Southeast Asia has become an element of competition in national efforts to attract investment by companies in IT, telecommunications, and other multimedia technologies. *Asian Business* observed recently,

> When Singapore introduced censorship of the Internet through proxy servers last year, the move was publicly condemned by the US telecoms sector. Mahathir has since pledged not to censor the Internet within the MSC, but has asked for self-censorship among Internet service providers (Johnstone, February 1997: 51).

Recently, *Asiaweek* observed that, for now, the new paradigm of Internet regulation in Asia is Singapore's model of a two-tiered system: '. . . one of unrestricted access for commercial users less likely to brook interference for business reasons, and government-monitored access at home . . .' (*Asiaweek*, March 28, 1997: 11).

Academic analysis has demonstrated that four paradigms or dimensions are available to guide a country's approach to controlling the Internet; these include the precedents set by the various media of the post, print, broadcast, and computer. Ang concludes that no one of these paradigms will do; he proposes a 'cautious piecemeal approach' to the regulation of the Internet; 'such an approach offers room for the new medium to develop and to cope with new issues' (Ang, June 1–3, 1996).

To date, Singapore has followed just such an incremental and experimental approach. The sequence of actions and experiments above enables one to get inside this process, and possibly employ its lessons and experiences elsewhere (Table 2). Malaysia is taking the novel approach of developing cyberlaws for the nation, but is pledged not to censor for part of the country, i.e. policies, guarantees, and laws for corporations that have been granted Multimedia Super Corridor status. Further, Malaysia has taken a multidimensional approach by developing cyberlaws for multimedia, digital signatures, intellectual property, computer crime, telemedicine, and electronic government.

Increasingly, the regulation of the Internet will be going beyond national concerns. A recent case of an international Internet service provider in Germany being charged with distributing illegal pornography and neo-Nazi material, has raised questions of legal jurisdiction over the Internet. While legislatures and

Table 2 Singapore IT Development Process

- scanning external environment and intelligence gathering, continuously (via targeted conferences for knowledge exploration);
- consultation with foreign and local stakeholders;
- legal and regulatory framework established;
- close coordination among the Singapore planning and implementation actors;
- each principal actor plays out a designated role;
- high-level leadership and exhortation/campaigns;
- financial and facilitation incentives;
- self-financing;
- corporatizing;
- well-funded modern infrastructure;
- measures of evaluation, publically general;
- re-organizations and re-structurings, continuously;
- training and human resources development;
- moving personnel around a great deal;
- government intervention at all stages of the process.

courts have local, state or national authority, there are no national boundaries in cyberspace – and therefore, to date, no effective laws (Kehoe and Taylor, April 22, 1997: 4).

If the charges are upheld, the international Internet service provider might have to apply German regulations to its subscribers around the globe. As a consequence, one of the principal concerns is that the countries with more restrictive Internet regulations might have their controls applied to other countries. There is discussion of the value of having treaties for the international regulation of the Internet. While these debates proceed, Germany has introduced legislation creating the first 'cyber sheriff'. Such officials would monitor content provided from the Internet, and when offending material is discovered, officials would 'decide whether to prosecute the originator or the Internet provider or both' (Norman, April 22, 1997: 4).

While the Singapore Police Force has stated that it does not monitor the Internet for criminal activity, in contrast, Germany's Munich police department has a special unit for the investigation of the Internet. That department's six-person unit is the investigatory team that led to the indictment of Compuserve's managing director of its German division (Studemann, April 20, 1997). This specialist police unit searches and scans the Internet for any content banned by German law. Such material includes child pornography, as well as violence and illegal gambling. One of several problems, is that much of this illegal material originates outside German borders, that is in areas where the German police unit has no jurisdiction. Of the 110 cases of individuals distributing child pornography apprehended last year by the Munich unit, only a third lived in Germany (Studemann, April 30, 1997: 3). Based on its experience to date in investigating Internet crimes, the police of the Munich unit believe that the broadcasting of illegal content over the Internet would be reduced if such broadcasters had to declare their identity. This, and authority to access encrypted content, are powers being advocated by German police (Studemann, April 30, 1997).

The control of the Internet currently is dynamic, experimental, and highly interdependent with national policies for economic development and each society's culture and values. One can only speculate on the impact of such control measures on IT foreign investment in those Southeast Asian countries that are aggressively wooing Internet innovation.

As these cases of national and international Internet regulation continue to play out, we will learn much more about the weight and value of facilitative regulatory environments in the intense competition for IT investments among the Southeast Asian countries. This learning will be important. The Internet is new. Approaches to its regulation are even newer. Such control environments recently have been used to market Malaysia's Multimedia Super Corridor. Time will tell to what extent such marketing is effective.

Lastly, in synthesizing the principal lessons from some of the above cases, generic processes of IT development may be identified. Singapore is one of the world's first countries to rely significantly on IT in the planning and development of its society and territory. Because of its early IT innovation, Singapore has had the opportunities to experiment and perfect its IT development initiatives. From analysing Singapore's IT experiences and results, it is possible to identify a generalized IT development process.

CHAPTER 10

NEIGHBOURS – AUSTRALIAN AND INDONESIAN TELECOMMUNICATIONS CONNECTIONS

Peter J. Rimmer

INTRODUCTION

> It would be difficult to find two large neighbouring countries more unlike each other
> than Indonesia and Australia: one a country of relatively recent Western settlement,
> the other an ancient Asian country not long emerged from colonial domination; one
> an OECD-type rich industrial welfare state, and the other a developing, industrializ-
> ing, still relatively poor country; and one a country inhabited by 17 million people,
> the other an archipelago with nearly 200 million people (Arndt and Thee, 1994: 9).

Telecommunications have been afforded a strategic role in the trade in services
between Australia and Indonesia. A marked increase in demand for telecommunications services and related equipment in Indonesia since the mid-1980s has
been driven by rapid income growth and the opening of its economy to greater
international trade and investment flows. Bottlenecks in Indonesia's domestic
telecommunications have impeded economic growth and structural change. The
Indonesian Government has recognized the need to draw on foreign capital, technology and skills to address this problem. Australia is seeking to provide internationally competitive telecommunications services and related equipment for
Indonesian and other potential markets in the Asia–Pacific region (BTCE, 1991;
EAAU, 1992). The highly competitive nature of the Asia–Pacific region's trade in
telecommunications services and the role of international firms, provides an acid
test of Australia's intentions to become a major supplier of Indonesia's imports of
telecommunications services and related equipment in the 2000s. Australia's
geographical proximity to Indonesia is seen as an important asset in this quest.

Australia's presumed 'natural advantage' over its competitors in Indonesia's
large potential telecommunications market needs to be questioned. While spatial
realities may have some force in moving goods and people this is less true of
information. The problems of facilitating trade in information have to be couched
less in locational than in non-locational factors (e.g. access to markets). Time
zones may be more important than geographical location. There is a need,
therefore, to go beyond the cliché that Australia and Indonesia are 'neighbours'
and examine the structure, operation, and performance of the Australian and
Indonesian telecommunications industries.

Before undertaking this exercise a brief examination is made of regional trends
in economic growth within the Asia–Pacific region, and the networks of hubs and

hinterlands by which centers of economic activity are tied into international telecommunications systems. Attention is then centred on the restructuring of the Australian and Indonesian telecommunications industries. The effects of the restructuring on industry performance, based on the degree of fulfilment of selected reform objectives, is undertaken. Finally, consideration is given to the emerging issues in the vertical integration of communications, computing, and other entertainment and information media within Australia – these may have relevance for Indonesia once the network is rolled out. A major problem of undertaking a study of this nature is the lack of comparable data (cf. APEC, 1993, 1994). Australia is information rich on telecommunications and Indonesia information poor.

THE ASIA–PACIFIC REGION

Within the Asia–Pacific region the Australian and Indonesian economies are modest in size compared with the giant economies of Japan and the United States. In 1995, the Australian economy at purchasing power parity was 12% that of Japan, and 21% that of the Association of Southeast Asian Nations (ASEAN) (cf. Rimmer *et al.*, 1994). The Indonesian economy was about twice the size of the Australian economy and eleven times that of Singapore.

A direct positive correlation exists between economic growth expressed as per capita GNP and the number of telephones per 100 people (i.e. teledensity) in countries within the Asia–Pacific region (Figure 1). Indonesia, like other Southeast Asian countries, had maintained growth rates of 6–7% until the economic crisis of 1997–98. This contrasts with the Australian economy which is unlikely to achieve a sustained growth rate much higher than 3.5% without a dramatic improvement in savings and investment.

INTERNATIONAL TELECOMMUNICATIONS

During the 1980s the explosive growth of international telephone calls saturated the capacity of the Pacific INTELSTAT satellite and gave rise to the development of submarine optical fiber networks (Figure 2). Both Australia and Indonesia are linked into the ASEAN optical fiber system (Australia-Indonesia-Singapore, Medan-Penang, Singapore-Hong Kong-Taiwan, Okinawa-Luzon-Hong Kong, and Taiwan-Luzon). Although satellites will continue to be used, the new networks will carry the majority of growth in business services. These include the next generation of FAX, high definition television, international video-conferencing and value-added services for financial transactions and computer-aided design. The 'superhighways' created by optical fiber networks will add a new dimension to the speed and availability of business communications.

Principal Australian and Indonesian cities do not lie on the trunk routes of international telecommunications networks. This is partly a matter of location, and partly a matter of the level and dispersion of traffic. As a consequence, both

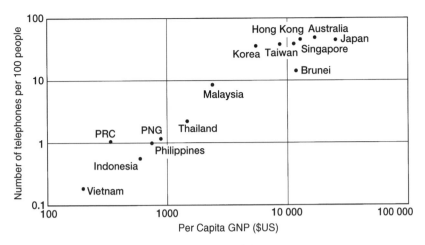

Figure 1 *Relationship between teledensity and GDP per capita*
Source: EAAU, 1992: 222.

countries have to explore ways of connecting better with global networks. International telecommunications centers will need to be developed and links with their hinterlands improved. Indonesia's proximity to Singapore means that it is much better placed than Australia to achieve this objective (though it precludes Jakarta becoming an important international telecommunications center). Australia's main cities are not way-ports for high-density international traffic.

Australia's originating and terminating international traffic was five or six times greater than that of Indonesia in the 1980s (see BTCE, 1993 for detailed discussion of Australia's international traffic). Annual growth in international public-switched telephone traffic in Australia between 1991 and 1994 was 20–30% annually. Indonesia's 30–40% growth rate in international traffic for the same period was closer to the norm for developing countries, reflecting its lower starting point compared to Australia.

Indonesia did not rank in Australia's 'top 15' largest telecommunications routes in 1995 (Staple, 1996). Conversely, Australia ranked fourth in Indonesia's 'top 10' largest telecommunications routes after Singapore, the United States, and Japan with over 8.5% of its outgoing traffic. The 'top 5' telecommunications routes in Australia accounted for 54% compared with almost 58% for Indonesia.

Indonesia had made an early start in telecommunications when it used its oil-windfall receipts to enter into advanced telecommunications with the inauguration of the Palapa-A1 satellite. This was developed by the Hughes Corporation in 1976 and was the fourth in the world and the first in a developing country.[1] Although

---

[1] Since 1976, Indonesia has launched six satellites: the Palapa-A series comprising two satellites; and since 1983 the Palapa-B series comprising four satellites. The Palapa-C series was launched in January 1996 (two more are planned). All have been built by the Hughes Space and Communications Company of the United States. Palapa-C is superior to the earlier Palapa-A and B series in coverage, power and flexibility.

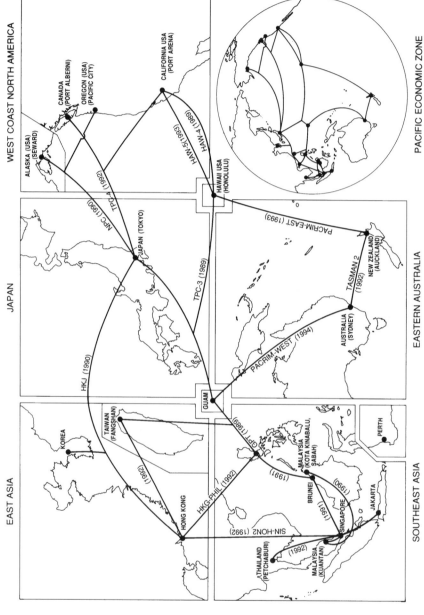

Figure 2 Optic fiber network in the Asia-Pacific region

the early start enabled the Indonesian archipelago to receive telephone, radio, and television from all over the world, demand for telecommunications outstripped supply. This is obvious from a comparison of Australian and Indonesian telecommunications industries. Rather than discuss the marked differences in the records of the two countries attention here is focused on the restructuring of their respective telecommunications sectors.

Sector Restructuring

Before 1988, Australian and Indonesian telecommunications had much in common. Telecommunications services in Australia were traditionally supplied by two carriers, with state monopolies in their respective areas of operation. The Australian Telecommunications Commission (Telecom) was created as a statutory authority in 1975 and took over the telecommunications functions of the Post Master General's Department to serve the domestic market; and the Overseas Telecommunications Commission (OTC) was established in 1946 to serve the overseas market.[2] In Indonesia, two state monopolies fulfilled similar roles – the domestic market was served by Perumtel (the National Public Company for Telecommunications) and the overseas market by PT Indonesia Satellite Corporation (PT Indosat).[3]

Australia's Telecom, as the incumbent monopoly provider, had exclusive rights to the domestic supply of fixed and mobile network services, and infrastructure. Also, Australia's Telecom performed certain regulatory functions relating to customer equipment, private networks and value-added services. In Indonesia, the Ministry of Tourism, Post, and Telecommunications controlled both Perumtel and PT Indosat through the Directorate General of Telecommunications, which also acted as the regulator.

Contracts for constructing state utilities in Australia were subject to an open bidding process. Conversely, telecommunications in Indonesia were used as a principal source of patronage. As detailed in the tendering process for the installation of new telephones lines in Jakarta between 1988 and 1991, this system involved well-known identities becoming 'local agents' to international bidders (Table 1). The system has delayed the upgrading of Indonesia's telephone system and may have resulted in the payment of unnecessarily high prices for contracts.

As demonstrated in discussing telecommunications reforms in Indonesia, this business culture of political access peddling has been a recurrent feature of telecommunications development. This contrasts markedly with Australia. A major problem for the Indonesian Government has been to shake off the country's reputation for non-transparent public sector procurement procedures.

---

[2] Aussat was established as a statutory authority in 1984 to operate the domestic satellite system.

[3] PT Indosat was a unit of the American International Telephone and Tariff Company until it was acquired by the Indonesian Government in 1980.

Table 1 *Key Dates in the Bidding Process for Installing New Telephones in Jakarta, 1988–1991*

Date	Event
September 1988	• Invitation to international suppliers to bid for US$300 million project as a joint venture with a local manufacturer to add 350,000 new telephone lines to Jakarta's telecommunications grid. • Bimantara Group (Bambang Trihatmodjo, second son of President Soeharto) preselected as local manufacturer.
November 1989	• Three foreign bidders selected from a final shortlist of five culled from initial eleven bidders. • Fujitsu of Japan (agent President Soeharto's daughter Siti Hardijanti Rukmana, nicknamed 'Tutut'). • AT&T of the United States (agent Hutomo Mandala Putra nicknamed 'Tommy', President Soeharto's youngest son). • NEC/Sumitomo of Japan (agent Bambang Trihatmodjo). • Fujitsu bid was discarded.
February 1990	• Tender declared void and foreign finalists requested to resubmit bids.
October 1990	• Five bids resubmitted.
November 1990	• Contracts for 375,000 lines each awarded NEC/Sumitomo and AT&T (the two highest tenders).
January 1991	• Citra Telekomunikasi Indonesia (75% owned by President Soeharto's daughter Siti Hardijanti Rukmana ('Tutut') and 25% Minister Habibie's brother) established in July 1990 was awarded the contract to be local manufacturing partner to AT&T rather than Lembarga Elektronika National, the government-run agency with telecommunications experience.

Source: Derived from Schwartz, 1994: 144–145.

FIRST ROUND REFORMS

Since 1989, both Australian and Indonesian Governments have restructured their regulatory frameworks to pursue economic liberalization. During the initial phases there were strong parallels in their actions. Both sought to 'corporatize' the operations of government-owned carriers. In 1989, Telcom, OTC, and Aussat were put on a more commercial footing as government-owned business enterprises. Since 1989, Perumtel and PT Indosat have been allowed to participate in cooperative ventures with licensed private organizations (i.e. cooperatives and national companies) and on a revenue sharing basis (e.g. in cellular mobile services).[4] In

---

[4] In 1989, PT Bakrie Brothers, for example, was one of the pioneer companies to be awarded a profit sharing contract with PT Telkom (known as PHB joint ventures). These contracts have involved the completion of lines around Jakarta. Bakrie Brothers have sold a 30% stake in its telecommunications business to PTT Telcom BV, a subsidiary of Koninklijke PTT Nederland (KPN), for US$90 million (Chia, 1995). In 1993, Radio Telepon Indonesia (PT Ratelindo) was established as a joint venture of PT Telkom (45%) with the Bakrie Group (45%) and PTT

1991, Perumtel was reorganized as the fully commercial, state-owned limited liability company PT Telekomunikasi Indonesia (PT Telkom). Like its Australian counterparts, the new company was charged with developing its own hiring and compensation policies, and formulating its own budget and business policy.

Both countries distinguished between basic and value-added services. In 1989, Australia removed restrictions on value-added services and opened them up to full competition. In 1993, Indonesia permitted joint ventures, joint operations, or management contracts in value-added services between its state enterprises and the private sector. This was to induce a more competitive environment. Australia went a stage further than Indonesia when the Telecommunications Act 1989 removed technical and regulatory functions from Australia Telecom and created the Australian Telecommunications Authority (Austel) to act as an independent industry regulator. No parallel legislation was passed in Indonesia. Australia also provided for competition in the supply of customer premises equipment by removing Telecom's monopoly. After the initial set of reforms Australia and Indonesia have pursued different strategies.

SECOND ROUND REFORMS

In 1990, the Australian Government outlined a detailed plan leading to full and open competition by 1997.[5] The chief goal of these reforms was to position Australia's telecommunications industry to make the industry globally competitive in the next century. The three elements of the Government's approach were to:

- introduce genuine and sustainable network competition;
- create a world class telecommunications industry able to compete internationally; and
- foster industry development.

Conversely, the Indonesian Government eschewed full and open competition.

The Indonesian Government was partial to 'big government' because state-owned enterprises were seen as a necessary counterweight to large Chinese-owned and operated conglomerates (Schwarz, 1994). Although lacking enthusiasm for privatization, economic realities – reduced prices for oil and increased competition for foreign investment – forced the Indonesian Government to adopt this option. The Indonesian Government's strategy has been to introduce a sweeping financial deregulation package to support planned privatization of telecommunications, by offering the assets of state firms for sale to the private sector. Privatization has involved opportunities for private firms to operate businesses which

---

Telecom BV (10%) to operate Indonesia's first, private cellular digital radio telephone system. The system is offered in Jakarta in areas distant from the installed telephone networks of Telkom. Two kinds of devices are used – multiple subscriber units (maximum 96) for housing complexes, offices or markets and a single subscriber unit for individuals.

[5] Already, concern has been expressed over whether new entrants will be given a 'free ride' after 30 June 1997 or will be forced to share some of the development costs.

were previously state-run firms. Both revenue sharing and Build, Own and Transfer (BOT) arrangements have been used by the Indonesian Government to enlist private support (Symon, 1994).

Australia's competitive strategy embodied in the Telecommunications Act 1991 was aimed at improving the quality and diversity of services and reducing costs to residents and business users. The Act's key components were:

- the creation of a transitional duopoly, until July 1997, in fixed network services (involving the merger of Telecom and OTC to form first, Australian and Overseas Telecommunications Corporation (AOTC) and then Telstra, and the sale of Aussat for US$600 million to establish a second carrier, Optus Communications Ltd, owned by Australian institutions and BellSouth Corporation and Cable & Wireless plc);[6]
- the licensing of three public cellular mobile carriers – the 'triopoly' of Telstra, Optus, and Vodafone – to provide competition in the provision of public mobile telephone services;
- the lifting of all restrictions on the resale of domestic and international telecommunications capacity;[7] and
- the increase in Austel's regulatory responsibilities to include jurisdiction over interconnection arrangements between the duopoly carriers.

These transitional arrangements, introduced in 1992, applied until June 30, 1997, after which there has been unrestricted entry for all carriers (APTA, 1997a).

The Indonesian approach has avoided putting the award of telecommunications contracts out to tender. The plan has been to sell shares in state enterprises in foreign markets to repay a portion of Indonesia's external foreign debt (estimated at US$61 billion in 1995). As outlined in the Five Year Plan (Repelita VI 1994–1999), the Indonesian Government's strategy has been:

- to create PT Satelit Palapa Indonesia (PT Satelindo) in January 1993 (without any open bid) to operate the new Palapa Series of satellites, compete with PT Indosat for international traffic, and operate the Global System for Mobile (GSM) Communications;[8]

---

[6] The initial shareholders in Optus were BellSouth Corporation Inc. (24.5%); Cable & Wireless plc (24.5%) and Optus Pty Ltd (51%). In turn, Optus was owned by Mayne Nickless Pty Ltd (49%), AMP Society 19.6%, AIDC Telecommunications Fund (19.6%), and a diverse group of Australian fund and investment groups. By 31 December 1997 Optus was required to provide domestic long distance and international services to 100% and Mobile Digital phone service to 80% of Australian homes (Optus, 1994).

[7] In 1992, Telecom Australia and the Overseas Telecommunications Corporation were merged to form the Australian and Overseas Telecommunications Corporation. In April 1993, Telstra became the legal corporate name for the Group. Since 1973, it has traded internationally as Telstra but continued domestically as Telecom Australia until July 1995.

[8] Originally, PT Satelindo was 60% owned by the private company PT Bima Graha, which in turn, was 60% owned by the Bimantara Citra Group, run by former Present Suharto's second son Bambang Trihatmodjo and by the Artha Graha Group owned by prominent businessman Tomy Winata (who had a close link with the Armed Forces). Of the remaining

- to list PT Indosat on the Jakarta and New York stock markets in October 1994 as the first step in the internationalization of state companies in Indonesia; and
- to restructure PT Telkom by retiring 6,000 of its 42,000 employees and enabling it to win long-term exclusivity rights for telephone services and to negotiate joint ventures to shore up its position before privatization;[9] and then in November 1995 to list the company on the New York, London, and Jakarta stock markets (APTA, 1994).[10]

State companies which have gone public through the domestic or local stock exchanges have to meet full disclosure requirements and have, therefore, become more transparent. Unlike the United States, there is no equivalent to the Federal Commission in Indonesia to oversee telecommunications liberalization. Thus, immense power remains with the Minister.

Privatization in Indonesia

Privatization reduced the Indonesian Government's stake in PT Indosat to 65%. Of the 35% that was sold, 10% went to Indonesian investors and 25% was sold in New York. Buoyed by PT Indosat's success, the Indonesian Government turned to the privatization of PT Telkom, which was enjoying 30% annual revenue growth and had plans to double telephone capacity by 1999. The original intention was to realize US$ 2.5–3.1 billion from the initial public offering by placing 12.5% shares domestically in Jakarta and Surabaya, and 15% on world markets through New York and London.[11] Domestic shares were fully subscribed. Share prices for the 70

---

stock, 30% was held by PT Telkom and 10% by PT Indosat. Following the sale of 25% of Satelindo for US$586 million to Deutsche Telekom Mobilfunk Gmbh (DeTeMobil) of Germany (a subsidiary of Deutsche Telecom) the revised percentages are PT Bima Graha 45%, PT Telkom 22.5% and PT Indosat 7.5% (JP, 1995). Originally, Cable & Wireless had been favoured for the stake but offered US$550 million and wanted a right to veto over acquisitions in excess of US$940,000.

[9] Privatization of PT Telkom was first mooted in 1988 by Johannes Sumarlin, the then Finance Minister. Management changes and an internal reorganization were required before it was ready for the initial public offering.

[10] PT Telkom has exclusive rights to provide local fixed line and wireless local loop telecommunications services nationally for a minimum period of 15 years from January 1, 1996 and 10 years exclusive rights to nationwide long distance services from the same date. PT Indosat and PT Satelindo have exclusive rights over international calls until 2005. PT Indosat has taken over cross-border calls from PT Telkom. PT Satelindo can also serve cross-border calls once it has established international gateways in border areas. In 1995 Satelindo's share of international traffic was less than 5%. By 1999 it is expected to be 15%.

[11] Involved in PT Telkom's sale were three global coordinators – Merrill Lynch for the US tranche, Goldman Sachs for Asia and Lehman Brothers/S.G. Warburg for the European syndication and local security firms (Bahana, Damareska, Jardine Fleming Nusantara, and Makindo Securities). Bahana and Damareska were later given a global coordinating role (EM, 1995). Merrill Lynch has an affiliation with PT Tirtamas Majutama (controlled by Hashim Djojohadikusumo, the President's son-in-law's brother); and Goldman Sachs has an operating agreement with Bahana Pembinaan Usaha Indonesia, owned 82% by the Bank of Indonesia and 18% by the Ministry of Finance. Warman and Lehman had less need for

million American Depository Shares offered in offshore markets were expected to range between US$19.90–US$24.50.

Lack of demand by foreign investors stemming from an oversupply of telecoms issues, particularly in the United States, resulted in the offer being more than halved by the Indonesian Government to US$1.59 billion or 19% of the company.[12] Only US$520 million was raised from selling 30 million American Depository Shares to foreign investors at a starting price of US$18.[13] Undoubtedly, this poor showing in off-shore markets will prompt the Indonesian Government to rethink its plans to sell off state assets, to repay the high interest portion of its external foreign debt and fund a major telecommunications investment programme.[14] Unlike the Indonesian Government's thrust, Australia's arrangements for 'administered competition' until July 1997 required a regulatory and policy framework featuring competition, consumer protection, and industry development (Figure 3).

Pro-competition and Deregulation in Australia

In Australia, Telstra responded to imminent total deregulation of the Australian telecommunications sector by committing $A40 billion (US$29 billion) to protect its market dominance. Telstra's strategy was to upgrade and streamline its telecommunications infrastructure (e.g. fully digitized telephone service); to develop new interactive media (multimedia) services by launching a broadband network; and to concentrate its overseas activities on the Asia–Pacific market. Consequently, competitive safeguards were introduced to prevent the former incumbent carrier (Telstra) abusing its previous monopoly presence in the market (i.e. through its customer base, infrastructure, and control of information). These arrangements prompted Austel to tilt the playing field in favour of Optus (Van der Vries, 1996). According to the Australian Government, without this safeguard, the market access and pricing arrangements of a mature market would have been slow to emerge and confined to niche markets offering few long-term benefits to consumers.

Safeguards were introduced in Australia to ensure consumers benefited from the lower prices stemming from the reforms and were not exploited in areas of little competition. The critical consumer safeguards were:

---

high profile connections because they had been long-term financial advisers to the Indonesian Government. The unsuccessful Morgan Stanley was allied in a venture with Makindo securities house in which Siti Hardijanti Rukmana (Tutut), the President's eldest daughter has an interest. Makindo, however, was included in the domestic underwriting syndicate.

[12] As the underwriters exercised their 'green shoe' option a further 1% was floated to bring the sum to US$1.69 billion. About 60% of the domestic shares were reserved for government pension funds and insurance companies, and PT Telkom employees and other domestic institutions. These funds were 'locked up' to safeguard small investors.

[13] PT Telkom became the first Asian company to offer shares in Japan without being listed on the Tokyo Stock Exchange.

[14] In January 1996, the Indonesian Government's team of officials supervising privatisation was disbanded. Then, in May 1996, Setyanto Santosa, president-director of PT Telkom was replaced by Asman Akhir Nasution and former Present Suharto's son, Bambang Trihatmodjo, appointed as the new president-commissioner.

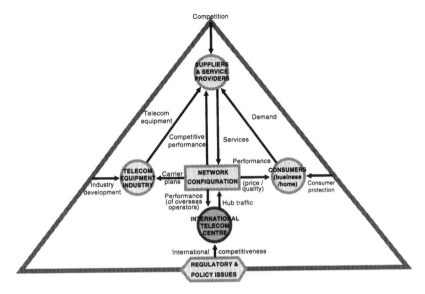

Figure 3 *Key features of the Australian telecommunications network*

- a price cap on selected Telstra services;
- continued access to untimed local calls; and
- a universal service obligation guaranteeing all Australians reasonable access on an equitable basis to standard telephone services and payphones (a similar provision applied in Indonesia).

The key industry development initiatives included 'Industry Development Arrangements' for potential equipment exports and 'Partnerships in Development' to encourage international companies to engage in joint ventures in information technology and telecommunications (BIE, 1994). The competitive and consumer safeguards covered interconnection arrangements, equal consumer access, non-discrimination provisions, price control arrangements, transparency mechanisms, and universal service.

When the existing duopoly was replaced on July 1, 1997 the previous Labor (Keating) Government's reform package had provided for an unlimited number of carriers; an end to the distinction between mobile and general carriers; open access to carrier's networks, customers' equipment and subscriber management systems; replacement of Telstra's obligation to offer non-discriminatory prices to all markets; and a freeze on local call charges. After being merged with the Spectrum Management Agency, Austel retained its technical and standards functions but economic regulation was taken over by the Australian Competition and Consumer Commission (ACCC) to ensure non-discriminatory access to telecommunications and other utilities. Some changes to these arrangements occurred with the election of the Liberal-National Coalition (Howard) Government in March 1996.

In a Green Paper designed to provoke debate on redrafting the former Labor Government's 1995 Telecommunications Bill the new Coalition Government reaffirmed the past government's commitment to a more competitive telecommunications market in Australia after July 1997. The Green Paper 'restates the goals of achieving a world class infrastructure with the latest market driven technology mix, a multitude of service providers, with equal non-discriminatory access to carrier facilities and contestable market strategies' (APTA, 1996a: 3). Electricity companies are positioned to become telecoms carriers and disturb the balance between telecommunications and the cable TV industries but this has yet to eventuate (APTA, 1996b).

The Coalition Government's plan to abandon the pro-state Telstra policy is discussed in the Epilogue because assessments of the restructuring of the Australian and Indonesian telecommunications industries refer to the period before its implementation.

PERFORMANCE

Monitoring the impact of the restructuring of the Australian and Indonesian telecommunications industries is not an easy task. Lacking intensive data sources, attention is limited to:

- examining networks and services (with a brief reference to financial performance);
- price but not quality of service;
- the development of Australia and Indonesia as international telecommunications centers; and
- the equipment industry.

International benchmarking has been used by Xavier (1996) to monitor deregulation in Australia but the study excludes Indonesia.

NETWORKS AND SERVICES

Varying degrees of competition have been developed in international trunk and mobile services in Australia and Indonesia. Since June 1992 Australia's publicly-owned Telstra – offering a wide range of telecommunications services – has competed in trunk, international and mobile services with Optus.[15] Optus had rolled out its network by 1997. This infrastructure duopoly has ended and new carriers have entered the market including AAPT Telecommunications, backed by Singapore Telecom and Primus Telecommunications Ltd. linked to Australia's electric utilities, and the Global One alliance of Sprint, France Telecom and Deutsche Telekom (APTA, 1998a). The former is concentrating its network on the central business districts of four or more state capitals and the latter on a 1,400 km network.

---

[15] In 1993–94, Telstra earned revenue of $A13.4 billion and achieved a profit of $A1.7 billion; and Optus earned $A835 million and incurred a loss of $A98 million. Excluding Telstra, revenue from service providers ranged up to $A750 million (BTCE, 1995a).

Table 2 *Analogue and Digital Operators in Australia*

	December 1993	June 1994	December 1994	June 1995	December 1995
ANALOGUE (AMPS)[1]					
Subscribers	920,000	1,185,000	1,568,000	2,000,000	2,550,000
Optus share (%)	27	34	34	30	29
Telecom share (%)	73	66	66	70	71
DIGITAL (GSM)					
Subscribers	18,400	35,000	176,000	309,000	584,000
Optus share (%)	10	26	30	37	40
Telstra share (%)	n.a.	n.a.	n.a.	37	37
Vodafone share (%)	n.a.	n.a.	n.a.	26	23

Source: APTA, 1996d: 3.

Note: [1] Scheduled to be shut down in 2000 (except in certain rural areas when equivalent digital services became unavailable).

In Indonesia, PT Telkom has maintained its monopoly over domestic services but there has been competition for international traffic between PT Indosat and PT Satelindo. (Although PT Satelindo has not captured much international traffic it is emerging as the country's long-term telecommunications giant). A wide range of new services has been introduced in both Australia and Indonesia but attention here is concentrated on personal mobile telephone services.

Personal Mobile Telephone Services in Australia and Indonesia

Australia and Indonesia are in the process of changing from analogue to digital mobile phones. In Australia's mobile services market both Telstra and Optus compete with the privately-owned Vodafone (Table 2).[16] (Vodafone's network had to cover 80% of Australia's population by the end of 1996). The three companies have 2.7 million analogue systems and 775,000 Global Standard for Mobile Communications (GSM) handsets.[17] Aggressive marketing by all three carriers is driving cellular growth in Australia, together with the convenience of mobile phones in outer suburbs and rural areas and the proven appetite of Australians for any new technology. Lower tariffs and cheaper service costs have also been contributing factors to the Australian boom in mobile phones. In Indonesia, there were only 80,000 mobile phone subscribers, in a population of 190 million in 1994, with the majority being in Jakarta.

---

[16] The major shareholder in Vodafone is Vodafone International, a UK-based company. It had a revenue of $A8.5 million in the year to March 1994 and incurred an operating loss of $A24.7 million.

[17] The greater number of analogue phones was because they were cheaper than digital varieties, had a wider geographical coverage and had a more convenient technology. However, the Australian Government will phase out the country's Analogue Mobile Phone System (AMPS) in 2000.

Analogue and digital mobile phones in Indonesia are handled by separate companies. There are four analogue cellular companies, which were established before 1993 under a revenue sharing agreement (Table 3). Since 1993, cooperation between PT Telkom and PT Indosat and private firms must take the form of a management contract, joint operation scheme or joint venture arrangement. These new arrangements have been extended to two of the analogue operators and applied to GSM operators.

The GSM cellular system was originally developed by PT Telkom on the Batam Island of Riau (part of the Singapore-Johor-Riau growth triangle) and in Jakarta by PT Satelindo (Table 4).[18] The Indonesian Government has also licensed PT Telkomsel to operate a nationwide mobile system as a joint GSM venture between PT Telkom (55%) and PT Indosat (45%). Once Indonesia's GSM operators were licensed the next step was to seek strategic partners from overseas.

In November 1995, Telkomsel sought fresh capital by asking 12 foreign companies to bid for a 25% stake. Australia's Telstra and Cable & Wireless and PTT Telecom of the Netherlands were shortlisted. Local companies, including the Rajawali Group, were also interested in the opportunity.[19] There were fears a local company would 'flip' the shares to a foreign company at a premium (Lopez, 1995). Offering US$392 million PTT Telecom Netherlands and PT Setdco Megasel Asia were successful.[20] This set back Telstra's plans for making Indonesia a key part of its Asian expansion. Subsequently, there was speculation that PTT Telecom Netherlands had overpaid for its stake, particularly given the strength of PT Satelindo's competition and the entry of a third licensed GSM operator, Excelcomindo, in 1996.[21]

Competition to Satelindo, Telkomsel, and Excelcomindo, in turn, is expected from the Personal Communication Network (PCN) and the Personal Communications Handy-phone Service (PHS).[22] The GSM operators were expected to reach their technical limit of 650,000 before the year 2000 (Table 5). Already, 120 potential applicants have been identified as willing to provide the new generation of digital mobile cellular telecommunications. They include most of Indonesia's existing fixed line and cellular companies, and unknown firms boasting executives

---

[18] The installation of the Global Standard for Mobile Communications was awarded to Alcatel; against the wishes of Indonesia's Ministry of Research and Technology which has a rule requiring switching equipment to be purchased from suppliers within the country. After Satelindo's discussions with Siemens and AT&T were unfruitful, the Ministry waived the ruling. Meanwhile the Ministry of Research and Technology had fast tracked the Batam Island Project before Satelindo's national project could commence (Pickles, 1994).

[19] The stakes of PT Telkom (51%) and PT Indosat (49%) have been consolidated into a joint holding of 77.72%.

[20] The Setdco Group was controlled by Indonesian businessman, Setiawan Djody, and associated with former President Suharto's son, Hutomo Mandala Putra.

[21] PT Excelcomindo Pratama has four shareholders: PT Telkom (62.8%), Nynex Network System Co. (23%), Mitsui & Co. Ltd. (4.2%) and an Indonesian businessman, Nugraha Santana (10%).

[22] PCN is a digital remote telephone system which uses light, inexpensive handsets with long-life batteries to communicate using low-powered antenna. Like PHS the new system operates on 1,800 or 1,900 megahertz. Their coverage includes expressways and tunnels.

Table 3 Analogue Operators in Indonesia, 1996[1]

Company	System	Owners	Area of operation
PT Rajasa Hazanah Perkasa (established 1986). Now Mobil Selular Indonesia.[2]	Nordic Mobile Telephones (NMT-450) 26,000 subscribers (March 1995)	PT Rajasa Hazanah Perkasa (70%), the family company of Ahmad Tahir, a former Minister of Tourism, Post and Telecommunications (which includes International Wireless Corp (US)). Rajasa is partly owned by International Wireless Corporation which is controlled by PT Bina Reksa Perdana and owned by former Present Suharto's youngest son Hutomo Mandala Putra. Telkom (25%), Telkom's employee pension fund (5%).	Jakarta and Bandung extending to Lambang, South Sumatra, Lombok, West Nusantara before going nationwide.
PT Centralindo Panca Sakti (established 1991). Now Metro Selular Nusantara.[3]	Advanced Mobile Phone System (AMPS-800) 20,000 subscribers (March 1995)	Centralindo (64%) owned by the Napan Group owned by businessman, Andyai Yasa, PT Telkom (20.17%); Telkom's employees pension funds (9.83%); DT Djati Yudha Cellular (5%) and Armed Forces (1%).	East and Central Java extending to Maluku and Irian Jaya.
PT Komunikasi Selular Indonesia (Komselindo) (established in 1991).[4]	Advanced Mobile Phone System (AMPS-800) 50,000 subscribers (March 1995)	Joint venture between Elektrindo Nusantara (65%), part of the Bimantara Group controlled by former President Suharto's second son Bambang Trihatmodjo and PT Telkom (35%).	Nationwide.
PT Telekmindo Primabhakti (established in 1992).[5]	Advanced Mobile Phone System (AMPS-800) 6,000 subscribers	Rajawali Corporation (54%); Telkom pension fund (22%); PT Telkom (10%); Armed Forces (10%); Telkom employees cooperative (Kopnatel) (2%); Tri Daya Foundation (2%).	Bali, East Kalimantan and South extending to East Nusa Tengara, East Timor, Riau, Jambi, Bengkulu and West Kalimantan.

Notes: [1] A fifth analogue mode owned by PT Telkom using the mobile facilities produced by the state-owned PT Inti has been phased out.
[2] Rajasa has become PT Mobil Selular Indonesia (Mobilsel) which is now expanding throughout Java, Lampung, South Sumatra and Lombok with a target of 80,000 subscribers.
[3] PT Centralindo has become PT Metro Selular Nusantara and aims to extend its coverage to East Maluku and Irian Jaya with 150,000 lines. Shareholders are now Centralindo 36%, Telkom 24%, First Pacific 35% and others 5%.
[4] Komselindo shifted from analogue to digital in 1997.
[5] Rajawali now has 84% shares, Telkom 10% and others have 5%.

Source: Various.

Table 4 *Digital Operators in Indonesia, 1996*

Company	System	Owners	Area of operation
PT Satelindo[1]	Global System for Mobile Communications (GSM)	PT Satelindo was 60% owned by the private company PT Bima Graha, which in turn, was half-owned by the Bimantara Citra Group (run by former President Suharto's second son Bambang Trihatmodjo), 30% by PT Telkom and 10% by PT Indosat.	Nationwide
PT Telkomsel[2]	Global System for Mobile Communications (GSM)	PT Telkom (51%) and PT Indosat (49%).	Nationwide
PT Excelcomindo Pratama[3]	Global System for Mobile Communications (GSM)	PT Telkom (62.8%), Nynex Network System Co. (23%), Mitsui & Co. Ltd (4.2%) and an Indonesian businessman, Nugraha Santana (10%).	Nationwide

Notes: [1] Satelindo's sold 25% of its business for US$586 million to Deutsche Telekom Mobilfunk Gmbh (DeTeMobil) of Germany (a subsidiary of Deutsche Telekom). The revised percentages are PT Bima Graha 45%, PT Telkom 22.5% and PT Indosat 7.5% (JP, 1995). Originally, Cable & Wireless had been favoured for the stake but offered US$550 million and wanted a right to veto acquisitions over US$940,000. PT Jakarta International and Development (JIHD) has acquired a 21.3 % indirect stake in PT Satelindo by purchasing 65% of PT Graha Jakarta Sentoda which owns 50% of BimaGraha.
[2] The stakes of PT Telkom (51%) and PT Indosat (49%) have been consolidated into a joint holding of 77.72% with PTT Telecom Netherlands taking 17.3% and PT Setdco Megasel Asia 5%.
[3] Subsequently, PT Telkom's share was reduced to 60%; there was no change at Indocel (23.2%, and Mitsui (4.2%); and AIF Indonesia took the remaining 12.7%.

Source: Various.

with good connections. Their proposed foreign partners include Canada's Northern Telecom, Japan's NTT, Hong Kong's Hutchison, Malaysia's Sapura, Sweden's Ericsson, Thailand's Shinawatra, and the United States' Motorola.

The evaluation process is touted as Indonesia's first 'open public tender' in cellular history, reflecting pressure from the World Bank for transparency in the allocation of licenses. More likely, the outcome will be decided behind closed doors (APTA, 1996c). The winners of the tender will be expected to join one of two consortia which have been licensed to operate PHS and PCN pilot projects in Jakarta and Surabaya respectively. They are PT Celnet and the Association of Retired Army Officers (*Pepabri*), and PT Inti, the equipment manufacturer, and the Foundation of Military Headquarters (*Yamabri*).[23] As PCN and PCS are considered to be basic services they must be run jointly with PT Telkom.

[23] PT Celnet is owned by businessman Sudwikaymono, a foster brother of former President Suharto and his daughter, Siti Hutami Endang Adiningsih; and PT Inti is a state-owned telecommunications equipment manufacturer supervised for the Management of Strategic Industries.

Table 5 *Cellular Operators in Indonesia and Growth Projections – Subscribers and Growth Projections*

Cellular company	March 1996 Total	March 1996 Jakarta	December 1996 Total	December 1996 Jakarta	December 2000 Total	December 2000 Jakarta
ANALOGUE						
Komselindo	75,000	60,000	95,000	75,000	220,000	187,000
Mobilsel	25,000	20,000	35,000	28,000	100,000	84,000
Metrosel	11,000	0	14,000	0	30,000	0
Telekmindo	10,000	0	12,000	0	25,000	0
Sub-total	121,000	80,000	156,000	103,000	375,000	271,000
DIGITAL						
Satelindo	120,000	105,000	200,000	170,000	380,000	325,000
Telkomsel	15,000	3,000	85,000	70,000	220,000	175,000
Excelcomindo	0	0	25,000	21,000	225,000	180,000
Sub-total	135,000	117,000	310,000	261,000	900,000	680,000
SUBSCRIBER TOTAL	256,000	197,000	466,000	364,000	1,275,000	951,000

Source: APTA, 1996e.

Service providers in both Australia and Indonesia use the facilities and services of licensed carriers to supply telecommunications services as resellers, suppliers of value-added services, and private network services – there has been little price competition and profitability has been reported to be low. In Australia, service providers have been increasing their share of the market though their combined share of net revenue is less than one-tenth that of Telstra, the major carrier.

The major carriers in both Australia and Indonesia had been profitable since the reforms. In 1995–96, Telstra, one of Australia's top 25 publicly-listed industrial companies, earned a revenue of $A15.2 billion and accrued a profit in excess of $A2.3 billion (the largest in Australian corporate history) (Telstra, 1996).[24] Optus Communications recorded a maiden profit of $A59 million on revenue of $A1.2 billion in 1995–96. In Indonesia, both PT Telkom and PT Indosat ranked first and second among Indonesia's top 200 corporate taxpayers in 1993. In 1993, PT Telkom's assets had grown to 6.82 trillion rupiah from 5.75 million in 1992. By 1995, PT Indosat recorded net profits of 459.4 billion rupiah compared with 289 billion rupiah in 1994.[25] After privatization, PT Indosat had become a major world stock and expected an annual growth rate of 32% until the year 2000. Most improvement is expected to come from a reduction in PT Indosat's tariff payment to PT Telkom. PT Indosat pays 35% of its foreign billings to PT Telkom in return for use of its domestic lines. This tariff was cut to 25% in 1996.

[24] Telstra also belongs to AT&T World Partners, a loose carrier alliance comprising KDD (Japan), Singapore Telecom, United (Canada) and AT&T (USA). Optus is part of the tight Cable & Wireless (C&W) alliance (ITU, 1994). Telstra was involved in separate talks with BT-MCI and IBM about forming a global alliance. Such an alliance would have had a marked impact on Telstra's value.

[25] Indosat retains a monopoly of its core IDD business but it has been susceptible to competition from discount telecommunications operators. The company has reacted by taking a 20% stake in USA Global Link – the world's largest discount operator.

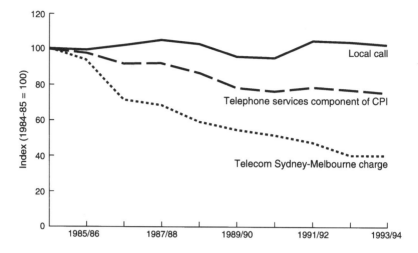

Figure 4 *Selected indices of telecommunications prices in real terms between 1984–85 and 1993–94*

Source: BTCE, 1995: 97.

PRICE

After the introduction of competition in Australia the performance of its telecommunications industry improved, particularly in the international, mobile and domestic long-distance markets (Xavier, 1996). The key features include:

- a reduction of overall prices in real terms;
- an increase in technical efficiency (i.e. total factor productivity rates of 6–7% which are higher than the economy as a whole);
- an increase in the range of services (e.g. public access to cordless telephone service); and
- a growth in telecommunications equipment exports (BTCE, 1995a).

No assessment is available of trends in Indonesia.

As it is difficult to satisfactorily determine overall trends in the quality of service in Indonesia attention is concentrated on the changes in price in Australia (BTCE, 1992). An examination of selected indices of telecommunications prices in real terms between 1984–85 and 1993–94 in Australia shows that the price of local calls fluctuated but had remained virtually unchanged (Figure 4). The telephone services component of the consumer price index based on weighted average prices for service rental, local calls, trunk calls, and international calls incurred by households shows a declining trend. Telstra's STD rate between Sydney and Melbourne shows a decline of 9.6% over the ten-year period. Other evidence derived from price cap information suggests in real terms the price of international calls declined at a much greater rate than domestic calls. Historically, the decline in international prices has been at a much slower rate than the decline in the cost of facilities. This outcome suggests the need for a more dynamic charging regime which is sensitive to market forces and reductions in costs.

As competition is still evolving in Australia it is difficult to comment on the achievement of genuine and sustainable network competition.[26] Preliminary observations suggest the entry of new carriers has radically altered the Australian telecommunications industry. There has been active marketing of services, changes in price structures, and a reduction of prices. However, the benefits of falling prices have been too heavily focused on business consumers and residential consumers with a high usage of telecommunications services.

Optus had secured over 30% of the market in mobile services by late 1995, more than 20% of the international market but only 14% of the domestic long-distance market (APTA, 1995a). Before any final assessment of the impact of the reforms on the performance of the telecommunications industry can be made other factors, such as changes in technology (e.g. optical fiber cable) and economic conditions have to be determined. International comparisons provide one option for identifying this contribution in Australia and Indonesia.

INTERNATIONAL COMPETITIVENESS

Australia – Improving Australia's competitiveness in the provision of telecommunications services has to be seen in the development of its cities as regional hubs (Langdale, 1991, 1992a,b). Domestic and international revenue from telecommunications hubbing was estimated at $A300–400 million per annum in the early 1990s. Many multinational corporations have established regional headquarters (RHQs) in Australia (e.g. Cathay Pacific, Data General, IBM, Knight Rider, and L.M. Ericsson). It is difficult to isolate the impact of telecommunications on corporate locational decisions. Available evidence on Australia's international competitiveness suggests its telecommunications infrastructure is not as modern as the United States, the United Kingdom, Canada, or New Zealand and Telstra is operating below world's best practice in some aspects (BIE, 1995). Prices have to fall further. Telstra's service quality, however, ranked in the second quartile of 24 OECD countries (BTCE, 1995a). Progress in mobile telephony by Telstra has to be offset against a re-emergence of problem areas – servicing of faults, call losses and sluggish performance in connecting new telephone lines. More information is required on user perceptions before changes in Australia's attractiveness as an international telecommunications center can be measured.

Indonesia – Jakarta has not been cast as an international telecommunications center because of the proximity of Singapore. Although successful long-distance call ratios in 1994 increased to 40% and local calls to 50% and the number of

---

[26] Effective competition is difficult to define. Several factors need to be considered including market shares, profitability, financial condition, ability of carriers to take customers from each other, the extent to which each carrier has to take account of other operators, and responsiveness to consumers.

out-of-order lines declined (1.9 per 100 customers from 2.7 in 1993) it does not rank with Hong Kong, Singapore, Sydney and Tokyo as a regional telecommunications hub. Away from the major cities of Jakarta, Bandung, Surabaya, and Medan the basic telephone services are 'patchy and limited in quality' (Symon, 1994: 19). Waiting lists for new connections have been growing at 12% per year. Paradoxically, only 2.5 million of 3.7 million telephone lines in Indonesia have been sold and the fiber-optic line between Jakarta and Surabaya, the second largest city, is poorly utilized. This has led to Indonesia being targeted by corporations from Australia and other countries; not as an international telecommunications center but as a growth market for telecommunications equipment exports.

INDUSTRY DEVELOPMENT

Much emphasis in Australia has been placed on deriving exports from the local telecommunications equipment industry to compensate for the small Australian market (Allen Consulting Group, 1991).[27] Australia's fortunes will be dictated by the purchasing policies of Telstra and Optus (providing 70% of local needs). Asia–Pacific markets for switching systems and optical fiber and submarine cable have also been identified.[28] Although local arms of major overseas companies, such as Alcatel and Ericsson, dominate the Australian industry's output, significant local operations include Exicom and Olex Cables (which has a relationship with NEC).[29] Scope also exists for managing network facilities and training.

Telstra wants to be seen as the pre-eminent telecommunications provider throughout the Asia–Pacific – a regional rather than a global strategy. As yet, it is not a big player outside Australia. It hopes to increase the amount of revenue offshore to compensate for losses from increased domestic competition. Already, Telstra has assisted the development of network systems and services in Cambodia, Laos, Kazakhstan, Sakhalin, and Vietnam (BTCE, 1995a: 48). However, much of the prospective investment is in low-return telephone services rather than in the higher yielding international network. Joint ventures have been undertaken in India, Hong Kong, Sri Lanka, and Thailand. Telstra also has a licence to operate a digital mobile service in New Zealand and a public telephone licence in the United Kingdom (with Ericsson Ltd).

On occasions, Telstra's regional ambitions have been thwarted. Its partnership with Hutchison Communications in Hong Kong has been dissolved. Proposed deals with Benpres Holdings (owned by the Lopez family) in the Philippines did not

---

[27] ITU (1994: 1) estimated global revenue at US$120 billion – the Australian industry accounting for 2% of the total.

[28] In 1993, the turnover of the Australian telecommunications equipment industry was estimated at $A3.2 billion. Exports totalled $A550. Research and development by local equipment suppliers was estimated at $A170 million (5.3% of industry turnover) (BTCE, 1995a).

[29] Questions have been asked whether the winners in this new export push into the Asia-Pacific region will be indigenous companies or locally-based multinationals.

come to fruition. The proposed link with the Binariang Group was aborted because of the reluctance of the Malaysian Government to support a foreign carrier. Telstra's emphasis is now on Indonesia which, like Vietnam, is seen as a high growth market for Australia's telecommunications initiatives.[30]

Most telecommunications expenditure in Indonesia will be on carrier activities, with up to three-quarters spent on services rather than equipment (BTCE, 1991). In 1993, Indonesia's exports of telecommunications products reached US$400 million (Steel, 1994). Much of the Indonesian market is closed to Australian companies through various restrictions on entry (unless they can be overcome through bilateral and multilateral agreements). For example, rivals Optus and Telstra have teamed up in a joint venture, Jasurus, and are cooperating with PT Indosat in a $A120 million supply contract. The contract, awarded to the Sydney-based company Alcatel, is to build a 2,000 km high-speed broadband communications network between Port Hedland in Western Australia and Jakarta.

Even where Australian manufacturers have had access to the Indonesian market there will be intense competition from other exporting countries, notably Japan and the United States. (Both the Japanese banks and the US Ex-Im Bank are willing to invest in Indonesia's telecommunications system.) Symptomatic of the nature of the competition in Indonesia is the creation of PT NEC Nusantara Communications to design, produce, sell, install, and maintain digital switching systems. This is a joint venture between NEC and PT Humpuss.[31] The main customer is PT Telkom. Another insight into the Indonesian way of doing business is provided by the private sector's participation in telephone development.

Private Participation in Indonesia – The KSO Contracts

The Indonesian Government decided to maintain PT Telkom's monopoly over fixed-line services but invited private participation in the building of 2 million telephone lines in different parts of the country other than Jakarta and East Java. These lines were part of the 5 million targeted in the present Five Year Development Plan, 1994–1999 (*Repelita VI*) – the other 3 million will be built by PT Telkom in Jakarta and Surabaya (APTA, 1994).[32] The increase in Indonesia's switching capacity from 3 million lines to 8 million lines will cost $US6 billion. Previously, PT Telkom offered a profit-sharing arrangement (known as *Pola Bagi Hasil* or PBH joint ventures).[33] PT Telkom's new strategy was to offer joint operation schemes (known as a *Kerja Sama Operasi* or KSO contracts) as a means of

---

[30] The attention of Australian firms will be concentrated on cellular mobile paging, data communications and value-added services. Although there will be few opportunities on the physical data network there may be scope for value-added operators to offer electronic mail, voice messaging and electronic data interchange (Langdale, 1992b).

[31] PT Humpuss is headed by former President Suharto's youngest son, Hutomo Mandala Putra (Tommy) Suharto.

[32] The target of 5 million lines includes 400,000 mobile connections.

[33] Nine revenue sharing projects have been established under *Pola Bagi Hasil* with the revenue split 70:30 between Telkom and the private party.

handing over the less profitable parts of the domestic system for competing foreign operators to manage.[34]

In response to the initial tender for 2 million lines, 138 companies registered for the joint operations scheme – 120 companies buying the prequalification documents. Of these, 12 consortia (comprising Indonesian and international companies) passed the prequalification phase for the 2 million telephone lines. One of the shortlisted consortia included Australia's Telstra (Table 6).[35] Significant omissions from this second list were BellSouth, Bell Atlantic and PTT Telecom of the Netherlands; the names of Indonesia's Maharani and Elektrindo Nusantara companies linked to President Suharto's second daughter, Siti Hediati Prabowo, and second son, Bambang Trihatmodjo, respectively; and the Salim and Lippo groups, Indonesia's leading Chinese-owned conglomerates. Instead, there were major ethnic Indonesian (*pribumi*) firms such as Alatief Corporation and Intidaya, the government-run PT Indosat and the Astra Group, the country's largest conglomerate.

Five winners were chosen for the joint operations scheme. Australia's Telstra was one of five winners with Japan's NTT. The winners were asked to team up with one of the seven losers by the Minister of Telecommunications, Joop Ave, to form larger consortia (APTA, 1995b).[36] Cable & Wireless of Britain and New Zealand Telecom dropped out, but the proposed marriages with the remaining five did not eventuate. Consequently, agreements were signed with the five winners in November 1995 to operate existing lines and build 2 million lines in five of Indonesia's seven regions. The five winning consortia will Build, Own and Operate (BOO) the regional networks under PT Telkom's umbrella in West Java, Central Java, Sumatra, Kalimantan, and Eastern Provinces. Collectively, these regions possessed 47% of the lines then in service (Table 7). Three regions – Greater Jakarta area (Jabotabek), Bandung, and East Java – remain in PT Telkom's hands.

The consortia were given until March 1999 to install the specified lines (though some analysts do not believe the line installation targets were feasible). One stipulation was that the private operators employed existing Telkom staff in their operations – a departure from usual BOO agreements. Significantly, there will be no further rights to additional lines in their franchise areas after that date. As compensation for the joint operation scheme PT Telkom will receive initial payments, Minimum Telkom Revenue (MTR) and a share of distributable income from each consortium (70:30 for existing lines and 30:70 for new lines).

After 15 years the networks will revert to PT Telkom. By then PT Telkom should have netted US$6.7 billion. As these deals weighed heavily against the

---

[34] The *Kerja Sama Operasi* (KSO) is similar to privatization on a Build Operate and Transfer (BOT) basis but Indonesian authorities prefer to describe it as a Joint Operations Scheme (JOS) with profit sharing.

[35] Telstra has an investment in a private trunk network in Jakarta, Bandung and Surabaya (SI, 1994).

[36] Reportedly, France Telecom and Astra were asked to team up with the Sinar Mas Group and Deutsche Telekom; the Rajawali Group and Nynex with Tiga-A and US West (which were not among those shortlisted); Telstra and Indosat with the Maharani Group; and Bukaka and Singapore Telecom with either the Bimantara Group and Cable & Wireless and Kanematsu, or Nusa Telekomindo and GTE of the US (APTA, 1995c,d).

NEIGHBOURS – AUSTRALIAN AND INDONESIAN TELECOMMUNICATIONS CONNECTIONS

Table 6 Pre-qualified Bidders for the Private Installation of Telephone Lines, 1994

Indonesian partner	Indonesian affiliation	Foreign partner	Target market
PT Widya Duta Informindo	PT Indosat	Telstra (Australia)	Central Java/ Sumatra
PT Intertel Nusa Perdana	Astra Group	France Telecom	Central Java/ Sumatra
PT Bukaka Telekomindo	Fadel Muhammad	Singapore Telecom International	Eastern Indonesia (sole bidder)/ Sumatra
PT Kartika Eka Mas Nusantara	Sinar Mas Group and Yayasan Kartika Eka Paksi (Army Foundation)	Deutsche Bundespot Telekom	Central Java/West Java
PT Maharani and PT Tripatra Engineering	Siti Hutami Endang Adiningsih ('Mamiek') former President Suharto's youngest daughter	Telecom New Zealand, Nissho Iwai	Central Java
PT Telekomindo	Rajawali Group	Nynex(US) Tomen Corp. (Japan)	Not known
PT Centralindo	Jatikusomo Family	Bell Canada Mitsui Corp. (Japan)	Sumatra
PT Elektrindo Nusantara	Bimantara Group (controlled by President's son Bambang Trihatmodjo)[1]	Cable & Wireless (UK), Kanematsu (Japan)	Sumatra/West Java
PT Intidaya Sistelindo Mitra	Alatief Corp.	Malaysia Telecom American International Group	Kalimantan/ Sumatra
PT Nusa Telekomindo Internusa	Arifin Pangigoro, Rianto Nurhad	GTE (US)	Sumatra
Aditarina Sumatera	Poco Sutowo	Sprint (US)	Not known
PT Krisna Duta	Bambang Yoga	Korea Telecom	Kalimantan/ Central Java

Note: [1] Other shareholders include PT Karya Teka Panca Murni (25%), Azbindo Nusantara (14%), Adipta Adidhana (5%) and Astagina Praksatama (5%).

Source: *Project and Trade Finance*, June 30, 1994; APTA, 1995b,c.

188

Table 7 Details of the Five Consortia Awarded Contracts by the Indonesian Government to Build Two Million Telephone Lines, November 1995

Consortium	Minimum lines (Region)	Foreign Partners	Indonesian Partner
PT Pramindo Ikat Nusantara	517,000 lines (Division I Sumatra) Cost US$570 million Existing lines 417,417 (Operational HQ Medan)	French Cable et Radio (subsidiary of France Telecom) (35%); Marubeni (Corp. 8%); Nichimen (1%), International Finance Corp. (4%); and Commonwealth Development Corp. (4%)	PT Astratel Nusantara (subsidiary of Astra International group) (60% reduced to 42.5%); Prinkopparpostel, staff cooperative of Ministry of Tourism, Post and Telecommunications (2%) and PT Intertel Pratama Media, the cooperative of telecoms ministry employees (3%)
PT Aria West International (Tiga-A)	500,00 lines (Division III West Java) Cost US$600 million Existing lines 266,841	US West Inc.(35%)	Asian Infrastructure Fund (12.5%); PT Arimas Kencana Murni (52.5%) and PT Aria Bahtera Internusa. Tiga-A is connected with Ari Sigit, former Present Suharto's grandson.
Mitra Global Telekomunikasi	400,000 lines (Division IV Central Java) Cost US$640 million (Operational HQ Semarang) Existing lines 241,792	Telstra Corp Ltd (20%); Nippon Telegraph and Telephone (10% increased to 15%); Itochu (1.25%); Sumitomo (1.25%)	PT Widya Duta Infomindo (subsidiary of PT Indosat) (30%). Others (30%) Note: Kokarindo and PT Krida Salindo Sentosa. Cooperatives Kopnatel (5%) and Kopindosat (2.4%) were later dropped and their shares taken by foreign companies.
PT Daya Mitra Malindo	237,000 lines (Division VI Kalimantan) Cost US$250 million Existing lines 94,937	Telekom Malaysia Bhd (25%) later replaced by Cable & Wireless; American International Assurance Group (AIA), Singapore (9.68%); TM Communications (UK) Ltd of Hong Kong (9.68%)	PT Alatief Nusakarya Corporation owned by Abdul Latief, Minister of Manpower (1993–98) (24%); Intidaya Sistelindomira owned by PT Telkom and Tanri Abeng, an executive of PT Bakrie and Brothers (29.03%); and Kopthindo, a tea producers cooperative (2.42%)
PT Bukaka Singtel International	403,000 lines (Division VII Eastern region – Sulawesi, Irian Jaya, Maluku and Nusa Tenggara) Existing lines 271,137	Singapore Telecom International (40%)	PT Bukaka Telokomindo International (60%) owned by Fadel Muhamad.

Source: Various.

foreign company and local partner, some concessions were barely profitable.[37] The international companies hope that their presence will provide an opportunity for future, more lucrative contracts. Malaysia Telkom has already pulled out of the Kalimantan region and has been replaced by Cable & Wireless.

The changes in the composition of the Daya Mitro Malindo have delayed the securing of loan agreements to finance the project. Telstra's group, Mitra Global Telekomunikasi, the Central Java KSO, was the third group to finalize finance after Primindo Ikat, the Sumatra KSO, and Aria West, the West Java KSO, though the other group, Bukaka Singtel, had also made arrangements (APTA, 1996f). After an initial delay over which members of the consortium would take charge of the funding of Mitra Global both Australian and Japanese banks, anxious to support Telstra and NTT respectively, have taken charge. Funding has been attracted from 16 banks led by Australia's ANZ Bank, Japan's Dai Ichi Kangyo and Deutsche Morgan Grenfell Asia.

In seeking markets in Indonesia, Australian producers of telecommunications services and related equipment should not ignore Indonesian capabilities. Already, PT Indosat has won a tender for telecommunications facility construction and refurbishment in Cambodia.

FUTURES

The information revolution has yet to occur in both Australia and Indonesia. Telephones are still an instrument for voice communications for the average consumer; personal computers are far from being universal in the home; and television is still used principally for free-to-air broadcasts (though the video cassette market is significant) (Cheah, 1994). Mega-deals between USWest/Time Warner and AT&T/McCaw Cellular Communications have signalled future strategic directions for both countries. Interests in Indonesia have been more concerned with network rollout and penetration (though PT Matahari Lintas Cakrawala is the pioneering operator of Indovision direct broadcast satellite TV service). Within the more mature Australian market major local and overseas commercial interests are restructuring their organizations, to introduce new consumer services through a range of delivery platforms. These will be discussed before returning to implications for Indonesia.

The restrictions on pay-TV in Australia were removed in 1992. This led to the formation of new partnerships such as Pay Television Australia comprising News Corporation, three commercial networks, and Telstra (Chadwick, 1995). Referred to as the Packer, Murdoch, and Telstra or PMT consortium, this partnership was dissolved in September 1994 because the group failed to win a licence to deliver

---

[37] The KSO units are trying to keep down infrastructure costs by using wireless local loop technology for 25% of the 2 million total line commitments. This technology is very useful in areas with high line densities. Other wireless technology is expected to be used in sparsely-populated and geographically difficult concessions (e.g. East Indonesia and Kalimantan).

Table 8 *Cross Media Links in Australia*

Telcos	Pay-TV	Free TV	Print
Telstra (Public ownership)	Foxtel Australis (Murdoch 20%/ Telstra)	Seven (Murdoch 14.9%)	News Ltd (Murdoch)
Optus (51% local, 49% US & UK interests)	Optus Vision (Optus, Packer, US interests)	Nine (Packer)	Fairfax (Black 25%, Packer 17.25% as at 17/2/95, Murdoch 5%)
	Visionstream (Murdoch/Telstra)	Ten (Can West and assorted locals)	Publishing & Broadcasting Ltd (Packer)
	ABS-Fairfax Venture	ABC (Public ownership)	APN (O'Reilly)
	PAN TV (SBS, Stokes, O'Reilly)	SBS (Public ownership)	Canberra Times (Stokes)

Source: Chadwick, 1995: 3.

pay-TV by satellite.[38] The winner was Australis Media's pay-TV unit, Galaxy Television. Further strategic alliances between telecommunications, pay-TV, free-TV and the print media have occurred – the old print media being the springboard into the new media (Table 8). Telstra and Murdoch joined together in Foxtel pay-TV (which sought unsuccessfully to merge with Australis) to compete against the other cable partnership Optus Vision which included Packer.[39] Pay-TV profits were not the sole motivation of these alliances – pay-TV provided an entry point into the potential profits to be derived from the integration of pay-TV, telephony (including the local call market), and broadband services (Joseph, 1993).[40] Mirroring activity in the United States, the alliances were 'aimed at a combination of improved financial backing and financial risk taking; some arise from changes to the regulatory framework and the joining of different skills' (BTCE, 1994d: 125–6).

---

[38] A merger between Foxtel, the cable venture of Telstra and News Ltd, and Australis, the satellite and microwave broadcaster, to offer entertainment, publishing and communications services to Australians was disallowed by the Australian Competition and Consumer Commission (ACCC). The ACCC considered the joint venture lessened competition in the pay-TV and telephony markets with Optus Vision (a partnership between Optus Communications, Continental Cable Vision of the US, and Seven and Nine TV networks). In December 1994, the Seven and Nine TV Networks withdrew because the communications ministry would not grant closed access to the cable network after 1997. Seven TV returned later.

[39] As both the cable companies – Foxtel and Optus – had movie channels, much depended on their access to the top audience-drawing local sport. Foxtel was originally favoured by the Federal Court's decision on 4 October 1996 acceding to News Corporation's plans for a Super League rebel rugby league in competition with the official Australian Rugby League for which Optus had pay-TV rights (Deakin, 1996).

[40] After ten years the entire Australian pay-TV market will generate $A1.4 billion whereas telephone revenues already exceed $A15 billion (APTA, 1995e).

The alliances highlight a quantum leap in the vertical integration of Australia's information, entertainment, computer, consumer electronics, and communications industries which raise a range of both new and predictable technical, economic, social, and regulatory issues for government. This process was further influenced by the priority given by the Clinton Administration in the United States to the establishment of the National Information Infrastructure (NII). More generally, it was affected by developments such as the Internet, mobile communications, private data banks, 'multimedia', and the prospects of a Global Information Infrastructure (GII) (US Secretary of Commerce, 1994). These fundamental changes prompted the Australian Government to establish the Communications Futures Project (CFP) and the Broadband Services Expert Group (BSEG, 1995).

AUSTRALIA'S COMMUNICATIONS FUTURES PROJECT

The task of the Communications Futures Project has been to explore the technological changes occurring in telecommunications between 1995 and 2005; the potential market responses to technology options; and the implications for regulatory structures of telecommunications, commercial broadcasting, and radio communications (BTCE, 1994a; 1995b). Four streams of activity have been pursued:

- emerging information, entertainment and communications services (content – voice, audio, video, and data – and marketing) (BTCE, 1994b,c);
- delivery technologies (including the extension of Australia's fiber optic network to the majority of houses, businesses and educational institutions) (BTCE, 1994d,e,f,g);
- market behavior (i.e. emerging pattern of commercial relationships within and between traditional industries); and
- policy and regulation.

Papers have been published on the first two streams (the third stream is unlikely to be published for commercial confidentiality reasons). The final report also considers policy and regulatory matters (BTCE, 1995b).

A key feature of the study of emerging information, entertainment, and communications services has been the identification of the main information and communication service markets in Australia and determination of their relative value by users (Table 9). Five categories were identified as being of obvious value to users: home entertainment and related services; communication services; transactional services; business information systems; and on-line information systems. The main focus of the Communications Futures Project was on residential networks (the pay-TV market and the prospects of other broadband products such as video-on-demand, video-telephony, and the transmission of high quality pictures). Not only were residential networks a key area of policy concern, but they were a neglected research focus in Australia, amenable to economic analysis and possessing more data than the business communications market.

Information on delivery platform technologies was derived from the Broadband Study – an expert group established to look at extending Australia's optical fiber network to houses, schools, and educational institutions (BSEG, 1995). The

Table 9 *Categorization of the Main Information and Communication Markets in Australia Showing Indicative Relative Values*

	Entertainment	Communications	Information
Business or intermediate services	Low value	High value (e.g. telephone, fax, E-mail, Internet)	High value (e.g. IT, PCs, Info systems)
Relative value		♦ ♦ ♦ ♦ ♦ ♦ ♦ ♦ ♦	♦ ♦ ♦ ♦ ♦ ♦
Home or consumer services	High value e.g. television, electronic and video games	High value e.g. telephone	Moderate value (e.g. newspapers, magazines, books)
Relative value	♦ ♦ ♦ ♦ ♦	♦ ♦ ♦ ♦	♦ ♦ ♦

Source: BTCE, 1994b: 139.

Broadband Study focused on the preconditions for technical, economic, and commercial viability of the widespread delivery of broadband services by optic fiber. A complementary study by the Bureau of Transport and Communications Economics (BTCE, 1994d) examined existing two cable-based systems – copper wire and coaxial cable – and wireless-based systems (terrestrial broadcasting, multipoint distribution systems, satellite and mobile communications).

The Communications Futures Project analysed both future cable-based (e.g. asymmetric digital subscriber lines and optic fiber) and wireless-based platform technologies using digital compression. Then, it assessed their commercial implications for Australian investors and regional satellite operators. Given the risks in the industry and high costs in establishing broadband cable networks the Project's conclusions heralded platform pluralism and many channels for Australia (the country is unique in that satellite, microwave and cable television commenced virtually simultaneously).[41] Network evolution is likely to commence with wireless platforms which will be overtaken by cable systems in urban areas.

Competing platforms and channel abundance challenge many of the assumptions underlying the present regulation of telecommunications and broadcasting. Of particular interest is the possibility of upgrading the universal service obligation, providing all Australians with reasonable access to the telephone system in a market less densely settled and more geographically dispersed than many other advanced capitalist countries (BTCE, 1994g). Assuming all households take up the different levels of service, Net Present Values for supplying hybrid fiber cable services to different geographical areas, for example, shows a deficit for rural and

---

[41] Australia is still a greenfields site as it adopted pay-TV later than the United States, Europe and other countries (BTCE, 1995b). Regulatory regimes differ between Australia and other countries. Australia's two telecommunications carriers are free to provide broadband services including pay-TV, whereas telecos are prohibited from engaging in such services in the United States. British Telecom can provide switched broadband services (e.g. video-on-demand) but not broadcast video services.

Table 10   Indicative Total Costs of Alternative Hybrid Fiber Cable-based Universal Service Obligations ($A million)

	Inner urban	Outer urban	Provincial cities	Rural	Remote
Distributive (pay-TV services)	1,500	–150	100	–5,200	–3,200
Interactive home recreation/ Centralized home transactions	2,600	1,100	750	600	0
Communicative home video	5,200	2,100	2,100	2,200	500
Total	9,300	3,050	2,950	–2,400	–2,700

Note: Inner urban – metropolitan area (household density 500 sq. km^2; outer urban – metropolitan area (household density 500 km^2; provincial cities population 5,000 households and household density 200 km^2; rural not provincial – areas less than 100 km from a provincial center; and remote – areas greater than 100 km from a provincial or urban center.

Source: BTCE, 1994g: 16, 71.

remote areas (Table 10). Apart from some inner urban areas dual rollout between cable providers is unlikely to be economic and broadband services providing home transactions are unlikely to be viable, until after the year 2000. In short, the proponents Telstra and Optus Vision have underestimated the costs of connecting inner and outer suburbs and overestimated penetration rates of pay-TV and cable telephony services.

These findings by the Communication Futures Project suggest that the broadband cable networks proposed by Telstra (using underground cabling) and Optus (using power poles for its cabling) will reach about 50% of the houses in Australia, at a cost of more than $A3 billion (US$2.25 billion) each.[42] Neither is likely to be viable based on pay-TV.[43] Wireless services based on satellite/microwave technology offered by Australis have inherent cost advantages but the Australian 'time rich and income poor' market may be simply too small to make them cost-effective.[44] (By 1997 Telstra had laid a $A3.9 billion digital cable network to reach

---

[42] Optus Vision's aerial cable TV and telephony network in Melbourne and Sydney is experiencing vocal opposition because it involves 17mm thick black cable suspended from power poles. Optus, like Telstra and Vodafone, has been exempt from the operation of state, territory and local government laws when erecting, installing and maintaining telecommunications facilities (COA, 1996: 148). These powers were conferred in the Telecommunications Act 1991 to facilitate rapid and efficient rollout of telecommunications networks, particularly during the period of facilities-based competition between 1991 and 1997. The hybrid coaxial cable being laid may be obsolete within ten years (COA, 1996: 144).

[43] The costs of connecting all households to the new services in Australia would be huge. Likely costs for the hybrid optic fiber coaxial cable was an estimated $A25 billion for the initial distributive network; an additional $5 billion for centralized services such as video-on-demand and $A11 billion for limited communicative services such as video-telephony (BTCE, 1995b: xvi).

[44] Paradoxically, most of the established players discounted the satellite/microwave technology. Microwave offered only a poor coverage over Australia's irregular terrain and no possibility of interactive services. Although satellite offered a wider coverage and faster return on capital investments a parallel telephone network was required for interactive services.

2.5 million of the 4 million targeted homes).[45] Telstra has also asked Belcore, the research arm of the United States regional carrier, to design software to transfer its telephony services to its cable network – a strategy offering huge cost savings through lower maintenance and running costs of an integrated network.

The Communications Futures team admits little is known of what Australians want from the new multimedia technology; or the social benefits and costs, even after publishing substantial work-in-progress papers and a final report. Promotion of telecommunications by the Australian Government as part of an efficient and internationalized economy has to be counterbalanced by minimizing the geographical and social inequalities brought about by the uneven spread of the broadband network (Langdale, 1996). Bringing forward Telstra's broadband cable plans for full interactive media services, however, has the advantage of generating skills which could be exported to Asia when interactive multimedia is in vogue.

Indonesia, for instance, will have a population of 290 million by 2020 (Edwards *et al.*, 1994). Already, the prospects offered by this market have been anticipated by News Corp Ltd. Its Asian satellite television broadcaster, Star TV, has forged an alliance with Indonesia's pay pioneer, PT Matahari Lintas Cakrawala, to bring its new subscription channels to the country – the Indonesian-owned satellite Palapa B2P will be used for the purpose. By complementing face-to-face meetings, Australian broadband telecommunications and interactive media could spur trade with Indonesia in education, health, and tourism services.

CONCLUSIONS

All economies – developed and developing – are information economies. An examination of Australian and Indonesian telecommunications has highlighted the issue of 'information rich' economies versus 'information poor' economies. This issue still looms large in the Asia–Pacific region and underlines the fact that half the world's population is not within two hours of a telephone (Lamberton, 1994). Australia's challenge is to capture the benefits of competition, positioning itself to provide high quality innovative infrastructure and advanced services within the Asia–Pacific region.

Concerns in Australia include the degree to which competitive success hinges on administered decisions rather than market place competition and the inevitability of increased competition leading to improved economic performance (Van der Vries, 1996; Joseph, 1993). The concerns are most apparent in issues involving local telephone networks and pay-TV on which, according to Quiggin (1996: 123), Australian decision-makers have 'flunked'. 'Duplication of telecommunications infrastructure [by Telstra and Optus] makes no economic sense, since the same service could be provided with a single network at round half the capital cost'. These concerns highlight that Australia is further along the road of

---

[45] Subsequently, Telstra decided to scale back on its broadband infrastructure plans (APTA, 1997d).

liberalization than Indonesia. The challenge for Indonesia is still network rollout and penetration.

Both countries have used their telecommunications industries to pursue national objectives. Australia has sought to create a world class industry capable of being internationally competitive in the next century. Indonesia has pursued investments in telecommunications as the 'essential engine' to boost skills formation and develop a national research and development programme. This programme is based on the application of information technology to industrialization. Clearly, Indonesia's aim is to benefit from the multiplier and linkage effects of the information sector such as business services (Karunaratne and Jussawalla, 1988). An improvement in the performance of Indonesia's telecommunications industry offers Australian producers of telecommunications services opportunities to develop stronger international linkages, joint ventures, and technology transfers.

Australia's structural adjustment and labor market reforms have increased international competitiveness and contributed to the development of a more outward looking business culture. Indonesia's deregulation of its financial sector and increasing liberalization of its productive activities have opened up the economy to foreign investment and improved its export performance. In telecommunications, the Indonesian Government has opened the door to overseas firms, but has retained the key by declaring any basic services must be operated by state-owned companies.

EPILOGUE

The distinction between the Australian deregulatory approach towards open competition and the Indonesian privatization approach which underpinned this chapter has become blurred. The Australian Government is now moving towards Indonesia's position on privatization. Indonesia's position has been affected by the Asian economic crisis following the targeting of the Indonesian rupiah on 21 July 1997. Before discussing the abnormal effects of Indonesia's predicament the change in Australian policy is outlined.

AUSTRALIAN PRIVATIZATION

The Coalition Government's original policy was to sell one-third of Telstra. While the Government had the numbers to pass the Telstra (Dilution of Public Ownership) Bill 1996 in the House of Representatives, it did not have a majority in the Senate (APTA, 1996g). Consequently, the Senate was able to send the Bill for consideration by its Environment, Communications and the AAJ Reference Committee. Subsequently, the Committee produced a report entitled *Telstra: To Sell or not to Sell?* (COA, 1996). Predictably, two diametrically opposed views were presented by Opposition and Government Senators.

The Committee found:

- the proposed sale would reduce the value of the public sector;[46]
- competition and regulation, not ownership, were the primary drivers of efficiency in telecommunications;
- privatization would hurt Australia's R&D effort in telecommunications and retard the development of its telecommunications equipment industry;
- privatization would have an adverse effect on rural and regional Australia.

On these grounds the Committee recommended Telstra should remain in public ownership; and the legislation should be divided into two Bills – one for the private sale and the other for the Consumer Service Guarantee.

A minority report by the Government Senators (COA, 1996: 1–95) rejected the Committee's key recommendations. The main thrust of the minority report was that 'part privatization' will:

- make Telstra more efficient operationally when gauged by OECD benchmarks on digitalization, revenue per employee and lines per employee;[47]
- give Telstra more commercial freedom (including greater access to capital and greater capacity to form joint ventures);
- give Telstra greater clarity of purpose by freeing it from political interference;
- bring benefits to users similar to those derived from the sale of British Telecom – a dramatic improvement in service quality, a 50% reduction in business bills and a 20% reduction in low use residential bills.[48]
- bring national economic benefits, boost public savings, benefit the supplier industry, and create economic activity – employment gains would occur in rural and regional Australia through a reduction in the cost of non-metropolitan communications.

The Government Senators, however, did not entertain a structural separation of Telstra, such as the mobile phone business or the Yellow Pages, before any sell-off. This strategy would not only realize more cash but reduce the concentration of market power yielded by Telstra.

In 1997, the Coalition Government was able to pass the necessary legislation to sell one-third of Telstra after attracting the support of two non-Government Senators (in return for special benefits for the States of Queensland and Victoria).[49] Prior to part privatization, Telstra was required by the current Australian Government to complete its network digitalization and offer universal access to its

---

[46] In evidence to the Committee Professor Quiggin estimated the value of Telstra in public ownership was $A54.4 billion, based on savings in public debt interest represented by the flow of profits to the enterprise' (COA, 1996: 59).

[47] Australia has 123 lines per employee compared with 160 for the United Kingdom, 187 for Canada and 223 for the United States (COA, 1996: 23).

[48] The privatisation of Telcom New Zealand, according to the minority report, has resulted in similar benefits (COA, 1996: 35).

[49] The key features of the privatization plan are a strict 35% foreign shareholding limit, service guarantees and price caps to allay fears about control shifting overseas, prices rising and service to rural areas declining.

Integrated Services Digital Network (ISDN) network by June 1997, rather than by its previous deadline of 2000. Also, Telstra has shed 24,000 of its 76,000 full-time employees to achieve OECD benchmarks on main lines per employee and revenue per employee. The sale of Telstra for A$14.3 billion was seen as so successful by the Coalition Government that, once re-elected it passed the Further Dilution of Public Ownership Act 1999 and sold an additional 16.6 per cent (and would like to sell the remaining 51 per cent but does not have the support of the Senate). Although there was political opposition to the sale because of Telstra's public service obligations the greatest threat to investor confidence is likely to come from the Australian Competition and Consumer Commission's (ACCC) action to open the network on more favourable terms to its competitors following deregulation on July 1, 1997. The ACCC is likely to order Telstra to provide unbundled local call resale 30% below the current retail price (APTA, 1998b).

Further, the Australian Government is under pressure from the Australian Telecommunications Users' Group (ATUG) to impose a charter on Telstra. This would require Telstra to concentrate on its core domestic telephony business rather than on pursuing high-risk overseas public network licences unless there was some benefit to its Australian consumers – a criterion that Telstra's Indonesian interests may not be able to satisfy.

INDONESIA IN CRISIS

Paradoxically, Indonesian telecommunications firms have been urged to seek jobs in other countries with foreign partners. PT Linthasartha was established by PT Indosat, private banks and joint ventures to engage in cooperative projects with PT Telkom (PT Telkom owns 25%, PT Indosat 18.8% with the balance being owned by cooperatives, state-owned banks, and foundations affiliated with the telecommunications industry). This thrust has been curtailed by the economic crisis of 1997–98 which has resulted in a negative Gross National Product. What are the other implications of the crisis on telecommunications? As it is not possible to catalogue the list of Indonesian telecommunications projects delayed or postponed (including many Personal Communications Handy-phone Service projects and satellite launches) attention is focused on the key items featured in this chapter – PT Telkom, PT Indosat, cellular phones, and KSO contracts (APTA, 1997b,c, 1998c,d,e).

- *PT Telkom* – As its overseas loans were not well hedged, the company experienced heavy foreign exchange losses in 1997 (Rp 722 billion). From April 1, 1998 it has increased its own local and long distance charges by 15% to reflect the devaluation of the rupiah. Telephone subscription charges have increased. The local telephone pulse rate has increased from Rp 125 to Rp 145. International calls have risen by 25% in rupiah terms. These increases are deemed inadequate as they were based on Rp 5,000 to the US dollar rather than the rate of Rp 10,000.
- *PT Indosat* – The company has increased international tariffs because the devaluation of the rupiah and cheaper costs in Indonesia could generate a foreign currency loss.

- *Cellular phones* – Little or no growth is expected in the cellular market. In rupiah terms the cost of a cellular phone has increased fourfold and dealers have reduced their cellular phone inventories. Cellular airtime charges have been increased by 20% (Rp 325 per minute) and further rises are anticipated if the rupiah does not strengthen against international currencies. A net decline in cellular users is anticipated with the departure of expatriates and pressures on corporate customers to restrict their use. Analogue users are worst hit with Komselindo losing one-third of its subscribers. No account has been taken of defaulters who switch to another operator. Subscription fraud is rife and the three GSM operators are exchanging information on delinquent subscribers. The prospect of increasing the ceiling on foreign investment would assist local operators though the market is unattractive until the currency stabilizes.

- *KSO Contracts* – The likelihood of joint operation schemes (the *Kerja Sama Operasi* or KSO contracts discussed earlier) failing to fulfil their rollout contracts led to PT Telkom waiving the conditions of default for an agreed period but it was reluctant to change the minimum telecom revenue arrangements or give the KSO operators a more favourable sharing formula. In particular, the KSOs are heavily reliant on long-distance revenues. When the KSO operators signed their contracts the rupiah was at 2,246 to the US dollar. The five KSOs are now exposed to debts estimated at between US$300 million and US$550 million each. Four out of five KSOs have stopped their rollout. Only the Mitra Global Telekomunikasi consortium supported by Telstra and NTT has continued because it had hedged against foreign exchange losses.

Analysts are predicting the consolidation of the Indonesian telecommunications industry may be more difficult to achieve because of the institutional and structural rigidities discussed in this comparison with Australia.

ACKNOWLEDGEMENTS

Assistance in obtaining literature was received from Maurice Haddad, former Director of the Bureau of Transport and Communications Economics and the staff of its library. Sandra Davenport provided research assistance and Elanna Lowes and Christine Tabart editorial assistance. The figures were drawn by Nigel Duffey and Ian Heyward, Cartographic Section, Research School of Pacific and Asian Studies, The Australian National University, Canberra.

CHAPTER 11

THE ECONOMIC DEVELOPMENT OF PERIPHERAL RURAL AREAS IN THE INFORMATION AGE

Ranald Richardson and Andrew Gillespie

INTRODUCTION

This chapter is concerned with the prospects for the economic development of rural places in the 'information age'. It critically reviews a series of policy measures which have been undertaken over the past decade aimed at creating the information economy in rural areas, particularly those relating to employment. It argues that policy approaches have been too narrowly focused around the supposed distance-shrinking powers of new technology and, in particular, have failed to take into account the realities of market relationships between urban and rural areas.

'Rurality' is not easy to define, but our focus is on 'deep rural' places (Huws *et al.*, 1996) rather than the rural hinterlands of urban areas. By 'deep rural' we mean regions which are physically remote from major centers of population, which are relatively inaccessible, and are sparsely populated, though they may include some small urban centers which are more accessible. Economically, these places tend to be characterized by income levels below the national average, and by over-reliance on agriculture, extractive industries, and basic processing industries, which in many areas are in decline.

Reading some of the most influential commentators' reflections on the information society, one might expect a bright future for peripheral rural regions. Early commentators such as Toffler (1980) suggested that the new communications technologies have 'anti-centralist' tendencies. Early speculation on the spatial-organizational tendencies of new technologies by Nilles also suggested a shift towards decentralization (Nilles *et al.*, 1976; Nilles, 1985). Nilles (1985) proposed a four-stage locational model for the service sector that is derived from the product model of manufacturing (Glasmeier and Howland, 1994). In the first stage, employment centralizes in urban areas. In the second stage, decentralization occurs, primarily through the outflow of back-office type functions. A third stage may involve relocation of central functions. A fourth phase occurs when employees work at home, connected to their office electronically (Nilles, 1985). This final stage chimes well with Toffler's prediction of a post-industrial economy comprised of 'electronic cottages'.

More recent (otherwise diverse) commentators have also been implicitly or explicitly decentralist, emphasizing the capacity for the new technologies to overcome the friction of distance and the tyranny of geography; thus, Microsoft's

Bill Gates envisages 'friction-free capitalism' (Gates, 1995), in which the lowering of transaction costs is emphasized, Nicholas Negroponte (1995) anticipates the 'digital planet' in which geography has been abolished, and Howard Rheingold (1994) predicts 'virtual communities'.

This rhetoric, which suggests that the natural tendency of the new technology is towards decentralization, has had an extremely powerful effect on policy-makers, including those concerned with regional development. In some respects this influence has been positive in that it has helped energize the debate on rural development, suggesting a different trajectory to those traditionally envisaged. The discourse has also had a negative effect, however, in that its proponents have tended to be guilty of what the American communications scholar James Carey has labelled the 'rhetoric of the technological sublime' (Carey and Quirk, 1989). In this rhetoric, the limitations and/or ills of present society will be overcome by the assumed liberating logic of new, space-shrinking technologies. This rhetoric often fails to take account of historically created differences between places, differences which despite the assumptions embodied in this technological utopia keep re-asserting themselves (Hepworth and Robins, 1988; Gillespie and Robins, 1989; Robins, 1995; Gold, 1991).

In the context of rural development, these rhetorics have led some policy-makers to seek a technological resolution, based on investing in telecommunications infrastructure, to the long-standing structural inadequacies of rural areas. On occasion, this has been accompanied by hyperbole which sees the balance of rural and urban development shifting radically, with rural areas 'leap-frogging' urban areas.

There seems little prospect, however, of the fundamental reordering of the space economy between urban and rural places which is implicit in the writings of some technology enthusiasts. Indeed, several commentators, although accepting that some economic activity will decentralize, have suggested that telecommunications may have a spatially *centralizing* effect on other economic activities, particularly higher order activities, in that they complement and create new demand for face-to-face contact, rather than substituting for it (Boden and Molotch, 1994). Boden and Molotch (1994) have suggested that what they term the 'compulsion for proximity' may even result in a '"decisive re-agglomeration" of certain aspects of economic activity as the scattering made possible by the new technologies . . . intensif(ies) the need for copresence among those who co-ordinate dispersed activities and interpret the information pouring in from far-flung settings' (Boden and Molotch, 1994: 274). It should be added that many others may seek to remain physically proximate to these key actors in order to enhance their own career or business prospects, thus helping to slow the process of decentralization. Referring specifically to producer services, the presence of which is likely to be crucial to the development of rural areas, Beyers and Lindahl (1997), whilst acknowledging that an expansion of the use of new technologies such as file transfer and fax machines is taking place, conclude that:

> . . . it is clear that face-to-face communications is still the primary way in which the work force in producer services communicates with clients, and is still a very important aspect of the production process (Beyers and Lindahl, 1997: 12).

Not only is there a danger that, for such reasons, productive economic activity will not shift to rural areas through decentralization, there is also a danger that what Grimes has termed 'telecolonization' will occur (Grimes, 1992). As telecommunications and transportation advances provide urban firms with relatively easy access to rural markets, it is argued, urban-based producer firms are able to reach into rural areas and provide efficient and cost-competitive services to businesses and to final consumers (Kirn, Conway and Beyers, 1990). This contention received support from a study for the European Commission by Price Waterhouse (1990), which noted a 'double edge effect' connected with investment in new technology in peripheral places and concluded that while the growth of electronic transaction services would benefit people living and working in rural areas, by improving access to a wider variety of products and services at lower prices, they might also lead to employment loss in these areas, as some rural businesses would be unable to withstand the pressure from urban competitors. A more recent study for the European Commission on technology and rural areas provides empirical evidence to support that view (Ó Siochrú et al., 1995). For example, it cites the case of an Italian bank – The Instituto Bancario San Paolo – based in Turin which undertook a major expansion by taking over smaller banks in towns and rural areas. Using advanced communication systems, the bank experienced phenomenal growth, but at the expense of hundreds of jobs in remote locations, as services to branches are concentrated in Turin, yielding great economies of scale.

The growth of new technologies, then, clearly does not automatically result in the decentralization of economic activity. In this chapter, we argue that the new communications technologies do present some opportunities for economic development in peripheral rural areas (though not a fundamental re-ordering of economies), but do so only within a context of an accompanying and integrated set of policy measures aimed at the economic and social development of these places. Without such policies the positive effects of ICTs, in terms of economic development, will be limited and may even be outweighed by the negative impacts, resulting in rural places falling even further behind core urban regions in the information age.

In the next section we turn to critically examine some of the main policy thrusts which have been developed over the past decade. We look firstly at what we term the infrastructuralist approach and then turn to consider policies aimed at assisting and attracting particular forms of economic activity – small firms, teleworkers, telecottages, and large (mainly inward investing) firms.

INCORPORATING RURAL AREAS INTO THE INFORMATION SOCIETY

AN 'ENDOGENOUS' MODEL

The response that initially dominated information society policies for rural areas can be described as 'infrastructuralist' (Richardson and Gillespie, 1996). This approach appeared to suggest that simply by building a telecommunications infrastructure which could support advanced services, such as digital switching, rural communities would seize the opportunity to take part in the new service-based 'information society'. It soon became clear, however, that infrastructure investment would not, of itself, lead to economic development or employment growth, and policy-makers began to develop initiatives to promote service *demand*, through encouraging the uptake of new technologies amongst local actors. In recent years an 'endogenous' economic development model has come to dominate policy thinking, at least in Europe (see Figure 1(a); Richardson and Gillespie, 1996). This model assumes that advanced infrastructure provision, plus encouragement and support to local economic actors, will result in enhanced access to core markets, and thus will lead to endogenously created employment. The main focus of this approach has been the small- and medium-sized enterprise (SME) sector, taken to include new micro-businesses exploiting the information society opportunities. This focus partly reflects the relative importance of small businesses to rural economies and the general absence of significant employers (beyond perhaps primary industries) in rural areas, but can also be seen as reflecting a more widespread belief among policy-makers that it is this sector which offers the best prospects for employment growth in the information society. It may also reflect the individualistic and 'small is beautiful' ideological stance which permeates much writing on new technologies.

This endogenous approach to rural development is to be applauded in that it recognizes the problems associated with over-dependence on external capital which in the end limited the economic potential of many places in the industrial era. There are, however, a number of deficiencies with the approach, two of which we highlight here. First, evidence suggests that SMEs, whether rural or urban, are slow to adopt advanced telecommunications. Stimulating the adoption of new technologies by this sector in rural or peripheral areas will, therefore, not be straightforward and is likely to take some time.

Second, the model takes only a limited account of the wider socio-economic and spatial characteristics of modern market economies – in particular it does not take account of the reality of market relations between the core and periphery. The model appears to suggest that by providing the advanced infrastructure and services, in conjunction with other demand stimulation measures, rural and peripheral industry will be 'well placed' to gain access to core markets. However, although these elements would be necessary parts of a strategy to integrate firms based in remote regions into core markets, they will not, by themselves, be sufficient. At least two additional elements are required if core markets are to be accessed. First, firms in rural and peripheral regions must have highly developed competencies and skills in order that they can compete effectively in highly open and competitive markets. Second, they must have social, business, and institutional *networks* and *contacts* to enable these competencies and skills to be successfully deployed and marketed. There are good reasons for believing that these conditions will be difficult to meet, imposing a major barrier to the effectiveness of the endogenous model of telecommunications-aided rural development. Research in North America in the 1980s, for example, suggested that rurally-based service firms can be significant exporters, but that those which export tend to be larger, non-locally owned firms (Glasmeier and Borchard, 1989; Stabler and Howe, 1988).

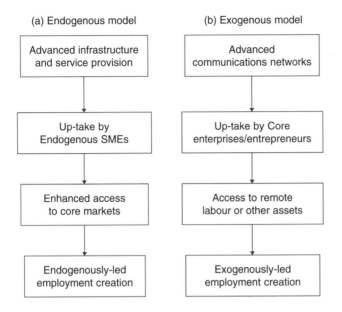

Figure 1 *Models of advanced communications and rural employment growth*

AN ALTERNATIVE TO THE ENDOGENOUS MODEL

An alternative to the endogenous model, and one which for some rural places perhaps more accurately reflects current development trajectories, is set out in Figure 1(b). In this model, rather than peripherally-based firms using advanced communications to access core markets, enterprises based in the core will use advanced communications to access the productive and reproductive capacity of certain rural regions (Richardson and Gillespie, 1996). In doing so, exogenous actors can help overcome some of the problems of market entry which firms in peripheral rural areas face. This may take several forms and will vary from region to region, including both (a) entrepreneurs wishing to relocate for predominantly 'quality of life' reasons, these entrepreneurs having already developed the necessary competencies and networks to allow them to gain access to core markets; and (b) large, often multinational, firms seeking to unlock new sources of good quality, inexpensive labor (Richardson and Gillespie, 1996).

This latter model, based on *exogenously*-led rural development, has, however, its own problems in terms of sustainable economic development. The problems associated with over-reliance on inward investment are well known and will be reflected upon in the context of the information society later in this chapter. However, we believe that unless sustained policies can be developed to success-fully promote relevant endogenous skills and competencies in rural areas and to promote mechanisms to gain access to non-rural markets, rural areas will come to be reliant on inward investment to introduce (a limited number) of information skills and to gain access to remote markets.

We turn now to examine these points in relation to the potential contribution of a range of forms of ICT-facilitated economic activity and of ICT-based modes of working to contribute to rural economic development. Each of them has had considerable interest shown from policy-makers keen to promote rural development. We begin with considering the potential of ICTs to stimulate economic activity through the *existing SMEs* operating in rural areas; we pose the question of the extent to which the adoption of new ICTs is likely to enhance the competitiveness of rural SMEs, through, for example, improving their access to remote markets. The second type of economic activity considered is that of *electronic home working*, which again has been heralded as a means by which rural areas could overcome their problems of distance and remoteness from markets. A variant of this model of electronically-supported working which is then considered is that of *telecottages*, which are shared facilities able to provide access to a range of ICTs. Each of these three types of electronically-supported economic activities conform to the endogenously-led model of rural development outlined above, in which rurally-based economic actors take advantage of the potential of new technologies. The fourth and final type of economic activity considered is that of back offices and call centers, in which externally-located actors take advantage of the new technologies in order to incorporate rural areas into their spatial structures of service production.

OVERCOMING CONSTRAINTS ON ENTERPRISES THROUGH ICTS?

Small and medium sized enterprises have been the focus of a number of information society related rural economic development initiatives, particularly in Europe, notably under the EU's TELEMATIQUE and ORA (Opportunities for Rural Areas) Programmes. The main thrust of these initiatives has been to promote the use of communications technologies by SMEs in peripheral regions and rural areas. Several studies, however, including those which have specifically examined the impact of these initiatives, suggest that this is a far from easy task. They make it clear that SMEs, in both urban and rural areas, tend to be slow to adopt the new technologies (Ilbery *et al.*, 1995; Richardson and Gillespie, 1996; Granger, 1996). This partly reflects the fact that small companies lack the technical personnel capable of designing, implementing, and developing information technologies applications, specifying clearly their technological needs, or carrying out maintenance functions (Granger, 1996). Studies specifically focused on rural areas confirm this. For example, an extensive survey of firms in a number of peripheral rural regions of Europe, for the European Commission, found marked differences in the technology adoption curves of large and small firms, with small firms lagging far behind (Ó Siochrú *et al.*, 1995). The survey found a number of reasons for these firms failing to adopt advanced communications, including the cost of equipment, costs of connection/service, the lack of expertise of users, the limited number of existing subscribers, and the lack of familiarity with the technologies/services. Another study found similar problems and argued persuasively that:

there are many barriers or resistances to the adoption of telematic services by SMEs in rural areas and it is not clearly obvious that the provision of telematics will lead to endogenous rural development (Ilbery *et al.*, 1995: 57).

In many cases small firms simply do not see a need for the new technologies; they do not see how such technologies can affect their 'bottom-line'. This finding may be explained in part by a *perception* gap on behalf of SMEs, which could be reduced by awareness campaigns or by demonstration projects designed to help SMEs understand the business benefits of ICTs. However, it also reflects the fact that for many SMEs there may in *reality* be few business benefits to be obtained from adopting new communications technologies. Evidence suggests that these new technologies are particularly useful for managing organizational complexity and for coping with a requirement for communicating at a distance, for example with remotely located customers; many SMEs are organizationally simple and many serve only or principally local markets, and in such instances the business case for adopting ICTs may be quite low. This suggests the need for greater targeting of resources on firms for which communication technologies offer a genuine opportunity, rather than assuming that all will be able to benefit equally.

Simply targeting technology and service support at those SMEs for which ICTs represent a potential opportunity will not, however, automatically lead to enhanced competitiveness. For an opportunity to translate into competitive advantage, the adopting firms must possess both the desire to innovate, and the managerial competence to enable them to do so effectively; neither the desire nor the competence can be assumed to exist in abundance in the population of existing rural SMEs (Grimes and Lyons, 1994; Ilbery *et al.*, 1995), and as a result policy efforts to raise the competitiveness of rural SMEs through encouraging ICT adoption will often fail to deliver the intended benefits.

USING THE INTERNET

One type of opportunity for rural SMEs which is receiving increasing attention and policy interest is that of using ICTs – particularly the Internet and its 'World Wide Web' – to 'break free' of the constraints imposed by local markets. This line of argument runs that by being able to serve remote (i.e. core) markets through 'electronic commerce', all or most of the market-access limitations associated with peripherality and remoteness will be overcome. Richardson (1996), for example, observes that:

> Rural food producers in North America now use the Internet to sell a wide variety of products . . . Rural craft and manufactured goods producers sell everything from clothing to furniture over the Internet. . . . The Internet represents a global storefront for such rural and remote businesses, providing them with access to customers never before possible (Richardson, 1996: 10).

However, these claims, as yet, appear difficult to sustain, at least within the context of the European Union. The EU-funded WOLF project, for example, worked closely with 150 SMEs drawn from ten of Europe's less favoured (Objective 1) regions, with the aim of assisting the firms to take advantage of the WWW for business benefit (WOLF Consortium, 1997). Although many of the firms reported a much greater degree of optimism about the potential of the Web at the end of the 18-month project than they had at the beginning, the optimism largely concerns future opportunities. Even though the SMEs involved in the project were hand-picked according to the extent they were likely to be able to benefit from the Internet, and despite the considerable assistance they received from external consultants during the course of the project, there were very few instances of increases in sales reported as a result of the firms' use of the Internet. Of course, this could be due to the relatively short duration of the project, or to the current limitations of the Internet for electronic commerce which will soon be overcome by secure trading standards; the explanation could also be, however, that, although the Internet will undoubtedly become a widely used business tool, it is not likely, in any generalizable sense, to overcome problems of market access associated with distance. Much evidence suggests that gaining access to new markets requires intense face-to-face interaction in order to build up trust, to provide an environment in which negotiation can take place, to provide after-sales support, and so on. While the Internet has a role to play within the process of marketing goods and services, it seems unlikely, in most instances, to be able to substitute entirely for direct market presence. We can then expect the Internet to become a useful tool for rural SMEs, but a tool that will need to be complemented by other mechanisms for gaining access to external markets.

Further, we need to recognize that gaining access to external markets will only be viable for those firms which are price and quality competitive in terms of the goods and services they can offer, prior conditions which cannot be taken for granted amongst rural SMEs. Indeed, the local markets which many rural SMEs serve are extremely unlikely to provide the type of 'home base' (Porter, 1990) which would lead to high levels of product or service innovation, or to the economies of scale which would lead to price competitiveness. Rather than providing viable opportunities for rural SMEs to 'break free' of their local markets, it may well be that the main impact of the Internet will be to open up rural markets, previously protected by their very remoteness and limited scale, to services provided by more efficient or more innovative suppliers located in cities and core regions. Just as did roads before them, the new electronic highways such as the Internet can support two-way traffic.

ELECTRONIC HOMEWORKING AND RURAL AREAS

Ever since Toffler (1980) put the electronic cottage at the center of his 'Third Wave' society, one of the great hopes for the regeneration of rural areas through the use of ICTs has been teleworking from home, which we term here 'electronic homeworking' (EHW). If we examine the literature on EHW, however, it is difficult not to agree with a recent report for the United Kingdom's Rural Development Commission which 'revealed a widespread scepticism about the extent to which (home-based) teleworking represents an opportunity for rural areas . . .' (Huws *et al.*, 1996). A number of findings emerge from the (admittedly scanty) literature, few of which are positive from the point of view of rural development.

First, and notwithstanding the well-publicized cases which appear in the media, overall levels of EHW, in Europe at least, are low and the phenomenon is growing only slowly (Huws, 1991, 1993; Huws *et al.*, 1996; Breton, 1993; Korte *et al.*, 1994; Qvortrup, 1992; Gillespie *et al.*, 1995).

Second, EHW is overwhelmingly an urban phenomenon (Huws *et al.*, 1996; Gillespie *et al.*, 1995; Korte *et al.*, 1994; PATRA, 1996). For those electronic homeworkers who have an employer (as opposed to those who are self-employed), this is related to the need to be close to the employer or to clients (for fuller discussion see Gillespie *et al.*, 1995; Huws *et al.*, 1996). One reason for this is that most employed teleworkers typically spend a quarter of their time at their employer's premises and a further quarter of their time elsewhere, often with clients (Huws *et al.*, 1996). A three year research study for the EU on Psychological Aspects of Teleworking in Rural and Urban Areas (PATRA, 1996) found that 70% of employees spent more than half their time working back in the office. Given the urban concentration of firms with the type of work that can be undertaken electronically, EHW's are likely to remain close to urban areas. This situation is unlikely to change in the foreseeable future as the two areas of most rapid growth in employee-EHW – namely, what has been termed 'ad-hoc' teleworking (that is to say professionals, managers, and others who take work home with them when they do not need to be in the office: Murray *et al.*, 1997), and, second, nomadic workers who increasingly divide their time between their clients' premises and a home-office – clearly need to be close to either their employer or their clients. Again, these are likely to be located in urban areas.

Third, there is evidence to suggest that rural-based workers have lower rates of job satisfaction from teleworking than do their urban counterparts, complaining of isolation and being passed over for promotion (PATRA, 1996). Further, case studies of fully home-based workers in 'deep rural' areas engaged in information processing work (mainly data entry), suggest that such work is unlikely to make a significant contribution to economic development. These workers tend to be poorly paid, may receive minimal training and may have to buy their own equipment (Huws *et al.*, 1996).

THE FREELANCE TELEWORKER

One important group which is missing from the foregoing analysis is the self-employed or freelance home-based teleworker. Given the trend towards 'downsizing' by organizations and the concomitant 'outsourcing' of work, often to former employees, many of whom, it could be hypothesized, will work from home using electronic communications, it is likely that one of the main areas of EHW growth will be amongst freelance workers. Census analysis in the United Kingdom suggests that rural areas seem to be over-represented with potential freelance teleworkers in terms of the incidence of the types of occupations which studies have found to have relatively high incidences of teleworking from home (Huws *et al.*, 1996).

Whether that potential translates into actual EHWs, however, is by no means certain, as most freelance work is found through contact networks which are difficult to develop and sustain in isolated areas (Huws *et al.*, 1996). In practice, in the United Kingdom at least;

> . . . the majority of freelance teleworkers appear to live within easy reach of their clients and where they have moved further afield they have done so only after establishing a client base in a non-rural area . . . thus the distribution of freelance teleworking . . . appears to follow fairly closely that of partially home-based teleworking . . . [and] exists in 'prosperous rural' areas to a significant extent, but is less prevalent in 'remote rural' ones (Huws *et al.*, 1996: 84–85).

Examples can nevertheless be found of teleworkers, both employees and freelance, working from home in rural areas, making a small but significant contribution to employment generation. A study of the Highlands and Islands of Scotland by Richardson and Gillespie (1996), for example, found a number of businesses having been established at home in areas which were remote by any standards. However, in the case of freelance workers, the study also suggested that teleworkers tended to be in-comers or returners to the area rather than people who had been based in the area most of their lives. The principal explanation for this was that in order to be commercially successful, teleworkers need to have both marketable skills and a product to offer by means of telecommunications, neither of which are likely to have been generated in remote areas, and to have well-established market-contacts. To develop such contacts initially from regions remote from central markets is obviously problematic. On the whole, teleworkers in the Highlands have moved there for quality of life reasons, whilst maintaining their externally-established business contacts.

EMPLOYED TELEWORKERS

In the Highlands and Islands Study, in the case of employed (and quasi-employed) teleworkers it was also clear that work was being facilitated by in-comers to the region who had previously built extensive or intensive contacts with relevant players. One example of a successful and relatively large-scale teleworking company in the Highlands is Crossaig. Crossaig was a private company, formed in 1990, to provide value-added services for publishing houses (the company has since been acquired by Thomson International). The company subcontracts work to mainly home-based workers located in the Highland Region. The workforce is connected with the company by means of ISDN links. Crossaig was the first ISDN user in Scotland and uses ISDN specifically to enable and extend teleworking practices.

Crossaig's main client is the UK–Dutch publisher Reed-Elsevier, which specializes in medical and health care journals. The company extracts information from medical journals, indexes and abstracts it and electronically transfers the information to the Netherlands. There are three segments to the operation within Crossaig. The journal is electronically scanned and placed in a queue ready for transmission for basic processing. Each worker retrieves work from the queue on a first-come first-served basis via ISDN. Upon receiving the journal they carry out basic information extraction and indexing for each of the articles in the journal. The journals are then returned to the file server where they are assigned to an expert, based on an expertise profile, and placed in a queue. Each expert retrieves his/her article, via ISDN, and prepares an index and an abstract for each article and then returns them to Crossaig's office, from whence they are sent electronically to the Netherlands, for inclusion on Elsevier's medical abstract database.

By 1994, over 30 home-based teleworkers were employed by Crossaig. There are a variety of skills involved, from basic data processing, mainly carried out by female returners, to highly-skilled experts including pharmacists, doctors and health science specialists. These workers are coordinated and managed from a small office in Helensburgh, near Glasgow. In 1996, the company spun-off some of its work to a new EHW organization, created locally with help from the economic development support organizations, specifically to take the work to even more remote areas, suggesting that it is possible to build on the work of projects initially brought in from outside the region.

COMMUNITY BASED TELECENTERS AND TELECOTTAGES

Early advocates of teleworking suggested that one way of overcoming some of the problems associated with teleworking from home (such as social isolation for the employee and perceived lack of control by management), while at the same time achieving some of the social and economic benefits (including decentralization of work, reduction in commuting, and higher worker productivity) could be achieved by establishing shared facility centers, either in the form of 'neighbourhood work centers' (catering for up to ten workers) or of 'local work centers' (designed to accommodate a larger – unspecified – number of workers) in residential areas (see Qvortrup, 1992: 85–86). Shared facility centers are envisaged as offices equipped with various forms of new technology facilities for both on-site work and for communicating at a distance. As their name suggests, these offices would be shared by a number of users who may be employees of different companies, independent freelance professionals, or small businesses unable to afford such facilities on their own. These centers would be located in residential areas and would be financially supported by different employers and/or public authorities. The evidence suggests that these centers, particularly in the United States and Japan, have been mainly peri-urban phenomena, the main impetus behind them being to reduce commuter-related congestion and environmental pollution and improve the quality of life of commuters (Gillespie *et al.*, 1995; US General Services Administration, 1995).

THE 'TELECOTTAGE'

A similar but more rural-oriented concept is the community teleservice center or 'telecottage'. The definition of these centers adopted by the International Association of Community Tele-Service Centres is:

A center where IT apparatus is placed at the disposal of the citizens of a specific local community with in a rural or peripheral area, so that communal use may be made of the facilities available. The purpose of the Centre is to counteract some geographically determined disadvantages which affect the local community, whether they are of an economic, educational or cultural nature, or whether those disadvantages concern employment, services, or other infrastructure facilities.

Telecottages, therefore, have a broad ambit and are not regarded merely as employment-generating enterprises, though it is this role with which we are primarily concerned here. Telecottages probably represent the main rural ICT-related policy response by economic development authorities in north-west Europe, particularly in Scandinavia (where the concept originated), the United Kingdom and Ireland. Most telecottages have been sponsored by public authorities and have attracted significant levels of public money for development, though in the current environment of tight expenditure controls many funding authorities are placing time limits on subsidies, expecting the centers to become commercially viable within a relatively short period (Gillespie *et al.*, 1995).

According to Hillman (1993) by the early 1990s there were around 100 telecottages in Scandinavia, with 40 in Sweden alone (Paavonen, 1993). The concept has thrived in the United Kingdom and Ireland and by mid-1997 the Telecottage Association covering these two countries had 160 members (Teleworker, 1997). The telecottage concept has been extended into the 'televillage' following some of the ideas emerging in the United States, notably those developed in Teluride, Colorado, though as yet only small scale pilots of limited duration have transpired. Telecottages are predominately (though not exclusively) a rural phenomenon. A study of UK telecottages suggested that a quarter of all telecottages are located in remote rural settings, another quarter in small villages, and half in towns, mainly small market towns situated in rural areas (Gillespie *et al.*, 1995).

THE LIMITED IMPACT OF TELECOTTAGES

The limited study evidence available regarding the ability of telecottages to contribute directly towards rural employment creation suggests that their impact will be limited. Two studies carried out in the United Kingdom in 1995 (Gillespie *et al.*, 1995; Murray, 1995) were in broad agreement that telecottages on average employed only 1.5 full-time workers and around four part-time staff. These staff tended to be engaged in managing the operation or in training-related activities. Few examples were found of remote teleworking from telecottages.

This lack of teleworking in telecottages suggests that these organizations may face some of the same problems to which SMEs and home-based teleworkers in rural areas are subject; in particular, the lack of necessary skills, identifying potential customers beyond the (mainly training-related) local market, and marketing capabilities to those customers. Even when external customers have been identified and contracts won, however, telecottages face a battle to retain the work. These points can be illustrated by reference to a telecottage which was formerly regarded as a 'jewel in the crown' of the telecottage movement in the United Kingdom in terms of remote working.

The Antur Tanait Cain Telebureau was set up near Oswestry in Wales, an area suffering from rural deprivation and an outflow of young people (Moindrot, 1991). The 'Telebureau' emerged, in the mid-1980s, out of the IT element of a local training project under the UK Government's Community Programme. Antur Tanait Cain was held up as an example of a telecottage which was able to overcome its peripherality and gain access to markets, thus creating employment opportunities which would not otherwise have been available. The Telebureau came to the attention of an executive of the computer company ICL who happened to have moved to the area, and it subsequently won a contract to input data from the company's clients who were switching over to computerized text management systems. At its busiest period the center employed up to 40 people in data processing tasks, at a rate of pay far higher than that provided by other jobs available to those people in the locality. The work also provided a useful element in the telecottage's training provision for the local population.

Unfortunately, Antur's remote working operation did not last. After successfully fulfilling its initial contracts – essentially data-processing tasks – one client insisted that the work be done using scanning. The client assumed that such scanning would reduce the amount of work involved and thus the cost of that work. However, the skill base of the work force meant that scanning work took longer than the data-processing, the result being that the amount earned per hour by workers fell. There was also a considerable cost in up-dating technology in order to keep pace with clients' demands. Furthermore, in the late 1980s when the recession began to hit ICL, the company contracted out less work to the Telebureau, preferring to use its own teleworkers. Today, although Antur still has many of the skills required to enable it to carry out remote working, this represents only a small part of its business.

The initial success of Antur illustrates how important it is to have someone locally who can identify, develop and organize local competencies. It also illustrates the need for a mechanism to market those skills to companies outside the area. In this case an ICL consultant happened to be living in the area and was able to forge the market link. There is a need for economic development actors to replicate this process where, as in most instances, it does not occur fortuitously. Nascent attempts are underway (such as in Wales and in the EU TeleMart project) to form networks of telecottages to integrate their competencies and to market those competencies. Telecottages will face increasing competition from commercial organizations, both in their own countries and off-shore, however, and it is likely that if they are to be successful, in terms of remote working, public sector work will have to be diverted to them, as a matter of policy.

Over the longer term, telecottages, if properly funded, have the potential to play an important role in training, in technology awareness raising, and in building confidence in local communities. If successful in these roles, peripheral communities may be better able to gain access to core markets in the longer run. What is clear is that without the kind of training and awareness-raising activities carried out by telecottages, peripheral rural communities will be further marginalized as we progress into the 'information age'. However, solutions to the problems identified above will need to be found if the newly trained workforce is to find teleworking employment.

BACK OFFICES AND CALL CENTERS

As illustrated above, one of the key problems in promoting employment growth in rural areas, particularly for SMEs and micro-businesses, is gaining access to distant export markets. This can be overcome when in-comers or returners to a rural area have already established networks that they are able to continue to tap into. Not all rural areas, however, will be attractive to such people, and, in any event, the number of jobs created is likely to be small. Another way for rural areas to overcome the problem of access to external markets is to attract footloose firms, which already have access to core regions, and which can then export their product from the periphery. This approach has been adopted for less favoured regions and some rural regions for several decades, but usually in respect of manufacturing work.

The advent of new communications technologies allows this approach to be adopted in respect of certain forms of service work and some companies have realized that they face immense opportunities for combining appropriate skill levels with low-wage labor (Glasmeier and Borchard, 1989). In the short run, at least, this approach seems to offer a more realistic prospect of rapid employment growth for those rural areas that can offer low wage workers with the appropriate skills. Commenting on the US experience, Parker and Hudson (1995: 2) note that 'in the 1980s, rural communities updated the rural development strategy of "smokestack chasing" to lure telemarketing and other "back office" industries'. Parker and Hudson point to several examples of firms relocating to rural areas of America; Breda, Iowa, a town with just 500 inhabitants, attracted a branch office of Sitel, a major telemarketing firm, after the local telephone company linked the town to the fiber optic network of a long-distance carrier (Parker and Hudson, 1995), and Glasmeier and Borchard (1989) comment more generally that there has been a dispersal of low-skilled back-office jobs to locales remote from headquarters control centers. Glasmeier and Howland (1994) introduce a note of caution, however, pointing to the difficulty that many rural areas will have attracting those investments because of the lack of an appropriate labor force.

In Europe the phenomenon of information-related service work moving to rural areas is less advanced than in the United States, but recent experience suggests that given adequate infrastructure provision, certain processing work can be attracted to at least some rural European regions. By the early 1990s, US insurance and banking firms were already relocating back office processing work to rural Ireland, taking advantage of the declining costs and increasing capacity of new communications technologies. The availability of advanced telecommunications provision and low labor costs and good transport infrastructure, notably air transport, added to a shared language, and an advantageous time difference, which allowed US firms to process data 'overnight', were crucial to the decision of these firms to locate in rural Ireland (Wilson, 1991; Grimes and Lyons, 1993). Another important factor was the role of the government agency charged with economic development in Ireland, the Irish Development Agency (IDA), which both promoted Ireland as a location and offered significant financial incentives for locating there.

Experience in the United Kingdom suggests that back offices have generally located in urban, or rather suburban, sites, but there are now some examples of more rural back offices, such as the Atomic Energy Authority's pensions operation at Thurso, virtually the most northerly point of the Scottish mainland. It is not clear, however, whether simple processing work will continue to create mobile employment in the coming years. The move to increasingly large back offices on the one hand, for which rural areas cannot provide adequate labor pools, and the rise of distributed processing on the other, together with the growing use of scanning technologies and an increasing tendency to send processing work offshore, will all militate against information or clerical processing employment growth in rural areas.

SECRETARIAL SERVICES

One example of back office work which may still offer opportunities for rural areas is remote secretarial services, though this may be limited to some extent by innovations in voice processing technology. An example of a remote outsourced secretarial bureau can be found in Barnard Castle, a small town in a rural area in the North East of England, where the French company Telergos has established an office which provides remote secretarial services for clients based both in other parts of the United Kingdom and in Paris. Telergos has three other offices based in rural villages in North-East France and a head office in Paris (Qvortrup, 1994). Telergos was established in 1989 and functions as a third party back office for major companies who do not wish to take on more secretarial and processing staff, but have insufficient staff to cope with peaks of activity. Initially, Telergos concentrated on word processing of mail and reports, and although the company is currently diversifying activities into more value-added services (desk-top publishing, graphic design, translation, etc.) its main market remains insurance companies based in Paris, though the firm is attempting to extend its markets into the United Kingdom (Gillespie *et al.*, 1995).

CALL CENTERS

Another development in services, the emergence of the call center, clearly presents opportunities for employment growth for those peripheral places which can offer low cost labor, advanced telecommunications, good transport infrastructure, and fiscal incentives (Richardson, 1994, 1997). These centers potentially bring new forms of work to rural areas. To take one example, Hoskyns Group plc (part of Cap Gemini, one of Europe's largest computer services companies) established a

Business Process Outsourcing Centre at Forres, near Inverness in the Highlands of Scotland. Hoskyns' target client groups include local authorities, banks, insurance companies and other organizations with heavy administrative loads.

The Hoskyns call center started off in 1994 with 30 staff. By late 1997, the company had a second site, in Inverness, and employed around 120 people. The Forres operation is principally concerned with collecting money on behalf of other bodies. Most interestingly, the company collects parking fines on behalf of a number of local authorities in London, in partnership with another firm which handles the traffic warden side of the operation. Offenders are given a PO Box to write to and a London local call rate number to telephone, from which the calls will flow automatically to Forres. The Forres operation carries out both traditional back office administration functions and 'call center' functions.

The Hoskyns operation does not require a sophisticated, technologically skilled workforce. Training is intense but carried out over a relatively short period and on the technology side involves mainly keyboard skills and becoming familiar with the PC and telephone systems. Skills are required, but these tend to be customer-relations skills. These forms of inward investment, however, clearly bring new opportunities to people living in rural areas. A detailed survey of employees in call centers in the Highlands and Islands of Scotland, for example, showed the following results. First, new employment has been generated in both full-time and part-time work. Second, that work is of a higher order than that offered by many of the jobs in which workers formerly worked. Previously much of the work had been seasonal. Third, the majority of jobs, including supervisory grades, had been taken up by local people. Fourth, the investment added to the base of types of job available in the region, creating new skills and utilizing existing (under-exploited) skills (Richardson and Gillespie, 1996).

The work carried out in the Hoskyns call center is fairly basic and deals only with the UK market. It may be more problematical for peripheral rural areas to attract centers which deal with more complex activities, particularly those requiring technical and, importantly in the European context, linguistic skills. In Ireland, for example, the IDA has focused much energy in attracting call centers which aim to serve pan-European markets, positioning the country as the 'Call Centre of Europe'. Ireland has had considerable success in this strategy, but the vast majority of these centers (79%) has located in or around the capital, Dublin (see Figure 2). Furthermore, over 90% of technically-oriented, pan-European call centers have located in greater-Dublin. In spite of great efforts by the IDA to disperse investment away from the capital, relatively few call centers have located in rural Ireland and those tend to be providing reservation-type activities (Richardson, 1998).

To sum up this section, back offices and call centers clearly offer opportunities for some, though probably not all, rural areas to attract information-related employment. Most of the employment created by such investment, however, is confined to the lower-skilled range of activities. These investments may 'pull-through' telecommunications infrastructure and accelerate property investment. They may also enhance the skills base to some extent and also bring new ways of working and promote new cultural attitudes to work. These elements, in turn, may

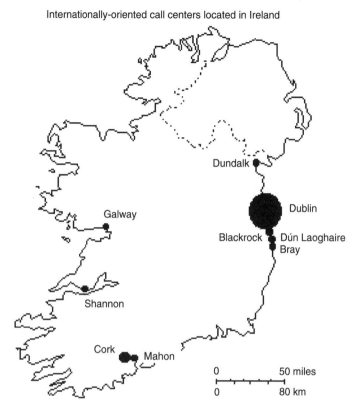

Internationally-oriented call centers located in Ireland

Figure 2 *The location of internationally-located call centers in Ireland (Summer 1996)*

Source: Richardson (1998).

contribute to the longer term economic health of a region. Several caveats must be entered as to the development potential of these investments, however; they offer little in the way of career development for the workforce; they bring new skills but the skills are limited and are unlikely to develop further over time; there are low multiplier effects in that they do not provide an environment which will encourage entrepreneurs and they tend to buy services externally to the region; finally, there are questions as to the sustainability of jobs they bring, as they will be most susceptible to technological displacement and under-cutting by lower-cost locations.

CONCLUSIONS

There are clearly opportunities for employment creation in some rural areas through the introduction of new advanced technologies. Such growth is unlikely, however, to be automatic. Constraints on the endogenous model of rural economic growth seem likely to remain, in spite of new communications technologies. Rural regions tend to be dominated by small firms, which are mainly oriented towards local markets, markets which have historically been protected by their peripherality. Research suggests that these firms are slow to adopt new technologies, failing to realize their potential or to construct strategies around them. Efforts have been made, particularly in the European context, to raise the awareness of small firms, and to strengthen their capacity to successfully adopt the new technologies, but with only limited success. The main problem facing rural small firms, however, and this applies equally to rural teleworkers, is developing and sustaining market contacts, particularly in core regions, at a distance. Although new technologies appear to be implicated in thickening existing relationships between rural SMEs, particularly supply-chain relations (NEXUS *et al.*, 1996), there is little evidence that they are allowing small firms to find new markets. Furthermore, technologies sustain existing relationships only where the technology is relatively stable, or where the firm can afford to continually up-grade, to keep pace with developments within the client firm. The key question facing rural firms is how to establish trust with clients or potential clients. The process of establishing trust often relies on being part of networks, usually with some face-to-face element, within which intelligence and information flows. Contracts are often won by 'being in the right place at the right time' and by 'who you know not what you know'. It is difficult to see how new technology, on its own, can overcome this constraint, though the creation of trading communities around the Internet may offer some glimmer of hope.

The exogenous model of economic growth appears to offer a better prospect of employment creation in the short-term for some rural areas. The facility to attract professional teleworkers through quality of life considerations, will be limited to relatively few places. The attraction of back office and call center work will be an option for more rural areas, as this type of work becomes more codified and industrialized, and as service firms seeking to reduce costs become more comfortable with the concept of managing operations remotely. The evidence presented in this chapter suggests that the attraction of such firms overcomes the problem of market entry and sustaining market relations. A number of reservations have also been expressed, however, as to the 'dynamic' impact of these activities on rural development.

Clearly, a successful rural region would need to both attract inward investment and build its endogenous capacity. For many rural places the 'recipe' for the former is fairly simple, *viz.*, telecommunications infrastructure, a reasonably educated labor force, real estate, and financial inducements. Building endogenous capacity is much more complex. Existing policies such as infrastructure investment, awareness raising and training need to continue. Information society policies, however, need to be integrated more closely with other support policies and should not be seen as stand-alone responses. So, for example, policy towards SMEs, would include advice on how firms could most sensibly use new technologies. This might be best done with tight targeting on firms which have or are capable of developing products which are marketable beyond their own region. Those firms which do have the capacity to develop such products should then be supported in marketing those products. This may involve technology-related solutions, but these solutions are likely to be complemented by other means; examples might include appointing a marketing executive in key core regions to market a rural area and to gather intelligence, subsidizing visits of targeted SMEs to trade fairs, inviting and subsidizing visits of likely SME partners to the rural area. There needs also to be support for firms in managing and fulfilling contracts, as only by successfully doing so can they build long-term partnerships. The technology would be then principally used to support and develop those partnerships.

CHAPTER 12

TELEMATICS, GEOGRAPHY, AND ECONOMIC DEVELOPMENT – CAN LOCAL INITIATIVES PROVIDE A STRATEGIC RESPONSE?

David Gibbs, Keith Tanner and Steve Walker

INTRODUCTION

The social and economic implications of the new information and communications technologies (ICTs or telematics) are complex and frequently contradictory. They have been identified as having the potential both to centralize (Innis, 1951; Genosko, 1987; Mulgan, 1991) and decentralize (Gottman, 1977; Kellerman, 1993) economic development activities. They have been associated with both employment creation, although there remains doubt over their additionality in relation to productivity, growth and output, and encouraging capital investments to displace employment (CEU, 1996). They are seen to support time-space compression (Janelle, 1968; Leyshon, 1995) and have implications for the geography of production and trade at the macro-level (Brotchie *et al.*, 1991; Dicken, 1992), as well as for organizational developments at the micro-level (Webster, 1988; Goddard, 1991; CEU, 1995; Molina and Fleck, 1995). The new telematic infrastructures and applications are increasingly used to support organizational change in manufacturing and service employment (Attewell and Rule, 1984; McNerney, 1995), as well as influencing the wage relation and skills demands in local areas. The diffusion and upgrade of telecommunications infrastructures has been observed as having a direct causal and effective relationship with national economic development prospects (Cronin *et al.*, 1991). Increases in telecommunication investment are therefore seen to produce increases in economic development and vice versa.

The relationship, at the macro-level, between investment, infrastructure development and economic growth is believed to translate down to local outcomes (Cornford *et al.*, 1991). However, physical barriers, cultural relations, market forces, policy motivations and political intervention can lead to uneven geographical patterns of usage, uptake, and access to these technologies (Castells, 1989; Nijkamp *et al.*, 1990; Kellerman, 1993; Graham and Marvin, 1996). Telematics is believed to offer economic development potential at urban (Hepworth, 1989; Graham, 1992, 1993; Tanner and Gibbs, 1996) and rural scales (Rural Development Commission, 1989; Hansen *et al.*, 1990; Henderson, 1992; Taylor and Williams, 1990; Harrison, 1990; *Sociomics*, 1993; Richardson and Gillespie, 1995) as well as at regional, national, and international levels. However, this potential is not uniform and can be to the comparative advantage of some areas and to the disadvantage of others, although given that many of the developments are innovative, local outcomes are not pre-determined and remain contestable. As Clark *et al.* (1995) illustrate, the advantages to businesses in urban areas outlined by Dabinett and Graham (1994) are not necessarily experienced by businesses in rural areas. The technologies may act either to reinforce or reset the balance of existing spatial hierarchies (Cornford *et al.*, 1991). Thus, while telematics offer potential for the economic revival of cities and the integration of peripheral areas, at the same time they expose localities to the exploitation of their resources by external agents (Gibbs, 1993). For example, these technologies can support distance working, distance learning and yet further increase the footloose nature of investment capital.

From the early 1980s onwards a range of telematics policies and initiatives have been developed by the European Commission which form a strong political drive to develop a European 'information society'. These have been embodied in a series of reports and White Papers, including the Delors' *White Paper on Growth Competitiveness and Employment* (CEC, 1993), the *Bangemann Report* (CEC, 1994), and the *First Reflections of the High Level Group of Experts* (CEC, 1996b), on the social and societal aspects of the information society, and a range of regulatory, technological, and structural initiatives to stimulate its development. These have attempted to encourage experimentation with telematics uptake and have focused on such developments as providing infrastructure for peripheral areas, enabling them to be more pro-active in working with core areas, to regional initiatives aimed at promoting an integrated approach to policies for an 'information society'. The European Commission argues that new jobs and more efficient services will arise from the plethora of new technologies now coming to maturity.

The United Kingdom has been at the forefront of the regulatory dimension of telematics, with the early privatization, liberalization and deregulation of its telecommunications provision and services (Tunstall and Palmer, 1990; Westerway, 1990) and has been seen as the 'telematics laboratory' of Europe (Graham, 1993). Other European countries have followed suit, liberalizing nationally owned telecommunications industries. UK policies at the national level have been oriented toward the creation of a competitive telecommunications market, rather than attempting to develop integrated policies which seek to promote telematics as social and economic goods (Tanner and Gibbs, 1996), although there is discussion and debate on the development of policies toward the 'information superhighway' (Dutton *et al.*, 1994). Where telematics' policies have been developed these are essentially national initiatives situated within the context of developing a competitive environment, for example the Department of Trade and Industry's Information Society Initiative (ISI), IT for All and the 1999 White Paper on Competitiveness.

European intervention has sought to support disadvantaged areas. Yet across the United Kingdom European grant aid is unevenly distributed, allocated via competitive bidding and is multifarious in its objectives. Across the divided political economy of local authority areas in the United Kingdom this equates to creating another level of uneven policy distribution, competition between areas, and absence of real policy presence. This situation, combined with the activities of private sector investors, further exacerbates the uneven use of telematics for local economic and social development across the United Kingdom, both in terms of infrastructure and application. Locally-oriented initiatives which aim to support economic development through the applications of telematics must engage with processes of national and European policy initiatives and of technological change. These processes are determined by actors typically operating at global, European and national levels, creating a context in which the development of local initiatives takes place. Many local initiatives can be seen as defining themselves in terms of these processes, for example through trying to compensate for the perceived failings of increasingly market-driven infrastructure development, (for example through attempts to combat the creation of an 'information poor' layer of society) or by promoting the uptake of technologies and applications whose impacts are seen as in some way positive (for example, through attempts to promote applications believed to generate competitive advantage for local companies). Increasingly reliant on European funding, these initiatives must reconcile perceived local needs with the opportunities and constraints provided by European policies and the rapidly changing technological landscape. In the following sections of this chapter we provide:

- A brief overview of key European-level policies promoting the 'information society'. European policy-makers, through a range of structural, R&D and regulatory mechanisms, have sought to promote the 'information society' as a central means of combating unemployment and promoting regional development;
- A brief overview of some recent and current technological developments and market trends, which provide the other main influences on the development of local-oriented initiatives;
- Case study material drawn from primary and secondary research, with a focus on the North West of England;
- A summary section which considers the benefits of local public activities in relation to these developments and the activities of the private sector. In this section we compare differing local strategies for responding to, and shaping, both national and European policy, and the evolution of the technical infrastructure.

OVERVIEW OF EUROPEAN POLICIES FOR THE INFORMATION SOCIETY

The European Union has as one important policy-goal that of transforming Europe into an Information Society. This goal is outlined in a number of policy documents. Thus, the Delors *White Paper* (1993) views the information society as a powerful engine for employment growth that will bring benefits to all regions and all parts of society, if there is solidarity between more prosperous and less favoured regions. The *Bangemann Report* (1994) similarly views the development of an information society as a positive development for regions, particularly peripheral regions. How this is to be achieved is not evident in the Report, although considerable stress is placed upon the capacity of the free market to deliver these benefits. The European Council meeting in Corfu (1994) took note of the *Bangemann Report* and requested greater co-ordination on the issues raised in the Report through the designation of a ministerial level appointment in each member state. These themes were elaborated upon in the action plan from the European Commission (1994), *Europe's Way to the Information Society*, which summarized information society initiatives already under way, or planned, by the Commission. Developing a new regulatory framework received most attention, while problems of regional cohesion and balance were only treated in brief. The specific regional implications were addressed at two points: in welcoming the emphasis on aspects of the information society in the Community Support Framework and in the Single Programming Documents agreed for Objective 1 regions for 1994–99. The Commission launched a study of the impacts and benefits of the information society for regional, economic and social cohesion. Besides this, only pilot projects and specific networks were envisaged in cooperation with cities and regions.

A European Council meeting in Essen (1994) stressed that the information society will bring new jobs, new forms of solidarity and stronger regional cohesion. The document produced from the meeting inaugurated a Forum on the Information Society and the installation of a Group of High Level Experts to deal with social and societal issues. This group produced the *Working Document on the Social and Societal Aspects of the Information Society* in 1995. The document stated that economic cohesion could be enhanced through the use of electronic networks by:

- Improving access to markets and sources of information;
- Bringing work to areas of high unemployment;
- Increasing the competitiveness of businesses at a regional level;
- Reinforcing positive externalities through shared infrastructures.

This group pointed out that telematics usage may not automatically lead to enhanced cohesion and that they could lead to greater centralization of jobs and services and to a 'fast' and 'slow track' information society. The questions asked by the Group in relation to this were:

- What are the regional and urban development consequences of disparities in infrastructure provision and service levels? What can be done to assist less well-equipped regions and areas?
- How do different levels of provision affect social cohesion at both regional and urban levels? What can be done to increase the accessibility of these new essential services?
- How can regions and towns be helped to optimize their use of the new possibilities of telematics services?
- How can telematics be used to improve the quality of life in the towns and regions of Europe, by allowing innovation in urban government and greater accessibility of services?

Preliminary answers to these questions were given in the Interim Report of the High Level Group of Experts *Building the European Information Society for Us All: First Reflections of the High Level Group of Experts* (1996). This outlined both the threats and opportunities that telematics present for peripheral regions and suggested a number of policy measures. The need for an integrated EU approach to the information society in order to increase social cohesion was stressed, as well as the need for a more focused approach to infrastructural support and to secure access to a reasonable service level at a reasonable price for different social groups.

Overall, it can be argued that European Commission and Council documents on the Information Society pay only limited attention to the impact of telematics upon the EU's regions and, while they are optimistic about the impact, do not adopt a critical approach to verify this, although the inauguration of the High Level Group of Experts indicated an awareness that problems may exist. This work, and other related European initiatives are still very much at the level of the European Commission. The fact remains that the policy measures identified by Europe are, as yet, not incorporated into national policies for the United Kingdom.

OVERVIEW OF TECHNOLOGY AND MARKET TRENDS

Underpinning all telematics applications – by definition – is the telecommunications infrastructure and the availability of IT. Rapid and continuing changes in both the technology and market structure of the infrastructure provides an essential part of the context in which local activities are placed. At a technological level, advances have occurred in the development of both the medium, largely through the replacement of copper by increasingly sophisticated types of fibre, and in the way information is compressed to allow more efficient use of that capacity, which have transformed the nature of the infrastructure. For example, the capacity of transatlantic communications infrastructure trebled in five years from 1988 to 1993. Similarly spectacular trends can be seen in the historic and projected capacities of other hardware and software technologies which underpin telematics applications, such as computer memories (ITU, 1995) and the increasingly powerful World Wide Web browsers. However, for locally-oriented initiatives the capacity of the local loop which links into these backbone networks, and which is available to domestic consumers and SMEs, is at least as important as the capacity of the backbone links. Here, technologies are similarly developing rapidly: the speed of 'conventional' modems which use the standard telephone network has increased 100 fold since the 300bps[1] devices of the early 1980s to 56,000bps widely available now.

More strategically, a range of technologies are contenders to become standards in high-capacity network provision to the domestic or small user, in a competition driven largely by industry structure and regulation. At the moment, the most

---

[1] bps = bits per second; kbps = kilo bps; and Mbps = Mega bps.

widely deployed of these technologies is ISDN which provides end-to-end digital connections at transmission speeds from 144,000 bps – capable of supporting moderate quality desk-top video-conferencing. The UK cable companies are, however, preparing to exploit their fibre networks by deploying services accessible using very high speed 'cable modems'. Cable modems available in the United States in the mid-1990s used cable TV networks to send data typically at 200kbps–2Mbps and receive at 3–10Mbps with maximum receive speeds of up to 36Mbps. In the United States, the first such services are currently being deployed (*Cable Datacom News*, 1996). The first UK trials were held in Salford as part of the GEMESIS initiative, which brought together the University of Salford, Salford City Council and Nynex, the local cable franchise holder. Telecommunications companies such as BT are responding by implementing DSL[2] technology that can provide high-capacity links capable of receiving data at between 1.5 and 6Mbps across their existing copper networks. BT currently expect to begin offering such services during 1997 (*Communications Week International*, September 23, 1996).

These technologies make new generations of multimedia applications possible. To transmit video at the quality of a domestic VCR requires transmission capacity of around 2Mbps, and to transmit at broadcast quality, around 6Mbps. Among the most immediate applications for these technologies will be access to the Internet, allowing, for example, the development of Internet World Wide Web sites that are effectively video-on-demand services. The availability of these infrastructures will not be spatially uniform. There is a tendency towards the evolution of 'hot spots' of information-intensive activity which attract increased competition in service and infrastructure provision, leading to lower costs and higher levels of innovation, reinforcing the attractiveness of a location to user organizations (Graham and Marvin, 1996). While technologies such as DSL, which have been developed to exploit the existing copper-based infrastructures of national operators, may become available relatively quickly at a national level, optic-fibre based technologies will inevitably be available differentially depending on the strategies of local cable TV franchise holders (where they exist at all) and other telecommunications operators (for example, regional utility companies).

In order for advanced applications to be available requires not only that end-users have access to high-capacity links but that applications' developers have access to high-capacity backbone infrastructures. In a number of UK cities, 'semi-public' broadband networks are being built (for example, the G-MING Network in Manchester) typically involving consortia of universities, further education colleges, local authorities, and other public bodies. The central role of universities in the development of such local infrastructures, using academic funding to complement the national higher education SuperJANET network, has meant that while they are technically advanced, they are restricted in the way these networks can be used to support private sector and domestic users. By sharing costs and pooling public resources where no individual class of application or user justifies the investment in advanced infrastructure (in applications such as distance

---

[2] DSL – Asynchronous Digital Subscriber Loop family of technologies.

learning, public information, and tele-medicine, for example), these partnership initiatives may nevertheless play an important role in stimulating the development of new public-service applications. This contributes to generating a 'critical mass' of users and service suppliers sooner rather than later, by 'recruiting' types of user into the 'information society' who may have been bypassed by market-only mechanisms, but who nevertheless can help to stimulate the market in digital products and services (for example, by increasing the potential audience for digital advertizing).

The relative diffusion of these competing technologies will be affected by a range of factors, including: diffusion of standards; availability and cost of end-user equipment; the evolving regulatory environment; and the commercial strategies of the various telecommunications, cable, IT and media companies. Difficulties in predicting the future of technologies in such a rapidly evolving field poses problems for those involved in local initiatives. Where projects aim to stimulate local demand for technologies and applications (for example, with the aim of gaining some form of competitive advantage through earlier adoption), the risks of selecting 'wrong' technologies – those that are supplanted in the market by others, or which prove to be unsuited to the intended application – will be higher. Similar issues relate to debates around the likely development of the so-called 'network computer' as a replacement in many contexts for the conventional desk-top computer. When Microsoft's Bill Gates can almost miss the significance of a technology such as the Internet, while planning the Microsoft Network, the problems of technology foresight that confront economic development practitioners, local authorities, and their partners are clear.

What these technological advances mean for local economies is still a matter of conjecture. However, in market economies, where there has already been serious concern over the potential of networks to 'suck out' skills from a local area, and where advanced infrastructures have been seen to displace employment with redundancy, policy-makers are increasingly charged with addressing these social concerns (Gibbs, 1993). The public sector, and, more broadly, from a political economy perspective, agents of local governance, are poorly equipped to address technological infrastructure inequalities. The financial resources necessary for technological investments are huge. Despite this, agents of local governance do possess the capacity to *enable* and *facilitate* local activities which can assist with the development of new telematic advances and subsequently these agents may be able to develop policy responses in conjunction with central government, the European Union, and the private sector itself.

DEVELOPING LOCAL TELEMATICS INITIATIVES – A CASE STUDY OF NORTHWEST ENGLAND

Research at the national scale in Great Britain has highlighted the high level of interventionist activity occurring at local levels through the strategic use of telematics by local authorities and associated partners, such as the Training and Enterprise Councils (TECs) (Tanner, 1997; Tanner and Gibbs, 1996). Often these are attempts to add value to the local economy, such as skills training for the labor market, information networks for community development, or new commercial services targeted at local business. These activities are based on the belief that new telematics infrastructure and applications have a vital role to play in the regeneration and/or sustainability of the local economy. This is all seen within the changing context of local competitiveness combined with national and international economic growth and development. Case study material has been selected from three initiatives on-going in the Northwest of England – one of six pilot regions of the EC-sponsored 'Inter-Regional Information Society Initiative' (IRISI)[3] and where the role of telematics for regional development has been explored through a number of local initiatives (Tanner and Gibbs, 1996). We use these case studies to look at three different locally-oriented telematics strategies and projects, and some of the ways they are influenced by and respond to broader developments both in national and European policy-making, and in technology and technological markets.

Much of the activity and development of the following case studies began prior to the selection of the North West as an IRISI region. Three main examples are presented. First, the Manchester case study describes the evolving telematics policies and activities of what has been termed a leading edge metropolitan authority (Graham and Dominy, 1991), in a city with a residential population of around 432,000 and a conurbation-wide population of 2.25 million. The second study of Burnley, Lancashire, identifies telematic policy developments and local activities at a smaller scale within a very 'local' economy having a residential population of around 90,000, where 83% of the workforce live and work in the local area. The final study, the case of the Lancashire College Consortium, illustrates a sectoral focus on further education which unites a range of partners, all with an active involvement in local economic development, and exemplifies a sub-regional focus in an area with a comparable residential population to that of Manchester.

MANCHESTER CASE STUDY

Manchester City Council (MCC) was among the pioneers in attempting to apply telematics to a local economic development strategy, originally through its sponsorship of the Manchester Host and Electronic Village Hall (EVH) initiatives in the early 1990s (Graham and Dominy, 1991) against a background of continued industrial change which has seen large contractions in manufacturing employment (Peck and Emmerich, 1992). Telematics has continued to act as a focus for the local authority's economic development strategy supported largely by external funding, and has grown to include dozens of distinct projects with total public sector support of several million pounds.

A semi-formal network of players has evolved, co-ordinated through the framework of the Manchester Telematics and Telework Partnership (MTTP). The MTTP

---

[3] The other 'pilot' regions were Saxony, Germany; Nord Pas de Calais, France; Piemonte, Italy; Macedonia, Greece; and Valencia, Spain.

is a partnership led by the local authority and the Manchester Metropolitan University (MMU) and includes the North West Arts Board and a number of other educational, cultural and community organizations. The MTTP also works closely with private sector IT companies, in particular Reed Personnel, ICL and Apple Computers. An increasing formalization of earlier loose relationships has been necessitated by the growing scale of projects, and the greater number of organizations involved. Increasingly, activities have focused on participation in cultural activities and the promotion of telematics-facilitated networking among those involved in 'content production'. Drawing on the perceived lessons of New York's growing concentration of small 'new media' producers, the local authority now prioritizes the creation of an organizational and physical infrastructure that will 'empower . . . the more innovative individuals and enterprises in the labor market' (Carter, 1996).

The various initiatives within the MTTP framework have been supported with resources from a range of public and private agencies. Public support for the original projects – Manchester Host and the EVHs were supported under the now-defunct government-funded Urban Programme. Subsequent initiatives have gained support from a range of European programmes. Training programmes have been supported by the European Social Fund, including its New Opportunities for Women (NOW) and Horizon programmes. Some support has been available under the central government's Single Regeneration Budget, but by far the greatest source of support has been the European Regional Development Fund (ERDF). Various ERDF-supported programmes have been used to extend the range of the network, from an original group of perhaps half a dozen core members (City Council, the MMU, Manchester Host and three Electronic Village Halls) to include around thirty cultural and community organizations, SMEs, and educational establishments. Dave Carter, the primary local authority officer responsible, has described this process as the 'long hard slog of alliance building, experimentation, campaigning and self-organization' (Carter, 1996).

In addition to the construction of local alliances and networks, the City Council and MMU have also devoted considerable effort to participation in broader European networks. These involve the Telecities network (a network of European cities actively involved in the development of telematics and of which Manchester held the first Presidency) and the Inter-Regional Information Society Initiative (IRISI), a pilot programme supported by the European Commission of six EU regions including the Northwest of England, and which was subsequently superseded by an enlarged network of 29 regions comprising the Regional Information Society Initiative. These networks have been used to inform and lobby policy-makers at the European level and to create partnerships to bid for resources under other EU programmes. One immediate example of the success of this broader network-building has been Manchester's participation in a successful multi-million ECU proposal under the TEN[4]-Telecom by the 'Infocities' consortium, along with seven other European cities.

---

[4] TEN – Trans European Network

Inevitably, there are tensions between the needs of those involved in European policy networks and the needs of those involved on the ground – for example in community groups or small businesses with limited access to resources of their own, as well as tensions within each network. Resources are needed to sustain the network, and MTTP now acts as a bridging-point or gatekeeper between the global networks controlling resources and the local actors. As European policies have evolved, gaining access to resources has required the reconfiguration of local priorities (and actors) to respond to changing funding environments. While the MTTP can use the broader networks to influence policy 'on behalf of' some of the local agencies, this is inevitably a longer, slow process and provides only a weak feedback. Consequently, a premium is placed on the MTTP's ability to respond rapidly to policy and programme developments at the European level in order to sustain itself, perhaps at the expense of responsiveness to local demand.

The other major global influence on local telematics initiatives is the development of technologies and the technological marketplaces. Manchester's telematics initiatives began with the commission of a technology infrastructure: the Manchester Host computer network (Leach *et al.*, 1991). The Host was originally designed to provide narrowband services such as electronic mail, database access and simple conferencing. In 1991, the first version of Mosaic (the first World Wide Web browser) was released, stimulating the growth of the Internet and revolutionizing the business models of on-line service provision. Previously, on-line information services and on-line messaging (particularly electronic mail) were provided by the same service providers and the information available varied greatly from system to system. Gateways allowing access to information held on other systems, where they existed at all, were generally crude. This stands in marked contrast to the model of the World Wide Web, where access to information services is determined independently of access to the network (and basic services) itself. All on-line service providers (e.g. CompuServe, MSN, Prodigy) were forced to respond to these developments in the early to middle 1990s, to respond to the growth of small, private-sector Internet Service Providers (ISPs). The Manchester Host had to respond in similar fashion and now competes directly with other local, regional and national Internet service providers (ISPs). Given the subsequent evolution of the on-line services market, the Host is now merely one of a number of competing ISPs available to users in the City. The more recent entry into end-user Internet provision of companies such as Microsoft and BT has subsequently created an even more competitive, and rapidly evolving, on-line service provision market nationally. The main value of the Host will therefore have been realized primarily in the period before 1994 when the Internet began to become a widely-used medium beyond academe, in raising awareness and helping to stimulate others to experiment with the technology.

Although the Host remains an important component of the Manchester network, a new technical infrastructure is being developed to support the 'Manchester Multimedia Network' (MMN). The network will provide higher-capacity network linkages from local access centers around the city to a Multimedia Centre based at the Manchester Metropolitan University, with further links into the G-MING

Network[5] and the Internet. The Multimedia Centre will provide training and development facilities, some of which may be accessible remotely. Within the Network, an advanced ATM[6] network is available, which it is envisaged will also be used to link at least some of the remote sites, albeit at lower transmission speeds. The Centre has a close relationship with Apple Computers, supporting the links to the cultural industries where Macintosh computers are currently seen as the *de facto* standard.

BURNLEY CASE STUDY

The Borough of Burnley has been experimenting directly with interventionist strategies around IT and telematics since the mid-1980s. The town successfully launched, and until recently sustained a local Information Technology Centre (ITeC), one of the first in Lancashire. This was an IT training and awareness center, sponsored originally by the DTI, and supported by the Borough Council and private training contracts. This center is now managed by the local college and collaborates closely with the Council and private businesses. More recently, through a partnership with the local college, the Borough Council has supported an investigation into telematic market trends, employer need, and potential training developments that may assist with growth strategies for both local employment and business development. This work has been grant funded with assistance from the European Structural Funds. Associated projects have developed from this research and now include a local business support project integrating business planning and telematics in the pursuit of technology exploitation for business benefit.

Within the Borough the ITeC and Burnley College have continued to focus on training needs, but to date this has been aimed at demand. A perceived issue in the local economy of this East Lancashire town is the lack of awareness as to what telematics may be capable of supporting, for the Borough to achieve its strategic ambitions of employment and business growth. Thus, there have been a series of awareness seminars (supported by the EU and national government funds made available from the Borough's successful Single Regeneration Budget (SRB) bid in 1994), an increase in training activities and a range of developmental projects linking the local area, which is geographically discrete, with regional actors such as Lancashire Enterprises plc (an economic development agency that developed from Lancashire County Council), the East Lancashire Chamber of Commerce and Industry (ELCCI), and members of the North West IRISI network. A KONVER project has supported the networking of Burnley with other local district councils to share economic development information and a new project, the Burnley Learning Network centered around the strategic vision of Burnley College, is set to

---

[5] A broadband network linking Manchester's four universities, the local authority and other partners.
[6] ATM – Asynchronous Transfer Mode – an advanced data communications standard to support multiple multimedia applications.

integrate businesses, community groups and educational establishments (the College, University of Central Lancashire, and local schools) to the wider world of communications and information. Allied to this there are plans for an SME learning center and a design resource center. Indeed, for Burnley, there is a growing concern that it is 'information' and 'communication' that are key resources to aid the development of the Borough and that the technology is only a tool to support this.

The Council is now reviewing its strategic policies and operational intentions with regard to telematics. It both perceives the need for specialist involvement but remains conscious of the fact that it is representing the needs of the Borough and its residents. It has therefore sought to involve a wide local partnership with both a community and business focus to derive the necessary needs and demands relating to any telematic strategy and in so doing is looking to build a resource base from local, national, and European funding to support its development strategy. An additional benefit of the local development is that it is strategically tied to a range of associated economic development activities, and as such is the basis for further integration with local policy frameworks such as the Borough's regeneration strategy and its economic development plans.

In 1996, a local technology and communications partnership (TCP) was formed and this has directly involved specialists from the private sector working with the local partnership to exploit the value of telematics for local economic development activities. Unlike activities in Manchester, the focus of Burnley has been very local. While the area has representation in world-class aerospace and defence sectors, much activity is centered on re-skilling workers and new entrants to the labor market with necessary awareness and telematic skills. There has only been limited dialogue with other regional partners and national organizations, although links within the East Lancashire area are actively being pursued.

LANCASHIRE COLLEGE CONSORTIUM CASE STUDY

The Lancashire College Consortium (LCC) has taken a very strategic view of how telematics can aid its developmental plans. Partners include seven Lancashire colleges and others from neighbouring areas, along with private sector consultants. The Consortium was established in the early 1990s as a forum through which coordinated College activities could take place across the sub-region. Much of the focus of the LCC is on accessing European and other external funding resources, but more recently it has looked to developmental partnerships with Colleges in other areas, such as Greater Manchester, Scotland and London, and to alliances with the private sector, including IBM, ICL, Cable & Wireless and NETG. Recent activities include promotional events for staff training, input to national panels on the development of multi-media training (involving the BBC), and lobbying of policy developments directly affecting the consortium's interests, such as the reformulation of the Greater Manchester, Lancashire and Cheshire (GMLC) Objective 2 Single Programming Document.

Due to the changing nature of the training market, and a resultant reconsideration of the value of vocational training to support skills development in businesses (Painter, Wood and Goodwin, 1995), telematics have been seen by many colleges as tools to support training in the work place and enhance education in traditional environments. This has led to an increase in the development of materials to support resource based learning (RBL), itself now being seen as a new market opportunity.

Through its relationship with commercial consultants and regional economic development agencies, such as the TECs, the local councils, and the ELCCI, the LCC has sponsored large funding applications to the European Union and the national government. A series of 'building blocks' have been positioned to gain the necessary funding to create a 'business knowledge network'. This has resulted in successful funding, now in excess of £3 million grant aid from a range of national and European sources, to support the creation of a business-based telematic network. This will enable the connection of approximately 500 companies to a regional training network. There have been complementary developments alongside the 'physical' network. These include training in the use of telematics; the development of RBL materials for a range of business needs; and staff development of local human resource infrastructure to manage distance learning. In addition to these developments, the network will support business advice and guidance services. The infrastructure itself is based upon the nationally available BT telephone network and the local cable infrastructure. The business computer resources, the front-end access point to the network are to be supplied by IBM and other commercial providers (as are some of the training products and software applications). More recently, tenders have been issued for the provision of a private ISDN network to provide a link between Lancashire colleges (several of which are in the LCC). The activities of the LCC, to date, have only been achieved through regional collaboration within the sector, through the sharing of knowledge and information with the private sector (namely IBM and the local cable company), and via the lobbying of other regional economic development activists that could otherwise have posed as competition. This has, in part, been driven by criteria set by funding agencies, such as the EU, who now stipulate the need for local partnerships.

The benefit of the LCC initiative is that it is explicitly focused on business need, is matched against the national ambitions to promote national vocational qualifications (NVQs), and meets the organizational and institutional needs of the colleges in their pursuit to develop a more pro-active and longer term business training market. However, it is still very much a pilot project. There is no evidence to date to suggest that it will add significantly to the potential of the local economy to reduce unemployment or the threat of redundancy, nor that it will add to the economic robustness of local businesses in a wider economic context.

DISCUSSION

Thus, there is ample motivation, not least because of the availability in many localities of real financial support, for the development of telematic initiatives at local levels although the direction of such initiatives may be imposed through the values of extra-local agencies. Often, when led by the public sector, local policies and initiatives are aimed at stimulating economic development for business and/or the community across a range of spatial scales. However, the case studies presented in this chapter indicate that such initiatives rarely involve the monitoring, evaluation or appraisal of economic development indicators through any formal policy process. While outputs may be achieved, such as individuals into training, numbers of businesses in networks, networks formed, and even job placements, it is not possible to see what real added value has occurred in terms of local economic development. Even where such developments are alluded to, they are not situated within a more holistic and wider geographical evaluation to calculate job displacement effects. There is, therefore, a lack of 'regional' monitoring of economic benefits. Thus, while a local picture may show achievements of outputs these may be counterweighted by negative outcomes in other adjacent local areas (Eisenschitz and Gough, 1993).

The lack of suitable indicators and methodologies creates difficulties in evaluating the cost-effectiveness of technological initiatives. As the Manchester example shows, technical and economic models in this area can be rapidly superseded. The original technologies for the Manchester Host were superseded by the Internet, and the rapidly developing market greatly reduced the significance of the Manchester Host as an infrastructure. Its real value may have been in its role as a catalyst for other initiatives in the city – something that may not best be measured by the original criteria set for it. Actor network theory offers some conceptual tools for analysing the creation and importance of such municipal telematics initiatives. The Manchester example can readily be described in terms of 'local network', 'global network' and the 'obligatory point of passage' between the two (Law and Callon, 1992), represented by leading actors in the MTTP. Actor-network theory may allow the setting of the 'local' strategy into wider economic development contexts. The strengths of the networks can be identified as the responsiveness to the 'obligatory point of passage' to policy shifts in the 'global network' of European policy making. The initiatives' responsiveness to developments in the related global networks of communications technologies may be less effective. The actor-network concept of 'heterogeneous networks', in which technologies can themselves be interpreted as actors, is helpful here. This theoretical approach requires further consideration for the analysis of the use of telematics as a strategic tool for local economic development.

So, for the United Kingdom at least, we have:

- isolated public-driven local activities operating within ill-defined parameters attempting to address perceived market failures;
- national activities stimulating profitable market developments across a range of spatial scales;
- a confused geography of potentially competing telematic developments.

In terms of their true economic development potential the actions of public sector agencies may actually achieve only marginal economic gains, if any at all. The lack of suitable indicators and methodologies creates difficulties in evaluating the cost-effectiveness of technological initiatives.

The Manchester case study shows that:

- Technical and economic models in this area can be rapidly superseded. The original technologies for the Manchester Host were superseded by the Internet, and the rapidly developing market greatly reduced the significance of the Manchester Host as an infrastructure. One economic development value may lay in the role it has played as a catalyst for other initiatives in the city – something that may not best be measured by the original criteria set for it;
- individuals can be linchpins, which, in the public arena may lead to a lack of democracy and unstable policy agenda;
- there is added value in the inclusion of a range of agencies who share common ambitions, but within this there is a need to placate tensions. Thus the human networks need management;
- there is a need for flux and change to be built into developments that are sustained through grant funding;
- there is a need to work with the private sector both for market awareness and to satisfy funding regime criteria.

The Burnley case study shows that:

- a focus on businesses and business need has led to a redefinement and reconsideration of many existing local policies. Information strategies are being seen as more important than infrastructure developments;
- the community dimension is not absent from local activity but provision is centered on existing community services (e.g. the ITeC and the College) and not through the instigation of new agencies;
- a wider partnership in the first instance has assisted in the development of a representative body (public and private, business and community) aiming to affect local economic development, but direction is not yet focused;
- external factors are deemed important, as are regional strategies and European policies;
- there can be a lack of direct involvement with the private sector;
- funding availability has driven policy and initiative.

The Lancashire College Consortium study identifies:

- a strategic approach at a sectoral level;
- the consideration of a 'grand plan' that integrates infrastructure and services to meet a commercial need, and hence to be sustainable outside grant funding;
- the value of collaboration to access funds and to entertain large private sector agencies (IBM and the local cable company);
- the advantages in being represented at a regional level to compete for limited funding against other agencies and other sectors. The LCC integrates and

interfaces with other local lead bodies for different sectors of local governance (e.g. the TECs);

- a focus on local strategy (at the level of the College) linked to a sub-regional strategy (across Lancashire) to identify resources to reach shared ambitions;
- the LCC is more collaborative than competitive and acts as a lobbying agency for the sector in the formulation of policy at a regional level (as in the objectives of the local Objective 2 Single Programming Document);
- consultancy support, connected to international networks across Europe, supports project development and successful applications for grant support.

CONCLUSIONS

In this chapter we have shown that there are a range of ways in which local agencies have sought to influence economic development through the use of strategy. However, it is apparent that these strategies are divergent. The policy direction of the European Commission is likely to have some effect within the UK policy environment with regard to telematics. But limited resources and the non-availability of a coherent national telematics strategy will result in uneven geographies of development. Technological change and private sector market activity further complicate evaluating the likely success of any local strategy. European intervention will certainly support an array of pilot projects at local levels with economic development as a stated ambition. European influence may therefore be seen as weak at the national level and stronger at the regional and local level, with a focus within the geographies of existing local authority boundary areas.

Technological change is a key consideration in all this, as is the value of information as an economic resource. Involvement with the private sector and an understanding of the current and newly developing technologies is necessary in any policy environment. Partnerships leading toward an identification of economic development objectives must aim to include as wide a range of interests as possible, but these partnerships must be appropriately managed. The crucial issue of limited resources available to local authorities and other local agents of governance means that they cannot sustain infrastructure projects, nor can they allow policies to be all things to all people. The case studies highlighted several concerns:

- Manchester illustrates that infrastructure is best supported by the private sector. The city council now focus economic development strategy on a specific growth sector, but retain a strong reliance on European grant funding to support human resources;
- Burnley shows the focus on shared local strategy, information as a resource and technological competence at basic skill levels. Partners share involvement and financial commitment. A range of resources are targeted to provide financial support. There is limited reliance on European finances for human resources;
- The LCC example shows how collaboration between local agencies in the same sector can give added value in identifying common strategies, sharing infor-

mation and targeting appropriate resources. It may illustrate to local authorities and other agencies of governance a more successful way to develop
common strategies to develop, what is for the most part, a communication
strategy for local areas in the context of national and international economic
development.

The final observation must be that it is still not known if telematic technologies,
infrastructure, and application, will add up to any greater local effectiveness in
terms of economic development, whether strategies are developed or not. Models
exist to illustrate the weaknesses and strengths of different approaches to policy
and activity but these alone cannot lead to economic development. The competitive nature of policies targeting inward investment, or training many for few
jobs do not stand as feasible objectives. A more coordinated inter-local strategy
may lead to more positive results but national policies are not geared toward
facilitating this. Thus national policies on the promotion and adoption of
telematics need to be addressed.

REFERENCES AND BIBLIOGRAPHY

Abler, R. (1995) 'Everywhere or Nowhere? The Place of Place in Cyberspace'. Mimeo.

Adam, P. (1995) 'A Reconsideration of Personal Boundaries in Space-time'. *Annals of the Association of American Geographers* **85**(2): 267–285.

Agnew, J. and Corbridge, S. (1995) 'Transnational Liberalism and Mastering Space or Empowering Communities'. In Agnew, J. and Corbridge, S. *Mastering Space: Hegemony, Territory, and International Political Economy.* Cambridge MA: Blackwell: 164–207 and 211–227.

Akrich, M. (1992) 'The De-scription of Technological Objects'. In Bijker, W. and Law, J. *Shaping Technology, Building Society: Studies In Sociotechnical Change.* London: MIT Press: 205–224.

Akwule, R. (1992) *Global Telecommunications: The Technology, Administration, and Policies.* Boston: Focal Press.

Allen Consulting Group (1991) *Australia's Telecommunications Industry: Market Opportunity, Industry Capability and Government's Role.* Canberra: Report to the Department of Industry, Trade and Commerce.

Amin, A. (1994) *Post-Fordism: A Reader.* Cambridge MA: Blackwell.

Anderson, B. (1989) *Imagined Communities.* New York: Verso.

Anderson, E. and Gatignon, H. (1986) 'Modes of Entry: A Transaction Cost Analysis and Propositions'. *Journal of International Business Studies:* **16**.

Anderson, P. and Tushman, M. (1991) 'Managing Through Cycles of Technological Change'. *Research Technology Management* **34**(2): 26–31.

Andersson, A.E. and Persson, O. (1993) 'Networking Scientists'. *Annals of Regional Science* **27**: 11–21.

Andrews, E.L. (1997) '67 Nations Agree to Freer Markets in Communications'. *The New York Times.* 16 February: 1 and 6.

Ang, P.H. (1996) 'Issues in the Regulation of the Internet'. Paper presented at the 25th annual conference of Asian Media, Information and Communication Centre, Singapore.

Anon (1987) 'How Stock Deals Move Around the Globe'. *Asian Wall Street Journal*, 10 Nov: 1.

Anon (1990) 'The Crunch That Competition Caused'. *The Economist, Survey on International Banking*, 7 April.

Aoki, T. (1995) *Intânettô to jôhô sûpâhaiuei.* Tokyo: Ômu Sha.

APEC (1993) 'Australia'. In *The State of Telecommunications Infrastructure and Regulatory Environment of APEC Economies*, Vol. 1. Singapore: APEC Telecommunications Working Group: 21–62.

APEC (1994) 'Indonesia'. In *The State of Telecommunications Infrastructure and Regulatory Environment of APEC Economies*, Vol. 2. Singapore: APEC Telecommunications Working Group: 23–64.

APTA (1994) 'Repelita VI: Indonesia Outlines Telecoms Blueprint for Rest of Century'. *Asia–Pacific Telecoms Analyst*, 1 June: 14–16.

APTA (1995a) 'Optus Asks Shareholders to Tip in Fresh Equity'. *Asia–Pacific Telecoms Analyst*, 20 November: 5.

APTA (1995b) 'Telkom Breathes Sigh of Relief on JOS'. *Asia–Pacific Telecoms Analyst*, 6 November: 9–10.

APTA (1995c) 'Anticipation Over JOS Project Winners'. *Asia–Pacific Telecoms Analyst*, 8 May: 6–7.

APTA (1995d) 'Jakarta Attempts to Keep all JOS Bidders Sweet'. *Asia–Pacific Telecoms Analyst*, 19 June: 7–8.

APTA (1995e) 'Spate of Programming Deals Destabilise Opus' Pay-TV Venture'. *Asia–Pacific Telecoms Analyst*, 18 December: 12.

APTA (1996a) 'Green Paper to Kick-start Debate on New Telecoms Bill'. *Asia–Pacific Telecoms Analyst*, 27 May: 3.

APTA (1996b) 'Power Companies May Rush into Post-97 Telecoms Market'. *Asia–Pacific Telecoms Analyst*, 5 February: 2–3.

APTA (1996c) 'Yellow Light for PCS in Indonesia'. *Asia–Pacific Telecoms Analyst*, 27 May: 5–6.

APTA (1996d) 'Half of Australians Will Own a Mobile by 2000, Says Optus'. *Asia–Pacific Telecoms Analyst*, 4 March: 3–4.

APTA (1996e) 'Troubles at Daya Mitra – Indonesian KSO Unit – Could Cause Difficulties'. *Asia–Pacific Telecoms Analyst*, 22 January: 12–13.

APTA (1996f) 'KSO Loans Prove Popular; Mitra Global Next in Line'. *Asia–Pacific Telecoms Analyst*, 7 October: 7–9.

APTA (1996g) 'Gaffe by Minister Raises Resistance to Telstra Sale'. *Asia–Pacific Telecoms Analyst*, 9 September: 3.

APTA (1997a) 'Deregulation Package Strikes Right Balance, Says Watchdog'. *Asia–Pacific Telecoms Analyst*, 10 February: 6–7.

APTA (1997b) 'Rollouts Grind to a Halt as Telcos Contemplate Collapse'. *Asia–Pacific Telecoms Analyst*, 1 December: 11–12.

APTA (1997c) 'Currency Crisis Still Making Waves in Asian Telco Circles'. *Asia–Pacific Telecoms Analyst*, 1 September: 10–13.

APTA (1997d) 'Telstra Broadband Go-slow is a Step in the Wrong Direction'. *Asia–Pacific Telecoms Analyst*, 18 August: 2–4.

APTA (1998a) 'New Telcos Set to Ditch Carrier Monopoly'. *Asia–Pacific Telecoms Analyst*, 2 March: 3–4.

APTA (1998b) 'Judges Swoon to GlobalOne's Tune in Power Companies' Beauty Pageant'. *Asia–Pacific Telecoms Analyst*, 16 February: 2–3.

APTA (1998c) 'Telcom Sector Still All Adrift as Telecos Struggle to Stay Afloat'. *Asia–Pacific Telecoms Analyst*, 23 March: 1–3.

APTA (1998d) 'More Projects Fall as Telecom Firms Sit Out Financial Storm'. *Asia–Pacific Telecoms Analyst*, 16 February: 7.

APTA (1998e) 'New Deal Likely for KSOs as Indonesia Nears Fiscal Abyss'. *Asia–Pacific Telecoms Analyst*, 2 February: 1–2.

APTA (1998f) 'KSOs Pull Out the Rug Just as Giri Gets Feet Under Table'. *Asia–Pacific Telecoms Analyst*, 20 April: 5–6.

Arndt, H. and Thee Kian Wie (1994) 'Great Differences, Surprising Similarities: Australia, Indonesia and Their Economic Relationship'. In East Asia Analytical Unit, Department of Foreign Affairs and Trade. *Expanding Horizons: Australia and Indonesia into the 21st Century*: 2–21.

Arnold, W. (1996) 'Beware: No E-mail is Safe from the Eyes of Strangers'. *The Asian Wall Street Journal* Weekly Edition, 29 April: 18.

Arnold, W. (1997) 'Hong Kong Takes a Hands-off Approach to Cyberspace'. *The Asian Wall Street Journal* Weekly Edition, 27 January: 15.

Arrowsmith, C. and Wilson, M. (1998) 'Telecom Tectonics Using Geographic Information Systems'. *Cartography* 27(1): 1–8.

Asakura, R. (1995) 'Bijinesu kara kaimono made kashikoi intânetto katsuyôhô (From business to shopping – Clever ways of using the Internet)'. *Gekkan Keiei Juku*, 15 November: 122–127.

Asian Business Review (1993) 'This is Asia Calling'. November.

Asia, Inc. (1997) 'Privacy and the Internet'. *Asia, Inc.*, March: 68–69.

Asian Media, Information and Communication Centre (1997) 'Impact of Globalization on Communications and Asian Values'. *Asian Mass Communications Bulletin* 27(1): 20.

The Asian Wall Street Journal Weekly Edition (1996) 'Asian Forum Focuses on Internet Policing'. *The Asian Wall Street Journal* Weekly Edition, 9 September: 11.

The Asian Wall Street Journal Weekly Edition (1997) 'China Ends Curbs on Some Net Sites by Western Media'. *The Asian Wall Street Journal* Weekly Edition, 20 January: 16.

Asiaweek (1996) 'Mega-solutions for Asia's Future Cities'. *Asiaweek*, 25 October: 48–51.

Asiaweek (1997) 28 March: 11.

Attewell, P. and Rule, J. (1984) 'Computing and Organisations: What We Know and What We Don't Know'. *Communications of the ACM* **27**(12): 1184–1191.

Auger, P. and Gallaugher, J.M. (1997) 'Factors Affecting the Adoption of Internet-based Sales for Small Businesses'. *The Information Society* **13**(1): 55–74.

Aurigi, A. and Graham, S. (1997) 'Virtual Cities, Social Polarisation and the Crisis in Urban Public Space'. *Journal of Urban Technology* **4**(1): 19–52.

Awang, A. (1995) 'Information Technology and Urban Development in Malaysia'. Paper presented at the Workshop on Informatics and Telecoms Tectonics: Information Technology, Policy, Telecommunications, and the Meaning of Space. Michigan State University, East Lansing, Michigan.

Baark, E. (1985) 'Towards an Advanced Information Society in Japan: A Preliminary Study of Sociocultural and Technological Driving Forces'. *Technology & Culture Occasional Series Report No. 13*. Lund Research Policy Studies.

Bakis, H., Abler, R. and Roche, E.M. (1994) *Corporate Networks, International Telecommunications and Interdependence: Perspectives from Geography and Information Systems*. London: Wiley.

Bakker, H., Jones, W. and Nichols, M. (1994) 'Using Core Competencies to Develop New Business'. *Long Range Planning* **27**(6): 13–27.

Baldwin, T., McVoy, D. and Steinfield, C. (1996) *Convergence: Integrating Media, Information and Communication*. London: Sage.

Batty, M. (1993) *The Geography of Cyberspace*. Environment and Planning B: Planning and Design **20**: 615–616.

Batty, M. and Barr, M. (1994) 'The Electronic Frontier: Exploring and Mapping Cyberspace'. *Futures* **26**: 699–712.

Bell, D. (1973) *The Coming of Post-Industrial Society*. New York: Basic Books.

Bellamy, E. (1897) *Equality*. New York: D. Appleton.

Benedict, M. (1991) 'Introduction'. In Benedict, M. (Ed) *Cyberspace: First Steps*. Cambridge MA: The MIT Press.

Beyers, W.B. and Lindahl, D.P. (1997) 'Endogenous Use of Occupations and Exogenous Reliance on Sectoral Skills in the Producer Services'. Paper presented to the RESER Conference, Roskilde University, Roskilde, Denmark, 25–26 September.

BIE (1994) *Information Technology and Telecommunications Industries: An Evaluation of Partnerships for Development and Fixed Term Arrangements Programme*. Canberra: Bureau of Industry Economics.

BIE (1995) *Telecommunications 1995*. Canberra: Bureau of Industry Economics.

Bingham, N. (1996) 'Objections: From Technological Determinism Towards Geographies of Relations'. Mimeo.

Blackwell, R. (1983) 'DP Rises to the Challenge of Electronic Banking'. *Canadian Datasystems* **15**(4): 34–39.

Blaine, M. (1994) *Co-operation in International Business*. Avebury: Aldershot.

Blaine, M. (1995) 'Comparative Contractual Governance'. In Boyd, G. (Ed) *Competitive and Cooperative Macromanagement: The Challenge of Structural Interdependence*. Brookfield VT: Edward Elgar Publishing Company.

Blainey, G. (1967) *The Tyranny of Distance: How Distance Shaped Australia's History*. Melbourne: Macmillan.

Boddewyn, J. (1988) 'Political Aspects of MNE Theory'. *Journal of International Business Studies* **18**(3): 341–63.

Boden, D. and Molotch, H.L. (1994) 'The Compulsion of Proximity'. In Friedland, R. and Boden, D. (Eds) *Nowhere*. Berkeley: University of California Press: 257–286.

Bolter, D. (1995) 'The Social Construction of Telepolis'. Mimeo.

Boyer, C. (1996) *Cybercities: Visual Perception in an Age of Electronic Communication*. New York: Princeton University Press.

Boyle, J. (1996) *Shamans, Software, and Spleens: Law and the Construction of the Information Society*. Cambridge MA: Harvard University Press.

Braudel, F. (1979) *Civilization and Capitalism, 15th–18th Century, Vol. II, The Wheels of Commerce*. New York: Harper & Row.

Breton, T. (1993) *Le Télétravail en France*. Paris: La Documentation Français.

Bridges, W. (1994) *Job Shift: How to Prosper in a Workplace Without Jobs*. Reading MA: Addison-Wesley Publishing Company.

Brotchie, J., Batty, M., Hall, P. and Newton, P. (Eds) (1991) *Cities of the 21st Century*. Melbourne: Longman Cheshire.

Brunn, S.D. (1981) 'Geopolitics in a Shrinking World: A Political Geography of the Twenty-first Century'. In Burnett, A. and Taylor, P. (Eds) *Anglo-American Essays in Political Geography*. Chichester and New York: Wiley: 131–56.

Brunn, S.D. (1984) 'Future of the Nation-State System'. In Taylor, P. and House, J. (Eds) *Political Geography: Recent Trends and Future Directions*. London: Croom Helm: 149–67.

Brunn, S.D. (1993) 'Cities of the Future'. In Brunn, S.D. and Williams, J.R. (Eds) *Cities of the World: World Regional Urban Development*. New York: Harper Collins: 478–92.

Brunn, S.D. (1996) 'The Internationalisation of Diasporas in a Shrinking World'. In Prevelakis, G. (Ed) *The Networks of Diasporas*. Nicosia: Cyprus Research Center: 259–72.

Brunn, S.D. and Cottle, C.E. (1998) 'Cyberboosterism: the "Selling" of Small States on the WWW'. *Geographical Review* **87**(2): 240–58.

Brunn, S.D. and Jones, J.A. (1994) 'Geopolitical Information and Communications in Shrinking and Expanding Worlds: 1900–2100'. In Demko, G.J. and Wood, W.B. (Eds) *Reordering the World: Geopolitical Perspectives on the Twenty-first Century*. Boulder CO: Westview: 301–22.

Brunn, S.D., Jones, J.A. and Purcell, D. (1994) 'Ethnic Communities in the Evolving "Electronic" State: Cyberplaces in Cyberspace'. In Gallusser, W. *et al.* (Eds) *Political Boundaries and Coexistence*. Berne: Peter Lang: 415–24.

Brunn, S.D., Husso, K. and Pyyhtia, M. (1998) 'Writing and Communicating in Cyberspace: A New World of Scholarly Discourse'. In Buttimer, A. and Brunn, S.D. (Eds) *Text and Image: Social Constructions of Regional Knowledge*. Leipzig: Institut fuer Laenderkunde.

Brunn, S.D., Husso, K., Pyyhtia, M. and Kokkonen, P. (1997) 'The GEOGRAPH Electronic Mailing List: The Emergence of a New Scholarly Community'. *Fennia*, **175**(1): 97–123.

Brunn, S.D. and Purcell, D. (1996) 'Ethnic "Electronic" Communities: New Immigrant Linkages in a Wired World'. In Klemencic, M. (Ed) *Ethnic Fraternalism in Immigrant Countries*. Maribor, Slovenia: Univerza v Maribor: 336–43.

Brunn, S.D. and Leinbach, T. (Eds) (1991) *Collapsing Space and Time: Geographic Aspects of Information and Communication*. New York and London: Harper Collins.

BSEG (1995) *Networking Australia's Future: Final Report*. Canberra: Broadband Services Expert Group.

BTCE (1991) *Demand Projections for Telecommunication Services and Equipment to Asia by 2010: An Australian Perspective – July 1991*. Occasional Paper 104. Canberra: Bureau of Transport and Communications.

BTCE (1992) *Quality of Service: Conceptual Issues and Telecommunications Case Study – Report 75*. Canberra: Australian Government Printing Service.

BTCE (1993) *International Telecommunications: an Australian Perspective. Bureau of Transport and Communications Economics – Report 82*. Canberra: Australian Government Publishing Service.

BTCE (1994a) *Communications Research Forum 1993 Papers, 30–31 August 1993*. Canberra: Bureau of Transport and Communications Economics.

BTCE (1994b) *Emerging Communications Services – an Analytical Framework. Communications Futures Project – Work in Progress Paper 1 (Module 1)*. Canberra: Bureau of Transport and Communications Economics.

BTCE (1994c) *Statistical Summary of the Communications, Entertainment and Information*

Industries, Attachment 1 to Communications Futures Project – Work in Progress Paper 1 (Module 1). Canberra: Bureau of Transport and Communications Economics.

BTCE (1994d) *Delivery Technologies in the New Communications. World Communications Futures Project – Work in Progress Paper 2 (Module 5)*. Canberra: Bureau of Transport and Communications Economics.

BTCE (1994e) *Networked Communications Services to the Home: Future Demand Scenarios. Communications Futures Project – Work in Progress Paper 4*. Canberra: Bureau of Transport and Communications Economics.

BTCE (1994f) *Diffusion of Communications, Entertainment and Information Services, Attachment 1 to Communications Futures Project – Work in Progress Paper 4*. Canberra: Bureau of Transport and Communications Economics.

BTCE (1994g) *Towards the Networked Home: The Future Evolution of Residential Communications Networks in Australia. World Communications Futures Project – Work in Progress Paper 6*. Canberra: Bureau of Transport and Communications Economics.

BTCE (1995a) *Telecommunications in Australia, Bureau of Transport and Communications Economics – Report 87*. Canberra: Australian Government Publishing Service.

BTCE (1995b) *Communications Futures: Final Report*. Canberra: Australian Government Publishing Service.

Buckley, P. and Casson, M. (1976) *The Future of the Multinational Enterprise*. London: Macmillan.

Budde, P. (1995) *Superhighways in Asia 1995–1996: Strategies, Trends and Developments on the Telecommunications and Television Markets in Asia*. Bucketty NSW: Paul Budde Communications Pty Ltd.

Burns, T. and Stalker, G.M. (1961) *The Management of Innovation*. London: Tavistock.

Business Week (1986) 'The Hollow Corporation'. *Business Week*, 3 March: 57–85.

Buttimer, A. (1982) 'Musing on Helicon: Root Metaphors and Geography'. *Geografiska Annaler*. **64B**: 89–96.

Cable Data Communications News (1996) Cable Modem FAQ http://www.cabledatacomnews.com/

Cairncross, F. (1997) *The Death of Distance: How the Communications Revolution Will Change Our Lives*. Cambridge: Harvard Business Press.

Callon, M. (1986) 'Some Elements of a Sociology of Translation: Domestication of the Scallops and the Fisherman of St Brieuc Bay'. In Law, J. (Ed) *Power, Action and Belief: A New Sociology of Knowledge*. London: Routledge: 196–232.

Callon, M. (1991) 'Techno-economic Networks and Irreversibility'. In Law, J. (Ed) *A Sociology of Monsters, Essays on Power, Technology and Domination*. London: Routledge: 196–233.

Carey, J. and Quirk, J.J. (1989) 'The Mythos of the Electronic Revolution'. In Carey, J.W. *Communication as Culture: Essays on Media and Society*. Boston: Unwin Hyman.

Carlos, A. and Nicholas, S. (1986) 'Giants of Earlier Capitalism: The Chartered Trading Companies as Modern Multinationals'. *Business History Review*. Autumn: 398–419.

Carmel, E. (1997) 'American Hegemony in Packaged Software Trade and the "Culture of Software"'. *The Information Society* 13(1): 125–42.

Carter, D. (1996) 'Creative Cities and the Information Society – The Role of Innovation and Cultural Development in Supporting Economic Regeneration: Manchester's experience as an "Information City"'. Economic Initiatives Group, Manchester City Council.

Castells, M. (1989) *The Informational City: Information Technology, Economic Restructuring and The Urban-Regional Process*. Oxford: Blackwell.

Castells, M. (1996) *The Rise of the Network Society*. New York: Blackwell.

Castells, M. (1997) *The Power of Identity: The Information Age – Economy, Society and Culture*. New York: Blackwell.

Castells, M. (1998) *End of Millennium*. New York: Blackwell.

Chadwick, P. (1995) '1995 – Another media watershed?' *Communications Update*. February: 2–3.

Chandler, A. (1962) *Strategy and Structure: Chapters in the History of the Industrial Enterprise*. Cambridge MA: MIT Press.

Chandler, A. (1990) *Scale and Scope: The Dynamics of Industrial Capitalism*. Cambridge MA: Belknap Press of Harvard University Press.

Chandler, A., Bruchey, S. and Galambos, L. (1968) *The Changing Economic Order: Readings in American Business and Economic History*. New York: Harcourt, Brace & World Inc.

Chandrasekaran, R. (1997) 'US Rejects Levying Tax on Internet'. *International Herald Tribune*. 1 July: 1.

Channel 4 (1994) 'Once Upon a Time in Cyberville'. London (Programme transcript).

Cheah, C. (1994) 'Communications Futures Project'. In BTCE (1994a) *Communications Research Forum 1993 Papers – 30–31 August 1993*. Canberra, Bureau of Transport and Communications Economics: 109–119.

Chen, K. (1996) 'China Blocks Internet Access to Dozens of Web Sites on News, Politics and Sex'. *The Asian Wall Street Journal* Weekly Edition, 9 September: 10.

Chia, W. (1995) 'Bakrie's Telecoms Focus Now Looks Good Move'. *Business Times* (Singapore) 7 July.

Choi, S.-Y., Stahl, D.O. and Whinston, A.B. (1997) *The Economics of Electronic Commerce*. New York: Macmillan.

Chua, C.H. (1997) 'Rules Have Not Hindered Internet, But Fine-tune Them, Says Advisory Body'. *The Straits Times* Weekly Edition, 4 October: 6.

Chua, R. and Zesiger, C. (1996) 'Vietnam's Emerging Net Faces Control Campaign'. *The Asian Wall Street Journal* Weekly Edition, 9 September: 1 and 11.

Chung, T.M. (1996) 'Steps Taken By Other Countries to Regulate Internet'. *The Straits Times* Weekly Edition, 16 March: 15.

Clark, D., Ilbery, B. and Berkley, N. (1995) 'Telematics and Rural Businesses: An Evaluation of Uses, Potentials and Policy Implications'. *Regional Studies* **29**(2): 171–180.

Clemons, E.K. and Row, M. (1988) 'A Strategic Information System: McKesson Drug Company's Economist'. *Planning Review* **16**(5): 14–19.

COA (1996) *Telstra: To Sell or Not to Sell? Consideration of the Telstra (Dilution of Public Ownership) Bill 1996. Report from the Senate Environment, Recreation, Communications and the Arts References Committee, The Parliament of the Commonwealth of Australia*. Canberra: Senate Publishing Committee.

Coase, R.H. (1937) 'The Nature of the Firm'. *Economica*: 386–405.

Coates, V.T. (1992) 'Technology and United States Stock Markets'. *Technological Forecasting and Social Change* **41**(1): 1–12.

Cohen, S.B. (1994) 'Geopolitics in the New World Era: New Perspective on an Old Discipline'. In Demko, G.J. and Wood, W.B. (Eds) *Reordering the World: Geopolitical Perspectives on the Twenty-first Century*. Boulder CO: Westview: 15–48.

Commission of the European Union (1994) *Europe and the Global Information Society: Recommendations to the European Council*. Brussels, May 26, 1994. http://www.iaehv.nl/users/red/bangem.html.

Commission of the European Union (1995) *Using Telematics in your Organisation*. DGXIII, CEU, Brussels.

Commission of the European Union (1996) *Information Technologies, Productivity and Employment*. DGIII, CEU, Brussels.

Communications Week International (1996) 'BT Reacts to Cable Threat with ADSL'. *Communications Week International*, 23 September.

Contractor, F. and Lorange, P. (Eds) (1988) *Cooperative Strategies in International Business*. Lexington MA: Lexington Books.

Corey, K.E. (1995) *Jean Gottmann, 1915–1994*. Annals of the Association of American Geographers. **85**(2): 356–365.

Corey, K.E. (1996) 'Digital Dragons and Cyber communities: The Application of Information Technology and Telecommunications Public Policies and Private Partnerships, to the

Planning of Urban Areas'. Paper presented at the International Symposium on Urban Sciences, Seoul City University, Seoul, Korea.

Corey, K.E. (1998) 'Information Technology and Telecommunications Policies in Southeast Asian Development'. In Savage, V.R., Kong, L. and Neville, W. (Eds) *The Naga Awakens*. Singapore: Times Academic Press: 145–200.

Corn, J. (1986) 'Epilogue'. In Corn, J. (Ed) *Imagining Tomorrow: History, Technology and the American Future*. Cambridge MA: MIT Press: 219–229.

Cornford, J., Gillespie, A. and Robins, K. (1991) 'Telecommunications and the Competitive Advantage of Cities in the European Urban System'. Paper presented at the Communications and Economic Development Conference, Manchester, May.

Cosgrove, D. (1996) 'Windows on the City'. *Urban Studies* **33**(8): 1495–1498.

Cronin, F.J., Parke, E.B., Colleran, E.K. and Gold, M.A. (1991) 'Telecommunications Infrastructure and Economic Growth: an Analysis of Causality'. *Telecommunications Policy* **15**: 529–535.

Cronin, M.J. (1996) *Global Advantage on the Internet: From Corporate Connectivity to International Competitiveness*. New York: Van Nostrand.

Culp and McIntyre, J. (1994) 'Competition in Japan's Information Technology Sector'. *Competitiveness Review* **4**: 1–12.

Cybriwsky, R. (1991) *Tokyo: The Changing Profile of an Urban Giant*. Boston: G.K. Hall and Co.

Dabinett, G. and Graham, S. (1994) 'Telematics and Industrial Change in Sheffield, UK'. *Regional Studies* **28**(6): 605–617.

Datta-Ray, S.K. (1995) 'How to Keep Singaporeans Out of Dark Alleys of Internet'. *The Straits Times*, 24 June: 32.

Davidow, W. and Malone, M. (1992) *The Virtual Corporation: Structuring and Revitalizing the Corporation for the 21st Century*. New York: Edward Burlingame Books/Harper Business.

Davis, S. and Lawrence, P. (1977) *Matrix Reading*. MA: Addison-Wesley.

Deakin, M. (1996) 'Super League: Full Federal Court Prefers Competition On and Off the Field'. *Communications Law Bulletin* **15**(4): 1–4.

Deans, P.C. and Kane, M.J. (1992) *International Dimensions of Information Systems and Technology*. Boston: PWS-Kent, especially 'Transnational Flows of Information Data': 64–92 and 'International Telecommunications and Global Community': 93–114.

Deans, P.C. and Karwan, K.R. (Eds) (1994) *Global Information Systems and Technology: Focus on the Organization and Its Functional Areas*. Harrisburg: Idea Group Publishing.

Dennis, E.W. (1993) 'Communication, Media, and the Global Marketplace of Ideas'. *Fletcher Forum of World Affairs* **17**(1): 1–8.

Dicken, P. (1992) *Global Shift: The Internationalisation of Economic Activity*. 2nd edition. New York: Guilford Press.

Dodge, M. (1999) *Atlas of Cyberspace*. http://www.cybergeography.org

Doxiadis, C.A. and Papaioannou, J.G. (1974) *Ecumenopolis: The Inevitable City of the Future*. New York: W.W. Norton & Company.

Drucker, P. (1988) 'The Coming of the New Organization'. *Harvard Business Review*, January–February: 45–53.

Dunning, J. (1977) 'Trade, Location of Economic Activity and the MNE: A Search for an Eclectic Approach'. In Ohlin, B., Hesselborn, P. and Wijkman, P. (Eds) *The International Allocation of Economic Activity*. London: Macmillan.

Dunning, J. (1979) 'Explaining Changing Patterns of International Production: In Defense of the Eclectic Theory'. *Oxford Bulletin of Economics and Statistics*, November: 269–95.

Dunning, J. (1980) 'Towards an Eclectic Theory of International Production'. *Journal of International Business Studies*, Spring/Summer: 9–31.

Dutton, W., Blumler, J., Garnham, N., Mansell, R., Cornford, J. and Peltu, M. (1994) 'The Information Superhighway: Britain's Response'. PICT Policy Research Paper 29, ESRC, Swindon.

Dymsza, W. (1984) 'Trends in Multinational Business and Environments: A Perspective'. *Journal of International Business Studies* 14: 25–46.

EAAU (1992) *Connecting the Region – Telecoms & Transport Markets. Australia's Business Challenge South-East Asia in the 1990s.* Canberra: East Asia Analytical Unit, Department of Foreign Affairs and Austrade: 221–234.

Editor (1996) 'No Big Brother in Cyberspace'. *The Straits Times* Weekly Edition, 12 October: 12.

Edwards, C., MacIntyre, A. and Asra, A. (1994) 'New Complementarities: Changing Demographics and the Demand for Services'. In *Expanding Horizons: Australia and Indonesia into the 21st Century.* Canberra: East Asia Analytical Unit, Department of Foreign Affairs and Trade: 23–49.

Economic Development Board (1997) 'Global City with Total Business Capabilities'. http://www.sedb.com

The Economist (1993) 'The Japanese Economy: From Miracle to Mid-life Crisis'. 6 March.

The Economist (1994) 'Offices'. 6 August.

The Economist (1995) 'A Survey of Telecommunications: the Death of Distance'. **336**: 7934. 30 September.

The Economist (1995) 'Malaysia's Edifice Complex'. **336**(7930): 39.

The Economist (1996) 'Electronic Cities: Move over, Mickey'. **338**(7956): 28–29.

Egelhoff, W.G. (1991) 'Information-Processing Theory and the Multinational Enterprise'. *Journal of International Business Studies* **22**(3): 341–368.

Eisenschitz, A. and Gough, J. (1993) *The Politics of Local Economic Policy: The Problems and Possibilities of Local Initiative.* Basingstoke: Macmillan.

Elg, U. and Johansson, U. (1993) 'The Institutions of Industrial Governance'. *International Studies of Management and Organization* **23**(1): 29–46.

EM (1995) 'Indonesia: The Brawl for PT Telkom'. *Euromoney*, September: 38.

Far Eastern Economic Review (1987) 'Japan Banking and Finance', 9 April: 47–110.

Far Eastern Economic Review (1998) 'New Internet Control' **161**(2): 13.

Ferguson, M. (1992) 'The Mythology About Globalization'. *European Journal of Communication* **7**: 69–93.

Frederick, H.H. (1993) *Global Communications and International Relations.* Belmont CA: Wadsworth.

Galbraith, J. (1973) *Designing Complex Organisations.* Reading MA: Addison-Wesley.

Garcia, D.L. (1997) 'Networked Commerce: Public Policy in a Deregulated Communications Environment'. *The Information Society* **13**(1): 17–32.

Gargan, E.A. (1996) 'A Boom in Malaysia Reaches for the Sky'. *The New York Times.* 2 February: C1 and C3.

Gates, B. (1995) *The Road Ahead.* New York and London: Viking.

Gelerntner, D. (1991) *Mirror Worlds: The Day Software Puts the Universe in a Shoebox . . . How It Will Happen and What It Will Mean.* New York: Oxford University Press.

Genosko, J. (1987) 'The Spatial Distribution of Telematics: Modelling and Empirical Evidence'. *Technological Forecasting and Social Change* **32**: 281–293.

Gershon, R.A. and Kanayama, T. (1995) 'Direct Broadcast Satellites in Japan: A Case Study in Government-business Relationships'. *Telecommunications Policy* **19**(3): 217–231.

Gershuny, J.I. (1978) *After Industrial Society?: The Emerging Self-Service Economy.* Atlantic Highlands NJ: Humanities Press.

Ghoshal, S. and Nohria, N. (1993) 'Horses for Courses: Organisational Forms for Multinational Corporations'. *Sloan Management Review* **34**(2): 23–35.

Gibbs, D.C. (1993) 'Telematics and Urban Economic Development Policies: Time for Caution?'. *Telecommunications Policy* **17**(4): 250–256.

Gibson, W. (1984) *Neuromancer.* London: Harper and Collins.

Giddens, A. (1979) *Central Problems In Social Theory.* London: Macmillan.

Gillespie, A. (1992) 'Communications Technologies and the Future of the City'. In Breheny, M. (Ed) *Sustainable Development and Urban Form.* London: Pion: 67–77.

Gillespie, A., Richardson, R. and Cornford, J. (1995) *Review of Telework in Britain:*

Implications for Public Policy. Report prepared for the UK Parliamentary Office of Science and Technology, CURDS, University of Newcastle upon Tyne.

Gillespie, A. and Robins, K. (1989) 'Geographical Inequalities: the Spatial Bias of the New Communications Technologies'. *Journal of Communications* **39**(3): 7–18.

Gillespie, A. and Williams, H. (1988) 'Telecommunications and the Reconstruction of Comparative Advantage'. *Environment and Planning A* **20**: 1311–21.

Gilroy, M.B. (1993) *Networking in Multinational Enterprises: The Importance of Strategic Alliances*. Columbia SC: University of South Carolina Press.

Glasmeier, A. and Borchard, G. (1989) 'From Branch Plants to Back Offices: Prospects for Rural Service Growth'. *Environment and Planning A* **21**: 1565–1583.

Glasmeier, A. and Howland, M. (1994) 'Service-led Rural Development: Definitions, Theories, and Empirical Evidence'. *International Regional Science Review* **16**(1–2): 197–229.

Goddard, J.B. (1991) 'New Technology and the Geography of the UK Information Economy'. In Brotchie, J., Batty, M., Hall, P. and Newton, P. (Eds) *Cities of the 21st Century: New Technologies and Spatial Systems*. Melbourne: Longman Cheshire.

Goh, A. (1996) 'Unrestricted Net Access to Continue for Business'. *The Straits Times* Weekly Edition. 7 September: 2.

Gold, J.R. (1991) 'Fishing in Muddy Waters: Communications Media, Homeworking and the Electronic Cottage'. In Brunn, S.D. and Leinbach, T.R. (Eds) *Collapsing Space and Time: Geographic Aspects of Communications and Information*. London: HarperCollins Academic.

Gôtô, M. (1990) 'Jôhô kanyôron (Information environment theory)'. In Tôkyô Daigaku Shimbun Kenkyûjo (Ed) *Kôdo Jôhô Shakai no Komiyûnikêshon (Communication in the Advanced Information Society)*. Tokyo: Tôkyô Daigaku. Shuppankai: 28–50.

Gottmann, J. (1961) *Megalopolis: The Urbanized Northeastern Seaboard of the United States*. New York: The Twentieth Century Fund.

Gottman, J. (1977) 'Megalopolis and Antipolis: the Telephone and the Structure of the City'. In Pool, I.S. (Ed) *The Social Impact of the Telephone*. Cambridge MA: MIT Press.

Gottmann, J. (1982) 'Urban Settlements and Telecommunications'. *Ekistics* **302**: 411–416.

Grabher, G. (Ed) (1993) *The Embedded Firm: On the Socioeconomics of Industrial Networks*. London: Routledge.

Graham, S. (1992) 'The Role of Cities in Telecommunications Development'. In Blackman, C. (Ed) *Telecommunications Policy*. Oxford: Butterworth-Heinemann.

Graham, S. (1992) 'Electronic Infrastructures and the City: Some Emerging Municipal Policy Roles in the UK'. *Urban Studies* **29**(5): 755–781.

Graham, S. (1993) 'Changing Communications Landscapes: Threats and Opportunities for UK Cities'. *Cities*. May: 158–166.

Graham, S. (1996) 'Imagining the Real-time City: Telecommunications, Urban Paradigms, and the Future of Cities'. In Westwood, S. and Williams, J. (Eds) *Imagining Cities: Scripts, Signs and Memories*. London: Routledge: 31–49.

Graham, S. (1996) 'Networking the City: A Comparison of Urban Telecommunications Initiatives in France and Britain'. PhD thesis, University of Manchester.

Graham, S. (1997) 'Cities in the Real-time Age: Telecommunications as a Paradigm Challenge to the Conception and Planning of Urban Space'. *Environment and Planning A* **29**: 105–27.

Graham, S. and Dominy, G. (1991) 'Planning for the Information City: The UK Case'. *Progress in Planning* **35**(3): 169–248.

Graham, S. and Marvin, S. (1996) *Telecommunications and the City – Electronic Spaces, Urban Places*. London: Routledge.

Granger, J. (1996) 'Advanced Telecommunication Infrastructure Programmes and Regional Development'. Paper presented at Europe and the Developing World in the Globalised Information Society: Employment Education and Trade Implications Workshop, UNU/ INTECH, Maastricht, 17–19 October.

Greenfeld, K.T. (1994) *Speed Tribes: Children of the Japanese Bubble*. London: Box Tree.

Grimes, S. and Lyons, G. (1994) 'Information Technology and Rural Development: Unique

Opportunity or Potential Threat?' *Entrepreneurship and Regional Development* 6(3): 219–238.

Gross, L.S. (1995) *The International World of Electronic Data*. New York: McGraw-Hill.

Hakansson, H. and Johanson, J. (1993) 'The Network as a Governance Structure: Interfirm Cooperation Beyond Markets and Hierarchies'. In Grabher, G. (Ed) *The Embedded Firm: On the Socioeconomics of Industrial Networks*. London: Routledge.

Halal, W.E. (1994) 'From Hierarchy to Enterprise: Internal Markets are the New Foundation of Management. *Academy of Management Executive* 8(4): 69–83.

Hamada, Y. (1995) 'Seijika wa jidai okure (Politicians are behind the times)'. *Aera* 25 November: 20–30.

Hamlin, K. (1997) 'Singapore Inc. Will Stay Ahead'. *The Straits Times* Weekly Edition, 29 March: 13.

Handy, C.B. (1994) *The Age of Paradox*. Boston: Harvard Business School Press.

Hannan, M. and Freeman, J. (1977) 'The Population Ecology of Organizations'. *American Journal of Sociology* 82: 929–64.

Hannan, M. and Freeman, J. (1988) *Organizational Ecology*. Boston: Harvard University Press.

Hansen, S., Cleevley, D., Wadsworth, S., Bailey, H. and Bakewell, O. (1990) 'Telecommunications in Rural Europe: Economic Implications'. *Telecommunications Policy* 14: 207–222.

Harasim, L.M. (Ed) (1993) *Global Networks: Computers and International Communication*. Cambridge MA: MIT Press.

Haraway, D. (1991) 'A Manifesto for Cyborgs: Science, Technology, and Socialist-feminism in the Late Twentieth Century'. In Haraway, D. (Ed) *Simians, Cyborgs and Women: The Reinvention of Nature*. New York: Routledge: 149–181.

Harding, J. (1997) 'China Crackdown on Internet "Subversion"'. *Financial Times*, 31 December: 4.

Harries, K. and Brunn, S.D. (1978) *The Geography of Laws and the Administration of Justice*. New York: Praeger.

Harrigan, K.R. (1985) *Strategies for Joint Ventures*. Lexington MA: Lexington Books.

Harrison, M. (1995) 'Visions of Heaven and Hell'. London: Channel 4 Television.

Harrison, R.T. (1990) 'The Nature and Extent of Innovative Activity in a Peripheral Regional Economy'. In ter Heide, H. (Ed) *Technological Change and Spatial Policy*. Nederlande Geografische Studies 112: 135–157.

Harvey, D. (1985) *The Urbanisation of Capital*. Oxford: Blackwell.

Harvey, D. (1989) *The Condition of Postmodernity: An Enquiry into the Origins of Cultural Change*. New York: Blackwell.

Harvey, D. (1993) 'From Space to Place and Back Again: Reflections on the Condition of Postmodernity'. In Bird, J., Curtis, B., Putnam, T., Robertson, G. and Tickner, L. *Mapping The Futures: Local Cultures, Global Change*. London: Routledge: 3–29.

Hatta, K. and Takeuchi, N. (1995) 'Facility Supply and Demand of the Trunk Line Network: Some Aspects of Competition in the Japanese Telecommunications Market'. *Telecommunications Policy* 19(3): 201–216.

Hattori, K. (1990) *Tokyo wo Shiru (Discovering Tokyo)*. Tokyo: Doyukan.

Hau, B.L. (1996) 'Internet Security: No Need to Worry, Say Service Providers'. *The Straits Times* Weekly Edition, 20 January: 7.

Hayes, D. (1996) 'Japan: A Domestic Profile'. *Asian Communications* July: 15–18.

Hayles, K. (1993) 'Virtual Bodies and Flickering Signifiers'. October 66: 69–91.

Healey, P., Cameron, S., Davoudi, S., Graham, S. and Madani Pour, A. (Eds) (1995) *Managing Cities: The New Urban Context*. Chichester: John Wiley.

Henderson, D.M. (1992) 'The Use of Telecommunications to Regenerate a Rural Area'. In *Institution of Electrical Engineers (IEE) International Conference on Data Transmission – Advances in Modem and ISDN Technology and Applications*. London: IEE.

Hennart, J.-F. (1989) 'Can the "New Forms" of Investment Substitute for the "Old Forms"? A Transaction Cost Perspective'. *Journal of Intentional Business Studies* 19(2): 211–33.

Hepworth, M. and Robins, K. (1988) 'Whose Information Society? A view from the Periphery'. *Media, Culture and Society* 10: 323–343.

Hepworth, M. (1989) *The Geography of the Information Economy: Studies in the Information Economy*. London: Belhaven.

Hepworth, M. (1990) *Geography of the Information Economy*. New York: Guilford.

Hepworth, M. (1991) 'Information Technology and the Global Restructuring of Capital Markets'. In Brunn, S. and Leinbach, T.R. (Eds) *Collapsing Space and Time: Geographic Aspects of Communication and Information*. London: HarperCollins Academic: 132–48.

Hill, C. (1990) 'Cooperation, Opportunism, and the Invisible Hand: Implications for Transaction Cost Theory'. *Academy of Management Review* 15(3): 500–13.

Hill, R. (1997) 'Electronic Commerce: The World Wide Web, Minitel, and EDI'. *The Information Society* 13(1): 33–42.

Hill, S. (1988) *The Tragedy of Technology*. London: Pluto.

Hillman, J. (1993) *Telelifestyles and the Flexicity: A European Study*. Dublin: European Foundation for the Improvement of Living and Working Conditions.

Ho, W.F. (1997) 'No Delay in MSC Project, Says Mahathir'. *The Straits Times* Weekly Edition, 20 September: 10.

Honma, M. (1995) 'Ima koso yûzâ no shiten ni tatta denki tsûshin seido no kaikaku o (Now is the time for user-based reform of the electrical communications system). *Gekkan Keiei Juku* 15 November: 103–107.

Hunt, E.S. (1994) *The Medieval Super-companies – A Study of the Peruzzi Company of Florence*. Cambridge: Cambridge University Press.

Huws, U. (1991) 'Telework: Projections'. *Futures* 23(1): 19–31.

Huws, U. (1993) *Teleworking in Britain. Employment Department Research Series No. 18*. Sheffield: Employment Department.

Huws, U., Honey, S. and Morris, S. (1996) *Teleworking and Rural Development. Rural Research Report No. 27*, Rural Development Commission. London: Rural Development Commission.

Hymer, S.H. (1960) 'The International Operations of National Firms'. Ph.D. Diss. MIT. (published by MIT Press in 1976).

IBM World Trade Corporation and Institute Sultan Iskandar (1996) Johor State Information Infrastructure (JII) Draft Final.

Ilbery, B., Clark, D., Berkely, N. and Goldman, I. (1995) 'Telematics and Rural Development: Evidence from a Survey of Small Business in the European Union'. *European Urban and Regional Studies* 2(1): 55–68.

Innis, H.A. (1951) *The Bias of Communications*. Toronto: University of Toronto Press.

International Business Studies 23(1): 133–145.

International Telecommunications Union (1999a) *Basic Indicators*. http://www.itu.int/ti/industryoverview/at_glance/basic98.pdf

International Telecommunications Union (1999b) *Cellular Subscribers*. http://www.itu.int/ti/industryoverview/at_glance/cellular98.pdf

Ishizawa, M. (1994a) 'NTT–Microsoft: Match Made in Heaven?' *Nikkei Weekly*, March 28: 8.

Ishizawa, M. (1994b) 'Software Houses Latecomers to Downsizing'. *Nikkei Weekly*, July 4: 8.

Ishizawa, T. (1987) *Tokyoken 2000nen no Ofisu Biru (Buildings in Tokyo in the Year 2000)*. Tokyo: Toyokeizaki.

Israel, J.I. (1989) *Dutch Primary in World Trade 1580–1740*. Oxford: Clarendon Press.

Israel, J.I. (1995) *The Dutch Republic: Its Rise, Greatness, and Fall 1477–1806*. Oxford: Clarendon Press.

IT Asia (1997) 'NCB To Come Under MTI Umbrella'. *IT Asia* 11(3): 5.

ITU (1994) *World Telecommunications Development Report 1994*. Geneva: ITU.

ITU (1995) *World Telecommunications Development Report*. Geneva: ITU.

Ives, B. and Jarvenpaa, S. (1991) 'Applications of Global Information Technology: Key Issues for Management'. *MIS Quarterly* 15(1): 33–49.

Janelle, D. (1968) 'Central Place Development in a Time-space Framework'. *Professional Geographer* 20(1): 5–10.

Johansson, J. and Mattsson, L.-G. (1987) 'Interorganizational Relations in Industrial Systems: A Network Approach Compared with the Transaction-cost Approach'. *International Studies in Management and Organization* **17**(1): 34–48.

Johns, R.A. (1983) *Tax Havens and Offshore Finance: A Study of Transnational Economic Development*. London: Frances Pinter.

Johnson, M. (1990) 'Why Japan isn't the Hottest IT Spot in Asia'. *Datamation*, 15 June: 149–153.

Johnstone, H.J. (1997) 'Entering the Twilight Zone'. *Asian Business* **33**(2): 48–51.

Joint Venture: Silicon Valley Network (1995) The Joint Venture Way: Lessons for Regional Rejuvenation, Joint Venture: Silicon Valley Network, San José.

Joint Venture: Silicon Valley Network (1996) Joint Venture's Index of Silicon Valley 1996, Measuring Progress Toward a 21st Century Community, Joint Venture: Silicon Valley Network, San José.

Joseph, R.A. (1993) 'Converging Telecommunications Technologies: Challenges Facing Governments and Regulators in Australia and New Zealand'. *Telecommunications Policy*. September/October: 493–503.

JP (1995) 'Indonesia Satelindo Reforms Billing System'. *Jakarta Post*, 13 December.

Junne, G. (1988) 'The Emerging Global Grid: The Political Dimension'. In Muskens, G. and Gruppelaar, J. (Eds) *Global Telecommunication Networks: Strategic Considerations*. Dordrecht: Kluwer Academic Publishers.

Jussawalla, M. (1987) *The Calculus of International Communications: A Study in the Political Economy of Transborder Data Flows*. Littleton CO: Libraries Unlimited.

Kageki, N. (1994a) 'KDD Asks for Whom the Bell Rings'. *Nikkei Weekly*, 7 March: 8.

Kageki, N. (1994b) 'NTT to Break into Interactive TV'. *Nikkei Weekly*, 4 April: 8.

Kang, S.L. (1996) 'Malaysia's First Cyberlaws to be Implemented 97'. *Business Times* (Malaysia). htttp://www.mdc.com.my/archive/press/press_g.html.

Karunaratne, N.D. and Jussawalla, M. (1988) 'The Information Economies of Indonesia, Malaysia and Thailand'. In Jussawalla, M., Lamberton, D.M. and Karunaratne, N.D. (Eds) *The Cost of Thinking: Information Economies of Ten Pacific Countries*. Norwood, N.J.: Abex: 165–194.

Keen, P.G.W. (1991) *Every Manager's Guide to Information Technology*. Boston: Harvard Business School Press.

Kehoe, L. (1997) 'US Court Strikes Down Law on Internet Decency'. *Financial Times*, 27 June: 1.

Kehoe, L. and Taylor, P. (1997) 'The Law Catches Up With the Internet'. *Financial Times*, 22 April: 4.

Kellerman, A. (1993) *Telecommunications and Geography*. London: Belhaven Press.

Kesler, M., Kolstad, D. and Clarke, W.E. (1993) 'Third Generation R&D: The Key to Leveraging Core Competencies'. *Columbia Journal of World Business* **28**(3): 34–44.

Kester, W.C. (1992) 'Industrial Groups as Systems of Contractual Governance'. *Oxford Review of Economic Policy* **8**(3): 24–44.

Kilduff, M. (1992) 'Performance and Interaction Routines in Multinational Corporations'. *Journal of International Business Studies* **23**(1): 133–145.

KK (1984) *Nihon 21 seiki e no tenbô – kokudo kukan atarashi miraizo o megutte (Observations of Japan in the Twenty-first Century – Our New Future Image of Land Space)*. Tokyo: Kokudocho Keikau/Choseibu.

Killing, P. (1983) *Strategies for Joint Venture Success*. New York: Praeger.

Kindleberger, C. (1968) *International Economics*. Homewood IL: Richard Irwin Inc.

Kindleberger, C.P. (1974) *The Formation of Financial Centers. Princeton Studies in International Finance*. Princeton NJ: Department of Economics, Princeton University.

Kirn, T., Conway, R. and Beyers, W. (1990) 'Producer Services Development and the Role of Telecommunications: A Case Study in Rural Washington'. *Growth and Change* **21**(4): 33–50.

Kirsch, S. (1995) 'The Incredible Shrinking World? Technology and the Production of Space'. *Environment and Planning D: Society and Space* **13**: 529–555.

Kitahara, Y. (1983) *Information Network System: Telecommunications in the Twenty-first Century*. London: Heinemann Education Books Ltd.

Kogut, B. (1988) 'Joint Ventures: Theoretical and Empirical Perspectives'. *Strategic Management Journal* 9: 319–32.

Koh, B.S. (1997) 'Internet: S'pore Takes Enlightened Approach'. *The Straits Times* Weekly Edition, 8 February: 4.

Koh, L. (1997) 'Internet Adviser Calls for Fewer Fences in Cyberspace'. *The Straits Times* Weekly Edition, 11 October: 15.

Konsynski, B.R. (1993) 'Strategic Control in the Extended Enterprise'. *IBM Systems Journal* 32(1): 111–143.

Koron, G. (1996) Personal communication, Hewlett Packard Company, Kansas City, Missouri. 1 May

Korte, W.B., Kordney, N. and Robinson, S. (1994) 'Telework Penetration, Potential and Practice in Europe – Results from Representative Surveys Carried Out in the TELDET Project', mimeo, Empirica.

Kozin, M.D. and Young, K.C. (1994) 'Using Acquisitions to Buy and Hone Core Competencies'. *Mergers & Acquisitions* 29(2): 21–26.

Kynge, J. (1996) 'Singapore Cracks Down on Internet'. *Financial Times*, 12 July: 7.

Kynge, J. and Nakamoto, J. (1997) 'NTT Joins Venture to Develop Malaysia Cybercity'. *Financial Times*, 7 May: 1 and 16.

Lakshmanan, T. and Okumura, M. (1995) 'The Nature and Evolution of Knowledge Networks in Japanese Manufacturing'. *Papers in Regional Science* 74: 63–85.

Lamberton, D. (1994) *Diffusion of new information technologies and products. Diffusion of Communications, Entertainment and Information Services, Attachment 1 to Communications Futures Project – Work in Progress Paper 4*. Canberra: Bureau of Transport and Communications Economics: 1–36.

Lanegran, D.A. (1992) 'Communication'. In Abler, R., Marcus, M. and Olson, J. (Eds) *Geography's Inner Worlds*. New Brunswick NJ: Rutgers University Press: 187–211.

Langdale, J. (1985) 'Electronic Funds Transfer and the Internationalisation of the Banking and Finance Industry'. *Geoforum* 16: 1–13.

Langdale, J.V. (1989) 'The Geography of International Business Telecommunications: The Role of Leased Networks'. *Annals of the Association of American Geographers* 79: 501–522.

Langdale, J.V. (1991) *Internationalization of Australia's Service Industries*. Canberra: Australian Government Publishing Service.

Langdale, J.V. (1991) 'Telecommunications and International Transactions in Information Services'. In Brunn, S. and Leinbach, T. (Eds) *Collapsing Time and Space*. London: HarperCollins Academic: 193–214.

Langdale, J.V. (1992a) *Regional Administrative Headquarters and Telecommunications Hubs: Australia and the Asia–Pacific Region*. Canberra: Construction and Services Division, Department of Industry, Technology and Commerce.

Langdale, J.V. (1992b) *Australia and Southeast Asia: Internationalization of Service Industries*. Canberra: Construction and Services Division, Department of Industry, Technology and Commerce.

Langdale, J.V. (1996) 'Geographical Perspectives on Broadband Telecommunications and Interactive Multimedia in Australia'. Unpublished paper presented to the Workshop on Exploring Electronic Space: Economic Policy and Social Dimensions of Information Technology. Hikone, Japan, May 1996.

Latour, B. (1987) *Science in Action: How to Follow Scientists and Engineers Through Society*. Milton Keynes: Oxford University Press.

Latour, B. (1993) *We Have Never Been Modern*. London: Harvester and Wheatsheaf.

Latzer, M. (1995) 'Japanese Information Infrastructure Initiatives'. *Telecommunications Policy* 19(7): 515–529.

Law, J. and Bijker, W. (1992) 'Postscript: Technology, Stability and Social Theory'. In Bijker,

W. and Law, J. *Shaping Technology, Building Society: Studies In Sociotechnical Change*. London: MIT Press: 290–308.

Law, J. and Callon, M. (1992) 'The Life and Death of an Aircraft: A Network Analysis of Technical Change'. In Bijker, W. and Law, J. (Eds) *Shaping Technology/Building Society – Studies in Sociotechnical Change*. Boston: MIT Press: 21–52.

Lawrence, P. (1981) 'The Harvard Organization and Environment Research Programme'. In Van De Ven, A. and Joyce, W. (Eds) *Perspectives on Organization Design and Behavior*. New York: John Wiley & Sons.

Lawrence, P. and Lorsch, J. (1967) *Organization and Environment: Managing Differentiation and Integration*. Boston: Division of Research, Graduate School of Business Administration, Harvard University.

Leach, B., Girbash, C. and Walker, S. (1991) *The Manchester Host Feasibility Study*. CER, Manchester Polytechnic and Soft Solution Ltd.

Lee, T. (1996) 'Religious Groups Unsure of New Cyberspace Rules'. *The Straits Times*, 31 May: 58.

Lee, T. and Goh, A. (1996) 'Internet to Link Key Services Soon'. *The Straits Times* Weekly Edition, 7 September: 4.

Lefebvre, H. (1984) *The Production Of Space*. Oxford: Blackwell.

Leinbach, T.R. and Brunn, S.D. No publication date. 'Cities, Firms and Regions in the Worlds of Electronic Commerce: Does Geography Matter in Competitive Advantage?' unpublished manuscript.

Leyshon, A. (1994) 'Under Pressure: Finance, Geo-economic Competition and the Rise and Fall of Japan's Postwar Growth Economy'. In Corbridge, S., Martin, R. and Thrift, N. (Eds) *Money, Power and Space*. Oxford: Blackwell.

Leyshon, A. (1995) *Annihilating Space?: The Speed-up of Communications*. Milton Keynes: Open University.

Lipman, A., Sugarman, A. and Cushman, R. (1986) *Teleports and the Intelligent City*. Homewood IL: Dow Jones.

Lopez, L. (1995) 'Indonesia: Suharto's Son in Controversial Bid for Telekomsel Stake'. *Business Times* (Singapore), 3 November.

Lyons, G.M. and Mastanduno, M. (1992) *Beyond Westphalia: International Intervention, State Sovereignty, and the Future of Intentional Society*. Dartmouth NH: Dartmouth University.

Maddox, T. (1994) 'The Cultural Consequences of the Information Superhighway'. *Wilson Quarterly* **18**: 29–36.

Mahathir, B.M. (1991) 'Malaysia: The Way Forward'. Working paper presented at the Inaugural Meeting of the Malaysian Business Council, Kuala Lumpur.

Mahathir, B.M. (1996) 'Keynote Address'. Speech given at the opening of Multimedia Asia on Multimedia Super Corridor, Putra World Trade Centre, Kuala Lumpur, 1 August.

Mahathir, B.M. (1996) 'Malaysia's Multimedia Super Corridor'. *I-Ways* **19**(3): 49–55.

Mansell, R. (1994) 'Introductory Overview'. In Mansell, R. (Ed) *Management Of Information and Communication Technologies*. London: ASLIB: 1–7.

Mariti, P. and Smiley, R.H. (1983) 'Co-operative Agreements and the Organization of Industry'. *The Journal of Industrial Organization* **31**(4): 437–51.

Martin, R. (1994) 'Stateless Monies, Global Financial Integration and National Economic Autonomy: The End of Geography?' In Corbridge, S., Martin, R. and Thrift, N. (Eds) *Money, Power and Space*. Oxford: Blackwell: 253–78.

Marvin, C. (1988) *When Old Technologies were New: Thinking About Electric Communication in the Late Nineteenth Century*. Oxford: Oxford University Press.

Masai, Y. (1989) 'Greater Tokyo as a Global City'. In Knight, R. and Gappert, G. (Eds) *Cities in a Global Society*. Newbury Park CA: Sage Publications.

Massey, D. (1993) 'Power-geometry and a Progressive Sense of Place'. In Bird, J., Curtis, B., Putnam, T., Robertson, G. and Tickner, L. *Mapping the Futures: Local Cultures, Global Change*. London: Routledge: 59–69.

McFarlan, F. Warren (1983) 'The Information Archipelago'. *Harvard Business Review* **83**(1): 145–56.

McFarlan, F. Warren (1984) 'Information Technology Changes the Way You Compete'. *Harvard Business Review* **62**(3): 98–103.

McGee, J. Jr (1991) *Implementing Systems Across Boundaries: Dynamics of Information Technology and Integration*. Ann Arbor: UMI (Doctoral Thesis).

McLuhan, H. (1964) *Understanding Media – The Extension of Man*. London: Sphere.

McNerney, D.J. (1995) 'Welcome to Virtual HR'. *HR Focus* **72**(8): 3.

McNulty, S. (1998) 'Loan for Malaysian Hi-tech Hub'. *Financial Times*, 21 January: 9.

McNulty, S. (1998) 'Malaysia's "Multimedia Super Corridor" in Danger'. *Financial Times*, 14 January: 7.

Mesher, G. (1996) 'The Internet's Impact'. *Asian Communications*, March: 28–32.

MIMOS (1995) 'MIMOS First Ten Years'. Malaysian Institute of Microelectronic Systems, Kuala Lumpur.

Mitchell, W. (1994) 'Building the Bitsphere, or the Kneebone's Connected to the I-Bahn'. *I.D. Magazine*, November.

Mitchell, W. (1995) *City of Bits: Space, Place and the Infobahn*. Cambridge MA: MIT Press.

MITI (1994) *Programme for Creating New Markets (Programme 21)*. Tokyo: Ministry of International Trade and Industry.

Moindrot, P. (1991) 'Managing a Major Telework Project'. Paper presented to ACRE seminar Telecottages and Teleworking, 13 May.

Molina, A. and Fleck, J. (1995) 'An Approach to Innovation and Technology Development'. Paper prepared for PICT International Conference on Social and Economic Implications of Information and Communication Technologies, London, May 10–12.

Morley, D. and Robins, K. (1995) *Spaces of Identity: Global Media, Electronic Landscapes and Cultural Boundaries*. London: Routledge.

Morris, D. and Hergert, M. (1987) 'Trends in International Collaborative Agreements'. *Columbia Journal of World Business*. Summer 15–21.

Morris-Suzuki, T. (1996) 'The Information Superhighway and the Political Economy of Knowledge: Some Thoughts on the Japanese Experience'. Paper presented to the International Seminar on the World Today Center for Research in the Humanities and Sciences. Autonomous National University of Mexico: January.

Morse, L. (1994) 'Shift Away from US Continues'. *Financial Times*. 16 November.

Morton, S.S. (Ed) (1991) *The Corporations of the 1990s: Information Technology and Organizational Transformation*. New York: Oxford University Press.

Mosco, V. (1996) *The Political Economy of Communication*. London: Sage.

Moss, M. (1987b) 'Telecommunications, World Cities, and Urban Policy'. *Urban Studies*, **24**: 534–546.

MRI (1993) *Total Forecast: Japan 1990s* (Ed N. Makino). Tokyo: Mitsubishi Research Institute.

Mulgan, G. (1991) *Communication and Control: Networks and the New Economies of Communication*. Oxford: Polity Press.

Mulqueen, J.T. (1987) 'Networking Dollars and Sense: ATMs Uniting Nationwide'. *Data Communications* **16**(11): 85–92.

Multimedia Development Corporation (1997) Overview. http://www.mdc.com.my/infras/overview/index.html

Multimedia Development Corporation (1997) Bill of Guarantees. http://www.mdc.com.my/incent/bill/index.html

Multimedia Development Corporation (1997) Policies & Cyberlaws. http://www.mdc.com.my/infras/cyberlaw/index.html

Multimedia Development Corporation (1997) Questions and Answers. http://www.mdc.com.my/faq/qa/index.html

Murai, J. (1995) *Intânetto sengen (The Internet Declaration)*. Tokyo: Kôdansha.

Murakami, T. (1985) 'Inception of INS Experience: Model System Sets in Service'. *Japan Telecommunications Review* **27**(1): 2–17.

Murdock, G. (1993) 'Communications and the Constitution of Modernity'. *Media, Culture and Society* **15**: 521–539.

Murphy, A.B. (1994) 'International Law and the Sovereign State'. In Demko, G.J. and Woods, W.B. (Eds) *Reordering the World: Geopolitical Perspectives on the Twenty-first Century*. Boulder CO: Westview: 29–24.

Murray, W. (1995) *Vital Statistics: Results of the Telecottage Survey. Teleworker No. 7*, February–March.

Murray, B., Murray, C. and Cornford, D. (1997) *Corporate Telework Survey*. Small World Connections, Manchester.

Naisbitt, J. and Aburdene, P. (1991) *Megatrends 2000 – Ten Directions for the 1990s*. New York: Avon Books.

Nakamura, H. and White, J. (1988) 'Tokyo'. In Dogan, M. and Kasarda, J. (Eds) *The Metropolitan Era Volume 2: Mega-Cities*. Newbury Park CA: Sage.

National Computer Board (1995) 'LIVEwire Pilot, an Experiment in Information Infrastructure Building: The Beginning'. National Computer Board, Singapore.

National Computer Board (1996) 'A New Mission, a New NCB'. *IT Focus* April/May: 1–2.

National Computer Board (1997) 'NCB to Come Under MTI Umbrella'. http://www.ncb.gov.sg/ncb/press/Ncbmove.html

Negroponte, N. (1995) *Being Digital*. London: Hodder and Stoughton.

Newfield, T. and Hôjô, S. (1996) 'Seishinkoku Amerika ni manabu bijiretsu seikôjutsu (Learning from Developed America's successful business methods). *Jitsugyô no Nihon* 99 January: 36–40.

Newman, K. (1993) *Declining Fortunes: the Withering of the American Dream*. New York: Basic Books.

The New Straits Times (1997) 'Body Will Enforce Digital Signature Act'. *The New Straits Times*. 14 May: 8.

NEXUS Europe, CURDS and Culture and Communications Studies (1996) *An Assessment of the Social and Economic Aspects of the Development of an Information Society in Europe. Volume 3: Barriers and Strategies to Effective Participation in the Information Society in the Cohesion Regions*. Final Report to DGXIII and DGXVI of the CEC. Nexus Europe, Dublin.

Ng, C.A. (1996) 'Internet paedophilia an Issue to be Addressed'. *The Straits Times* Weekly Edition, 5 October: 23.

Nijkamp, P., Rietveld, P. and Salomon, I. (1990) 'Barriers in Spatial Interactions and Communications: A Conceptual Exploration'. *The Annals of Regional Science* **24**: 237–252.

The Nikkei Weekly (1997) 'Malaysia High-tech Project Swamped by Companies'. *The Nikkei Weekly* **35**(1772): 15.

Nilles, J.M., Carlson, R.R., Gray, P. and Hanneman, G.J. (1976) *The Telecommunications–Transportation Tradeoff: Options for Tomorrow*. New York: Wiley.

Nilles, J. (1985) 'Teleworking From Home'. In Forester, T. (Ed) *The Information Technology Revolution*. Oxford: Basil Blackwell.

Nishi, K. (1995) 'Nihonjin ga miotoshita marchimedia no YTT (The Multimedia YTT: Overlooked by the Japanese). *Daiyamondo* 23 December: 45–48.

Noam, E.M. and Sato, H. (1995) 'Kobe's Lesson: Dial 711 for "Open" Emergency Communications'. *Telecommunications Policy* **19**(8): 595–598.

Norman, P. (1997) 'Bonn Outlines its Plans for First "Cyber Sheriff"'. *Financial Times*, 22 April: 4.

NTT (n.d.) *INS (Information Network System)*. Tokyo: Nippon Telegraph and Telephone Corporation.

Nun, A. (1995) 'Putrajaya the Intelligent City: A Strategy Towards the Digital Economy'. Paper presented at Infotech 95 Malaysia, Kuala Lumpur.

Nun, A. (1995) 'Putrajaya: The Intelligent City Spearheading the Malaysian Multi-media Super Corridor Development'. The Third Leadership Seminar, Johor Bahru.

Nun, A. (1996) Personal electronic communication. 29 August.

Nye, J.S. Jr and Owens, W.A. (1996) 'The Information Edge'. *Foreign Affairs* **75**(2): 20–36.

O'Brien, R. (1992) *Global Financial Integration: The End of Geography*. London: Pinter.

Office of Technological Assessment (1995) *The Technological Reshaping of Metropolitan America*. Washington: Congress of the United States.

O'Lear, S. (1996) 'Using Electronic Mail (E-Mail) Surveys for Geographic Research: Lessons from a Survey of Russian Environmentalists'. *The Professional Geographer* **48**: 209–17.

Optus (1994) *Corporate Environmental Plan*. Optus Communications (no place of publication given).

Ó Siochrú, S., Gillespie, A.E. and Qvortrup, L. (1995) *Advanced Communications for Cohesion and Regional Development*, Final Report to DGXIII, CEC, ACCORDE Project (T1015) 'Telework 94' Initiative.

O'Toole, T. (1993a) 'Firms Joining Global Computer Net'. *Nikkei Weekly*, 15 Nov: 8.

O'Toole, T. (1993b) 'PC Networks to Forge First Links'. *Nikkei Weekly*, 6 Dec: 8.

O'Toole, T. (1994a) 'NEC Inching Toward IBM Standard'. *Nikkei Weekly*, 14 Feb: 8.

O'Toole, T. (1994b) 'US Firm Points Way to Data Highway'. *Nikkei Weekly*, 21 Feb: 8.

Ôtsuki, H. (1995) 'Kôseinô nettowâku' koso muruchimedia o sasaeru kiban da (The 'high-performance network' is the base which supports multimedia)'. *Gekkan Keiei Juku* 15 November: 50–59.

Ouchi, W. (1980) 'Markets, Bureaucracies, and Clans'. *Administrative Science Quarterly* **25**: 129–41.

Ôzaki, S. (1995) 'Wâpuro wa ikinokoru ka (Will wordprocessors survive?)'. *Aera* 25 November: 15–17.

Paavonen, W. (1993) 'Telework in Sweden'. Paper presented to the Telematics and Innovation: New Ways of Living and Working in Europe Conference, Palma, Majorca, 17–19 November.

Painter, J., Wood, M. and Goodwin, M. (1995) 'British Local Governance Beyond Foredooms: A Regulationist Perspective'. Paper presented at ESRC Local Governance Programme Conference, Exeter, 19–20 September.

Palvia, S., Palvia, P. and Zigli, R. (1992) *The Global Issues of Information Technology Management*. Harrisburg: Idea Group Publishing.

Panos/D'Monte, D. (1995) 'Access Denied'. *Asian Review*, September: 22.

Parker, E.B. and Hudson, H.E. (1995) *Electronic Byways: State Policies for Rural Development Through Telecommunications*. Washington DC: The Aspen Institute (2nd Edition).

Parliament of Singapore (1993) The Computer Misuse Act 1993 Bill No. 17/93. Parliament of Singapore, Singapore.

Parry, J.H. (1967) 'Transport and Trade Routes'. In Rich, E.E. and Wilson, C.H. (Eds) *Cambridge Economic History of Europe. Vol. 4 (The Economy of Expanding Europe in the Sixteenth and Seventeenth Centuries)*. Cambridge: Cambridge University Press: 155–222.

Pascal, A. (1987) 'The Vanishing City'. *Urban Studies* 24: 597–603.

PATRA Consortium (1996) *Psychological Aspects of Teleworking in Rural and Urban Areas*. Final Report to the European Commission.

Pawley, M. (1995) 'Architecture, Urbanism and the New Media'. Mimeo.

Peck, J. and Emmerich, M. (1992) 'Recession, Restructuring and the Greater Manchester Labour Market: An Empirical Overview'. Spatial Policy Analysis Working Paper 17, School of Geography, Manchester University.

Pereira, G. (1996) 'Net Users Not Being Monitored, Says SBA'. *The Straits Times* Weekly Edition, 28 September: 2.

Pereira, G. (1996) 'New Moves to Regulate the Internet Here'. Southeast Asia Electronic Discussion List. 6 March.

Pereira, G. (1996) 'Singapore's Internet Regulation Starts July 15th'. Southeast Asia Electronic Discussion List. 15 July.

Pickles, M. (1994) 'First National GSM System'. *Asian Communications* **8**(4): 22.

Pickles, J. (Ed) (1995) *Ground Truth: The Social Implications of Geographic Research Systems*. London and New York: Guilford.

Pile, S. (1994) 'Cybergeography: 50 years of Environment and Planning A'. *Environment and Planning A* **26**: 1815–1823.

Pile, S. and Thrift, N. (1996) 'Mapping the Subject'. In Pile, S. and Thrift, N. (Eds) *Mapping the Subject: Geographies of Cultural Transformation*. Routledge: London: 13–51.

Piore, M.J. and Sabel, C.F. (1984) *The Second Industrial Divide: Possibilities for Prosperity*. New York: Basic Books.

Pipe, G.R. (1997) 'Special Report, Privacy and Security'. *I-Ways*. First Quarter: 40–54.

Porter, M. (1990) *The Competitive Advantage of Nations*. London and Basingstoke: Macmillan.

Poster, M. (1990) *The Mode of Information. Poststructuralism and Social Context*. Chicago: University of Chicago Press.

Poster, M. (1995) *The Second Media Age*. Cambridge MA: Blackwell.

Powell, W. (1990) 'Neither Market nor Hierarchy: Network Forms of Organization'. In Straw, B. and Cummings, L.L. (Eds) *Research in Organizational Behavior*. **12**: 295–336. Greenwich CT: JAI Press Inc.

Prahalad, C.K. (1993) 'The Role of Core Competencies in the Corporation'. *Research Technology Management* **36**(6): 40–47.

Price Waterhouse (1990) *The Economic Impact of Information Technology and Telecommunications in Rural Areas*. Final Report to DGXIII.F, Commission of the European Communities. London: Price Waterhouse.

Pugh, D.S. and Hickson, D.J. (Eds) (1989) *Writers on Organizations*. Newbury Park CA: Sage Publications Inc.

Pura, R. (1995) 'Malaysia Will Soon Commence Carving a High-tech Capital Out of the Palms'. *The Asian Wall Street Journal*, 4 September: 11 and 15.

Pura, R. (1996) 'Will This Great Mall Top China's Wall?' *The Wall Street Journal*, 11 July: A12.

Pyle, K.B. (1988) 'Japan, the World and the Twenty-first Century'. In Inoguchi, T. and Okimoto, D.I. (Eds) *The Political Economy of Japan: Vol. 2: The Changing International Context*. Stanford: Stanford University Press: 446–486.

Quiggin, J. (1996) *Great Expectations: Microeconomic Reform and Australia*. Sydney: Allen & Unwin.

Qvortrup, L. (1992) 'Telework: Visions, Definitions, Realities, Barriers'. In OECD (Ed) *Cities and New Technologies*. Paris: OECD.

Qvortrup, L. (1994) 'Advanced Communications and Regional Development – The Case of Finnmark'. Mimeo.

Raban, J. (1988) *Soft City*. London: Collins Harvill.

Rada, J.F. and Pipe, G.R. (Eds) (1984) *Communication Regulation and International Business*. Amsterdam: North-Holland.

Rapoport, A. (1985) *General Systems Theory*. Tunbridge Wells, Kent: Abacus Press.

Revzin, P. (1995) 'Info-Highway Builders Seek to Change African Nations' Development Priorities'. *Wall Street Journal*, 9 June: A5C.

Rheingold, H. (1993) *The Virtual Communities: Homesteading on the Electronic Frontier*. Reading MA: Addison-Wesley.

Rheingold, H. (1994) *The Virtual Society: Finding Connection in a Computerised World*. London: Secker and Warburg.

Richardson, D. (1996) *The Internet and Rural Development: Recommendations for Strategy and Activity: Final Report and Executive Summary*. Report prepared for the Food and Agriculture Organization of the United Nations. http://www.fao.org/waicent/faoinfo/sustdev/Cddirect/CDDO/contents.htm

Richardson, G.B. (1972) 'The Organisation of Industry'. *The Economic Journal*. September: 883–96.

Richardson, R. (1994) 'Back-officing Front Office Functions – Organisational and Locational Implications of New Telemediated Services'. In Mansell, R. (Ed) *Management of Information and Communications Technologies: Emerging Patterns of Control*. London: ASLIB.

Richardson, R. (1997) 'Network Technologies, Organisational Change and the Location of Employment: The Case of Teleservices'. In Dumort, A. and Dryden, J. (Eds) *Economics of the Information Society*, OECD–European Commission.

Richardson, R. (1998) 'Call Centres and the Prospects for Export-oriented Work in the Developing World: Evidence from Western Europe'. In Mitter, S. and Bastos, M.I. (Eds) *Europe and the Developing World in the Global Tele-Economy: Employment and Distance Education*. London: Routledge/UNU Press.

Richardson, R. and Gillespie, A. (1996) 'Advanced Communications and Employment Creation in Rural and Peripheral Regions: A Case Study of the Highlands and Islands of Scotland'. *Annals of Regional Science* **30**: 91–110.

Rimmer, P.J. (1988) 'The Dialectic of the External and the Internal: A Perspective on Australia's Future Transport-land Use Activity'. Invited Speakers: 14th ARRB Conference August 28–September 2, 1988: Proceedings Part 1. Melbourne: Australian Road Research Board: 221–238.

Rimmer, P. (1991) 'Exporting Cities to the Western Pacific Rim: The Art of the Japanese Package'. In Brotchie, J., Batty, M., Hall, P. and Newton, P. (Eds) *Cities of the 21st Century*. Melbourne: Longman Cheshire.

Rimmer, P.J., Dick, H., Papanak, J. and Siregar, M. (1994) 'Facilitating Trade: Problems on the Periphery'. In *Expanding Horizons: Australia and Indonesia into the 21st Century*. Canberra: East Asia Analytical Unit, Department of Foreign Affairs and Trade: 147–190.

Roach, S. (1994) 'Premier 100: Lessons of the Productivity Paradox'. *Computerworld*. September 19: 55.

Robins, K. (1995) 'Cyberspace and the World We Live In'. *Body & Society* **1**(3–4): 135–155.

Robins, K. (1995) 'Cyberspace and the World We Live In'. In Featherstone, M. and Burrows, R. *Cyberspace/Cyberbodies/Cyberpunk*. London: Sage: 135–156.

Robinson, R. (1981) 'Background Concepts and Philosophy of International Business from World War II to the Present'. *Journal of International Business Studies*. Spring/Summer: 13–21.

Roche, E.M. (1992) *Managing Information Technology in Multinational Corporations*. New York: Macmillan.

Roche, E.M. and Blaine, M.J. (Eds) (1996) *Information Technology, Development and Policy*. Aldershot: Avebury.

Root, F. (1984) 'Some Trends in the World Economy and their Implications for International Business'. *Journal of International Business Studies* **14**(1): 19–32.

Rosenberg, H. (1994) *Exploring the Black Box: Technology, Economics, and History*. Cambridge: Cambridge University Press.

Rowles, G. (1975) *Prisoners of Space. Exploring the Geographical Experiences of Older People*. Boulder CO: Westview.

Rural Development Commission (1989) *Telecommunications in Rural England*. Rural Development Commission Research Report No. 2 RDC.

Sanders, S.R. (1995) 'The Web of Life'. *Utne Reader* **68**: 68–71.

Sassen, S. (1991) *The Global City: New York, London, Tokyo*. Princeton NJ: Princeton University Press.

Saunders, H.H. (1991) 'The Historic Challenge to Rethink How Nations Relate'. In Volkan, V. et al. *The Psychodynamics of International Relations*. Lexington MA: Lexington Books: 1–30.

Savage, J. (1988) *Financial Centre Prospects for New Zealand*. Wellington: New Zealand Institute of Economic Research, Research Monograph No. 41.

Sawhney, H. (1996) 'Information Superhighway: Metaphors as Midwives'. *Media, Culture and Society* **18**: 291–314.

Saxenian, A. (1994) *Regional Advantage: Culture and Competition in Silicon Valley and Route 128*. Cambridge MA: Harvard University Press.

Schenker, J.L. (1997) 'OECD is Seen Adopting Policy for Encryption'. *Wall Street Journal*, 27 March: B19.

256

Schroeder, R. (1994) 'Cyberculture, Cyborg Post-modernism and the Sociology of Virtual Reality Technologies'. *Futures* **26**(5): 519–528.

Schuler, D. (1996) 'Creating Public Space in Cyberspace: The Rise of the New Community Networks'. Paper presented at the Annual AMIC Conference, Singapore.

Schuler, D. (1996) *New Community Networks: Wired for Change.* New York: ACM Press.

Schwartz, A. (1994) *A Nation in Waiting: Indonesia in the 1990s.* Sydney: Allen & Unwin.

Scott, A.J. (1993) *Technopolis: High-technology Industry and Regional Development in Southern California.* Berkeley: University of California Press.

Seager, J. (Ed) (1990) *The State of the World Atlas.* New York: Simon and Schuster.

Seager, J. and Olson, A. (1986) *Women in the World: An International Atlas.* New York: Simon and Schuster.

Sesit, M.R. (1987) 'Crash Exposes Perils of Global Market'. *Asian Wall Street Journal.* 16 November: 24.

Shariffadeen, T.M.A. (1996) Personal discussion. Stanford University, Palo Alto, California. 10 September.

Shelley, F.M., Archer, J.C., Davidson, F.M. and Brunn, S.D. (1996) 'Political Geography of the Twenty-first Century'. In Shelley, F.M. (Ed) *Political Geography of the United States.* New York and London: Guilford: 308–35.

Shuhaimi, A. (1996) 'Regulating the Internet: SBA Will Be Pragmatic'. *The Straits Times* Weekly Edition, 23 March: 23.

Shuhaimi, A. (1996) 'Singapore Launches Effort to Police Internet'. Southeast Asia Electronic Discussion List, 15 August.

SI (1994) *Australian Telecommunications: Competition and Beyond 1994–1995.* Melbourne: Strategic Information Pty Ltd.

Simpson, D. (1994) 'How to Identify and Enhance Core Competencies'. *Planning Review* **22**(6): 24–26.

Singapore Broadcasting Authority (1996) *Singapore Broadcasting Authority: An overview.*

Singapore Broadcasting Authority (1996) *Singapore Broadcasting Authority Inaugural Annual Report.*

Singapore Bulletin (November 1996) 'Practical Approach to Keep Out Net Abusers', *Singapore Bulletin* **24**(11): 13–14.

Singapore Telecom (1995) *Take Telecommunications Into a Future Address.* Telepark, Singapore Telecom, Singapore.

Slouka, M. (1995) *War of the Worlds: The Assault on Reality.* London: Abacus.

Smart Valley (1996) *Connect 96: The Global Summit on Building Electronic Communities.* Smart Valley, Inc., Santa Clara, California.

Smith, A. (1980) *The Geopolitics of Information: How Western Culture Dominates the World.* New York: Oxford

Smith, A. (1990) 'Media Globalism in the Age of Consumer Sovereignty'. *Gannett Center Quarterly* **4**(4): 1–16.

Smith, D. (1977) *Human Geography. A Welfare Approach.* New York: St. Martin's Press.

Smith, D. (1994) *Geography and Social Justice.* Cambridge MA: Blackwell.

Sociomics Ltd/Arkleton Trust (Research) Ltd (1993) *Exploratory Investigation of Employment Trends in Rural Areas Related to ECS, Employment Trends Related to the Use of Advanced Communications,* DG-XIII, European Commission, Luxembourg.

Spaeth, A. (1996) 'Bound for Glory'. *Time* 148(24) 9 December: 20–30.

Spinks, W. (1991) 'Satellite and Resort Offices in Japan'. *Journal of Transportation* **18**: 411–432.

Stabler, J. and Howe, E. (1988) 'Service Exports and Regional Growth in the Postindustrial Era'. *Journal of Regional Science* **28**: 303–315.

Stalk, G. Jr and Hout, T.M. (1990) 'Competing Against Time: How Time-based Strategies Give Technological Innovators the Competitive Edge'. *Research Technology Management* **33**(2): 19–25.

Stallabrass, J. (1995) 'Empowering Technology: The Exploration of Cyberspace'. *New Left Review* **211**: 3–32.

Staple, G. (1993) 'Telegeography and the Explosion of Place'. *TeleGeography, Global Traffic Statistics and Commentary*: 49–56.

Staple, G. (1996) *Telegeography 1996–97: Global Communications Traffic Statistics and Commentary*. Washington: International Institute of Communications.

Staple, G. and Mullins, M. (1989) 'Telecom Traffic Statistics – MiTT Matter: Improving Economic Forecasting and Regulatory Policy'. *Telecommunications Policy* **13**(2): 105–28.

The Star (1997) '25 Bills Passed in 28 Sittings'. 16 May: 10.

Steel, J. (1994) 'Indonesia's Imports Grow'. *Asian Communications* **8**(4): 21–22.

Stewart, H. (1996) 'NTT Strides On'. *Asian Communications February*: 33–38.

Stiglitz, J.E. (1997) 'The Role of Government in Economic Development'. In *Annual World Bank Conference on Development Economics 1996*. Bruno, M. and Pleskovic, B. (Eds) Washington: The World Bank: 11–23.

Stopford, J. and Wells, L. (1972) *Managing the Multinational Enterprise: Organization of the Firm and Ownership of the Subsidiaries*. New York: Basic Books.

Storper, M. and Scott, A.J. (1995) 'The Wealth of Regions: Market Forces and Policy Imperatives in Local and Global Context'. *Futures* **27**: 505–26.

The Straits Times (1996) 'US Urged to be Involved in the "Asian Century", Malaysia Planning its Own Silicon Valley'. *The Straits Times*, 21 May: 21.

The Straits Times (1996) 'Peep into Malaysia's First Cyber Township'. *The Straits Times*. 25 May: 21.

The Straits Times Weekly Edition (1995) 'Capital Investment in Johor Rose to [S]$1.16 Last Year'. *The Straits Times* Weekly Edition, 15 April: 11.

The Straits Times Weekly Edition (1996) 'KL Plans to Act Against Net Abusers'. *The Straits Times* Weekly Edition, 16 March: 10.

The Straits Times Weekly Edition (1996) 'River City'. *The Straits Times* Weekly Edition, 8 June: 10.

The Straits Times Weekly Edition (1997) '14 Major Companies to Pump $100m into S'pore ONE'. *The Straits Times* Weekly Edition, 1 February: 6.

The Straits Times Weekly Edition (1997) '10 Offices to be Set Up Abroad to Woo Firms to Multimedia Project'. *The Straits Times* Weekly Edition, 15 March: 8.

The Straits Times Weekly Edition (1997) 'Computer Hackers Face up to 7 Years' Jail Under New Bill'. *The Straits Times* Weekly Edition, 29 March: 10.

Studemann, F. (1997) 'Bavaria Gives Lead in Cleaning Net'. *Financial Times*, 30 April: 9.

Sugaya, N. (1995) 'Cable Television and Government Policy in Japan'. *Telecommunications Policy* **19**(3): 233–239.

Survey of Current Business (1992) 'US International Sales and Purchases of Services'. September: 116–127.

Swyngedouw, E. (1993) 'Communication, Mobility and the Struggle for Power over Space'. In Giannopoulos, G. and Gillespie, A. (Eds) *Transport and Communications in the New Europe*. Belhaven: London: 305–325.

Symon, A. (1994) 'A Country in Transition'. *Asian Communications* **8**(4): 19–20.

Takahashi, J. (1995) 'Tokyo: A World City in Transition'. Unpublished paper presented at Pre-Habitat Conference on the World Cities and the Urban Future. Tokyo August 23–25, 1995 organized by United Nations University Japan Habitat Society and National Institute for Research Advancement.

Takano, T., Nakamura, K. and Akao, C. (1995) 'Assessment of the Value of Videophones in Home Healthcare'. *Telecommunications Policy* **19**(3): 241–248.

Tampines Webtown (1996) 'About Tampines Webtown'. http://www.tampines.org.sg/about.html.

Tamura, T. (1995) 'Wâpuro dekitara pasokon tsûshin intânetto (Personal computers and internet – for those who can use wordprocessors)'. *Shûkan Tôyô Keizai*, 14 October: 38–40.

Tan, S.N. (1996) Personal interview, Head, Strategic Studies, Urban Redevelopment Authority, Singapore. 24 May.

Tan, T. (1996) 'All Homes to be Linked to Range of Services'. *The Straits Times* Weekly Edition, 8 June: 1.

Tanner, K. (1997) 'Telematics and Local Economic Development: The Case of Interventionist Strategies of British Local Authorities'. PhD thesis Manchester Metropolitan University.

Tanner, K. and Gibbs, D. (1996) 'Local Economic Development and Information and Communication Technologies'. In Simmie, J. (Ed) *Innovation Networks and Learning Regions*. London: Jessica Kingsley: 196–210.

Taylor, J. and Williams, H. (1990) 'The Scottish Highlands and Islands Initiative: An Alternative Model for Development'. *Telecommunications Policy* 14(3): 189–192.

Teo, C.H. (1995) 'National Computer Board – Restructuring for IT2000'. Speech at the National IT Forum, Singapore, 7 September.

Telecommunications Council (1994) *Reforms Towards the Intellectually Creative Society of the 21st Century: Program for the Establishment of High-Performance Info-Communications Infrastructure*. Report Summary: Tokyo.

TeleTech Park (1996) 'Asia's First Dedicated Telecommunications Research and Development Centre'. TeleTech Park, Singapore.

Teleworker (1997) 'Telecottage Map: British and Irish Telecottages'. *Teleworker* 4(5): 20–21. The Telecottage Association.

Telstra (1996) *Annual Report 1995/96*. Sydney: Telstra Corporation Limited (Note: the Minority Report is bound in this Report but has separate pagination).

Thompson, J.D. (1967) *Organizations in Action*. New York: McGraw-Hill.

Thrift, N. (1995) 'A Hyperactive World'. In Johnston, R.J., Taylor, P.J. and Watts, M.J. (Eds) *Geographies of Global Change: Remapping the World in the Late Twentieth Century*. Oxford: Blackwell.

Thrift, N. (1996a) 'New Urban Eras and Old Technological Fears: Reconfiguring the Goodwill of Electronic Things'. *Urban Studies* 33(8): 1463–1493.

Thrift, N. (1996b) 'Not a Straight Line but a Curve: or, Cities are not Mirrors of Modernity'. Mimeo.

Thrift, N. (1996c) 'Inhuman Geographies: Landscapes of Speed, Light and Power'. In Thrift, N. *Spatial Formations*. London: Sage: 256–310.

Thu Nguyen, D. and Alexander, J. (1996) 'The Coming of Cyberspacetime and the End of Polity'. In Shields, R. (Ed) *Cultures of Internet: Virtual Spaces, Real Histories, Living Bodies*. London: Sage: 125–132.

Toffler, A. (1970) *Future Shock*. London: Pan.

Toffler, A. (1980) *The Third Wave*. New York: Morrow.

Tokyo Mondai Kenkyukai (Tokyo Issues Research Committee) (1988) *Tokyo Mondai (Tokyo Issues)*. Tokyo: Gyosei.

Tokyo Metropolitan Government Planning Department (1989) *Tokyo Teleport*. Tokyo: Tokyo Metropolitan Government Information Center.

Trinet [no date] 'Internet For Everyone'. Trinet, Kuala Lumpur.

TSKJSK (1982) *Yutaka naru jôhôka shakai e no dohyo (Signposts to a Prosperous Information Society)*. Tsûshô Sangyôshô Kikai Jôhô Sangyô Kyoku Tokyo: Kompyuta Eji Sha.

TSKJSK (1994) *Kôdo jôhôka purogramu (High Level Information Program)*. Tsûshô Sangyôshô Kikai Jôhô Sangyô Kyoku Tokyo: Kompyuta Eji Sha.

Tunstall, J. and Palmer, M. (1990) *Liberating Communications: Policy Making in Britain and France*. Oxford: NCC Blackwell.

United States Congress, Office of Technology Assessment (US OTA) (1990) *Trading Around the Clock: Global Securities Markets and Information Technology – Background Paper*, OTA-BP-CIT-66. Washington DC: US Government Printing Office.

United States, Federal Communications Commission (1999) *Trends in the US International Telecommunications Industry*. http://www.fcc.gov/Bureaus/Common_Carrier/Reports/FCC-State_Link/Intl/itltrd99.pdf

Urban Redevelopment Authority (1991) *Living the Next Lap: Towards a Tropical City of Excellence*. Singapore: Urban Redevelopment Authority.

Urban Redevelopment Authority (1993) *Guidelines for Business Park Development*. Singapore: Urban Redevelopment Authority.

USA Today (1998) 'Cyber Smut'. *USA Today*, 21 January: 10A.

US General Services Administration (1995) *Federal Interagency Telecommuting Centers. Interim Report, Office of Workplace Initiatives*. Washington DC: US General Services Administration.

US Secretary of Commerce (1994) *National Information Infrastructure: Progress Report September 1993–1994. Information Infrastructure Task Force*. Washington: US Government Printing Office.

Van der Staal, P. (1994) 'Communication media in Japan: Economic and Regional Aspects'. *Telecommunications Policy* **18**(1): 32–50.

Van der Staal, P., Grassmuck, V. and Hatta, K. (1995) 'ISDN in Japan: Actors, Status and Expectations'. *Telecommunications Policy* **19**(7): 531–544.

Van der Vries, M.C. (1996) 'The Transition from Monopoly to Competition in Australian Telecommunications'. *Telecommunications Policy* **20**(5): 311–333.

Vasquez, J.A. *et al.* (Eds) (1995) *Beyond Confrontation: Learning Conflict-Resolution in the Post-Cold-War Era*. Ann Arbor: University of Michigan Press.

Venkatraman, N. and Loh, L. (1994) 'The Shifting Logic of the IS Organization: From Technical Portfolio to Relationship Portfolio. *Information Strategy: The Executive's Journal* **10**(2): 5–11.

Vignault, W. (1987) *Worldwide Telecommunications Guide for the Business Manager*. New York: John Wiley & Sons.

Virilio, P. (1993) 'The Third Interval: A Critical Transition'. In Andermatt-Conley, V. (Ed) *Rethinking Technologies*. London: University Of Minnesota Press: 3–10.

Virilio, P. (1995) *The Art of the Motor*. Minneapolis: University of Minnesota Press.

VISTAS (1997) 'Switching on Singapore ONE'. *VISTAS* (Vision, Telecommunication Authority of Singapore), Issue **2**: 30–35.

Vogel, E. (1986) 'Pax Nipponica?' *Foreign Affairs* **64**: 752–67.

Wallenstein, G. (1990) *Setting Global Telecommunication Standards: The Stakes, the Players & The Process*. Norwood: Artech House Inc.

Warf, B. (1989) 'Telecommunications and the Globalization of Financial Services'. *Professional Geographer* **41**(3): 257–271.

Warf, B. (1993) 'Back Office Dispersal: Implications for Urban Development'. *Economic Development Commentary* **16**: 11–16.

Warf, B. (1995) 'Telecommunications and the Changing Geographies of Knowledge Transmission in the Late Twentieth Century'. *Urban Studies* **32**: 361–378.

Waters, R. (1989) 'The Local Expert Has Much to Offer'. *Financial Times*, 26 October.

Webber, M. (1947) *The Theory of Social and Economic Organization*. New York: Free Press.

Webber, M. (1964) 'The Urban Place and the Non-place Urban Realm'. In Webber, M., Dyckman, J., Foley, D., Guttenberg, A., Wheaton, W. and Whurster, C. (Eds) *Explorations Into Urban Structure*. Philadelphia: University of Pennsylvania Press: 79–153.

Webber, M. (1968) *Economy and Society*. (Roth and Wittich, Eds. translation) New York: Bedminister Press.

Webber, M. (1968) 'The Post-city Age'. *Daedalus*, Fall.

Webster, J. (1988) 'New Technology, Old Jobs: Secretarial Labour in Automated Offices'. PICT Working Paper 8, PICT Working Paper Series, Edinburgh University.

Westerway, P. (1990) *Electronic Highways: An Introduction to Telecommunications in the 1990s*. Allen and Unwin.

White, G. Jr (1979) 'Electronic Banking and its Impact on the Future'. *Magazine of Bank Administration* **55**(12): 39–42.

Wigend, R. (1997) 'Electronic Commerce: Definition, Theory, and Context'. *The Information Society* **13**(1): 1–16.

Williams, F. (1997) 'IT Accord Will Scrap Tariffs by Year 2000'. *Financial Times*, 27 March: 9.

Williamson, O. (1975) *Markets and Hierarchies: Analysis and Antitrust Implications*. New York: The Free Press.

Williamson, O. (1979) 'Transaction-cost Economics: The Governance of Contractual Relations'. *Journal of Law and Economics*. **22**: 223–61.

Williamson, O. (1985) *The Economic Institutions of Capitalism*. New York: The Free Press.

Wilson, E. (1995) 'The Rhetoric of Urban Space'. *New Left Review* **209**: 146–160.

Wilson, M. (1991) 'Offshore Relocation of Producer Services: the Irish back office'. Paper presented at the Annual Meeting of the Association of American Geographers, Miami, Florida.

Wilson, M. (1995) *Telecom Tectonics*. Paper presented at E•Space: The Electronic Space Project Conference, Michigan State University.

Wilson, M. (1997a) 'The Office Farther Back: Location Determinants of Offshore Back Offices'. *Lusk Review*. Spring.

Wilson, M. (1997b) 'Offshore Back Offices'. In Sussman, G. and Lent, J.A. (Eds) *Global Productions: Labor in the Making of the "Information Society"*. Cresskill NJ: Hampton Press.

Wired Magazine (1996) 'The Wired Manifesto'. October: 42–46.

Wiseman, C. (1988) *Strategic Information Systems*. Homewood IL: Irwin.

WOLF Consortium (1997) *WWW and Internet Opportunities in the Less Favoured Regions. Project Final Report*. WOLF Consortium, Onyx Internet.

Wong, K.W. and Yeh, S.H.K. (Eds) (1985) *Housing a Nation: 25 Years of Public Housing in Singapore*. Singapore: Maruzen Asia.

Wood, P. (1991) 'Flexible Accumulation and the Rise of Business Services'. *Transactions of the Institute of British Geographers* **16**: 160–172.

Woodward, J. (1958) *Management and Technology. Problems and Progress in Industry* 3. London: HMSO.

Xavier, P. (1996) 'Monitoring Deregulation Through International Benchmarking'. *Telecommunications Policy* **20**(8): 583–606.

LIST OF CONTRIBUTORS

Colin Arrowsmith, Department of Land Information, Royal Melbourne Institute of Technology, 124 LaTrobe Street, Melbourne, Victoria 3000, Australia

Michael James Blaine, 1000 Urlin Avenue #1422, Columbus, OH 43212, USA

Stanley D. Brunn, Department of Geography, University of Kentucky, 1457 Patterson Office Tower, Lexington, KY 40506-0027, USA

Kenneth E. Corey, Dean, College of Social Science, Michigan State University, 203 Berkey Hall, East Lansing, MI 48824, USA

David Gibbs, School of Geography and Earth Resources, University of Hull, Hull, HU6 7RX, UK

Andrew E. Gillespie, Centre for Urban and Regional Development Studies, University of Newcastle, Newcastle upon Tyne, NEI 7RU, UK

Stephen Graham, Department of Town & Country Planning, University of Newcastle, Claremont Tower, Newcastle upon Tyne, NEI 7RU, UK

John V. Langdale, School of Earth Science, Macquarie University, North Ryde, NSW 2109, Australia

Tessa Morris-Suzuki, Division of History, Research School of Pacific and Asian Studies, Australian National University, PO Box 4, Canberra, ACT 0200, Australia

Edward Mozley Roche, The Chart Group, 135 E 54th Street #4B, New York, NY 10022-4509, USA

Ranald Richardson, Centre for Urban and Regional Development Studies, University of Newcastle upon Tyne, Newcastle upon Tyne, NEI 7RU, UK

Peter J. Rimmer, Department of Human Geography, Australian National University, Research School of Pacific and Asian Studies, PO Box 4, Canberra, ACT 0200, Australia

Keith Tanner, Burnley College, Shorley Bank, Ormerod Road, Burnley, BB11 2RX, UK

Steve Walker, Centre for Employment Research, Manchester Metropolitan University, Manchester, M15 6BY, UK

262
———

Barney Warf, Department of Geography, Florida State University, Tallahassee, FL 32306-2050, USA

Mark I. Wilson, Institute for Public Policy and Social Research, Michigan State University, East Lansing, MI 48825-1111, USA

INDEX

AAPT Telecommunications 176
ABS-Fairfax 190
academic communities 47–8
actor-network theories 23–5, 232
adaptive organizations 76
Aditarina Sumatera 187
Advanced Mobile Phone System (AMPS)
      177, 179
Afghanistan 31
Africa 30, 31, 36, 38
AIDC Telecommunications Fund 172
Alatief Corporation 186, 187, 188
Alcatel 178
American International Assurance Group
      (AIA) 187, 188
AMP Society 172
Amsterdam 69
analogue mobile phone systems (AMPS)
      177–8, 179, 181
Anderson Consulting 151
Antur Tanait Cain Telebureau 211
Apple Computers 130, 227, 229
areal uniformity 12–14, 15
Aria Bahtera Internusa 188
Aria West International (Tiga-A) 188,
      189
Arimas Kencana Murni 188
Artha Graha group 172
AsciiNet 107
Asia
   controlling the Internet in 153–64
   creating cyber communities in 136–53
   telecom tectonics 36, 37
   teledensity 30, 31
   see also named countries
Asia Connect 160
Asia-Pacific region
   economic activity and
         telecommunications 166–9
   international financial trading 95, 97
   Internet host distribution 129
   see also named countries
Asian Infrastructure Fund 188
Association of Southeast Asian Nations
      (ASEAN) 153, 166
Astra Group 186, 187, 188
Astratel Nusantara 188
asynchronous digital subscriber loop (ADSL)
   technology 224

asynchronous transfer mode (ATM)
   technology 109, 124, 125
AT&T 30, 104, 105, 107, 108, 110, 170,
      181, 189
Aussat 170, 172
Australia 33
   human rights issues 49–50
   telecommunications 165–98
      future 189–91
         Australia's Communications Futures
               Project 191–4
         Indonesia in crisis 197–8
      performance
         industry development 184–5
         international competitiveness 183
         mobile phone services 177, 181
         networks and services 176–7
         price 182–3
      privatization 195–7
      review of Asia-Pacific region 166–9
      sector restructuring 169–73
         pro-competition and deregulation
               174–6
      see also Indonesia
   teledensity 31
Australian Competition and Consumer
      Commission (ACCC) 175, 190
Australian and Overseas
      Telecommunications Corporation
      (AOTC) 172
Australian Telecom 169, 170, 171, 172,
      177
Australian Telecommunications Authority
      (Austel) 171, 174, 175
Australis 190, 193
automatic teller machines 79

back offices 212–13
Bahana 173
Bakrie Brothers 170, 188
Bandai 131
Bangladesh 31
banking and finance industry 89
   internationalization 90–3
      centralization and decentralization
            93–4
Barbados 30
Bekkoame Internet 131

264

Bell Cable Media 224
Bell Canada 187
BellSouth Corporation 172
bilateral governance 84
Bill of Rights 52, 54
Bima Graha 172, 173, 180
Bimantara group 170, 172, 179, 180,
    187
Bina Reksa Perdana 179
Black 190
Bloomberg 94, 98, 151
boundaries 4–5, 42
    erosion of 46–8
British Telecom 192, 224
Bukaka Singtel International 188, 189
Bukaka Telekomindo 187, 188
Burnley case study 229–30, 233, 234

Cable & Wireless 172, 178, 181, 187, 188,
    189, 224
cable modems 224
cable TV
    in Japan 103, 104, 109–10, 119, 126
    in Singapore 148, 151, 152
call centers 212, 213–15
Cambodia 31
Can West 190
Canada 31
canals 70
Canberra Times 190
Canon 104, 110
CAPTAIN 112
CD-ROMs 104
cellular phone services *see* mobile phone
    services
Celnet 180
Centralindo Panca Sakti 179, 187
centralization 86, 200
    of information processing 71, 72–3,
        74
    in international banking and finance
        industry 93–4
Chad 31
Channel Islands 31
chartered trading companies 69
Chicago Board of Trade (CBOT) 97, 98
Chicago futures exchanges 91, 94, 97
Chicago Mercantile Exchange (CME) 96,
    97, 98
China 159–60
Cisco Systems 107
Citibank 79
cities
    actor-networks 25

co-evolution of geographical and
    electronic space 17–20
power and divisions 22
as relational assemblies 27
urban dissolution 12–14
Citra Telekomunikasi Indonesia 170
client-server 71, 79
co-evolution
    cities 17–20
    place-based and tele-mediated
        relationships 16–17
    spatial fixes and space production
        20–2
Commonwealth Development Corporation
    188
community: new definitions 46
community based telecenters/telecottages
    209–12
computer games 129–30
computers 2
    in Japan 103, 107–8, 128, 129
    networks 130–1
contingency theory 75–6
contractual arrangements 77, 82
    costs 85
core competencies 80
costs
    of alternative governance structures
        83–6
    cost barriers to using Internet
        132–3
    cost reduction and telecommunications
        31–3
    labor costs 39–40, 81
    mapping cost space 33–7
Cote d'Ivoire 31
Country Heights 138
Crossaig 208–9
cultural time regions 59
cyber communities
    defined 135–6
    see also Asia, creating cyber
        communities in
Cyberjaya 137–8
cyberspace *see* electronic space
Cyberview 138, 141
Cyberway 155
cyborgs 23

Damareska 173
data processing 70–2
    centralization 71, 72–3, 74
    decentralization 71
    linking 74

Daya Mitra Malindo 188, 189
DDI Corporation 110, 120
decentralization 199–200
  information processing 71
  in international banking and finance
      industry 93–4
Democratic Republic of Congo 31
Denmark 31
determinism see technological determinism
Deutsche Bundespost Telekom 108, 187
Deutsche Telekom 176
Deutsche Telekom Mobilfunk GmbH 173,
    180
Digital Media Lab 131
digital mobile phone systems 177–8, 180,
    181
dis-integration 79, 80, 85, 87
diseconomies 84, 85
distance, death of 2, 12–13
Djati Yudha Cellular 179
DOS/V 107

Electronic Arts 151
electronic cottages 199, 206
  see also telecottages
electronic democracies 50–1
electronic homeworking 204, 206–9
electronic space 1, 9
  conceptualizing space, place and
      information technology 9–28
  co-evolution 16–22
  diversity of cyberspace 24
  recombination 23–5
  spatial metaphors 9, 10–11
  substitution and transcendence
      11–16
  emergence 2
  geographies of 3–5
  roots of 2–3
  tectonics see telecom tectonics
  vehicles 30–2
electronic state: defined 43
electronic trading systems 93, 94, 97–8
Elektrindo Nusantara 179, 186, 187
Embay 138
Ericsson 184
ethical issues 52–5
Europe
  development of multinational enterprises
      (MNEs) 69–70
  EC policies for information society 220,
      221–3
    see also local telematics initiatives
  human rights issues 49

Excelcomindo 178, 180, 181
Exicom 184

Fairfax 190
Famicon 129, 130
Fiberoptic Link Around the World (FLAG)
    108
finance industry see banking and finance
    industry
Finland 31
First Pacific 179
'following the sun' 95
Fordist model 80, 102
foreign exchange trading 95
foreign subsidiaries 70, 72, 73
formalization 86
Foxtel Australis 190
France
  electronic space map 34
  futures exchange 98
  teledensity 31
France Telecom 104, 108, 176, 187,
    188
freelance teleworkers 207–8
Fujitsu 104, 107, 108, 131, 142, 170
Full Service Networks (FSNs) 13
futures industry
  internationalization 90–1
  role of telecommunications
      92–3
  24–hour trading 94–8

G-MING network 229
Galaxy Television 190
generalized interactivity 14
geography of electronic space 3–5
  see also electronic space; telecom
      tectonics
Germany
  electronic space maps 34, 37
  futures exchange 98
  Internet regulation 162–3
  teledensity 31, 32
Global Information Infrastructure
    Commission (GIIC) 161
global networks 27–8, 79
Global Standard for Mobile
    Communications (GSM) system 172,
    177–8, 180
'global village' 13
GLOBEX 94, 97–8
Golden Hope 138
Goldman Sachs 173

266

governance in multinational enterprises
67–88
pre-nineteenth century 68, 69–70
1860–1960 70–2
1960–1970 72–3
1970–1985 73–8
1985–1993 78–81
1993–present 81–3
future prospects 83–6
gross domestic product (GDP) 166, 167
GrR Homenet 126
GTE 187
Guinea 31

Hagenuk GmbH 104, 111
Hewlett Packard 151
hierarchical centralization 71
hierarchical governance
costs 84
development of 70–2
hierarchies of communications 60, 61
Hitachi 104, 110
holding companies 70, 72, 73
homeworking 204, 206–9
Hong Kong 31, 159–60
Hoskyns Group plc 213–14
housing 145, 147
Hughes Corporation 167
human rights and welfare 41–64
definitions 42–3, 46
in 'electronic world' 43, 55–7
erosion of boundaries 46–8
legal standards 45
mapping electronically connected and
unconnected worlds 57–62
maps of information and
communication 57–8
social justice and welfare issues 58–62
spatial dimension 44–5
states' rights and international rights
48–55
electronic democracies 50–1
legal, ethical and moral issues 52–5, 56
humanism 25
Humpuss 185

IBM 104, 107, 108, 131, 151, 231
ICL 227
IDO Corp. 111
impact 11–12, 26
Indonesia 69
telecommunications 165–98
economic crisis 197–8

future 189
performance
industry development 185
private participation/joint
ventures 185–9
international competitiveness
183–4
mobile phone services 177–81
networks and services 176–7
review of Asia-Pacific region 166–9
sector restructuring 169–73
privatization 173–4
see also Australia
Indosat 169, 170, 172–3, 177–8, 180, 181,
185–9, 197
industrial structure formation 69–70
information cycle 70, 71
information economies 2, 3
information network system (INS (Japan))
119–25, 127
information processing systems 71
information society 10
information superhighway 10
information transactions scale 60
infrastructuralism 201–2
Instituto Bancario San Paolo 201
integrated services digital network (ISDN)
223–4
inter-organizational systems (IOSs) 78–9
InterCon International 108
Interconnected Associates of Seattle
128
International Digital Communications 104,
105, 106
International Finance Corporation 188
International Labor Office (ILO) 161
international rights see states' rights and
international rights
international securities industry see
securities industry
International Telecom Japan 105, 106
International Wireless Corporation 179
Internet 9, 10, 43, 224
in Japan 103, 107, 127–9
cultural and cost barriers 132–3
political implications 131–2
regulation in Germany 162–3
regulation in southeast Asia 153–64
and global regulation 160–1
Hong Kong, China and Vietnam
159–60
Malaysia 157–9, 162
Singapore 153–7, 162, 163
and rural enterprises 205–6
Intertel Nusa Perdana 187

Intertel Pratama Media 188
Inti 180
Intidaya Sistelindo Mitra 187
Ireland 30, 39
  call centers/telecenters 210, 213, 214,
    215
Itidaya 186
Itochu 188

Japan
  cyberstructure and social forces
    117–34
    1980s vision and 1990s reality
      117–27
    predicting social uses of new
        technology
      computer games and computer
        networks 129–31
      corporate response and political
        implications 131–2
      cultural and cost barriers 132–3
      Internet see Internet, in Japan
  electronic space maps 35, 37
  information services in late twentieth
      century 101–14
    contrasts with United States 103–4
    deregulation of telecommunications
      104–7
    global economy 102–3
    recent developments
      cable TV, multimedia and
        videoconferencing 103, 104,
        109–10, 119, 126
      cellular phones 103, 104, 110–11
      computer networks 107–8
    Tokyo telecommunications
        infrastructure 111–12
  teledensity 31, 32
Japan Key Technology Center 110
Japan Telecom 110, 120
Japanese Satellite Broadcasting 110
Jardine Fleming Nusantara 173
Jasarus 185
Johor State 142–3
JUNET 127
Jusco Co. 110

Kanematsu 187
Kartika Eka Mas Nusantara 187
Kinki Nippon Railway 105, 109
Kinseki 111
Kintetsu Cable Network 105
Kokarindo 188

Kokusai Denshin Denwa (KDD) 104, 105,
    106, 108, 113, 181
Komselindo 179, 181
Komunikasi Seluar Indonesia 179
Koninklijke PTT Nederland 170
Kopindosat 188
Kopnatel 188
Kopthindo 188
Korea Telecom 187
Krida Salindo Sentosa 188
Krisna Duta 187
KSO contracts 185–6, 197, 198
Kuala Lumpur
  City Center Project 137
  international airport 139

labor costs 39–40, 81
Lancashire College Consortium (LCC) case
    study 230–1, 233–4, 235
Laos 31
LCV Corporation 109
legal issues
  and human rights 44, 45, 52–5, 56
  Internet regulation in southeast Asia
    153–64
  see also human rights and welfare
Lehman Brothers/S.G. Warburg 173
LIFFE 98
Linthasartha 197
Lippo Group 186
local area networks (LANs) 104, 107
local telematics initiatives 225–31
London futures exchange (LIFFE) 98

McCaw Cellular Communications 189
Maharani 187
Makindo securities 173, 174
Malaysia 136–44
  intelligent cities 137–8
  Internet regulation 157–9, 162
  Johor State 142–3
  Kuala Lumpur
    City Center Project 137
    international airport 139
  learning from Malaysia's IT and
      development projects 143–4
  Multimedia Super Corridor 139–40
    connecting the corridor 143
    flagship applications 140–1
    Multimedia Development Corporation
      138, 141–2
    Technology Park Malaysia 138
    WWW addresses 144, 158

Malaysia Telekom 187, 188, 189
Malaysian Institute of Microelectronic
    Systems (MIMOS) 138
Manchester case study 226–9, 232, 233,
    234
market trends: overview 223–5
Marubeni Corporation 188
Matahari Lintas Cakrawai 189, 194
MATIF 98
matrix form 68
Mayne Nickless Pty Ltd. 172
MEASAT 138
mechanistic organizations 75
Mediabank 109
'Megalopolis' 3
Merrill Lynch 95–6, 173
Metro Seluar Nusantara (Metrosel) 179, 181
Microsoft 104, 106, 109, 130, 151
Middle East 36
'mirror worlds' 15
Mitra Global Telekomunikasi 188, 189, 198
Mitsubishi 104, 109, 142
Mitsui 178, 180, 187
Mobil Seluar Indonesia (Mobilsel) 179, 181
mobile citizens 47
mobile phone services 31
    in Australia and Indonesia 177–81, 183,
        198
    in Japan 103, 104, 110–11
modems 68, 223
moral issues 52–5
Morgan Stanley 174
Motorola 104, 106, 107, 111, 151
multidivisional form 68, 70, 72–3
multimedia services 109–10, 125, 126,
    191–4, 224
multinational enterprises (MNEs),
    governance see governance in
    multinational enterprises
Murdoch 189, 190
Music Pen 151
Myanmar 31

NEC 107, 108, 131, 142, 151, 170, 185
Net 1500 123–4
network (virtual) companies 68, 78, 79,
    80–3
    costs and advantages of 83–6
    future prospects 86–8
    structural mechanisms 86
'new forms of investment'(NFIs) 77, 82
New York Stock Exchange 93
New Zealand Telecom 187, 196
News Corporation Ltd. 190, 194

Nextel Communications 104, 106, 110
Nichimen 188
Nifty-Serve 107, 128
Niger 31
Nihon Cisco Systems 107
Nihon Dempa Kogyo 111
Nintendo 129
Nippon Life Insurance 110
Nippon Motorola 104, 106
Nippon Telegraph and Telephone (NTT)
    113
    cellular services 110–11
    deregulation 104–7
    information network system 119–26
    investment in Indonesia 186, 188,
        198
    investment in Malaysia 138, 142
    multimedia services 109–10
Nissan Motor Company 110
Nokia 104, 111
Nordic Mobile Telephones (NMT) 179
normative integration 86
Northern Telecom 104, 106, 109, 110
Nusa Telekomindo Internusa 187
Nynex 126, 178, 180, 187, 224, 231

offshore financial centers 93–4
Olex Cables 184
Optus Communications Ltd. 172, 174, 176,
    177, 181, 183, 185, 190
Optus Vision 190, 193
Oracle 104, 109, 151
O'Reilly 190
organic organizations 75
Organization for Economic Cooperation and
    Development (OECD) 161
outsourcing 77, 79, 80, 81, 82
Overseas Telecommunications Commission
    (OTC) 169, 170, 172

Pacific Internet 155
Packer 189, 190
Pakistan 30
Palapa satellites 167, 172, 194
PAN TV 190
Paraguay 31
Pay Television Australia 189
PBH joint ventures 185
PC-Van 107, 128, 131
People World 131
Peremba 138
Performance Systems International
    108

Permodalan Nasional 138
Personal Communication Network (PCN) 178
Personal Communications Handy-phone Service (PHS) 178
personal extensibility 22
Perumtel 169, 170, 171
Petronas 137
Pioneer Electronics 109
place
  co-evolution with electronic space 16–22
  impacts of technology on 11–14
  importance of 2, 17
  relational assemblies 26–8
  transmission of 15
  virtuality 17
  see also electronic space, conceptualizing space, place and information technology
pornography 156, 162, 163
post-Fordism 102
power 21–2, 58
Pramindo Ikat Nusantara 188, 189
Primus Telecommunications Ltd. 176
Prinkopparpostel 188
Prodigy 108
Project A 98
public switched telecommunications network (PSTN) 92
Publishing and Broadcasting Ltd. 190
Putrajaya 137–8

quaternary economic activities 3
QUICK 92

Radio Telepon Indonesia 170
railroads 70
Rajasa Hasanah Perkasa 179
Rajawali Group 178, 179, 187
re-engineering of organizations 78–81
recombinant architecture 18
recombination: actor network theories 23–5, 232
Reed Personnel 227
Reed-Elsevier 208
regional information processing 71
relational assemblies 26–8
relational contracting 84
relational time-spaces 23–5
Renong 138
Reuters 92, 94, 97, 151
Rimnet 131

rural areas 199–217
  back offices and call centers 212–15
  community based telecenters and telecottages 209–12
  electronic homeworking (freelance and employed) 206–9
  incorporating into information society
    endogenous model 201–2
    exogenous model 203–4
  overcoming constraints on enterprises through ICTs 204–6
Rwanda 31

Salim Group 186
Sanyo 104, 110
Satelindo 172, 173, 177, 180, 181
satellite services 110, 194
SBS 190
Scandinavia 210
secretarial services 213
securities industry 89–99
  internationalization 90–1
    role of telecommunications 91–4
  24-hour trading in 94–8
Sega 104, 109, 126
Selangor State Government 138
Sembawang Media 155
Setdco Megasai 178, 180
Sharp 104, 110, 142
Shiki Satellite Office system 110
Shopping 2000 131
Sinar Mas Group 187
Singapore 31, 145–53
  futures exchange (SIMEX) 96, 98
  Internet regulation 153–7, 162, 163
  and Johor State 142–3
  learning from Singapore intelligent city 148–9
    National Computer Board 149–50
    Singapore Inc. 152–3
    Singapore ONE 150–2
  spatial organization and IT infrastructure 145
  technology corridors
    cable TV 148, 151, 152
    housing and recreation 147
    Northeastern Technology Corridor 147
    regional center anchors 147–8
    Southwestern Technology Corridor 146–7
  WWW addresses 144, 150, 152
Singapore Broadcasting Authority 154–5, 156, 157
Singapore Cable Vision 151, 152

270

Singapore Science Park 146
Singapore Technologies Pte Ltd 146
Singapore Telecom 104, 108, 146, 155,
   176, 181, 187, 188
Singnet 155, 156
Sitel 212
social justice 50, 58–62
social power 21–2, 58
social processes 10–11
   co-evolution with information
      technology 16–22
   recombination 23–5
   see also human rights and welfare; Japan,
      cyberspace and social forces
socialization 86
Softbank 109
software 108–9
Somalia 31
Sony 104, 110, 126
South Africa 31
South America 37
space see electronic space; place
spatial fixes 21
spatial metaphors 9, 10–11
spatial power 21–2
spatial rights 44–5
SPH Multimedia 155
Sprint 104, 176, 187
ST Telecommunications 155
Star TV 194
Starr Direct 128
states' rights and international rights 48–55
   in electronic democracies 50–1
   legal, ethical and moral issues 52–5
stockmarket
   crashes 89
   see also securities industry
Stokes 190
strategic systems 78–9
substitution and transcendence 11–16
   areal uniformity, urban dissolution and
      generalized activity 12–14
   concept of 11–12
   'mirror worlds', transmission of place and
      world transcendence 14–16
Suginami Cable Television 126
Sumitomo 188
Sun Microsystems 151
Sydney futures exchange 98

Tampines 147–8
technological determinism 10, 12
   criticisms of 17, 26
technological networks 24–5

technology, overview of developments in
   223–5
Technology Park Malaysia 138
Technology Parks Pte Ltd 146
Telecom BV (Netherlands) 170, 178,
   180
telecom tectonics 4, 29–40
   cost and distance 32–3
   electronic space vehicles 30–2
   implications
      equity 38
      production 39–40
   mapping electronic space 33–7, 57–8
Telecommunications Inc. (TCI) 126
telecottages 204, 209–12
Telefonaktiebolaget LM Ericsson 106
telegraph 68, 70, 72
Telekmindo Primabhakti 179, 181, 187
Telekomsel 178, 180, 181
telephones
   cellular services see mobile phone
      services
   cost space 31–3
      mapping 33–7
   historical significance 68, 70, 72
   teledensity 30–1, 166, 167
Telerate 92, 94
Telergos 213
TeleTech Park 146
Teleway Japan 104, 105, 120
teleworking 206–9
telex 68, 70, 72
Telkom 170, 171, 173–4, 177–81, 185–7,
   197
Telstra 172, 174–8, 181–90, 193–8
Tenaga Nasional 138
Thai Telephone and Communications
   Corporation 106
Thailand 30
Thomson International 208
Time Warner 189
time-zone differences 93–4
Tirtamas Majutama 173
TM Communications Ltd 188
Tokyo
   stock exchange 92, 111
   telecommunications infrastructure
      111–12
Tokyo Cable Television 105
Tokyo Communication Equipment 111
Tokyo Corporation 105
Tokyo Digital 104, 111
Tokyo Electric Power Company 105
Tokyo Telecommunications Network (TNN)
   105

Tokyo Teleport 112, 113
Tokyo-Seattle Bridge 128
Tokyo-Washington Internet Railroad 128
Tomen Corporation 187
Toshiba 104, 111
transactional diseconomies 84, 85
transcendence *see* substitution and
    transcendence
transmission of place 15
transnational corporations (TNCs) 20, 28,
    47, 95
Tri Daya Foundation 179
tribalisation 19
Tripatra Engineering 187
24–hour trading
    in international securities industry
        94–8
        extending operating hours 97–8
        options for acheiving
            linking exchanges 96–7
            linking firms 95–6
            linking locations 95

Ultra-High Speed Network and Computer
    Technology Laboratories 108
unitary form 72, 73
United 181
United Kingdom
    local telematics initiatives 221
    in NW England 225–35
    rural area developments 206, 207,
        208–9, 210, 211, 213–14
    telecom tectonics 31, 32
    telematics regulation 220
United States
    comparisons with Japanese
        telecommunications 103–4
    electronic space maps 35, 36
    futures trading 91, 97
    human rights issues 48–55

'Megalopolis' 3
    rural area developments 205, 209, 210,
        212
    telecom tectonics 31, 32
urban dissolution 12–14
US West Inc. 188, 189
USF Pacific 105

Venezuela 31
vertical hierarchy 68
Victor Corporation 126
video-on-demand 24, 123, 125, 126
videoconferencing 110
Vietnam 160
virtual companies *see* network companies
Virtual Reality (VR) 13, 14–15, 17
Visionstream 190
Vodafone 172, 177

Warman and Lehman 173–4
Weberian hierarchy 71, 81
welfare *see* human rights and welfare
Wellfleet Communications 107
wide area networks (WANs) 107
WIDE network 128
Widya Duta Informindo 187, 188
Windows 95, 130
wireless WANs 107
WOLF project 205–6
wordprocessing 128, 130
'world rejection' 15–16
world time regions 59
World Trade Organization 161

Yahoo 151
Yamaha Corporation 126
Yayasan Kartika Eka Paksi 187
Yokohama TV 105, 109, 126